# Internet Retailing and Future Perspectives

Since the first edition of this landmark textbook, online shopping has grown exponentially to the point that it now threatens to eclipse the high street. With online retail offering both advantages and challenges that are distinct from traditional commerce, this textbook provides new approaches to retailing and as such helps readers to take advantage of new digital technologies.

This long-awaited new edition provides a thorough and substantial update to its solid core principle of digital retailing and its relationship with conventional retail methods. These principles are explained clearly and practically to provide students, entrepreneurs and researchers with a reliable guide to the implementation and operation of a successful online retailing business.

Updates to this edition include:

- Search engine marketing and search engine optimization.
- New and updated case studies, including Tesco's virtual store, Ray-Ban's smart mirror, IKEA's mobile catalogue and Nordstrom's TextStyle.
- Social networks and electronic word-of-mouth communication.
- A new chapter on ubiquitous retailing.
- A brand new companion website to support tutors.

With accessibly written features such as key learning points, questions, think points and further reading, *Internet Retailing and Future Perspectives* is ideal for anyone using, studying or researching digital commerce.

**Eleonora Pantano** is a Lecturer in Marketing at Middlesex University London, UK.

**Bang Nguyen** is an Associate Professor of the Marketing Department at East China University of Science and Technology, China.

**Charles Dennis** is a Professor of Consumer Behaviour at Middlesex University London, UK.

**Bill Merrilees** is a Professor of Marketing at Griffith University, Australia.

**Sabine Gerlach** is a Lecturer in Marketing at the University of Lincoln, UK.

This book is an impressive repository of information on e-retailing and internet marketing. The comprehensive approach provided by the book shows the extent to which digital technologies have intervened in the processes that characterise the sale of goods and services online. This book will stand as an invaluable resource for students, academics and practitioners in the field.

– **Dr Alessandro Gandini,** *Lecturer in Digital Media Management and Innovation, King's College London, UK*

The second edition of *Internet Retailing and Future Perspectives* provides a comprehensive coverage of the key opportunities and challenges faced by retailers in a growing age of internet shopping and digital disruption. The text is well written and structured, and raises a series of critical questions about the operationalisation and growth of internet and digital platforms, illustrated using relevant case studies and practical examples. The glossary is also particularly useful. The text is an ideal companion for both undergraduate and postgraduate students studying business, as well as practitioners looking for insights on how to successfully navigate the world of internet retailing.

– **Jonathan Elms, PhD,** *The Sir Stephen Tindall Chair in Retail Management and Director of the Centre for Advanced Retail Studies (CARS), Massey University, New Zealand*

# Internet Retailing and Future Perspectives

## Second Edition

Eleonora Pantano, Bang Nguyen, Charles Dennis, Bill Merrilees and Sabine Gerlach

LONDON AND NEW YORK

First published 2004
As *e-Retailing* by Charles Dennis, Tino Fenech and Bill Merrilees

Second edition 2017
by Routledge
2 Park Square, Milton Park, Abingdon, Oxon OX14 4RN

and by Routledge
711 Third Avenue, New York, NY 10017

*Routledge is an imprint of the Taylor & Francis Group, an informa business*

© 2004 Charles Dennis, Tino Fenech and Bill Merrilees
© 2017 Eleonora Pantano, Bang Nguyen, Charles Dennis, Bill Merrilees and Sabine Gerlach

The right of Eleonora Pantano, Bang Nguyen, Charles Dennis, Bill Merrilees and Sabine Gerlach to be identified as authors of this work has been asserted by them in accordance with sections 77 and 78 of the Copyright, Designs and Patents Act 1988.

All rights reserved. No part of this book may be reprinted or reproduced or utilised in any form or by any electronic, mechanical, or other means, now known or hereafter invented, including photocopying and recording, or in any information storage or retrieval system, without permission in writing from the publishers.

Every effort has been made to contact copyright holders for their permission to reprint material in this book. The publishers would be grateful to hear from any copyright holder who is not here acknowledged and will undertake to rectify any errors or omissions in future editions of this book.

*Trademark notice*: Product or corporate names may be trademarks or registered trademarks, and are used only for identification and explanation without intent to infringe.

*British Library Cataloguing-in-Publication Data*
A catalogue record for this book is available from the British Library

*Library of Congress Cataloguing-in-Publication Data*
A catalogue record for this book has been requested

ISBN: 978-1-138-94051-2 (hbk)
ISBN: 978-1-138-94052-9 (pbk)
ISBN: 978-1-315-67430-8 (ebk)

Typeset in Bembo
by codeMantra

Visit the companion website: www.routledge.com/cw/pantano

**Eleonora Pantano:** To my lovely parents, Pietro and Assunta, who constantly supported me in this long project.

**Bang Nguyen:** To my family and my best friend, Harry.

**Charles Dennis:** To my wife Mary, to Janine, Trish and Juliet; and in memory of Joan and Ross.

**Bill Merrilees:** My contribution is dedicated to integrity as the core capability that helps you get through all sorts of crises; and to Dale as my integrity partner in life.

**Sabine Gerlach:** To my fiancé Wilhelm and our son Wilhelm Henry Maximus.

# Contents

List of illustrations — xi
List of contributors — xv
Acknowledgements — xviii
Introduction — xix
  Aim  xix
  Rationale  xix
  Key issues and success factors in e-retailing  xx

**1 The world of e-retailing** — 1
  What is e-retail?  2
  Disadvantages of e-retailing for retailers  5
  Advantages of e-retailing for retailers  7
  The (E-) retail mix: sale the seven Cs  8
  Growth and prospects for e-retailing  20
  Conclusions  22

**2 The business of e-retailing in practice** — 33
  What are the main e-retail product categories?  34
  Home electronics  36
  Amazon and Argos  36
  Books  37
  Music  39
  Video  44
  Digital piracy  46
  Groceries  47
  Online grocers  48
  Clothing and footwear  50
  Conclusions  60

CONTENTS

**3 Integration of e-retailing into an organisation**    77
Introduction   78
Why traditional retailers adopt e-retail   78
Strategies for integration   80
Loyalty-based integration strategies   87
Switching barriers and switching costs   90
Implementation: change management and resource implications   91
Conclusions   93

**4 Understanding and communicating with the e-consumer**    100
Introduction   101
Understanding e-consumer behaviour   101
The perceived risk of e-shopping   102
Introducing e-shoppers   103
What does e-shopping offer the e-shopper?   105
Disadvantages and advantages of e-shopping for consumers   106
Social and experiential aspects of e-shopping   110
Differences between male and female shopping styles   113
Electronic word-of-mouth (eWOM) and e-reviews   117
Consumer satisfaction: 'bricks' and 'clicks' shopping compared   118
The communications mix for the e-retailer   122
Conclusions   131

**5 Information search on the web**    142
'Clicks' and 'bricks'   143
The background to searching the internet and the web   143
Surveys on what people do and where people 'go' on the web   144
Searching and finding on the web   145
The average web session   146
Focus   146
Directories   147
Search engines   148
Monitoring the use of your webpages   153
Conclusions   154

**6 E-store design navigability, interactivity and web atmospherics**    159
What is e-store design?   160
The purpose and scope of e-store design   160
Why is store design more important for e-retailers?   161
Start e-store design with navigability   162
Progress to interactivity   163
Building e-relationships through interactivity   165
Enhancements through web atmospherics   166

*All together for an integrated approach to e-store design* 172
*The role of objectives and strategy in guiding e-store design* 174
*Conclusions* 174

## 7 E-service — 183

*E-service as the fourth stage of e-commerce development* 184
*Three approaches to e-services* 185
*A second taxonomy of e-services* 189
*The self-service myth* 189
*E-service performance* 192
*A critical incident approach to e-service performance* 192
*E-service metrics: a management tool* 197
*E-retail service quality: an alternative performance metric* 199
*Additional guidance on practical e-service provision* 202
*Conclusions* 202

## 8 Branding on the web — 210

*Introduction* 211
*Branding in conventional retailing* 212
*Different approaches to branding on the web* 212
*Branding as hype: the narrow meaning* 213
*E-brand development I: start with the brand concept* 214
*E-brand development II: build the brand platform* 215
*E-brand development III: implement through the brand elements* 216
*E-brand development IV: the special role of interactivity and trust in building strong e-brands* 216
*The role of the e-retail mix in branding* 220
*What is the overall e-retail offer?* 222
*A framework for choosing an optimal e-retail offer* 222
*Brand innovation on social media* 223
*Conclusions* 224

## 9 E-malls — 229

*Introduction* 230
*Conventional (bricks) malls* 231
*Lessons from conventional malls for online malls* 233
*Multiple category e-retailers* 234
*Shopping bots: intelligent shopper assistants or virtual mall?* 235
*Virtual reality mall* 236
*Portals and other quasi e-malls* 237
*E-malls as ports of entry for newly started businesses: the tenant perspective* 237
*Conclusions* 238

CONTENTS

**10 E-retailing models**     **247**
*What is a business model? 248*
*The retail participant groups in a retailer's environment 249*
*Distribution channels 251*
*Revenue streams 253*
*Assessment of the fit between organisational objectives
    and the business models 254*
*Assessment of product suitability for e-retailing using
    de Kare-Silver's electronic shopping ES test 261*
*Conclusions 268*

**11 M-shopping**     **272**
*Remote shopping continues to evolve, now into m-shopping 273*
*How has m-shopping come about? 274*
*What is needed to go m-shopping? 274*
*Features that distinguish m-commerce from
    traditional e-commerce 276*
*Contributors to the growth in m-commerce 276*
*Mobile payments 277*
*Profiling the m-shopper 279*
*Conclusions 280*

**12 U-shopping**     **286**
*Mobile retail evolution to ubiquitous retail 287*
*How has u-shopping come about? 287*
*What is needed to go u-shopping? 288*
*Features that distinguish traditional e-commerce,
    m-commerce and u-commerce 290*
*Conclusions 290*

**13 Multi-channel success and the future of e-retailing**     **295**
*Introduction 296*
*The hybrid retailer – the most likely winner in future retailing 302*
*What can you expect to see and hear in e-retailing? 304*
*Conclusions 311*

**Answers to chapter-end questions**     **317**

Index     329

x

# Illustrations

## FIGURES

| | | |
|---|---|---|
| 1.1 | Global online retail sector value and growth forecast | 4 |
| 1.2 | Web-rooming vs. Showrooming survey results | 21 |
| 2.1 | Most bought product categories online in Europe 2014 (millions of customers) | 34 |
| 2.2 | Where consumers have bought online in the past 12 months | 37 |
| 2.3 | Exemplar strategic positioning of books e-retailers | 39 |
| 2.4 | Paid-for content, mobile and online in 2014 | 43 |
| 2.5 | Physical and digital home video revenue in the US, 2010–2019 | 45 |
| 2.6 | Physical and digital video consumption | 45 |
| 2.7 | Annual UK grocery market predictions | 47 |
| 2.8 | Online grocery market shares UK | 49 |
| 2.9 | Reasons for switching online retailers | 53 |
| 2.10 | Reasons for cart abandonment | 59 |
| 2.11 | The importance of delivery and return services in online retail for UK shoppers | 60 |
| 2.12 | Visitors to UK e-retailers in May 2014 | 62 |
| 2.13 | Ansoff Matrix | 68 |
| 3.1 | E-commerce digitisation | 83 |
| 3.2 | Strategic options for retailers | 84 |
| 3.3 | The Online Retail Relationship matrix | 88 |
| 3.4 | The Purchaser-Purveyor Loyalty matrix | 90 |
| 6.1 | Simplified representation of a grid layout e-retail store | 169 |
| 6.2 | Simplified representation of a free flow layout e-retail store | 170 |
| 6.3 | Simplified representation of a free grid layout e-retail store | 170 |
| 6.4 | An integrated framework for e-store design | 173 |
| 6.5 | User interacting with Ray-Ban virtual mirror | 176 |
| 7.1 | Web ancillary services that influence e-retail trust | 190 |

ILLUSTRATIONS

| 8.1 | An integrated framework for e-branding | 218 |
| 8.2 | Snake position maps for three e-retail booksellers | 226 |
| 10.1 | Five rings of influence in the business environment | 248 |
| 10.2 | The Electronic Shopping ES test | 262 |
| 10.3 | Product characteristics and the five senses | 263 |
| 10.4 | Scoring product characteristics | 263 |
| 10.5 | Familiarity/confidence and electronic shopping | 264 |
| 10.6 | Scoring familiarity and confidence | 264 |
| 10.7 | Consumer categories and electronic shopping potential | 266 |
| 10.8 | Scoring customer attributes | 266 |
| 11.1 | IKEA mobile catalogue | 282 |
| 12.1 | Example of ubiquitous store in Barcelona, Spain | 291 |
| 13.1 | Interactive touch screen displays come in a variety of styles | 309 |
| 13.2 | Regent Street app (Regent Street, London, UK) | 311 |

## TABLES

| 1.1 | Internet penetration rates in Europe | 2 |
| 1.2 | European online retail sales 2014 and 2015 | 5 |
| 2.1 | Segmentation of the online retail sector in Europe | 35 |
| 2.2 | Evaluation of the e-shopping potential of CDs using the ES test | 42 |
| 2.3 | Relative quantities of purchases from Amazon for November 2015 | 62 |
| 4.1 | The principle benefits expected by consumers from e-shopping | 106 |
| 4.2 | The principle benefits expected by business customers from e-purchasing | 107 |
| 7.1 | Positive critical incidents affecting e-service (percentage) | 193 |
| 7.2 | Negative critical incidents affecting e-service (percentage) | 195 |
| 7.3 | Logit regression differentiating high-service and low-service sites | 196 |
| 7.4 | OLS regression determining overall site e-service rating | 197 |
| 9.1 | Determinants of brand attitudes in two Australian e-malls | 242 |
| 9.2 | Determinants of e-trust in two Australian e-malls | 243 |
| 9.3 | Determinants of interactivity in two Australian e-malls | 243 |
| 10.1 | Assessment of retail channels in meeting a retailer's objectives for customers | 255 |
| 10.2 | Assessment of retail channels in meeting a retailer's objectives for staff | 257 |
| 10.3 | Assessment of retail channels in meeting a retailer's objectives for shareholders | 258 |

| | | |
|---|---|---|
| 10.4 | Assessment of retail channels in meeting a retailer's objectives for suppliers, partners and dealers | 259 |
| 10.5 | Assessment of retail channels in meeting a retailer's objectives for the community | 260 |
| 10.6 | Examples of electronic shopping ES tests | 267 |

# Contributors

**Eleonora Pantano**

Dr Eleonora Pantano is a Lecturer in Marketing at Middlesex University of London (UK). Prior to joining Middlesex in February 2015, she was a Postdoctoral Research Fellow at the University of Calabria (Italy) and Researcher at Technical University of Eindhoven (The Netherlands). She holds a PhD in Psychology of Programming and Artificial Intelligence (2008) and a MSc in Business and Management Engineering (2005) from the University of Calabria (Italy).

Her research activities explore marketing management and mainly relate to consumers' attitude and acceptance towards new technology-based retail settings, and how business and retail models are implemented in terms of innovation and technology management.

Eleonora's findings appear in numerous international journals such as *Information Technology and People, International Journal of Information Management,* and *Journal of Retailing and Consumer Services.* She was also Guest Editor of special issues for the *International Journal of Electronic Commerce, Technology Forecasting and Social Change,* among others.

**Bang Nguyen**

Dr Bang Nguyen, PhD, is a member of the Marketing Department at East China University of Science and Technology (ECUST), School of Business (Shanghai, China). Previously, he held positions at Oxford Brookes University and RMIT University Vietnam and was a Visiting Scholar at China Europe International Business School (CEIBS). His research interests include customer relationship management, services marketing, consumer behaviour, branding and innovation management. Bang is the Associate Editor of *Journal of Marketing for Higher Education* and has published widely in journals such as *Internet Research, Industrial Marketing*

*Management, Journal of Business Research, European Journal of Marketing, Journal of Marketing Management, International Journal of Market Research*, among others. He has published more than 100 peer-reviewed scientific articles, books, conference papers and book chapters. In addition, he has edited four books, including *Ethical and Social Marketing in Asia* (Elsevier), *The Dark Side of CRM* (Routledge), *Services Marketing Cases in Asia* (Springer) and *Asia Branding* (Palgrave Macmillan).

## Charles Dennis

Professor Charles Dennis is a Professor of Consumer Behaviour at The Business School, Middlesex University of London (UK), and Associate Editor (Retailing) of the *European Journal of Marketing*. His main teaching and research area is (e-) retail and consumer behaviour – the vital final link of the Marketing process. Charles is a Chartered Marketer, elected a Fellow of the Chartered Institute of Marketing for helping to modernise the teaching of the discipline. Charles was awarded the Vice Chancellor's Award for Teaching Excellence for improving the interactive student learning experience at Brunel University. Charles has published in journals such as *Journal of Business Research* and *European Journal of Marketing*. Books include *Marketing the e-Business* (first and second editions) (joint-authored with Dr Lisa Harris); and research monograph *Objects of Desire: Consumer Behaviour in Shopping Centre Choice* (Palgrave). His research into shopping styles has received extensive coverage in the popular media including TV appearances with Sir Trevor McDonald OBE and Adrian Edmondson.

## Bill Merrilees

Professor Bill Merrilees is in the Department of Marketing, Griffith Business School, Griffith University (Australia), based on the Gold Coast campus. He has worked in both academia and the government. He has a Bachelor of Commerce (Hons I) from the University of Newcastle (Australia), and an MA and PhD from the University of Toronto (Canada). He has consulted with companies like Shell and Westpac at the large end, down to middle-sized companies like accountants and even very small firms like florists. Bill particularly enjoys conducting case research as it builds a bridge to the real world. He has published more than 100 refereed journal articles or book chapters. Some of his articles have been in the e-commerce field including the *Journal of Relationship Marketing, Journal of Business Strategies, Corporate Reputation Review* and *Marketing Intelligence and Planning*. This work includes innovative scale development in the areas of e-interactivity, e-branding, e-strategy and e-trust.

## Sabine Gerlach

Sabine Gerlach is a Lecturer in Marketing at the University of Lincoln (UK). She holds a MSc in International Marketing Strategy and a BA in International Business. A Chartered Marketer and Fellow of the Higher Education Academy, she also works as independent consultant for a number of large public events in the UK.

Her research interests are related to marketing strategies and marketing communications, consumer satisfaction and behaviour and engagement marketing.

# Acknowledgements

The authors thank the many people who have helped bring this book to completion. In particular, we are grateful to Nicola Cupit at Routledge whose input and patient support have gone far beyond the duty. The authors acknowledge the substantial input of Tino Fenech and thank Delia Vazquez and Mehtap Durmus for contributing cases.

# Introduction

## AIM

The aim of this research-based book is to demonstrate the success factors of e-retailing efficiency and effectiveness. It should be useful to readers, e-retailers and researchers seeking an understanding of or studying e-retail and related marketing at various levels and to enhance their selling a product or service to consumers (rather than businesses) via the Internet or other electronic channels. A key feature of the book is that it taps into the latest research studies and in some cases introduces new research findings. This aspect helps ensure that the book is as up-to-date as possible and has the sharpest edge in guiding best practice e-retailing.

## RATIONALE

> Rarely has the retail and consumer services sector been faced with a strategic challenge of such significant complexity and uncertainty which has grown in terms of that significance so rapidly.
> 
> (Reynolds, 2000)

Although Reynolds reviewed e-commerce at the time of a fall in Internet stock values from previous unrealistically high expectations (the 'dot.com crash') during the early days of e-retailing, this strategic challenge still holds today in 2016. E-retail has not become less complex, though, but since that time, it has progressed in acceptability to consumers and in market share. Reynolds also wrote that 'rarely has the academic world ... lagged so significantly behind the world of practice'. Research has exploded, across a wider range of platforms and technologies, and we contend that a modernisation of teaching and training in retail and marketing is overdue.

This is not just an academic issue. Since 2003, when the *Sunday Times* (UK) asked readers for their experiences of shopping online, and they received an 'avalanche of complaint' about poorly designed

# INTRODUCTION

sites, delivery, payment and many other problems (*Sunday Times Doors*, 9 February 2003), it received huge attention by both scholars and practitioners. This book attempts to address some of the problems by providing research material and resources on the essential issues and success factors in e-retailing for researchers, lecturers, trainers, students and practitioners.

## KEY ISSUES AND SUCCESS FACTORS IN E-RETAILING

|  | For a detailed discussion, see Chapter: |
|---|---|
| What is the mix of tools and techniques that e-retailers can use to provide value for customers? | 1 |
| What are the latest practices and trends in the e-retailing of the main product categories? | 2 |
| How can e-retailing be integrated into an organisation? | 3 |
| How can e-retailers understand and communicate with e-consumers? | 4 |
| How can satisfying consumers' needs for information increase sales? | 5 |
| How should the e-store be designed so as to make it easy and enjoyable to move around the site? | 6 |
| How can e-shopper loyalty be encouraged? | 6 |
| How can consumers' needs and wants for good service be better satisfied? | 7 |
| How can e-retail brands be developed and integrated with high street brands? | 8 |
| What are the benefits and problems for e-retailers of 'locating' under a single 'roof' or e-mall? | 9 |
| How can the suitability of products for e-retailing be assessed? | 10 |
| What are the problems and opportunities of retailing via mobile communication devices? | 11 |
| What are the problems and opportunities of retailing offered via ubiquitous technologies? | 12 |
| What are the likely issues and technologies facing future e-retailing developments? | 13 |

INTRODUCTION

## Case study
## LIVING THE DOT.COM LIFE

Started from an experiment of Matthew Wall in September 2003, after more than 10 years we tried to live our life totally online for few days. This is what we got:

It's 5 p.m. on Monday and I've been living my life online for 5 days. Shopping, banking, playing, working and meeting friends, I've done it online (or mobile). I can see live pictures of the shuttle speeding round the earth, and I can even get a pint of milk before tomorrow and a new lipstick for my next online meeting with my friends (by ordering before 12 noon today). It was not possible 10 years ago. It's been pretty amazing. I've bought groceries, clothes, presents, travels and just missed a pair of shoes and an iPhone on eBay. I've ordered a kebab and chatted to strangers.

Actually, the web has shifted from a niche for nerds to an essential for everyone. Even so, e-retailing is still not perfect. It's good for communications, research and transactions, but still has difficulty responding to impulse and emergency buying with fast collect in the store or next-day delivery, while Amazon is developing new forms of delivery to have your purchase in a few hours (through drones).

My online week started well with a cup of tea and pancakes I'd ordered at my favoured supermarket that delivered at 7:30 a.m. (as booked online). I check my e-mail and I got some notifications from my favoured brands that advise me about the new products on sale (online special offers). Unfortunately, I cannot get same-day delivery. It would have been quicker to go to the store, but they are online exclusives only.

Ok, I can book a delivery for tomorrow. When I came to pay, three out of five items ordered are out of stock. If customers can't get what they want, the key e-shopping benefits of convenience and wide choice evaporate. Are these products too exclusive?

I try with other retailers. Contact lenses from VisionDirect (www.visiondirect.co.uk) came free delivery (next day!). Electronics retailer Argos (www.argos.co.uk) is equally efficient. Similarly, books from Amazon (www.amazon.co.uk) came on same-day delivery.

Banking is a dream with my mobile banking app. I can see balances and statements for my mortgage, bank account and credit cards all on one page, transfer between accounts in seconds, set up bill payments in a minute or two – and they'll even text (SMS) my mobile to warn before I go overdrawn. It's great to set monthly payment dates so that I never miss a deadline, and I can easily manage my overdraft limit.

Renewing magazines online and in printed copy was a doddle from the website. I should share my experience online, probably through the magazine's page on Facebook (oh, look! Today it has more than 1,000,000 fans!).

**xxi**

## INTRODUCTION

Nowadays, the web is hardly a communal experience. The chat rooms that I found were full of youngsters talking gibberish. The web has also got a long way to go to rival cinema, TV and radio for entertainment. It will need some sort of 'megaband' to do that – and a wide-screen TV-style display. TV 'webcasting' is in its infancy and apart from music videos and news there isn't much around.

Music lovers who have broadband are well catered for, though, with a terrific audio quality, and I found tickets for my favourite artists.

I spend leisure hours checking the best deal for bars and restaurants checking out Groupon (www.groupon.co.uk), where I found an interesting deal for a cocktail making course.

In the midst of all this I manage to order food from a variety of proposals through Just Eat (www.just-eat.co.uk) which promise arrival in 25 minutes, because I pay by credit card. My food is still warm.

Work is also easy for me as a Lecturer, and my university provides me with remote access to university facilities such as access to academic journals and books I need to check. Moreover, I can interact with my students and provide them additional support for completing their coursework that must be submitted through the university platform by 5 p.m today.

I regularly browse the main newspapers and television to keep updated with the news (i.e. *Times*, www.times-online.co.uk, and BBC, www.bbc.co.uk). Up-to-the-second news is a click away.

The beauty of broadband is that I can multi-task, visiting several sites at once while listening to live radio and watching TV. I mainly use e-mail to file stories, reply to readers and receive breaking news and research newsletters. I don't even need to make calls, while interacting with friends and colleagues through WhatsApp. I have to remember to change my clothes for the Skype meeting with my line manager at 4:30 p.m.

So living online is nearly possible and the Internet is coming of age. How will it transform our lives in the next 20 years? I have one doubt: is meeting friends online and having a beer delivered at home comparable to going out and meeting them at a pub and ordering a fresh pint of Guinness?

## REFERENCE

Reynolds J. (2000) 'eCommerce: A critical review', *International Journal of Retail and Distribution Management,* 28 (10): 417–444.

# Chapter 1

# The world of e-retailing

### LINKS TO OTHER CHAPTERS

- Chapter 4 – Understanding and communicating with the e-consumer
- Chapter 6 – E-store design: navigability, interactivity and web atmospherics
- Chapter 7 – E-service
- Chapter 8 – Branding on the web

### KEY LEARNING POINTS

*After completing this chapter you will have an understanding of*

- What e-retail is, advantages and disadvantages for retailers
- The (e-) retail mix
- E-retailing trends

### ORDERED LIST OF SUBTOPICS

- What is e-retail?
- Disadvantages of e-retailing for retailers
- Advantages of e-retailing for retailers
- The (e-) retail mix: sale the seven Cs
- Growth and prospects for e-retailing
- Conclusions

- Chapter summary
- Case study
- Questions
- Glossary
- Further reading
- References
- Web links

## WHAT IS E-RETAIL?

E-retail has been defined as the sale of goods and services *via* the Internet or other electronic channels, for personal or household use by consumers (Harris and Dennis, 2002).[1] This definition includes all e-commerce activities that result in transactions with end consumers (rather than business customers), i.e. B2C rather than B2B. Some digital marketing activities that do not directly involve transactions, such as providing (free) information, or promoting brands and image are considered to be part of B2C but are not normally considered as being within the scope of e-retail. This is common for luxury products where the website acts as an informational tool, but does not sell the products online, e.g. Omega (www.omegawatches.com).

Internet retailing has been growing in recent years and is expected to continue at a slower rate for mature markets like North America and Western Europe. Other countries are still in their infancy and have stronger growth potential through increased Internet access and household income, e.g. parts of Asia and Eastern Europe (Marketline, 2014). The global online retail market is predicted a Compound Annual Growth Rate (CAGR) of 15.7% (Marketline, 2014) from 2014 to 2019.

**Table 1.1** Internet penetration rates in Europe

| Country | Internet penetration % |
| --- | --- |
| Norway | 97 |
| Netherlands | 93 |
| Sweden | 93 |
| Denmark | 90 |
| Finland | 89 |
| UK | 84 |

| | |
|---|---|
| Germany | 83 |
| Switzerland | 82 |
| Belgium | 81 |
| Austria | 80 |
| France | 80 |
| Slovakia | 79 |
| Estonia | 78 |
| Ireland | 77 |
| Czech Republic | 73 |
| Latvia | 72 |
| Slovenia | 72 |
| Croatia | 71 |
| Israel | 70 |
| Spain | 67 |
| Hungary | 65 |
| Lithuania | 65 |
| Poland | 65 |
| Italy | 58 |
| Serbia | 56 |
| Portugal | 55 |
| Greece | 53 |
| Bulgaria | 51 |
| Russia | 48 |
| Turkey | 46 |
| Romania | 44 |
| Ukraine | 34 |

*Source*: Adapted from Nielsen (2014)

The rise of multi-channel retailer and mobile technology adds to the convenience and attractiveness of e-retailing. Customers shop online more frequently and spend more money across a rising number of product categories; retailers who provide a smooth online experience will capture the most additional sales (Parro and Santorro, 2015).

The major growth areas comprise electrical/electronic goods, apparel including accessories and footwear, groceries, books, music, videos and furniture. The UK spent £104bn online in 2014, with orders made on mobile devices reaching 40% of the total by 2015 (IMRG, 2015). Research from RetailMeNot and the Centre for Retail Research projects that online sales will grow by 16.2% in the UK in 2016, with the average shopper expected to spend more than £1,000 online for the first time (Internet Retailing, 2014).

Giulio Montemagno, Senior Vice President at digital coupon marketplace RetailMeNot, said: "While the ecommerce sector is continuing to grow rapidly, we are starting to see the German, the UK and the US markets mature as shopping online becomes a commonplace activity" (Internet Retailing, 2014). Today, growth is being mainly driven by an increase in the frequency of consumers shopping online and spending more money through online channels, while in previous years growth came primarily from a growing number of first-time online shoppers.

The share of online retail of all retail sales grew from 6.3% in Europe and 10.6% in the US in 2013 to 7.2% and 11.6% in 2014, respectively (Internet Retailing, 2014). The online retail in the UK accounted for 12.1% of all retail sales in 2013 and increased to 13.5% in 2014 (Internet Retailing, 2014).

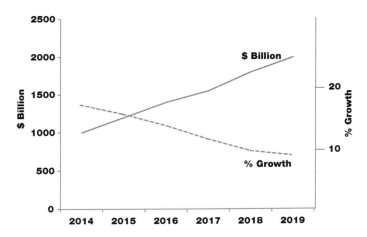

■ *Figure 1.1* Global online retail sector value and growth forecast
Source: Adapted from Marketline (2014)

**Table 1.2** European online retail sales 2014 and 2015

|  | 2014 Online retail sales £ | 2014 Growth % | 2015 Online retail sales £ | 2015 Growth % | 2015 Online retail sales € |
|---|---|---|---|---|---|
| UK | 45.0 | 15.8 | 52.3 | 16.2 | 61.8 |
| Germany | 36.2 | 25.0 | 44.6 | 23.1 | 52.8 |
| France | 26.4 | 16.5 | 30.9 | 17.0 | 36.5 |
| Spain | 6.9 | 19.6 | 8.2 | 18.6 | 9.6 |
| Italy | 5.3 | 19.0 | 6.4 | 19.0 | 7.5 |
| Netherlands | 5.1 | 13.5 | 5.9 | 16.8 | 7.0 |
| Sweden | 3.6 | 15.5 | 4.2 | 15.5 | 4.9 |
| Poland | 3.6 | 22.6 | 4.3 | 21.0 | 5.1 |
| Europe | 132.1 | 18.4 | 156.7 | 18.4 | 185.4 |

Source: Adapted from Centre of Retail Research (2013)

## DISADVANTAGES OF E-RETAILING FOR RETAILERS

Major traditional 'brick-and-mortar' retailers have taken up online retailing over the past years. However, luxury retailers[2] like Chanel, Céline, Hermes and Dior, as well as some small high-street retailers, are holding back due to perceived disadvantages and problems. Retailers, for example, may lack the technical know-how, the substantial investment required or the order fulfilment capabilities. The start-up costs for a website for small retailers are low, as providers like Etsy (www.etsy.com) or Notonthehighstreet.com (www.notonthehighstreet.com) provide a trading website without monthly fees[3] with templates and support. However, established retailers need to invest in order to provide a website which reflects their brand and fulfils various functions e.g. product videos, order tracking, personalised customer experience. In addition to the initial costs of website design and domain name registration, there are ongoing costs of website hosting and regular updating of the website to be considered. The rise of price comparison sites, e.g. www.pricerunner.co.uk, leads to increased price transparency and puts the online retailers in direct price competition with each other – with the result of prices being driven down even further.

Shipping costs influence the price conscious shopper in their final purchase decision and create a major disadvantage for smaller retailers. Major retailers often offer free shipping, or click-and-collect services, whereas smaller retailers cannot afford to bear delivery costs and have to pass them on to the consumer. For example, Country Attire (www.countryattire.com) offers free worldwide delivery to remove the barrier for its customers (Morrell, 2015). The footwear retailer Schuh (www.schuh.co.uk) offers a one hour buy and collect service on items held in store.

The opportunity to save time and/or money leads consumers to purchase from one of the major online retailers instead of from a small shop. One of the biggest pure players, Amazon, struggled to offer free shipping through its 'Super Saver Delivery' for their products the last few years, and therefore increased the minimum spend on orders in order to guarantee free shipping. In 2013, a £10 minimum spend was introduced to gain free delivery; this was raised to £20 in 2014. In 2015, Amazon introduced the Same-Day-Delivery for selected products in selected postcode areas in the UK, when the order is placed by midday. The service is free for Amazon prime members; otherwise the charge is £9.99. Return handling is required by law, but adds to further costs for small retailers through shipping costs and loss of sales.

The rising acceptance and popularity of click-and-collect services can be seen as a weakness for pure players due to the lack of physical stores. In any case, for each type of retailer, continuous costs will include fulfilment, warehousing and logistics. Successful e-retailers, such as Next (www.next.co.uk) and Lands' End (www.landsend.com), have had the advantage of already operating profitable mail order catalogues.

Internet fraud and security issues require investment in the latest security software to protect the transactions and the brand. Customer concern about online security and privacy increases loyalty to established retailers and directs them to well-known and trusted brick-and-mortar retailers.

There can be legal problems. For example, if purchaser and supplier are in different countries, there may be conflict between the laws and taxation in the two countries. A further disadvantage is that e-selling is less powerful than face-to-face selling. (It is easier to say 'no' to a computer.) This viewpoint is linked to a concern of traditional high street retailers that e-retailing offers a diminished role for their expertise. For example, there are obvious difficulties with products sold by 'atmosphere' – touch, feel, smell – and impulse purchases. The lack of passing trade and difficulty browsing influence sales, as shoppers know what they want to buy and therefore spend less online (Mintel, 2014). In addition, consumers have a perception of lower prices online. This puts pressure on margins for e-retailing, and can lead to shoppers expecting consistency with online pricing in store.

Online retail comes with the danger of cannibalizing in-store sales and traffic. Therefore, some luxury retailers opt to preserve the quality of the brand and sell their products exclusively in store.

Finally, after care can be difficult, especially if the shopper is overseas.

**Box 1.1**
**DISADVANTAGES OF E-RETAILING FOR RETAILERS**

- May lack know-how and technology
- Substantial set-up, investment and ongoing costs
- Complex logistics of fulfilment
- E-selling less powerful than face-to-face – uptake slow for goods selected by taste or smell
- Less impulse purchases
- Legal problems
- Less role for traditional high street retail expertise
- Pressure on margins and prices in-store
- After-sales care difficulties

## ADVANTAGES OF E-RETAILING FOR RETAILERS

On the other hand, there are a number of advantages for retailers. First, location is unimportant. According to some textbooks, adapting an old saying, the three most important elements in retail are 'location, location and location'. The best high street locations are therefore expensive. The e-retailer, though, can sell equally well to anywhere in the country and even overseas. Second, size does not matter – small e-retailers can compete on equal terms to large ones, and reach a larger audience than the high street – and be open 24 hours a day. For example, the independent, northern UK-based Botham's of Whitby has been a pioneer of e-retailing.

There are many other advantages. The socio-demographic profile of e-shoppers is attractive to many retailers, as the majority is affluent and therefore commercially attractive customers (Mintel, 2014). In theory at least, online selling saves on the wages costs of face-to-face salespeople and the costs of premises. The savings may be less than expected though, as there are still costs in Internet customer contact and packaging and delivery can be more expensive to provide. Perhaps a more substantial advantage is the ease with which e-retailing integrates with Customer Relationship Management (CRM) and micro-marketing systems – identifying

THE WORLD OF E-RETAILING

and treating the customer as an individual. This, together with the easier provision of product information, leads to greater opportunities for cross-selling and selling-up. Traditional 'brick-and-mortar' retailers are the late entrants to online retailing. They profit from diversifying its operation, enhancing sales and presence in other markets.

Overall, operating as an online retailer includes low fixed costs, easy access to suppliers and fewer regulations than a physical retail store.

The perceived consumer resistance among retailers is fading. According to Internet World Stats, global Internet access increased to 39% in 2013 (cited in Marketline, 2014).

Eurostats (2013) reported nearly 60% of EU28 Internet users aged 16 to 74 had shopped online. Among the European members the UK is the leading country in online retail. In 2013, 21 million households (83%) had Internet access and 72% shopped online (ONS, 2013).

### Box 1.2
### ADVANTAGES OF E-RETAILING FOR RETAILERS

- Location is unimportant
- Size does not matter
- Wages and premises costs are lower
- A larger audience can be reached
- There is a higher disposable income profile than average
- Orders are accepted 24 hours a day
- More opportunities are provided for CRM, micro-marketing, cross- and up-selling
- If we don't, our competitors will

## THE (E-) RETAIL MIX: SALE THE SEVEN CS

The (e-) retail mix is a shorthand term for the blend of tools and techniques that (e-) retailers use to provide value for customers. It is a development of the well-known marketing mix, more specific to retail and e-retail. As far back as the first half of the twentieth century, the job of the marketer was described as a 'mixer of ingredients' (Culliton, 1948). Marketers devise strategies and tactics aimed at providing satisfaction and adding value for customers. The various elements are blended into a 'marketing mix' – a phrase first coined by Neil Borden (1964) of Harvard Business School.

The marketing mix is most widely known as E Jerome McCarthy's (1960) '4Ps': Place, Product, Price and Promotion. 'Place' is not quite

# THE WORLD OF E-RETAILING

self-explanatory, but refers to the routes organisations take to get the benefits of the product or service to the intended customers – channels of distribution. 'Product' means both tangible product and also 'service' and all the ways that an organisation adds value. 'Price' means not just the price charged, but also all aspects of pricing policy including, for example, distributor margins. 'Promotion' is not just the more-specialised 'sales promotion', but also every way that a product is promoted to customers – from print advertising to websites to social media.

In recent decades there have been numerous attempts to update and revise the marketing mix. One development is particularly descriptive of the way marketers think about the customer. The '4Cs' (Lauterborn, 1990) imply more emphasis on customer wants and concerns than do the 4Ps. The 4Cs (in the same order as the equivalent 4Ps listed above) are **Convenience for the customer**; **Customer value and benefits**; **Cost to the customer**; and **Communication**. Reflecting the emphasis of long-term relationships with customers and the rise of social media marketing, we include **customer relationships** within the umbrella of the 'communication' C.

## C1 Convenience for the customer

'Place' (from the 4Ps), rather than implying managements' methods of placing products where they want them to be, can be thought of as '**Convenience for the customer**', recognising the customers' choices for buying in ways convenient to them. It can also include the convenience of delivery, e.g. door to door, in-store collection or parcel stations.

For the retailer, 'Place' incorporates what can be the most critical decision concerning 'location'. For the e-retailer, this is also important, as many customers prefer a multi-channel approach: they browse online, buy in-store or *vice versa* – or buy on the web, return to the store for a refund or even use 'click-and-collect' services. There are many digital touch points throughout the customer journey, e.g. online price comparison or a store finder app, which need to be integrated to provide a seamless customer experience. This perhaps goes some way towards explaining the success of high street and multi-channel retailers in e-retail, as compared to the pure players.

Physical location can also be important for the e-retailer, as many customers prefer to buy from, or are more likely to trust, an e-retailer based at least in the same country, where carriage costs and maybe taxes are cheaper.

'Location' for the e-retailer also means virtual location and the ease of finding the website. This entails search engine optimisation, social media presence, a memorable web domain and links from associates, to name a few.

All elements need to be in sync and support each other in order for the online retailer to be visible.

Convenience also includes key aspects of website design such as navigation, layout and ease of purchase. For the 'bricks' retailer, convenience decisions include shelf space allocation and layout. The equivalent in e-retail is web atmospheric including the user interface and user experience (UI/UX). Virtual store layout and design are considered in more detail in Chapter 6.

## C2 Customer value and benefits

'Product', rather than being something that a company has to sell, can be thought of as '**Customer value and benefits**' – meaning the bundle of service and satisfactions wanted by customers. People do not buy 'products' as such, but rather solutions to problems or good feelings. Retailers and e-retailers now specify (and sometimes design) products to a much greater extent than previously, reflecting closeness to the customer and appreciation of benefits that customers want. Customers demand customised and personalised product solutions, which transfers the power from the retailer to the customer. Customers are able to design their own product that will satisfy their needs and wants (Thirumalai & Sinha, 2011). For example, Adidas offers its customers personalisation of their own shoes, by offering a choice of material colours, individual prints and other options (www.adidas.com). Co-creation, which is defined as a collaboration-based process between participants (consumers) and organisations, creates benefits for both parties (Wittel et al., 2011). It is about developing ideas, sharing knowledge and participating in the process of creating a new service or product that could be of worth for other consumers as well. It is also used in the automotive industry, e.g. Audi offer 'Build your all-new R8' (www.audi.co.uk).

An essential task of retail and e-retail is selecting the range of products offered for sale – assembled for target markets from diverse sources. The wide and deep range that can be offered is one of the areas where the 'clicks' e-retailer can score relative to the 'bricks' retailer.

E-shoppers who need help in understanding a product are more likely to abandon the transaction and find an alternative supplier or even buy through a different channel. E-retailers, therefore, need to be particularly careful about describing products clearly in Customer value and benefits terms. Customer reviews on the product site, product presentation and visual product demonstration, e.g. videos of dresses being worn by a model on ASOS (www.asos.com), support the value and benefits for the customer.

## C3 Cost to the customer

'Price' may be what companies decide to charge for their products, but **'Cost to the customer'** represents "everything given by the acquirer in terms of money, time and effort to obtain the product" (Yudelson, 1999). The real costs that customers will pay, include, for example, in the case of 'bricks' retail, their own transport costs. For 'clicks' e-retail, there are also the costs of carriage and perhaps taxes to be added to the quoted prices, e.g. import tax when ordering products from China. High carriage charges may be one reason for the high rate of carts abandoned at the checkout. Customers also need to consider the costs of Internet access, product search and possible usage costs.

Consumers have a perception that prices should be lower online than in-store, and this can cause problems when customers buying *via* other channels realise that they are paying more than online customers. For example T-Mobile (t-mobile.com), a well-known telecommunications provider, despite having stores, has a number of attractive special offers only available online. Customers, who have looked up what they want online, and then go in the store to buy, can be irritated to learn that the extra discounts are not available offline.

'Brick' stores have started to offer price-matching services in order to avoid losing customers to online retailers. For example, both Best Buy and Target offer price-matching services in the US, and their brick-and-mortar stores will match prices from major retailers, such as Amazon and Wal-Mart.

Even John Lewis, a well-established department store in the UK, offers a price-matching service but under the condition that the company needs to own a high street store (no pure online players or mail order catalogues).

## C4 Communication and customer relationships

'**Communication**' is equivalent to the final 'P' in the 4Ps: 'Promotion'. Promotion suggests ways in which companies persuade people to buy, whereas communication is a two-way process also involving feedback from customers to suppliers. Reflecting an increasing control of elements of the retail mix by retailers rather than manufacturers, retailers spend more on advertising than manufacturers do (assisted by advertising allowances from manufacturers). Retailers are closer to the customer than are manufacturers and have more access to customer feedback.

Communication is not just advertising, though, but all the ways in which retailers communicate with their customers, including, for example, marketing research surveys, social media, public relations (PR), direct mail, e-mail, marketing databases and loyalty schemes. Successful e-retailers often use integrated marketing communications with a variety of online and offline elements linked together, e.g. through links or by sending direct mail after an online order. Online methods include social networking, Google ads and pop-ups (often incentivised), pay per click, search engine optimisation, and affiliate programmes. The rise of social media changed the way of communication between organizations, communities and individuals (Kietzmann et al., 2011). Platforms like Twitter, Facebook and Instagram enable direct and individual dialogue between the customer and retailer.

In addition to solving problems (see the 'Customer Value and Benefits' section), there is another reason for customers to buy products – to get good feelings. This is a particularly difficult area for e-retailers. The 'bricks' retail store and the face-to-face salesperson are often much better at identifying and satisfying customers' emotional needs and wants. The physical store uses atmospherics in the attempt to change mood and give shoppers a pleasant emotional experience when buying. Emotional cues may include visual (decor), olfactory (perfume), touch (smooth and cool or soft and cuddly) and acoustic (music). Instant satisfaction is another major reason for purchasing 'off-line'.

E-retailers can create web atmosphere (UX/ UI) using, for example, music and visuals such as 3D displays/demonstration videos. These atmospherics can be hungry for bandwidth but websites are able to customise/amend the experience based on the speed of consumers' broadband connections. Web atmospherics (UX/UI) are considered in more detail in Chapter 6.

**'Customer relationships'** are an area that successful bricks retailers such as Tesco (www.tesco.co.uk) have used to gain a major lead over competitors by introducing the loyalty card (Tesco Clubcard). In the section above, the importance of the emotional aspects of selling was mentioned. The sales representative selling face-to-face in the 'bricks' retail store can use verbal and non-verbal (body language) communication to build personal relationships with customers, enhancing the emotional value of products. In trying to replicate the physical buying experience, the e-retailer is at a disadvantage. On the other hand, with transaction data ready-digitised, the e-retailer is well placed to enhance product value using Customer Relationship Management (CRM) techniques. For example, data mining can be used to build a picture of products most likely to be wanted by individual customers. Products tailored specifically can be offered pro-actively. Amazon (www.amazon.co.uk), for instance, uses such a system to match new books to existing customers likely to be interested in them and show related products other customers bought or

# THE WORLD OF E-RETAILING

which are frequently bought together. This approach aims to emulate the personal recommendations given by traditional 'bricks' sales personnel.

Computer cookies can customise and enhance the usability of the website through more effective navigation, which contributes to building customer relationships.

There have been a number of suggestions for structuring a 'Retail mix', equivalent to the 4Ps, 4Es or 4Cs of the marketing mix, adding other aspects that may be key to retailer success. For example, McGoldrick (2002) uses a nine-element mix. In addition to those that can be incorporated into the 4Cs framework above, McGoldrick also includes factors such as 'brand image', 'logistics' and 'information'. Most versions of the retail mix are not as 'catchy' as the 4Ps or 4Cs of the marketing mix. Therefore we propose a simplified '**7Cs**' for the e-retail mix, adding **Computing and category management issues**; **Customer franchise**; and **Customer care and service**.

To some extent there is a parallel with Kearney's (2000) 7Cs for creating a rewarding customer e-shopping experience. In addition to convenience, communication and customer care, Kearney included 'content' and 'customisation' which we have included under 'Customer value and benefits', 'connectivity' (in our 'Convenience') and 'community' (in our 'Customer care and service'). Jones et al. (2001) added a further C: 'concern' which we have again included under the 'Customer care and service' heading.

## C5 Computing and category management issues

The success of retailers has been founded on supplying the products that customers want, in the right sizes and quantities, at the right time and in the right place. With the growth in consumer choice has come a proliferation of products. Superstores carry 20,000 plus branded products and department stores from 100,000 even up to a million or more. Efficient control of this degree of complexity needs effective computer and logistics systems.

Retail logistics have been changing rapidly in recent decades. First, the growth of retailer power has involved major retailers taking more control of their supply chains. The involvement of wholesalers has been reduced, tending to give way to contract logistics (under retailer control). At the same time, supply chains have become more efficient with computer network links between suppliers and retailers – many still based on Electronic Data Interchange (EDI).

Stock levels have been reduced using techniques such as Efficient Customer Response (ECR – the retailers' equivalent of Just-in-Time or JIT). EDI networks are expensive to install, costing at least hundreds of

13

THE WORLD OF E-RETAILING

thousands of pounds. There is a growing trend towards the use of the Internet, particularly for smaller businesses (suppliers and customers) and smaller order quantities. Increasingly, retailers such as Tesco are allowing Internet access to their suppliers for real-time Electronic Point-of-Sale (EPoS) data. Trusted supplier partners can thus respond more quickly to changes in customer demand.

Co-operation between suppliers and retailers has been key to improving the efficiency of satisfying customers while minimising stocks and costs. On a larger scale, this co-operative process is known as 'Category management' (CM), the retailer/supplier process of managing categories as strategic business units.

High efficiency of the computer-controlled logistics systems is largely behind the success of bricks-and-clicks retailers such as Tesco. Ironically, deficiencies in this area have been a major factor in the failure of a number of pureplay dot.coms that have concentrated on advertising and promotion at the expense of other areas of the e-retail mix. One exception is Amazon, which is founded on efficient logistics systems and customer care and service. In the UK, Amazon has used its logistics expertise to carry out distribution services on contract for bricks retailers such as WHSmith (www.whsmith.co.uk) and Toys "R" Us (www.toysrus.co.uk).

Apart from Amazon and the major bricks-and-clicks retailers, many of the e-retailers with the most efficient computer and logistics efficiency are established direct-selling businesses. For example, Quill (www.quillcorp.com) and Screwfix (www.screwfix.com), office supplies and tradesperson supplies, respectively, operate established mail businesses via a paper catalogue. Dell (www.Dell.co.uk) has been a pioneer in telemarketing and direct selling since the late 1980s, demonstrating that a complex product like a computer could be sold without face-to-face contact. Much of the success has been due to investment in computer-based mass customisation systems, along with excellent customer care and service. The company was one of the first e-retailers and holds the second largest market share (18%) for the global server market (Eweek, 2015).

## Mini case 1.1
## SCREWFIX

Screwfix (www.screwfix.com) started out as a UK trade wholesale supplier, but also sells extensively for DIY. Screwfix.com earned Retail Week's 'Retailer of the Year' award for 2002. Screwfix is an example of the successful niche e-retailer with 1.5 million unique website visitors each week (Kingfisher, 2014). Screwfix is owned by Kingfisher, i.e. in the same stable as the B&Q UK DIY stores. Although the branding, ordering and fulfilment are completely separate, the supply chains are integrated, resulting in economies of scale and buying power. Screwfix is the UK's largest omni-channel supplier of trade tools, accessories and hardware to trade professionals and DIY enthusiasts (Marketline, 2014). Sales soared by 17.6% to £665m in 2014 in the UK and Ireland due to a strong promotional strategy, extended opening hours (7 a.m. – 8 p.m. for all stores), successful click-and-collect offers and store expansion (DIY week, 2014).

The (e-) retail mix is summarised below.

**Convenience for the customer:** Express Shopping: if you have the catalogue, simply type in the quantities and catalogue number, or alternatively use 'Search' to find what you want.

A free phone telephone number is available 24 hours per day, plus fax and e-mail options, offering improved personal interaction.

Screwfix also offers a mobile app and SMS services for ordering. Their click/call-and-collect in-store service guarantees that the order is ready within 5 minutes if the stock is available in store.

Next-day delivery to the store or home address for 7 days a week is a standard procedure.

**Customer value and benefits:** Products include not only screws, bolts and nails, but also fixings, adhesives, tools, hardware, lighting, plumbing and cleaning products – the claim is 'Everything for the trade and DIY – next day', 100 percent stock availability of 6,000 products. Screwfix also offers an extended online range.

**Cost to the customer:** A number of Special Offers are always available. Most prices are significantly cheaper than in DIY retail sheds.

**Communication and customer relationships:** The homepage has many examples of good practice, for example:

Recommend a Friend – get a reward when they order for the first time;
Open a Business Account;
Testimonials – 'I have just received my order and felt I must congratulate you on an excellent service. Your site is well designed. The products are well laid out and the order processing excellent.' ... 'Your web site is brilliant; the designer needs a big pat on the back. Well laid out, and to order online is so easy.'
Register/Login: Optional registration makes ordering quicker and easier. Regular communications by mail with catalogues, 'What's new' and special offers for registered customers.

**Computing and category management issues:** Winner of best use of Supply Chain Management at the 2001 Internet Business Awards.

**Customer franchise:** Without the need for heavy advertising, Screwfix has quickly built up a reputation for cheap prices, with quick and reliable delivery based on actual performance.

**Customer care and service:** To test the service, we ordered a long, complex list of equipment and fittings at 4 p.m. on a Sunday. The complete, correct order was delivered by 8 a.m. on Monday.

*Sources*: Various, included authors' own site test and Reynolds (2002).

## C6 Customer franchise

The most successful 'bricks' retailers have invested heavily in quality and customer care and service in order to raise their standing in the assessments of customers. Some authors refer to the accumulated value of image, trust and branding as the retailer's **'customer franchise'**. As we detail in Chapters 4 and 7, consumers' lack of trust has been one of the main factors inhibiting the growth of e-retail. As McGoldrick (2002) pointed out, with greater choice, consumers choose the brands that they trust.

Many 'bricks' retailers have high-quality brands with clear personalities backed by long-term corporate promotion. These strong brands give 'bricks-and-clicks' retailers a head start over 'pureplay' dot.coms. Start-up brands must work hard on trust. For example, one of the few pure players to prosper, the auction site eBay (www.ebay.co.uk), includes five levels of safeguards including fraud protection and dispute resolution. Other successful pure players include ASOS (www.asos.com), Amazon (www.amazon.com) and Net-a-Porter (www.net-a-porter.com). The latter three have been awarded with pure player awards 2014 (Global e-commerce submit, 2014).

## C7 Customer care and service

According to McGoldrick (2002), retailing has traditionally been classified as a 'service industry' but, for most retailers, the preoccupation with service quality and services offered is of more recent origin. At the broadest level, most of a retailer's activities deliver a form of service to the consumer, creating assortments at competitive prices in accessible locations. These activities therefore all play major roles in creating customer satisfaction.

More specifically for the e-retailer, good service means, for example, reasonably fast and reliable deliveries at times convenient to the shopper; availability of online chat; telephone help, social media integration e.g. Facebook, Twitter and Instagram; and return and refund facilities. These are aspects on which many e-retailers have been lamentably poor, with many e-shoppers still having a sorry tale to tell.

For the 'bricks' retailer, even in self-service settings, store personnel play a crucial role in forming retail images and patronage intentions. The e-retailer is at a disadvantage, but elements for real-time support such as click-through online help, click to chat, click and reserve, web call-back, forums, click to call and video chat can help to make the e-shopping experience more interactive.

In general, the successful (e-) retailer sets out to make shopping more enjoyable, more convenient and/or less worrying for the customers by removing the element of uncertainty.

When buying high-priced items and those with a high 'personal' content such as cars, shoppers particularly value personal service. Audi collects the customer data via a pop-up window and provides information about the nearest Audi centre. A representative will contact the customer and invite him/her for a test drive. Retailers such as Nordstrom (http://shop.nordstrom.com) or Schuh (www.schuh.co.uk) use live-chat to overcome this above mentioned drawback with a live chat pop-up window 24 hours a day. Schuh has the option to video chat and the customer decides whether to turn the webcam on.

The extra 3Cs of the (e-) retail mix (in addition to the 4Ps or 4Cs of the marketing mix) can therefore be seen to be particularly critical for e-retailers. The computing, category management, supply chain and delivery systems are areas in which the early e-retailers, particularly pure players, have been sadly lacking, affecting trust, image and customer care and service. The stronger brands with greater customer franchise have higher sales and potentially higher profit, for example, Tesco (www.tesco.com) and Next (www.next.co.uk).

With few exceptions, it is already strongly branded 'bricks' retailers with established computer and supply chain systems who are making the running in e-retailing. Notable exceptions include Amazon (www.Amazon.co.uk) and Dell (www.dell.com), both well-known for efficient systems, quality, service, communications and interaction (see case studies).

**THINK POINT**

If people can shop online easily, why should anyone use the high street?

THE WORLD OF E-RETAILING

**Box 1.3**
**SALE THE 7CS – THE (E-) RETAIL MIX**

### C1 Convenience for the customer ('Place' from the 4Ps)

- Physical location
- Multi-channel options: browse the web, buy in-store or vice versa – or buy on the web, return to the store for a refund
- Virtual location and ease of finding the website: registration with search engines, and links from associates
- Website design: connectivity; navigation; 'shelf' space allocation and ease of purchase
- Layout: 'free-flow', 'grid' or 'free-grid'

### C2 Customer value and benefits ('Product')

- Satisfactions wanted by customers
- Solutions to problems or good feelings
- Specify (sometimes design) products reflecting closeness to the customer and benefits that customers want
- Selecting the range of products offered for sale – assembled for target markets from diverse sources
- Wide and/or deep range – where the 'clicks' e-retailer can score relative to the 'bricks' retailer
- Content: describing a compelling offer of products clearly in customer value and benefits terms
- Customisation of products to match the wants of customer segments as closely as possible

### C3 Cost to the customer ('Price')

- The real cost that customers will pay including transport, carriage and taxes
- Costs of Internet telephone access
- Customers' perceptions that prices should be cheaper online than in-store

### C4 Communication and customer relationships ('Promotion')

**Communication** is a two-way process also involving feedback from customers to suppliers, including:

- Marketing research surveys
- Public relations (PR)
- Direct mail
- E-mail

- Social media
- Offline advertising such as magazines and 'click here' sections of newspapers
- Online methods including banner ads and pop-ups (often incentivised); paid-for listings in search engines and directories; and affiliate programmes
- Atmospherics and web atmospherics including UI and UX: visual (décor, colour management, video clips, 3D), olfactory (perfume and samples), touch (smooth and cool or soft and cuddly – communicated by visuals or samples) and aural (music)

### *Customer relationships*

- In-store sales representatives use verbal and non-verbal (body language) communication
- Marketing database and loyalty schemes are used
- The e-retailer can enhance product value using Customer Relationship Management (CRM) and data mining to tailor products specifically to individual customers

### C5 Computing and category management issues

- Supplying the products that customers want, in the right sizes and quantities, at the right time and in the right place
- Efficient supply chains with computer network links between suppliers and retailers
- Minimising stocks and speed of response: Efficient Customer Response (ECR – the retailers' equivalent of Just-in-Time or JIT)
- Co-operation between suppliers and (e-) retailers aiming to improve the efficiency of satisfying customers while minimising stocks and costs. On the larger scale, this is 'Category management' (CM), the retailer/supplier process of managing categories as strategic business units.
- Efficient logistics systems are an important component of customer care and service.

### C6 Customer franchise

- Image, trust and branding – long-term investment in quality, corporate communications and customer care and service
- Safeguards including fraud protection and dispute resolution
- Safe shopping icons, e.g. a padlock or unbroken key icon for used encryption

### C7 Customer care and service

- Creating assortments at competitive prices in an accessible format
- Fast and reliable deliveries at times convenient to the shopper

- Availability of help; return and refund facilities
- For the 'bricks' retailer store personnel are crucial
- For the e-retailer click-through telephone help, click to chat, click and reserve, web call back, forums, click to call and video chat. To make the experience more interactive
- Addressing customer concerns, particularly for credit card security, e.g. displaying the 'padlock' secure site logo

*Source*: The authors, developed from McCarthy's (1960) 4Ps and Lauterborn's (1990) 4Cs.

## GROWTH AND PROSPECTS FOR E-RETAILING

### Geographic expansion and omni-channel innovation

The online retail market becomes increasingly global with the mature markets in Western Europe and North America and the emergence of the markets in East Asia and Latin America, which are expected to double the growth rates of the former over the next 5 years (Wigder et al., 2014).

Customers are seeking a seamless shopping experience with easy flow between laptops, tablets, mobile phones and stores. They already include multiple digital touch points to their shopping experience regardless of completing the transaction.

Web-rooming also known as 'reverse showrooming' describes the purchase where the transaction takes place online with the order fulfilment offline. Pure online players like Baidu in China or Snapdeal.com in India seek 'brick' partners, e.g. department stores, or invest in companies for their online fulfilment. This accelerates their growth and catch up with omni-channel retailers. Ebay (www.ebay.co.uk) has been using over 750 Argos stores across the UK as collection points for customers' orders since 2014. Amazon has installed lockers in various locations including shopping malls where customers can pick up their online orders.

Traditional retailers play a leading role in online retailing (Wigder et al., 2014) especially in North America, Europe and Latin America. Those with stores in various countries are expected to expand through international online orders and fulfilment in their local stores. An increasingly smooth integration between store, mobile and web is expected from traditional retailers to compete with the pure online players.

'Showrooming', where consumers touch, feel, try out a product in store before purchasing it online for a cheaper price is still popular, but according to Adler (2014) more people (69% in the US) are using online-to-offline (O2O) whereas only 46% engage in showrooming.

PricewaterhouseCoopers's (2015) report confirmed the trend with 70% of their global sample confirming that they use web-rooming and 68% use showrooming.

Both present opportunities for retailers while linking the online and offline experience, e.g. through automatic payment via mobile registration, in-store Wi-Fi, smartphone discounts.

## Mobile retailing

Penetration is twice as high for smartphones than for tablets in the US and UK, while in emerging markets it can be up to 10 times higher (Wigder et al., 2014). In developing markets, the mobile phone is often the first device to access the Internet. Therefore, online retailers need to put emphasis on mobile strategies, as responsive design is a critical factor to boost their sales. Tablets are used by affluent customers with higher conversion rates which lead to substantial growth in revenue for tablets. According to Nielsen (2014) those are used by nearly one third (31%) for online shopping[4] globally. As the penetration of tablets grows so will their use for online shopping.

All of the trends above help to strengthen the competitive position of omni-channel retailers.

To increase digital engagement, then, retailers must deliver on multiple shopper needs for lower prices, quality choices and peace of mind. Easy-to-navigate websites that offer a wide selection of well-described, unique products with plenty of images and have proper security protocols are a must (Nielsen, 2014).

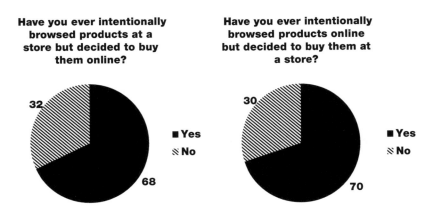

*Figure 1.2* Web-rooming vs. Showrooming survey results[5]

Source: Adapted from PricewaterhouseCoopers (2015)

The market leaders in their sectors were Amazon (books), Tesco (groceries), Dell (computers), Next (clothing) and Apple (personal communication devices) in the UK. Though perhaps not actually an e-retailer, eBay is the leader for online auctions and one of the most visited of all UK websites.

### Box 1.4
### HOW TO SHOP SAFELY ONLINE

- Always pay by credit card, in order to take advantage of the safe purchasing protection (and not by debit cards such as Switch or Delta).
- Check the policy for returning unwanted goods – shipping charges can be high.
- Provide payment details on secure sites only – check for the small padlock in the bottom-right corner of the screen.
- Check carefully for extra charges. For example, goods from outside the EU may be subject to customs and excise duty and/or VAT (check out www.hmce.gov.uk).
- Check for a privacy statement which informs you how the company protects your personal information and secures your credit card data and whether they sell information about their customers to other companies.
- Be cautious clicking on realistic-looking retail ads in pop-ups. Some are a phony operation designed to gather personal information. Most reputable retailers do not use pop-ups.

*Source*: Adapted from *Sunday Times* 'Doors', 27 June 2002.

### THINK POINT

With a Boots on every high street, why shop at the Boots online store?

## CONCLUSIONS

While many will regret the passing of the old-fashioned high street, change is inevitable. Consumers are overcoming reservations, e.g. credit card fraud on e-shopping. Market forces in action mean that the e-retailing survivors and leaders are the strong brands who are successfully addressing the customer care and service and fulfilment issues.

# THE WORLD OF E-RETAILING

Given the unstoppable progress of e-retailing, traditionalists can at least take comfort in the current e-success of the high street multi-channel retailers – hopefully preserving at least some vibrant 'bricks' shopping alongside the growing proportion of 'clicks'. In the following chapters, we will compare and contrast with the successes of conventional retailing to develop the theory and practice of e-retailing, finally speculating on the shoppers of tomorrow.

**THINK POINT**

For each of these e-retailers – Botham's, Next, Amazon, Marks & Spencer and Boots, what do you consider to be the reasons for their success (or otherwise) as e-retailers?

**CHAPTER SUMMARY**

E-retail is the sale of goods and services via Internet or other electronic channels, for personal or household use by consumers.

The well-known marketing mix of 4Ps (or 4Cs) can be extended by the addition of three more Cs to make a more catchy retail mix: 'Sale the 7Cs'. The three extra Cs are particularly relevant to e-retail success:

- Computing and category management issues
- Customer franchise, trust, image and branding
- Customer care and service

E-retail is growing, and the leaders are mainly those performing well on the three extra Cs.

The next chapter will outline the latest practice and trends in e-retailing the main products.

## Case study 1.1
## NEXT

Next is a top multi-channel retailer for street fashion. The first Next store opened in February 1982 with an exclusive co-ordinated collection of stylish clothes, shoes and accessories for women. They later introduced collections for men, children and

**23**

home products and have more than 500 stores in the UK and Ireland. It also operates 200 stores in 40 countries in Europe, Asia and the Middle East.

The successful mail order business, Next Directory, launched in 1988 with 350 pages, which has soared to 1,400 pages in 2015. Online shopping at Next began in 1999 and now the entire catalogue is available to shop from on the Internet including formalwear, casual wear, accessories, shoes, swimwear, lingerie, men's and children's wear. The Next Directory including the online and catalogue business has about 4 million active users (Marketline, 2014). The mail order expertise in order handling, fulfilment and customer care has proved invaluable, making the business one of the strongest retailers in the UK clothing e-retailing. The company's multi-channel retail model provides a competitive advantage and allows it to serve a diverse range of customers. Customers can purchase from the three main channels Next Retail (stores), Next Directory (catalogue and website) and Next International (franchised stores).

To shop online you have to set up an account. Revenue comes from its business segments including NEXT Retail (59.6% of the total, revenues during FY2014), NEXT Directory (35.9%), NEXT International Retail (2.3%), Lipsy (1.7%), NEXT Sourcing (0.3%), property management (0.1%) and other (0.2%) (Marketline, 2014).

## *The e-retail mix at Next*

**C1 Convenience for the customer** The Next website can easily be found using most search engines. The website is a convenient place to shop as it is well structured, easy to navigate and buy, pages download fast and there is general ease of access.

Their various delivery options are convenient and show a flexible, consumer-friendly approach to service, e.g. small charge for next-day delivery, but guaranteed if you order by 11 p.m., an evening slot delivery between 6 and 10 p.m. the next day or even a same-day delivery when ordered by 12 midday during the week, or store collection. Returns can be arranged via courier pick-up for free or through direct return to a high street shop. Next integrates the online and store channels seamlessly. Next continues to improve the functionality of its website, with particular emphasis on payment processing and account management screens, re-launch of the iPad and iPhone Apps in addition to a redesign of the mobile site (m.next.uk) (NEXT, 2015).

**C2 Customer value and benefits** There is a wider product range than can be found in the high street shops offering products that are available in the Next Directory.

In addition next.co.uk offers products exclusive to the website in their 'Online Exclusives' sections. Customer ratings and reviews about specific products are available on the website. Next also included a "yes, I recommend this product" option in the review section.

# THE WORLD OF E-RETAILING

**C3 Cost to the customer** Next does not offer online customers any discount. Customers also pay a £3.99 delivery charge no matter how large the order except for furniture where the charge is £8.99 at the time of writing. However, customers do save in terms of the time and travel costs of travelling to a 'bricks' store.

**C4 Communication and customer relationships** The Next website provides communication to customers through an electronic newsletter via e-mail. Customers can register to receive updates of forthcoming offers and promotions including details of the end-of-season sale. See the 'Web atmospherics' section for other communications aspects of the Next website. Next is present on main social media sites like Facebook, Twitter and Pinterest to engage with its customers and provide dedicated customer service including complaint handling.

Computer cookies enhance the experience by showing 'recently viewed' items at the bottom of the site for consideration.

However, Customer Relationship Management (CRM) techniques to offer customers a tailored experience and pro-actively offer products based on previous purchase history do not yet exist.

**C5 Computing and category management issues** The supply chain systems are slick and efficient, utilising ECR techniques to provide fast delivery from minimum stocks, keeping the customer informed of progress by an automated e-mail system. In-store assistance is able to check the stock levels in other stores and warehouses, but the service is not offered on the website as yet.

**C6 Customer franchise** Next has a trusted brand name for high street and Next Directory shopping and the website has inherited this.

Next targets customers in their 20s and 30s who are looking for stylish but affordable clothes to take them through the next fashion trend. Quality, style and value for money are core brand values.

**C7 Customer care and service** Next provides customer service via their social media sites with quick responses, a contact form on the website and a pop-up 'We can call you now' on the website as well as a 24/6 telephone number. If a customer wishes to return goods, he or she can do this with no extra charge. The customer can either take them back to a store or return them with a courier or by post (Next provides a pre-paid label). Purchases made before 11.00 p.m. are delivered the following day, excluding Sunday deliveries.

In order to enhance the customer service an online chat option at checkout would avoid abandoned shopping carts and therefore increase sales. Another opportunity would be the introduction of automated reminder e-mails if items have been added to the shopping cart without placing an order. The checkout is proven to be critical for online shopping due to the registration of details, display of total costs and delivery charges. Next offers various payment options for its customers from usual credit and debit cards, direct debit, PayPal and Next Directory Card which charges the Next Credit Account.

### *Web atmospherics - user interface and user experience (UI/UX)*

There is a lack of interactivity on the Next website and they do not sell any customised products. 'Extras' such as these could help compensate for the lack of personal contact. There is a separate login for customers who have bought online before, but apart from this, there is no personalisation or mass customisation found on the site.

The Next website is very simple which makes for good usability – something that many Internet retailers get wrong. The layout of the site is easy to navigate for people who are not computer literate. Purchasing from the website is very straightforward, without too many click-through pages.

Visually the Next site is appealing and sophisticated. Pictures of the products are available from all angles. The quality and colour of the pictures of the products are excellent. The text on the Next website is short yet contains all the required information.

In conclusion, the good all-round retail mix has made Next into one of the top Internet retailers. As a result, they are now looking to start sub-contract fulfilment services for other e-tailers.

As an improvement, Next could consider catwalk videos like ASOS do. This is simple to do and will help to make the purchase experience more pleasant to a customer due to the enhanced product view.

Another refinement could be to introduce a virtual changing room where items can be coordinated. This is the 'Style Builder' idea as used by Eddie Bauer (www.eddiebauer.com). A further improvement would be to implement a system for customers to see pictures of themselves wearing different garments. Records could be stored on a database for customers to refer to later. These kinds of ideas may encourage people to buy by making the experience more interactive and personal.

In order to improve customer service Next could e-mail registered customers when their desired product is back in stock or even a store nearby. Having a stock availability 'instant stock check' for stores next to the product description like Argos would encourage sales and customers to visit the store too.

## QUESTIONS

*Brief feedback to these questions is included at the back of the book.*

**Question 1.1** – What do you think would be disadvantages of e-retailing for an independent baker like Botham's (www.botham.co.uk/)?

THE WORLD OF E-RETAILING

**Question 1.2** – What do you consider are the main advantages of e-retailing for a small independent baker like Botham's?

**Question 1.3** – Why do you think Screwfix is separately branded from B&Q even though both are under the same ownership, selling many of the same products?

**Question 1.4** – Why do you think that the 7Cs of the e-retail mix represent a superior model to the traditional 4Ps and other versions of the retail mix?

## NOTES

1 Tickets, holidays, gambling and insurance are excluded because they are not classed as retailing.
2 Aside from cosmetics and fragrances.
3 Etsy charges 3.5% transaction fee per item and 4% + £0.20 payment processes (November 2015). Notonthehighstreet charges a joining fee of £238.80 including VAT and 25% commission (plus VAT) on each sale (November 2015).
4 Based on 30,000 respondents of the global online shopping survey.
5 19,068 survey participants in the Total Retail Survey by PwC 2015.

## GLOSSARY

'7Cs'   See *E-retail mix*.
B2B   Business-to-business e-commerce.
B2C   Business-to-consumer e-commerce.
'Bricks'   See *High street*.
'Bricks and clicks'   See *Multi-channel*.
Category management (CM)   A retailer/supplier process of managing categories as strategic business units, aiming to enhance results by focusing on delivering consumer value.
'Clicks'   See *E-shopping*.
Cookie   A file containing a unique user identifier that is placed in a user's browser by a website's server, allowing the user's interactions with the site to be tracked. Subject to the user's consent, e-retailers can use cookies to personalise communications with e-shoppers.
Customer franchise   An (e-) retailer's standing in the assessments of its customers: image, trust and branding.
Customer relationship management (CRM)   Techniques and systems for retaining existing customers rather than attracting new ones. The term is often used more narrowly to refer to computer-based systems that integrate information about customers with uses of that information.

# THE WORLD OF E-RETAILING

**Efficient customer response (ECR)**   The retail equivalent of *Just-in-Time (JIT)*. Focusing on the efficiency of the total supply system rather than individual components, ECR aims to reduce total system costs, inventories and physical assets, while improving consumers' choice. Elements of ECR include efficient:

**Replenishment,**   e.g. *EDI* or web links to shorten order cycles; and **store assortment,** e.g. *Category management (CM)* and space allocation.

**Electronic data interchange (EDI)**   Computer systems (usually operated by a third-party contractor and predating the Internet) designed to exchange large quantities of data between computers.

**Electronic point-of-sale systems (EPoS)**   Retail till systems that operate electronically, currently from the bar codes. The data can be fed directly into (e.g.) *EDI* or *ECR* systems to control stocks and re-ordering (Electronic funds transfer point of sale – EFTPoS – also enables payment *via* debit or credit cards).

**E-retail**   The sale of goods and services *via* Internet or other electronic channels, for personal or household use by consumers.

**E-retail mix (or Retail mix) ('7Cs')**   Short-hand term for the blend of tools and techniques that e-retailers (or retailers) use to provide value for customers. Based on the '4Ps' or '4Cs' of the marketing mix, the key elements of e-retail success can be summarised as the '7Cs': **C1 Convenience for the customer; C2 Customer value and benefits; C3 Cost to the customer; C4 Communication and customer relationships; C5 Computing and category management issues; C6 Customer franchise;** and **C7 Customer care and service.**

**E-shopping ('clicks')**   The purchase of goods and services by consumers using *e-retail* channels.

**High street ('bricks')**   The sale of goods and services from real shops in streets and shopping centres.

**Just-in-time (JIT)**   An IT-based system requiring flexible, efficient processes for ensuring that goods are produced so as to be available where and when wanted, with minimum order quantities and stock levels. The retailers' equivalent is *Efficient customer response (ECR)*.

**Mass customisation**   Producing individually designed products and communications to order on a large scale.

**Multi-channel**   Retailing *via* more than one channel, e.g. *high street* and Internet *e-retail* ('Bricks and clicks').

**Pure player**   ('clicks') A company who sells goods and services from the Internet only.

**Retail**   The sale of goods and services for personal, family or household use by consumers using any distribution channel or combination of channels.

**Retail mix (7Cs)**   See *E-retail mix.*

**UX/UI**   User experience (UX) encompasses all aspects of the end-user's interaction with the company, its services, and its products, e.g. usability, interface layout, copywriting, etc. (Nielsen and Norman, 2015). User interface (UI) is everything designed in a website which invites interaction and responds to it, e.g. help messages, click to chat.

**VAT**   Value-Added Tax, a tax payable on purchases in the UK.

**Web atmospherics** – known as user interface and user experience (UI/UX) The creation of the virtual environment of the e-retail store: includes structural design (e.g. frames, pop-ups, 1-click checkout); media (video, audio, graphics and colour management); layout and usability (search facilities, organisation and grouping of merchandise); sound and music; and personalisation. In theory, can also include touch and smell (which might be incorporated by offering to send samples).

## FURTHER READING

Adler E. (2014) *'Reverse Showrooming': Bricks-and-Mortar Retailers Fight Back,* [Online] Available at Business Insider: http://www.businessinsider.com/reverse-showrooming-retailers-fight-back-2014-9?IR=T.

Centre for Retail Research (2013) *Online Retailing: Britain, Europe, US and Canada 2015,* Centre for Retail Research, [Online] Available at Centre for Retail Research: http://www.retailresearch.org/onlineretailing.php.

PricewaterhouseCoopers (2015) *Total Retail 2015: Retailers and the Age of Disruption,* [Online] Available at PricewaterhouseCoopers: https://www.pwc.es/es/publicaciones/retail-y-consumo/assets/informe-total-retail-2015.pdf.

Thirumalai, S. and Sinha, K. K. (2011) 'Customization of the online purchase process in electronic retailing and customer satisfaction: An online field. study', *Journal of Operations Management,* 29 (5): 477–487.

Wigder Z. D., Johnson C. and Katz R. (2014) *Predictions 2015: Prepare for More Global eCommerce Players to Spread Their Wings,* [Online] Available at Forrester: http://www.pi2.ca/getdoc/622442a6-63bf-457e-a87a-02abb5ed041a/forrester_predictions-2015_global--ecommerce-playe.aspx.

## REFERENCES

Adler E. (2014) *'Reverse Showrooming': Bricks-and-Mortar Retailers Fight Back,* [Online] Available at Business Insider: http://www.businessinsider.com/reverse-showrooming-retailers-fight-back-2014-9?IR=T [Accessed 5 July 2015].

Borden N H. (1964) 'The concept of the marketing mix', *Journal of Advertising Research,* 4 (June); 2–7.

Culliton J W. (1948) *'The Management of Marketing Costs',* Boston: Harvard University.

DIY week (2014) *Kingfisher Results: Stellar Year for Screwfix,* [Online] Available at DIY week: http://www.diyweek.net/news/news.asp?id=17524 [Accessed 13 November 2015].

Eweek (2015) *HP, Dell Lead Growing Worldwide Server Market,* [Online] Available at Eweek: http://www.eweek.com/small-business/hp-dell-lead-growing-worldwide-server-market.html [Accessed 6 November 2015].

Harris L and Dennis C E. (2002) *Marketing the E-Business,* London: Routledge.

IMRG (2015) *Internet Mobile Accounts for 40% of All Online Retail Sales,* London, Interactive Media in Retail/Cap Gemini.

Internet Retailing (2014) *UK Retailers Expected to Make Online Sales of £45bn This Year: Study,* [Online] Available at Internet Retailing: http://internetretailing.

net/2014/03/uk-retailers-expected-to-make-online-sales-of-45bn-this-year-study/ [Accessed 2 July 2015].

Kearney A T. (2000) *'E-business Performance',* Chicago, A T Kearney.

Kietzmann J H, Hermkens K, McCarthy I P and Silvestre B S. (2011) 'Social media? Get serious! Understanding the functional building blocks of social media', *Business Horizons,* 54 (3): 241–251.

Kingfisher (2014) *Screwfix Investor Event Presentation 2-5-14,* [Online] Available at Kingfisher: http://www.kingfisher.com/files/presentations/2014/0614/Screwfix_Investor_Event_020514.pdf [Accessed 4 September 2015].

Lauterborn R. (1990) 'New marketing litany: 4Ps passé; 4Cs take over', *Advertising Age,* October 1.

Marketline (2014) *Global Online Retail,* [Online] Available at Marketline Advantage Database [Accessed 1 July 2015].

McCarthy E J. (1960) *Basic Marketing,* Homewood, IL, Irwin.

McGoldrick P. (2002) *Retail Marketing,* 2nd edition, Maidenhead, UK: McGraw-Hill.

Mintel (2014) *E-commerce-Uk-July-2014,* [Online] Available at Mintel Reports: http://store.mintel.com/e-commerce-uk-july-2014?cookie_test=true [Accessed 2 July 2015].

Morrell L. (2015) Conversion rate optimisation, *InternetRetailing Magazine,* 51.

NEXT (2015) *Annual Report and Accounts,* [Online] Available at NEXT plc: http://www.nextplc.co.uk/~/media/Files/N/Next-PLC-V2/documents/reports-and-presentations/2014/next-annual-report-2015-final-web.pdf [Accessed 2 July 2015].

Nielsen (2014) E-commerce: *Evolution or Revolution in the Fast-Moving Consumer Goods World?* [Online] Available at Nielsen: http://www.nielsen.com/us/en/insights/reports/2014/e-commerce-evolution-or-revolution-in-the-fast-moving-consumer-goods-world.html [Accessed 10 July 2015].

Nielsen J and Norman D. (2015) *The Definition of User Experience,* [Online] Available at Nielsen Norman Group: https://www.nngroup.com/articles/definition-user-experience/ [Accessed 15 November 2015].

Parro D and Santorro M. (2015) *Reinventing Retail: What Businesses Need to Know for 2015,* [Online] Available at WalkerSands: http://www.walkersands.com/pdf/2015-future-of-retail.pdf [Accessed 1 July 2015].

PricewaterhouseCoopers (2015) *Total Retail 2015: Retailers and the Age of Disruption,* [Online] Available at PricewaterhouseCoopers: https://www.pwc.es/es/publicaciones/retail-y-consumo/assets/informe-total-retail-2015.pdf [Accessed 4 September 2015].

Reynolds J. (2002) 'Charting the multi-channel future: Retail choices and constraints', *International Journal of Retail, and Distribution Management,* 30 (11): 530–535.

Thirumalai S and Sinha K K. (2011) 'Customization of the online purchase. process in electronic retailing and customer satisfaction: An online field study', *Journal of Operations Management,* 29 (5): 477–487.

Wigder Z D, Johnson C and Katz R. (2014) *Predictions 2015: Prepare for More Global eCommerce Players to Spread Their Wings,* [Online] Available at Forrester:

http://www.pi2.ca/getdoc/622442a6-63bf-457e-a87a-02abb5ed041a/forrester_predictions-2015_global--ecommerce-playe.aspx [Accessed 6 November 2015].

Witell L, Kristensson P, Gustafsson A and Löfgren M. (2011) 'Idea generation: Customer co-creation versus traditional research techniques', *Journal of Service Management*, 22 (2): 140–159.

Yudelson J. (1999) 'Adapting McCarthy's four P's for the twenty-first century', *Journal of Marketing Education*, 21 (1): 60–67.

# WEB LINKS

Try these sites to taste the flavour of e-shopping:

**Amazon:** www.amazon.co.uk – busy, friendly and informative; the market leader for books, music and much more.

**Dell:** www.dell.co.uk – market leader for computer sales

**Lands' End:** www.landsend.co.uk – simple, cotton clothes in a clean and airy site.

**Net-a-Porter:** www.netaporter.com – the market leader in luxury online fashion.

**Tesco:** www.tesco.com – top grocery supermarket online as well as in-store.

**Toys "R" Us:** www.toysrus.co.uk – fantastic range of thousands of toys.

**Wallpaperdirect:** www.wallpaperdirect.com – huge range of wallpaper styles.

**Wine Cellar Club:** http://winecellarclub.co.uk – good range of wines.

*Price-comparison sites*

These sites allow comparison of the prices of the same item from different e-retailers:

**Cheapperfumeexpert:** www.cheapperfumeexpert.com – is a fragrance price comparison site

**Gocompare:** www.gocompare.com – compares insurances for cars, home and travel

**Priceline:** www.priceline.com – creates a market or reverse auction. Enter the price you want to pay for a range of services such as air travel, vacations and car hire. The system searches for suppliers willing to sell at that price.

**Pricerunner:** http://www.pricerunner.co.uk – finds cheapest electrical equipment, compares products and prices.

**Skycanner:** http://www.skyscanner.net – compares cheap flights, hotels & car hire with numerous providers.

# THE WORLD OF E-RETAILING

*Auctions*

In the US, e-Auctions are the most active and popular way of e-shopping, with eBay the leader for fun (and risk?):

www.ebay.co.uk

*More e-retail and e-mall links*

For links to e-retailers plus statistics and press releases concerning *Verdict on Electronic Shopping* reports, see the following:

www.verdictretail.com

# Chapter 2

# The business of e-retailing in practice

### LINKS TO OTHER CHAPTERS

- Chapter 3 – Integration of e-retailing into an organisation
- Chapter 4 – Understanding and communicating with the e-consumer
- Chapter 6 – E-store design: navigability, interactivity and web atmospherics
- Chapter 7 – E-service
- Chapter 10 – E-retailing models

### KEY LEARNING POINTS

*After completing this chapter you will have an understanding of*

- Practice and trends in e-retailing the main tangible product categories

### ORDERED LIST OF SUBTOPICS

- What are the main e-retail product categories
- Home electronics
- Books
- Music
- Video
- Groceries
- Clothing and footwear

- Conclusions
- Chapter summary
- Case study
- Questions
- Glossary
- Further reading
- References
- Web links

## WHAT ARE THE MAIN E-RETAIL PRODUCT CATEGORIES?

As mentioned in Chapter 1, the top categories that account for the majority of all European sales comprise clothing, books, home electronics, cosmetics, music and movies, furniture, sport/leisure, children's wear and toys, car accessories and groceries. In addition, although perhaps not a category, auctions are among the most popular UK e-retailing sites.

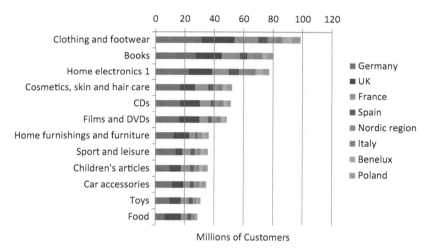

**Figure 2.1** Most bought product categories online in Europe 2014 (millions of customers)

Source: Adapted from Ecommerce news (2014)

### THINK POINT

Why do you think books, music and movies are among the most popular e-shopping products?

In Europe the most popular categories are durables and entertainment-related products. Consumables, e.g. groceries, make up only a small percentage of online retail so far. An increase is predicted due to the provision of attractive opportunities for online retailers and the frequency of purchases. Exceptions are the UK and France, where traditional hypermarkets and grocery retailers, e.g. www.tesco.co.uk and www.carrefour.fr, who offer online purchases on a wide range of products, are driving real change on consumers' buying habits (Burbank cited in Nielsen, 2014). Grocery online retail comprises 19% of all online retailing in the UK (Mintel, 2014). It is of note that currently only 5% of UK grocery sector sales are currently online.

In this chapter we look in more depth at some of the tangible products that have traditionally been mainstays of high street retailing: books, music and movies, groceries, and clothes. Other e-retailing categories, such as home electronics,[1] travel and tickets, although important, are too diverse to cover in depth in this chapter. Auctions, though not strictly an e-retailing category, are considered as a case study in Chapter 4.

If customers have a specific product in mind, such as a book or toy, they browse and usually purchase online. Burbank, cited in a Nielsen report (2014), emphasised that online browse-to-buy correlation rates for fast-moving consumer goods translate to loyal repeat customers for these categories. Other non-consumable categories have a lower buy-to-browse ratio, e.g. electronic equipment, mobile phones, computer hardware/software, sporting goods and cars/motorcycles. Reasons include the higher price and necessary physical examination before a buying decision is made.

The growth of social media, review sites, and price comparison sites has led to the emergence of an increasingly informed consumer in recent years. The research stage of the purchasing process becomes increasingly important with 77% of consumers in the UK looking at online reviews before making a purchase (Marketline, 2015). This constitutes a noticeable change in consumer behaviour.

**Table 2.1** Segmentation of the online retail sector in Europe

| Category | $ Billion sales 2014 | % |
| --- | --- | --- |
| Electronics | 83 | 25 |
| Clothing, accessories and footwear | 64 | 19 |
| Books, music and videos | 53 | 16 |
| Other | 138 | 40 |
| Total | 338 | 100 |

Source: Adapted from Marketline (2015b)

## HOME ELECTRONICS

Electronic goods are one of the largest online retailing categories in Europe with 24.5% (Mintel, 2015b). The category consists of four sub-categories: household appliances (large and small), computing and telecoms equipment, audio-visual and photographic equipment and electronic appliances for personal care (Mintel, 2015b).

In this category, the technological advancements and new products can impact the sales of older goods, e.g. tablets have had an impact on laptops, smartphones affected digital cameras.

Electronic goods purchases migrate to the pure-players and from store-based multi-channel retailers to online transactions. However, consumers value stores even when ordering online. Research by Mintel (2015b) demonstrates that 47% of consumers prefer to buy electronic items online from a retailer that has physical stores and 52% said they would like pure-players to open stores.[2] Multi-channel retailers compete with their purely online counterparts on services like click-and-collect, after-sales service and advice, e.g. pre-sales advice. In contrast, pure-players tend to lead on price, have a wide range of products and brands, and offer various delivery options and quick stock availability responses.

Mintel (2015) also found that most (64%) customers decide primarily on price when buying electronics. Such items are also bought based on product specification; and customers usually know exactly what they are ordering. Customers compare prices for identical products, for which the Internet provides plenty of dedicated platforms.

Amazon is leading the market as the single largest online operator (pure-player) in the electronic goods market, accounting for 26% of the total UK online market (Mintel, 2015). The second largest is Dixons Carphone with 13% market share, followed by John Lewis. The latter has been successful due to its price-matching promise "Never Knowingly Undersold" and extended warranties on electronic items (www.johnlewis.co.uk).

## AMAZON AND ARGOS

Both of these retailers have worked on making the purchasing process easier through one-click purchasing and convenience features, such as the ability to reserve products, same-day delivery and (in the case of Argos) Fast Track collection service in store.

Black Friday/Cyber Monday weekend, named the "biggest shopping day of the year," affects online spending. Both days started as shopping events for electronic goods with an online focus, but have expanded to a wide range of categories today. The Office for National Statistics (UK) reported a 22%

# E-RETAILING IN PRACTICE

**Figure 2.2** Where consumers have bought online in the past 12 months
Source: Adapted from Mintel (2015b)

jump in electronic goods specialist sales in November, with Black Friday clearly a driving force behind the increase (Marketline, 2015).

## BOOKS

Books, music and movies are another large e-retailing category in Europe. The category includes, among others, books, second-hand books, e-books, audio books and other digital content, such as music and movie downloads or streams. According to Mintel (2015c), books are increasingly bought online rather than in traditional bookshops. This is understandable in the light of books scoring highest in de Kare-Silver's (2001) ES (electronic shopping) test, detailed in Chapter 10. In de Kare-Silver's sample table, books score a total of 38 points out of a maximum of 50, ten points ahead of the next category (hotels). Books score highly on product characteristics, being low touch products that are simple to deliver by post; and familiarity and confidence, as customers usually know exactly what they are ordering. Finally, the higher-weighted consumer attributes parameter is particularly favourable to books.

In Europe books are sold online predominantly by Amazon, the market leader in many European countries, and through websites of chain bookshops. Customers are able to compare retailers on price and stock online before purchasing and choose the retailer with the best offer. The number of market players decreased with the increased competition and availability of information (Marketline, 2015c). 'Brick-and-mortar' booksellers are threatened by online sales of printed books, e-books and audiobooks.

# E-RETAILING IN PRACTICE

The book price laws vary across Europe, with printed books having 0% VAT in the UK, but 20% VAT for e-books and a reduced tax rate of 7% for printed publications in Germany. Some countries like France and Luxembourg have broken the ranks on VAT rates on e-books to encourage the digital industry in their country with 5.5% and 3%, respectively. The European Court of Justice (ECJ) required an increase of VAT on e-books to 20% (France) and 17% (Luxembourg).

Amazon is by far the leader of the book e-retail category in many European countries. Amazon's customers favour the convenience, reliability and customer service. Amazon has achieved worldwide success and brand recognition by attention to these considerations and heavy (offline) advertising, becoming one of only two dot.com brands in the Top 10 of the Interbrand world league table (Interbrand, 2015). It is an illustration of the power of branding that Amazon is the world's top e-retailer and way ahead of Barnes and Noble, its nearest competitor, for the title of the world's biggest bookstore.

Other dot.coms such as BestBookPrice (www.bestbookprice.co.uk) have attempted to exploit the Internet for quick and easy price comparisons, claiming that 'people know the products and price is driving them'. Indeed, a price comparison site such as Bookfinder4U (www.bookfinder4u.com) can often find prices for identical books significantly cheaper than Amazon. These cheaper prices often come from suppliers such as The Book People (www.thebookpeople.co.uk) that do not have Amazon's heavy marketing costs. Nevertheless, even competitors such as Tesco (strongly branded for groceries in the UK and a number of other countries), with offers like 'The top 100 books 10 percent cheaper than Amazon', have failed to make a substantial impact on the online books market. As Brynjolfsson and Smith (2000) put it, 'the most expensive is not always the least patronised', pointing out that Amazon.com maintained a US market share of 80 percent while charging 10 percent more than the cheapest. For more on Amazon, please refer to the case study.

> **THINK POINT**
>
> The first-mover and market leader for books, Amazon, is also the market leader for e-books. Why do you think this is?

The Internet is not only near ideal for selling new books, but also as a marketplace for secondhand books. Search results on Amazon indicate not only the new price but also the price at which associates sell the same

|  | Lower cost | Differentiation |
| --- | --- | --- |
| Broad target | Cost leadership<br><br>The Book People | Differentiation<br><br>Amazon |
| Narrow target | Disaster | Focus<br><br>Abe Books |

**Figure 2.3** Exemplar strategic positioning of books e-retailers
Source: The authors, based on Porter (1985)

title secondhand. Secondhand purchases through associates are covered by Amazon's usual safety-first guarantees. It has been our experience, though, that reliability and service can fall far below Amazon's own, and guarantee claims can be very slow to settle.

The real beauty of the Internet for book enthusiasts is the ability to track unusual titles. AbeBooks (www.abebooks.co.uk), for example, is a marketplace connecting those who buy books with those who sell them, and is one of the main sources used by professionals. Since 2008 a subsidiary of Amazon, AbeBooks is one of the biggest online marketplaces for secondhand, rare and out-of-print books, claiming to have a virtual inventory of more than 110 million books (AbeBooks, 2016).

In summary, the strategic positioning of books e-retailers can be neatly described using the generic strategies matrix (Figure 2.3), illustrating the Cost leadership, Differentiation and Focus strategies, respectively, of exemplar major players.

## MUSIC

From the suppliers' point of view, the music industry is largely not a happy story. The European music and video market has been in decline in recent years and the decline is expected to continue at least to 2019 (Marketline, 2015d). Physical CD and DVD sales have seen a decline due to competition from digital downloads and streaming services, which are growing fast (Marketline, 2015d). In contrast to traditional media, consumers are able to enjoy the product almost instantly, without having to leave the comfort of their own home.

Consumers have often complained about what are alleged to be unfairly high prices for CDs. On the other hand, the major companies tend to blame piracy and illegal Internet downloads for the slump (single tracks are obviously quicker and easier to download than albums), claiming global music piracy causes $12.5 billion of economic losses every year (Institute for Policy Innovation cited in Music Business Worldwide, 2014).

There is a noticeable shift in the market from physical music media to digital media, e.g. downloads via iTunes, with streaming services becoming increasingly popular. This digital revolution is illustrated by the UK sales of physical music media, which were down 4.9% in 2014, while paid-for digital downloads were down 14.9% during the same time; however, streaming was up by 65.1% compared to 2013 (Marketline, 2015e).

Subscription streaming services like Spotify, Deezer, Rdio and Apple Music manage to increase customer spending in this category due to their monthly/yearly fee. Those services might convert the digital downloads or cannibalise the industry altogether due to their instant availability, resistance to degradation in normal use and ease of use in portable devices, mainly smartphones.

However, the biggest issue to impact the market is piracy. Based on the ease of duplicating digital audio and video, the wide availability of pirated titles online through file sharing and streaming websites and the threat of substitution from counterfeit media have increased significantly in recent years (Marketline, 2015e). The national governments (e.g. UK with their Digital Economy Act 2010, Spain with Ley Sinde) and European Union are keen to stop piracy with various legislations, frequent shutdowns of file sharing sites and fining of alleged copyright infringers. In the US, the Recording Industry Association of America (RIAA) has taken legal action against hundreds of 'major offenders' alleged to have illegally distributed an average of more than 1,000 copyrighted music files. The US government managed to close one of the largest file sharing sites, Megaupload, in 2012. However, these efforts often seem to be in vain, as pirates simply move to multiple, smaller resources to get content, rather than sticking with one service (Aguiar et al., 2015).

Due to the rise of digital audio and video files and their characteristics, buyers easily switch retailers and tend to prefer online retail channels based on such factors as price, recommendations, availability, loyalty schemes and brand image. High street retailers try to diversify their product portfolio into related categories, e.g. games and electronic goods, to become an entertainment outlet for their customers in the effort to keep their brand current and strong, and as they are not likely to compete with the low prices online. The lower overhead costs for online retailers, compared to traditional brick-and-mortar stores, lead to intense price competition, which is a distinct advantage for online vendors.

The big players in the market, such as Amazon and Apple, are able to utilise their economies of scale to lower prices even further. They also benefit from their strong brand recognition and highly visible marketing campaigns.

# E-RETAILING IN PRACTICE

There is intense competition in the digital music and video market within the growing online retail sector, the illegal file sharing sites which enable downloads free of charge and streaming services, which experience phenomenal growth in many countries.

> **THINK POINT**
>
> Despite theoretical losses, do you think that the entertainment industry could actually benefit from piracy?

> **Box 2.1**
> **E-RETAILING CDS – THE ES TEST**
>
> The Electronic Shopping (ES) Test was developed by de Kare-Silver (2001) and is used to assess a product to evaluate the likelihood that it will be purchased online (see Chapter 10 for more details). According to de Kare-Silver, a product's potential for e-retailing can be judged by assessing three factors: 'Product characteristics', 'Familiarity and confidence' and 'Consumer attributes'. Consumer attributes are considered to carry more weight than the other two and are therefore loaded three times as highly in the model. The example of CDs follows below.
>
> **Product characteristics**
>
> A CD is a product that a consumer either wants or doesn't and is down to personal preference. The consumer gets the same product whether he or she buys from HMV or Tesco. A CD does not need to be tried on, smelt or touched before it is bought. The only thing that the customer may want to do is listen to it, and he or she will probably have heard the music already on the radio or TV. Score: 8 out of 10.
>
> **Familiarity and confidence**
>
> Consumers will usually be familiar and confident when choosing to buy a CD. They will buy a CD of their own taste whether rock, soul, hip hop, etc. Furthermore leading brands such as HMV sell online and CD Now uses Amazon as a channel to sell their CDs at cheaper prices. They are well-known brands so consumers are likely to feel confident buying from them. Score: 8 out of 10.
>
> **Consumer attributes**
>
> The typical music buyer is younger, better educated and in a higher socio-economic group then the general population, i.e. closely fitting the profile of the typical Internet user. Score: 22 out of 30.

**Table 2.2** Evaluation of the e-shopping potential of CDs using the ES test

| Product | Product characteristics (10) | Familiarity and confidence (10) | Consumer attributes (30) | Total |
|---------|------------------------------|----------------------------------|--------------------------|-------|
| CDs     | 8                            | 8                                | 22                       | 38    |

The total score for selling a CD online was 38 out of 50. de Kare-Silver stated that if a score is above 20 then the product has good potential of being bought by consumers online. The total score therefore indicates that CDs have a high potential to be purchased on the Internet, which justifies the reason why CDs (and now downloaded and especially, streamed music) have high sales online. This can be compared to basic clothing, which de Kare-Silver scored at only 19 in the ES test. This means that clothing has a lower potential for e-retailing compared with CDs.

*Source*: This box kindly contributed by Mehtap Durmus.

## Digital music downloads

Downloading music from Amazon, Google Play or iTunes means the file is transferred directly onto a device and stored there. Once stored, no Internet connection is needed to play. A one-time fee per song or per album is charged, which then may be transferred to other personal devices, depending on the service provider.

Industry insiders estimate that three times as much music is downloaded on the Internet (largely for free) as is being sold on physical formats (CD, Vinyl, Cassette). CDs are simply outdated, which is shown by the huge drop in sales in recent years, a trend that continues. In a similar vein, digital downloads are experiencing a slump. The sales of albums in CD format have dropped by 10.8%, digital album sales are down 2.8% and paid-for downloads of individual tracks even decreased by 12.5% (Nielsen, 2015).

In the US, physical album sales still exceed digital downloads, although both are declining. In contrast, on-demand audio streams have seen an increase of 83.1% from 2014 to 2015 (Nielsen, 2015).

Online-only releases of albums by established musicians have become more common, e.g. Radiohead released their 2007 album as download only, allowing buyers to pay their desired amount, including zero. It is interesting to note that artists like The Prodigy announced plans to stop releasing albums altogether, because the time-consuming album format restricts the quick release of music.

# E-RETAILING IN PRACTICE

### Box 2.2
### ONLINE PAID CONTENT

Paid content is not new. Financial news and pornography (now mainly downloaded videos and 'live' webcams) have been around since the early days of the web. What is new is the fast rate of growth of many other categories, as illustrated in the chart.

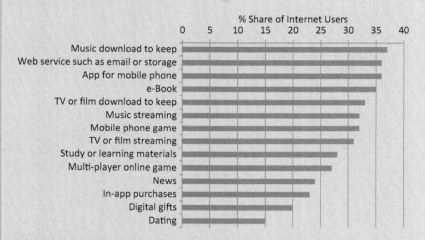

**Figure 2.4** *Paid-for content, mobile and online in 2014*

Source: Adapted from Statista (2015c)

This statistic ranks the most popular types of online and mobile content, which Internet users paid for in the past month as of the fourth quarter of 2014. During the survey period it was found that 32% of Internet users had paid for a music streaming service in the past month.

## Streaming services

Streaming music is different from downloading because the listener does not actually own the tracks; much like Internet radio, music is played on demand via Wi-Fi or mobile data. Many providers offer a free option (limited and often supported by advertising), while pushing for a premium subscription that offers unlimited access to large music libraries without any advertisement interruptions. Some even provide the ability to store music for offline listening.

Streaming services are on the rise with over 15 billion songs streamed in the UK in 2014, compared to 7.5 billion in 2013 (Marketline, 2015e), which accounts for 43.9% of the European online music streaming market value. The additional revenue for retailers through ad supported streaming was $40.6m overall in 2014 (Marketline, 2015e).

43

Due to the increasing popularity, competition is growing with newcomers such as Apple's streaming service Apple Music and Tidal entering the market. Both have a strong brand name, funding and contacts in order to acquire the distribution rights and to promote the business effectively. The competition between services means prices are continuously changing, family plans are being added and listening limits have been removed. The product offered is essentially identical, thus providers need to differentiate themselves based on prices, catalogues, music quality and accessibility. Monthly subscription fees of the biggest players at the time of writing are all close to £9.99 per user, for example Apple Music, Spotify, Rdio. Some providers also offer family plan pricing, to allow multiple users in a household to stream together.

Even for the biggest players in the music streaming business there are some limitations on the availability of music. The music of certain artists, e.g. The Beatles, Radiohead and AC/DC, is not available for on-demand streaming. Even Taylor Swift, one of the most streamed artists on Spotify, removed her back catalogue over a disagreement on royalty fees. Artists have more influence on the availability on streaming service than on the sales of their CDs.

## VIDEO

While the physical video market is in decline, this sector still represents a huge part of the total video market, and indeed the entertainment sector as a whole (Nielsen, 2015b). The digital evolution is on the way, as physical media sales, e.g. Blu-Ray or DVD, are now being overtaken by increasing digital download sales and on-demand streaming. According to Marketline (2015d), UK sales of DVDs declined by 12.1% in 2014, while digital home videos increased by 29.3% in the same period. A similar picture can be seen in the German market (DVDs down by 9% and digital home videos increased 29%). The rise of smart TVs in households encourages consumers to make use of digital streaming services, providing the benefit of consuming as many films and movies as desired for a fixed monthly fee. With easy access via apps on multiple devices, there is no more need to own a DVD or Blu-Ray player; a broadband Internet connection is sufficient.

DVDs and Blu-Ray movies are mainly available from the same suppliers as CDs; thus the same advantages for e-retailing apply (see Box 2.2). High street retailers struggle to keep up with the digital demand of the customers and e-retailers, especially pure-players, dominate the market. Although the UltraViolet (UV) system may help to retain the loyalty of those thinking about making the switch across to digital formats by giving purchasers of physical copies access to a digital file at no extra cost (Mintel, 2014), it lacks popularity and awareness among consumers.

# E-RETAILING IN PRACTICE

Facing the threat of declining sales of physical media by the emergence of online streaming competitors (PricewaterhouseCooper, 2015), such as Netflix, Hulu and iTunes, Amazon introduced its own streaming service, Amazon Instant Video, tied into its Prime membership.

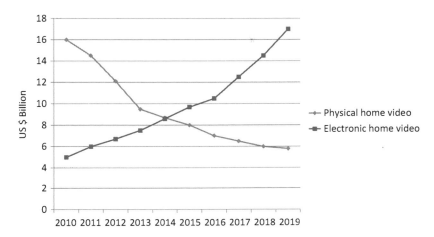

**Figure 2.5** *Physical and digital home video revenue in the US, 2010–2019*
Source: Adapted from PricewaterhouseCooper (2015)

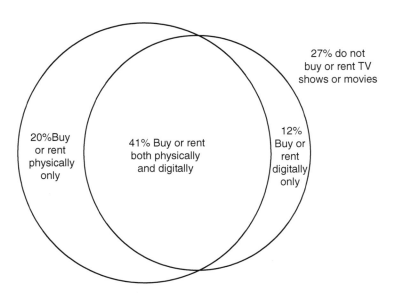

**Figure 2.6** *Physical and digital video consumption*
Source: Adapted from Nielsen (2015b)

Streaming services provide an abundance of available content that would have been nearly impossible to access via physical media. However, with each new iteration of the home viewing experience, the volume of available titles decreases. Many movies filmed on celluloid never made it to VHS, only a proportion of the movies on VHS are available on DVD, and not all of the movies available on DVD are streaming.

## DIGITAL PIRACY

File sharing via the Internet is one of the main challenges facing digital media creators, distributors and retailers – from Napster, which arguably brought file sharing to the masses in the 1990s, to BitTorrent, a mainstream peer-to-peer file sharing mechanism which is fast, efficient, and difficult to stop.

There are many potential motives for pirating digital media, e.g. the unwillingness or inability to pay the price requested, unavailability of the product in the country of the end-user, restrictions to the use of the legitimate product (DRM, region lock), and the desire to consume immediately, rather than waiting for official release. Despite security concerns and privacy risk, peer-to-peer file sharing is widely adopted, due to increasingly available Internet bandwidth, the widespread digitization of physical media, and the increasing capabilities of residential personal computers.

The origin and development of on-demand streaming services can be traced back to peer-to-peer networking and the development of file sharing software. These innovations proved the technical feasibility of offering the consumer potentially every film or song ever made, without the need for creating a costly centralised streaming hub. Spotify is one of the many legal services that make use of peer-to-peer distribution to better scale their platforms. BitTorrent as a platform is a popular alternative to legal streaming services, taking up 3.35% of global Internet bandwidth (Palo Alto Networks, 2016). Waldfogel (2011) claims that although file sharing has reduced revenue, other technological changes have reduced the costs of bringing creative works to market.

Both the music industry and the motion picture industry claim annual losses of billions due to copyright infringement, mainly due to lost revenue. In contrast, Aguiar and Martens (2013) have found that illegal music downloads can have a positive effect on legal music purchases. In a similar vein, Belleflamme and Peitz (2010) find that illegal copies can play a sampling role by attracting consumers and motivating them to purchase a legitimate copy later, and piracy can increase demand for goods that are complementary to the pirated content. Dilmperi, King and Dennis (2011) found that older respondents are more likely to pay for music and less likely to pirate it. These older consumers belong to a different generation where paying for music was the norm and will therefore reduce over time, which is obviously a concern for the industry. Following a review of all available research into the impact of piracy on sales, Smith (2016) concludes that piracy does not always harm sales, but it usually does.

## GROCERIES

Being one of the largest segments in global retail, grocery has seen a large impact by the adoption of the digital channel. Traditional retail chains are making huge investments into developing their online presences, to keep up with the evolution of the rapidly growing market.

Groceries are mainly non-durable necessities that need to be delivered quickly and in such a way that quality is not lost in the delivery process. Perishable groceries delivery can be difficult if the recipient is not available to receive them – unlike other goods that may be popped through the letterbox or left in a lockable delivery drop. Compared to products typically ordered online, such as Blu-Rays, many grocery items tend to be variable in characteristics and quality and are often selected by look, feel and smell (how do you select a ripe mango online?).

In a global survey, Nielsen (2015c) found that 25% of respondents are already ordering grocery products online for home delivery, and more than half (55%) are willing to do so in the future. The online grocery channel is particularly used by younger shoppers who are in full-time employment and have children at home (The Institute of Grocery

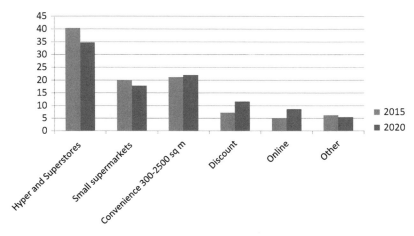

**Figure 2.7** *Annual UK grocery market predictions*
Source: Adapted from The Institute of Grocery Distribution (2015)

Distribution, 2013). Indeed, de Kare-Silver's ES test rates groceries at 27 (out of 50), well behind Books (38) and DVDs (39 by our estimation – see Chapter 10).

> **THINK POINT**
>
> If groceries are problematic for delivery and fulfilment, how does it come about that Tesco's e-grocery service is one of the largest e-retailers in the UK?

## ONLINE GROCERS

Despite its rise in popularity, online grocery shopping is unlikely to replace physical stores any time soon, as traditional stores have strong key advantages. One obvious in-store benefit is the immediate fulfilment of shopping needs without having to wait and pay for delivery. Personal interaction and powerful sensory experiences – smelling freshly baked bread and seeing and feeling the vibrant colour and texture of perfectly ripe strawberries – are virtually impossible to replicate online (Nielsen, 2015c).

Still, the global online grocery market is continually expanding, with some key players at the forefront of development. Tesco, once the undisputed king of online grocery retailing, is now facing tough competition, not only from its traditional competitors, but also from new, smaller players. With a market share of 38% in the UK, Tesco is still ahead of ASDA and Sainsbury's, each taking 15% of the market (Syndy, 2015). However, all are aggressively improving and expanding their online models, with Tesco aiming for omni-channel leadership, i.e. every arm of its business will feature a digital aspect.

Different operational models are employed by online grocers. The simple approach of employing pickers to select the goods from the shelves of local stores enables a supermarket to get its online grocery operation off the ground quickly and cheaply. When online orders are quiet, pickers can do other work. As the online market grows, existing players employ a combination of in-store pick-up, dark stores and dedicated ecommerce warehouses. Dark stores are simply warehouses full of groceries where staff, or rather, mainly a computer, selects the goods that have been ordered by an online customer. They are similar to normal supermarkets, without the atmosphere.

In contrast to the brick-and-click retailers, Ocado is the world's largest online grocery pure-player, having reported its first profitable year

# E-RETAILING IN PRACTICE

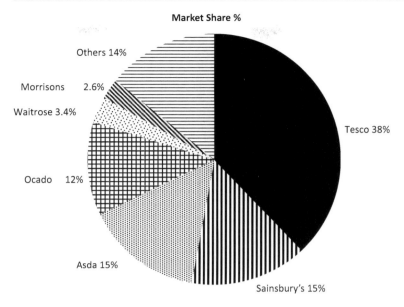

**Figure 2.8** *Online grocery market shares UK*
Source: Adapted from Syndy (2015)

in 2014. Their applications and algorithms are at the forefront of digital innovation, even offering a function that predicts a consumer's basket based on previous purchases. By offering its infrastructure and operating capabilities to third parties, Ocado enables traditional brick-and-mortar retailers to outsource the development of their online operations and rapidly build scalable and profitable online businesses (Syndy, 2015).

Traditional retailers not only need to keep up with current market developments, they also need to be innovative and provide value. However, no matter how well thought out their online services may be, there will always be new challenges, such as solving the "last mile" issue in same-day delivery. Amazon introduced Amazon Fresh, delivering fresh chilled and frozen food in less than 60 minutes in some areas. In the UK, Amazon's grocery service is called Pantry; however, instead of facing the competition head-on, they decided to ally with one of the largest supermarkets by adding hundreds of their products to its platform. Instacart puts another twist on the delivery model, using a mobile application and part-time personal shoppers, using their private cars to deliver orders. A customer places and pays for the order online, and the shopper collects the ordered items from the desired (local) store and delivers them to the customer. A similar service is offered by Google Express, in major US cities.

E-RETAILING IN PRACTICE

> **Box 2.3**
> **EIGHT WAYS TO CUSTOMER VALUE AND PROFITABILITY IN GROCERY E-RETAILING**
>
> (i) Customer density
> (ii) Loyalty
> (iii) Buying power
> (iv) Ordering efficiency and customer information
> (v) Operational efficiency and customer service level
> (vi) Large range of products
> (vii) Price level
> (viii) Shopping convenience
>
> *Sources*: (i) to (vi), Tanskanen et al. (2002), (v) to (vii), Ankar et al. (2002), i.e. (v) and (vi) appear as similar constructs in both sources.

Burt et al. (2015) discuss the key areas that an online grocery strategy should include. Retailers can interact with omni-channel shoppers with personalized offers (segmentation), pricing, and promotional strategies based on shopping preferences and previous purchases (value proposition). With individualised promotional offerings they can offer variety to shoppers and increase engagement. Convenience is important, but quality, assortment and price also matter tremendously. The value proposition and the marketing messages of online grocers should reinforce these elements (McKinsey, 2013).

While a physical presence remains crucial for connecting with customers, pure-play online grocers have an edge with their flexibility and speed to market. Traditional retailers can take advantage of their existing assets as they improve their digital capabilities and enhance their online offering (Burt et al., 2015).

## CLOTHING AND FOOTWEAR

Clothing is not an obvious product for e-retailing. First, of course, clothing is normally bought by look, feel and fit, all of which are difficult for the e-shopper to evaluate online. Second, clothing is bought not just for warmth and modesty, but also to express our self-image. Any purchase errors in (for example) style, therefore, carry a particularly high perceived risk. Nevertheless, clothing represents the second biggest category in Europe's e-retail market. Its value was an estimated $64.3bn in 2014,

# E-RETAILING IN PRACTICE

which is 19% of Europe's online retail sector (Marketline, 2015b). The two markets with continually rising online spend are Germany and the UK, with expected double-digit shares of the clothing category (Mintel, 2014b). In Germany and the UK, more than half of online shoppers, 54% and 53%, respectively, bought clothing and footwear online in 2013 (Postnord, 2014).

One reason may be that clothing has historically been one of the major mail order categories in the UK. Both shoppers and suppliers are used to home delivery channels for clothing. The clothing e-retail market leader, Next (www.next.co.uk), has been supplying fashion clothing by mail order since 1988 (see the Next case study in Chapter 1).

The largest pure-players in Europe are ASOS and Zalando, with Zalando trading in over 15 countries in Europe. Both of the online clothing retailers expanded rapidly over the years to reach fashionable consumers in provinces where retail stores are limited.

Farfetch (www.farfetch.com) is a "global community of over 400 visionary fashion boutiques offering an inspirational shopping experience to fashion-forward consumers" (Farfetch, 2016). The website enables small, independent brick-and-mortar boutiques to compete with the dominant brands in the marketplace, by showcasing more than 1,000 labels from independent designers across the globe. Having attracted much interest by investors, the company has been valued at over $1 billion within 7 years of being founded. The main revenue comes from selling well-known luxury brand items, although lesser known, emerging brands are key to the business.

One of the main threats of online retailing to offline clothes retailing is showrooming, where consumers use brick-and-mortar outlets for reference, but purchase the goods elsewhere, mainly after an online comparison of prices. Wilde Rooms (www.wilderooms.com) have introduced a link between online shopping and trying on apparel before the purchase. This premium service for online clothes shoppers pays for the customer's online order and delivers the order to a premium dressing room in leading shopping centres. Customers are able to 'try-before-you-buy' and unwanted clothing will be returned by Wilde Rooms. They attempt to create a luxurious atmosphere with a lounge area and café to enhance the shopping experience. According to Mintel (2015c), customers can touch and try on garments, without having to walk from shop to shop, and with the knowledge that their desired items are ready waiting for them (similar to click and collect). This strengthens costumers' convenience and accessibility to shop online without paying for the order in advance or waiting on deliveries. Further, it provides the opportunity to order from various retailers at once.

# E-RETAILING IN PRACTICE

> **THINK POINT**
>
> If clothing does not meet the requirements for a suitable product for e-retailing, how does it come about that clothing is one of the largest categories for UK e-shoppers?

Look and feel goods tend to be compared and evaluated before buying, i.e. they are high involvement. Enjoyment is often a motivation for in-store clothes shopping (and other comparison shopping). In the 'bricks' retail store, 'atmospherics' are often used to increase enjoyment and hence sales. The effectiveness of such techniques is well known in-store, but in Chapter 6 we argue that equivalent considerations are also important for the e-retailer. Emotional aspects such as enjoyment strongly predict shoppers' attitudes towards online shopping (Childers et al., 2001). According to Chicksand and Knowles (2002), equivalent features can be identified to help in overcoming the difficulties of selling 'look and feel' goods like clothing online. The equivalent stimuli for the 'clicks' store include sound, personalisation/customisation, usability of the website, visuals and text. Kim et al. (2009) found evidence that product presentation (3D versus flat) had a significant effect on consumers' emotional responses; and there were positive relationships among consumers' emotional, cognitive and conative responses. Unexpectedly, music had no effect on consumers' emotional responses. Hunter and Mukerji (2011) stress the importance of tailoring "website atmospherics" according to the characteristics of the target market. Mintel research (2014b) revealed that the main customer influences for switching to online apparel shopping are product descriptions, flexible delivery slots and 3D images.

As we demonstrate in Chapter 6, web atmospherics can help compensate for the lack of sensory experience in e-shopping. Nevertheless, the indications are that shoppers' needs for enjoyment (rather than just utilitarian) benefits are not being satisfied by e-retailers (Henderson and Kunz, 2002).

3D body scans are not new to the clothing industry, with Selfridges and New Look using the technology to drive up jeans sales. However, a new type of biometrics scanner used by New Look quickly calculates 100 measurements, and analyses the body shape and size to help the customer find the best fitted garments. The technology is only available in

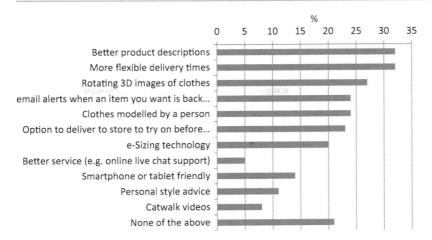

**Figure 2.9** *Reasons for switching online retailers*
Source: Adapted from Mintel (2014b)

the flagship stores, but free to access. Customers are able to save, store and access the information online, which can also be linked to retailers via a platform called PrimeSense.

Customisation is another key element of web atmospherics for clothing. Mass customisation refers to self-designed products. Shopper involvement in the design of the products adds considerably to the personal feel of the shopping experience. Shopper satisfaction can be enhanced by more closely matching to exact needs. In the case of Nike (www.nike.com), shoppers can customise shoes, not just colours and styles, but also, for example, with a name or message. A potential drawback of this system, though, is the concern over what happens if the customer wants to return the product for any reason. There are many clothing e-retailers, e.g. Eshakti (www.eshakti.com) or eDressit (www.edressit.com), that offer customisation for all shapes and sizes across their clothing range, e.g. choice of neckline, sleeves and lengths. These custom items are more expensive than non-custom ones, but many customers are prepared to pay more for customised products (Spaulding and Perry, 2013). eDressit offers free customisation or colour change of the garments, and charges 1.5 times the original price if both are required. Customised garments cannot be returned. Eshakti gives customers a satisfaction guarantee and has a satisfactory return policy in place.

E-RETAILING IN PRACTICE

**Mini case 2.1
ASOS**

Online fashion giant ASOS is one of the UK's leading pure-play retailers, dominating the e-retailing fashion market worldwide with increased revenues of 18% to £1.2bn during the year to August 2015. ASOS.com is a British online fashion and beauty store, primarily aimed at young adults. ASOS sells over 850 brands as well as its own range of clothing and accessories. Nick Beighton is the CEO of ASOS at the HQ in Camden, London. The company was founded in June 2000 by Nick Robertson and Quentin Griffiths, named As Seen On Screen Ltd. By 2004 annual sales had reached £8.3m and ASOS launched their first own label collection.

In 2005 sales climbed to £12.8m, the product range widened to 1,800, boosted by the launch of ASOS beauty and ASOS hit their target of 1 million unique visitors. By 2006 sales had hit £17.8m and ASOS Catwalk was launched giving ASOS the distinction of the first UK fashion retailer to launch a moving images catwalk. More top fashion brands such as Diesel and Firetrap joined Asos.com.

In 2007 ASOS magazine was launched, distributing 400,000 copies a month to customers, and ASOS own label Men arrived. In 2008, sales grew 90% to £71.7m, and ASOS Outlet opened selling last year's brands at 70% off. In 2010, the year of mobile and free shipping, ASOS reached 1.6m active customers and France, Germany and the US got country-specific websites. In 2011, tailored websites for Australian, Italian and Spanish customers went live and Asos iPhone and iPad apps were launched. In 2012, following the launch of the Russian language site, ASOS became truly global as the most visited fashion website by 18- to 24-year-olds in the world. The global reach was consolidated in 2013 with the opening of offices in New York, Lille, France, Berlin, Germany and Shanghai and the launch of the Chinese site. In that year, ASOS was awarded the Drapers and Retail Week Fashion Pure-Play Etailer of the Year award.

In 2014 ASOS launched mobile apps in Germany and France and opened the company's first European Warehouse in Berlin.

By 2015, retail sales reached £1,119.9m from 9.9m active customers. The cut-off time for UK next-day delivery was extended to midnight, and click-and-collect

# E-RETAILING IN PRACTICE

launched with Boots's wide range of high street stores. Although sales are buoyed by the international markets, profitability is muted due to intensive price competition. Nevertheless, according to a survey of 3,000 UK consumers by Jefferies, the research house, ASOS has a website that ranks ahead of rivals such as Boohoo, H&M and Next for content and ease of use.

*Sources*: Various, including http://www.asosplc.com/our-story.aspx accessed 19 April 2016 and *Financial Times*, 14 January 2016.

**THINK POINTS**

1  What do you think is an appropriate strategy for growth for ASOS globally for the next 5 years?
2  Should ASOS focus on China or the UK to grow to a £3bn business?
3  How important is mobile shopping in their future?
4  How important are social channels for future growth?

**Box 2.4**
**DIGITAL INFLUENCERS**

When 23-year-old Aimee-Rose Francis left university with a 2:1 degree in 2014, she already had a fashion blog, http://aimazin.london. By 2015 she had almost 30,000 followers on Instagram, the threshold at which brands start to take an interest. She can charge brands about £800 for a post to Instagram and up to £5,000 for bigger projects for brands such as Reiss, H&M and Armani Exchange. Aimee-Rose says 'you don't want it to look too sponsored; you must keep it personalised.' Other bloggers and the brands that pay them can be more circumspect about their financial dealings. But YouTube star Zoella (real name Zoe Sugg) (https://www.youtube.co.uk/user/zoella280390), who has 10 million followers of her everyday life, posted a profit of £397,000 for the eight months to November 2014, according to filed accounts. In the UK, the Advertising Standards Authority (ASA) stepped in after bloggers were paid to promote Oreo biscuits but the videos were not acknowledged as advertising. Paid-for videos will now have to state that they are ads in their titles although bloggers who accept free items who post blogs that are not subject to editorial control do not need to comply.

According to the London *Sunday Times Style* section, 'Haul girls [who show off their "hauls" of shopping in their blogs] are sweet, smart, fashion-savvy and funny.' They display their purchases creatively with storyboarded scenes and in a genuine way, they give us a glimpse into their lives 'At one with their purchases in a way advertisers and fashion mags are not'. And it certainly pays off, both for the bloggers and the brands that support them. Bethany Mota, the 20-year-old (in 2016) who *Sunday Times Style* dubs the 'Princess of the haul video', uploads videos of outfit ideas, makeup and hair tutorials, recipes, DIY and a wide range of lifestyle suggestions (https://www.youtube.com/user/Macbarbie07). She has more Internet followers than the top UK fashion magazines *Vogue, Elle, Marie Claire* and *Cosmopolitan* put together: 2 million on Twitter, 3.5 million on Instagram and 7 million YouTube viewers. Bethany was named as one of 'The 25 Most Influential Teens' by *Time* magazine in 2014 and 2015. As the *Sunday Times* puts it, 'traditional advertising techniques have been blown apart by social media.'

*Sources*: Various, including numerous issues of the *Sunday Times*, particularly 5 July 2015 and 13 March 2016; and *Evening Standard* 19 August 2015.

## Mini case 2.2
## INTHEFROW (www.inthefrow.com)

Inthefrow Social Media Metrics, accessed April 2016: Twitter 98,632, Instagram 60,408, Facebook 25,124, Pinterest 111,226, Google Plus 40,242, YouTube 465,767.

Inthefrow is Victoria; a mid-twenties writer, photographer and editor. Victoria established Inthefrow in late 2012 during the completion of her Fashion PhD and career as a Fashion Marketing Lecturer at the University of Manchester. Covering a variety of topics including Fashion, Beauty, Lifestyle, Travel and

Food, Inthefrow aims to offer its readers the latest on the subjects they enjoy the most. Within its first six months, Inthefrow won the Company Magazine Best Newcomer Blog Award, and the year later, the award for Best Established Blog. In 2016, Victoria was also nominated for a Glamour Woman of the Year Award.

Over the three years that the blog has been developed, Victoria has worked with a number of large established fashion and beauty brands including Burberry, Dior, Guerlain, Giorgio Armani, Viktor and Rolf, The Body Shop, Maybelline, Vauxhall, L'Oreal, Batiste, HP, Samsung, Clarisonic, ASOS, Topshop, Clinique, Vestiaire, Farfetch, Monnier Freres, LuisaViaRoma, Kenzo, Amanda Wakeley, Revolve Clothing and Reiss.

Victoria's purple, or now white, hair has become her recognisable trait, yet her defining characteristic would be her enthusiasm and passion for her brand. Her love for premium travel, beauty, food and fashion are all apparent within her writing, as she aims to create a hub for those who aspire and hope to be inspired.

Catch up with her latest hauls over on her **YouTube channel**, her newest styles and reviews **right here**, or see what she got up to today on **Instagram**, **Facebook**, **Twitter**, **Pinterest** and Snapchat as Inthefrow.

Awards, mentions, articles and coverage for Inthefrow
Company Magazine Personal Style Blog 2014 Winner
Company Magazine Personal Style Newcomer 2013 Winner
Glamour Woman of the Year 2016 Award Nominee

### *The evolution of blogging*

I guess right at the beginning, my thoughts were to start a beauty blog. I enjoyed reading both beauty and fashion, but then I was in a stage of absolute obsession when it came to the expansion of my makeup and skincare collection. I had become privy to all of this opinionated information regarding beauty products that I had no idea existed online, and as soon as that can of worms was open, I was hooked! I would spend hours every night reading blog posts and finding reviews for the latest releases and totally immersed myself in the whole industry. And finally after six months, I decided to create Inthefrow. I set up a web page on blogger, opened up all the social channels to match and went ahead designing something I could be proud of. And the hundreds of blog posts came right after that.

After a few months, I finally plucked up the courage to start talking about the clothing I was buying and how I was wearing it. I was studying a fashion PhD and had been educated in fashion for over 6 years, and yet the thought of including fashion wasn't a primary thought for me. Yet, time went on and my obsession shifted to fashion once again, and fashion became a secondary topic alongside the constant beauty postings.

And it's funny that even now, I speak to some people and they still see me as a beauty blogger primarily. For me, I find the blog to be a big mix of fashion, beauty and travel, all wrapped into the lifestyle bubble. So I guess someone could call me lifestyle where another could call me a fashion blogger. But for someone to still regard me as primarily beauty focused after such a shift to fashion over the last three years just shows you that how you initially start, truly does stick.

I still adore beauty and offering my own opinions, but I feel it is a sub topic amongst many others. Fashion, beauty, travel and lifestyle are the topics I love to cover and try to cover them as equally as I'm able to.

And the main evolution came last year [2015], when I decided to completely overhaul the look of the blog and go down a route that I was really passionate about. I adopted a luxury focus more heavily, incorporating luxury beauty and fashion in a way I personally had not seen many bloggers doing in such a saturated space. I wanted to show my love for premium products whilst still maintaining an accessibility and offering real and natural opinions and uses and this became a big fork in the road for me. Increasing the quality of my content, spending a lot more time on my writing and investing a lot in order to create content I was thoroughly proud of.

And I feel it was due to my circumstances and life changes. I was living in London, working with a lot of incredible brands and working extremely hard. I was visiting a number of wonderful places and living a new type of lifestyle and I guess it rubbed off on how I wanted to dress, the products I wanted to use and the way I wanted to portray myself. I think this would happen to anyone starting a new job, living in a new city and spending time with new people. You adapt to your environment and the choices you are able to make.

And that leads me to where we are now. A fashion, beauty and travel blog, which I guess you could round up into lifestyle, with a luxury focus and a more polished concept. And I couldn't be happier. It's been a pretty huge evolution, since I was stood in my bedroom, finding a tidy space in the corner of the room to take a photograph of my outfit. But I feel everything needs to evolve and become something greater in order to become something successful. So evolve I will, and hopefully you're happy to stick with me for the long haul.

*Source*: http://www.inthefrow.com/2016/04/the-evolution-of-blogging.html

# E-RETAILING IN PRACTICE

> **THINK POINTS**
>
> 1 Inthefrow's YouTube following is 465,767 subscribers. How important do you think her YouTube following is to her blog?
> 2 Which social media channel should Inthefrow be developing most prolifically over the next 5 years? Include new channels in your answer.
> 3 Is blogging the new marketing?
> 4 What role do bloggers play for consumers? Expert? Friend? Confidante? Mentor?
> 5 What strategies should major retailers and marketing companies employ in the future to work with bloggers?

Consumers want their shopping needs met in a way that minimizes uncertainty and inflexibility and maximizes efficiency, convenience and pleasure (PricewaterhouseCooper, 2015c). More than half of fashion shoppers in the UK (52%) frequently buy through digital channels (Tradedoubler, 2015), reflecting a trend that is growing globally. Only few (high end) major brands and retailers can afford to stick to traditional brick-and-mortar-only outlets; thus, when competing in the mass market, having an online shop is almost essential in order to retain a share of the market. Certain factors have to be considered to provide online shoppers with a similar experience to what is expected from a retail store visit. The website needs to be appealing, easy to navigate and the ordering process should be simple and straightforward. Clear information about deliveries, e.g. costs and status, is also relevant.

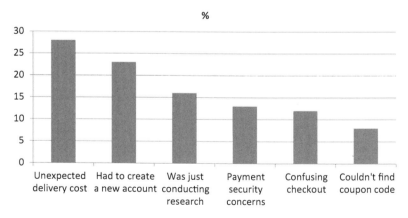

■ *Figure 2.10* Reasons for cart abandonment
Source: Adapted from Nagpal (2014)

# E-RETAILING IN PRACTICE

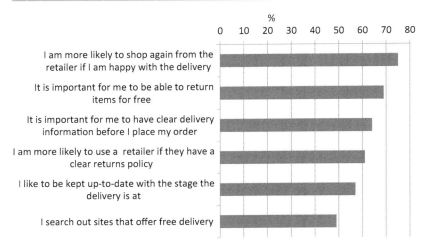

**Figure 2.11** *The importance of delivery and return services in online retail for UK shoppers*
Source: Statista (2015b)

## CONCLUSIONS

Online retailing has massively grown in recent years, and has even overtaken traditional forms of retail in some categories. This is mainly due to changes and advancements in technology and logistics, but also due to evolving products and services. Access to the Internet is available nearly everywhere, and the opportunities to purchase goods and services are nearly limitless. It is essential for traditional retailers to evolve and to embrace the digital age.

### CHAPTER SUMMARY

Amazon is by far the largest pure-player in online retailing and provides great customer experience in terms of choice, reliability and transactions. Amazon is a vast resource for consumers and is constantly innovating across categories, including logistics, payments and digital products. The sheer size, breadth and depth of the organisation make it a promising contender for many categories it has not dominated yet.

In a similar fashion to the domination of those markets by Amazon, first mover Tesco dominates e-groceries retailing. In addition to leveraging the brand value of the bricks stores, Tesco attributes much of the success to the store-picking model (only non-food products

# E-RETAILING IN PRACTICE

such as books, CDs and Blu-Rays are despatched from a non-store centre). Competitor Ocado is trying hard to compete on the basis of service and convenience benefits, using the custom distribution centre approach.

Next is still the leader for online clothing retail, built on the existing mail order systems. However, other pure-players are catching up and are likely to overtake in the near future.

The following chapter investigates the integration of e-retailing into an organisation.

## Case study 2.1
## AMAZON.CO.UK

This case illustrates Amazon.co.uk's retail mix and the application of the Ansoff matrix (see also the comparison with eBay in Chapter 8).

> I buy all my books at Amazon.com because I'm busy and it's convenient. They have a big selection, and they've been reliable. – Bill Gates

Amazon has established itself worldwide as an online retail success, the world's biggest e-retailer of books and way ahead of its nearest competitor Barnes and Noble or even eBay for the title of the world's largest bookstore, even though Amazon sells only online. The success is based on its operations as an online marketplace, with third-party merchants' sales via the site. The retail format and market position assist Amazon to target a larger customer base (Marketline, 2015f). From a start-up in 1995, annual revenue has grown to close to $89,000 million in the financial year 2014 (Marketline, 2015f).

The UK site, www.amazon.co.uk, was formed in 1998 by the takeover of Bookpages, and the UK is now Amazon's third largest market after the US and Germany (Campaign, 2016).

Amazon is clearly the UK market leader in Internet retailing, especially for books, CDs, movies and games and offers many other product lines including electronics, software, games, toys, travel and more (Guardian, 2015). Amazon UK accounts for 25% value share in 2015 and is the most dynamic of the leading players (Euromonitor, 2015). According to Euromonitor (2015), 96% of consumers in the UK have made a purchase from Amazon.co.uk in the past year. The general preference for the Amazon website is due to its wide range of product categories and the large amount of available products within these categories.

**61**

# E-RETAILING IN PRACTICE

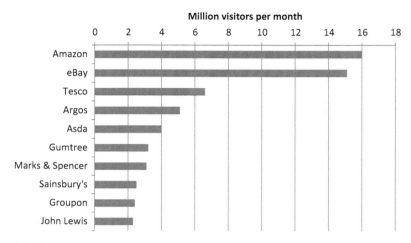

**Figure 2.12** Visitors to UK e-retailers in May 2014
Source: Adapted from Statista (2015)

**Table 2.3** Relative quantities of purchases from Amazon for November 2015

| Category | Count millions, November 2015 | % |
|---|---|---|
| Electronics | 96 | 22.0 |
| Phones and accessories | 72 | 16.5 |
| Digital music | 56 | 12.8 |
| Home and kitchen | 55 | 12.7 |
| Books | 55 | 12.7 |
| Clothing, shoes and jewellery | 25 | 5.7 |
| Sports and outdoors | 24 | 5.6 |
| Computers | 19 | 4.4 |
| Industrial and scientific | 18 | 4.2 |
| Collectibles and fine art | 16 | 3.6 |

Source: Adapted from Scrapehero (2015)

Amazon.co.uk is the market leader in the UK for selling online books based on its main advantage to deliver low cost books by saving on store, warehouse and inventory costs (Kotha, 1998). Amazon also dominates the market for e-books with its Kindle e-book reader. Amazon.co.uk has panels of experts in all the different areas such as music, kids and technology who write reviews from each perspective.

E-RETAILING IN PRACTICE

## Amazon's e-retail mix

### Convenience

Convenience plays an important role in gaining and maintaining new customers. There are several factors driving the level of customer convenience. First, Amazon invested heavily in multi-channel integration (there are seven different channels), enabling a consistent cross-channel experience which adds to the customer convenience despite a lack of physical stores.

During research by Internet Retailing (2016), the website loaded in just over a second, and was fully loaded in between 3 and 4 seconds – despite having as many as 35 page elements.

The usage of strong images and a clear design make the site visually appealing, while detailed product information keeps customers informed. The customer experience is also enhanced by the use of banners and signposts which aids a straightforward navigation.

The use of cookies including the customers' browsing history on amazon.co.uk offers related items which have been viewed before. The cookies, linking to customer needs and wants via a recommendation engine, is one of the reasons why customers start their shop/search on Amazon.

The search function can also be used, which helps customers finding their desired product quickly as only timely and relevant products are presented. According to OneHydra, more than 600,000 retail keywords are used by Amazon.co.uk, which were searched for more than 700 million times in November 2015 alone (cited in Internet Retailing, 2016). Once the result is located, it provides value-added services such as reviews and ratings and displays their price and a comparison price. Comparative pricing allows customers to see the value they are receiving from Amazon.co.uk, i.e. how much they are saving. Amazon makes it easy to source products, despite its range, by allowing filtering by brand and other attributes. They have also perfected their up-selling, cross-selling and down-selling function with personalised recommendations.

Reviews add to a depth of product information, while social validation enables browsers to share their finds and purchases easily (Internet Retailing, 2016). For instance, if you are looking at a product, the website will also display other products in the same category. This feature allows customers to have better choice. This online comparison adds convenience, as you are comparing two products while only looking at one screen. The facility increases sales, as customers can always find something that they want. Customers can view their account anytime, which includes information about their past orders along with shipment details. Account information is used to make recommendations about other books and products that customers may like.

# E-RETAILING IN PRACTICE

The purchase process and tracking of deliveries include easy-to-follow steps. The website offers a secure socket layer connection, which means that sensitive credit card information is transmitted in encrypted format. In some cases they even provide a guarantee that if unauthorized transactions are made they will reimburse the customer. All major credit and debit cards are accepted.

Second, the Amazon app is one of the leading retailer apps, next to Argos, for downloads in the UK. It provides the customer with one-click settings for purchasing products, wish lists, option to track orders when signed in with an existing Amazon account. There is also the opportunity to access previously filled shopping cart, payment and shipping options, which streamlines the customer buying process by storing personal information such as credit card number and shipping address, saving time and hassle.

The free app also enables smooth integration and interoperability across various devices to enhance the shopping experience. New technology allows customers to compare prices and check availability instantly by scanning a barcode or taking a picture of the product within the app, for more convenience and the reassurance of not having to pay too much. Additional features include fingerprint ID sign in and the ability to share product pages on social media (Internet Retailing, 2016).

The retailer is expanding its service offer and at the time of writing has started to introduce the Amazon Fresh service for some areas of London, which offers 1-hour chilled and frozen food deliveries (Euromonitor, 2015). It is one of the fastest delivery services for chilled and frozen groceries in the UK market. Currently (at the time of writing), the product range is limited to 50 fresh products and a minimum order value of £20. However, when Amazon Fresh is rolled out across the UK, it is likely to pose a major challenge to grocery retailers' Internet retailing sales.

Amazon caters to diverse customer needs by offering nine delivery and collection options for UK customers, including same evening delivery and collection from Amazon Pickup points (Internet Retailer, 2016).

Amazon concentrates on faster, premium delivery services and has introduced 1-hour delivery for members of its Prime subscription scheme to satisfy customer demand. Meanwhile, the threshold for free delivery has been raised to a minimum spend of £10 for books, and £20 for other items.

Returns are handled with care and customers are able to check the return status of refunds that are in the system.

One of the prime factors of convenience is based on availability. If any item is unavailable, Amazon will still take your order and will let you know when the title will be available. Amazon's main aim is to maximize customers' convenience, so they do not look anywhere else.

## Cost

Cost is one of the features that drive customers to shop online. Nevertheless, Jeff Bezos, Amazon's CEO, believes that online customers consider selection and convenience to be more important than price. This belief is probably justified, as Brynjolfsson and Smith (2000) pointed out that Amazon.com had a market share of 80% while charging 10% more than the cheapest (see Mini Case 2.1 for more book pricing examples). Therefore, Amazon does not seek to compete on price alone. Customers want to get the best price with excellent customer service. Most of the books at Amazon.co.uk are available at a discounted price ranging from 1% to 50% off the recommended retail price. Consumers are always shown three prices: 'Amazon price', 'New from price' and 'used from price'.

Consumer lifestyles and demands are changing, which lead Amazon to offer a range of delivery options from subscription-based delivery via Prime (£79 a year in 2016) including unlimited next-day deliveries and same-day deliveries in selected postcode areas to free deliveries, when spending a certain amount. Generally, Amazon charges reasonable delivery charges. Customers also have the choice between Royal Mail First Class and ordinary mail.

Amazon lockers are another alternative for receiving goods from the retailer via publicly available, secure storage. The number of Amazon lockers in the UK is around 300 (with more planned at Tube stations in London). This allows customers to collect the orders at their convenience, with no delivery charge.

## Communication

Amazon has established its brand name through customer intimacy and customer relationship management. From day one their aim has been to be a customer-centric company. It welcomes returning customers with their name, e.g. 'Hello, Charles', with the help of a cookie file stored on the user's computer. This has been referred to as the web equivalent of customizing a storefront to suit the taste of each person walking through the door.

Customers can opt-in if they wish to receive more information, for example, when a new novel comes out by their favourite author. Consumers can always opt-out as well, if they are not interested in receiving any more information.

Amazon monitors the customer's ordering process through its Oracle database environment that feeds all the content to its web site. It can track the speed and performance of each step in a transaction, including placement of an item in a cart, completion of an order and e-mail notification to the customer.

Amazon offers personalisation by recommending similar items according to what other customers have bought or recently viewed. For example, the personalised screen will say: 'Customers who bought titles by this author also bought titles by these authors'. These features help users to make up their mind quickly and they can also read spotlight reviews by other readers. Amazon is, to some extent, a virtual community where users express their views about purchased items.

Amazon.co.uk uses an integrated marketing communications strategy that encompasses advertising, public relations, promotions and online marketing. Offline advertising includes TV commercials and billboard. However, Amazon decreased their offline spending over the years to follow the strategy 'since customers shop online, online is where they will be found'. Online activity includes the associates program, sponsored search, portal advertising and e-mail marketing campaigns.

The associate program uses other sites to promote Amazon by links that directly take users to Amazon's site. In return, associates receive a small percentage commission on the total transaction value.

Amazon (2011) also utilises customer loyalty tools, e.g. free shipping, even though the costs are not part of their marketing expense. They say: "while costs associated with Amazon Prime memberships and other shipping offers are not included in marketing expense, we view these offers as effective worldwide marketing tools, and intend to continue offering them indefinitely".

*Computing*

Amazon uses a backend (warehouse) and front end (website). The company has developed a customised information system and dedicated ordering system, which is linked with suppliers to automatically order books and other items. The search engine employs XML and Oracle Database technologies, which bring up results in a matter of seconds. Once the book or an item is found, users sign in using the one-click system and the purchase is complete. The company's software processes the orders via electronic interfaces or Electronic Data Interchange with suppliers and all the stages in supply chain are computerised.

Black Friday 2015 saw a shift from previous high street overrun by customers to online purchases. Amazon was able to provide not only a wide range of product offers, but also managed the extensive traffic (double its usual amount of visits) to the website without any problems. Amazon UK stated that 2015 Black Friday was its strongest sales day to date in the UK, with over 7.4 million items purchased that day (Internet

Retailing, 2016b). Other major UK retailers' sites, e.g. John Lewis, Tesco, PC World, Argos and Boots, stopped working or crashed that day. With predicted millions lost for the retailers, this emphasises the importance of excellent backend systems.

Euromonitor (2015) suggests that 20% of overall UK Internet retailing sites crashed at points on Black Friday 2015, with this event clearly indicating the inadequacy of many store-based retailing players' Internet retailing provision.

The use of Amazon's mobile app increased by 125% on Black Friday 2015, compared to the usage in 2014, followed by Argos (115%), according to web traffic monitor SimilarWeb (Internet Retailing, 2016b).

Amazon Web Services (AWS), first introduced in late 2004, incorporates a collection of cloud services used by startups, companies such as Netflix and Instagram, and government agencies. It is a cloud-computing platform offered by Amazon.com which operates across the globe. The most central of these services arguably includes Amazon's Elastic Compute Cloud "EC2" and Amazon's Simple Storage Service "S3". AWS is a service that provides large computing capacity (storage, database, analytics, application and deployment services) quickly, with the ability to scale applications at much lower costs than building a company's own physical server farm.

The technology with a complex infrastructure helps other companies to handle traffic, to store video and to power databases, which in turn has enabled fast growth for many companies.

*Customer care*

Amazon invites customers to participate in online surveys to provide information on their experience with products. These surveys are hosted on the sites of third-party providers and offer an incentive for participants (Amazon.co.uk, 2016).

Amazon has a proven track record in creating an excellent customer experience due to best practice and continuous innovation.

The company currently takes second place, after John Lewis, in the UK Customer Satisfaction Index (UKCSI) (Institute of Customer Service, 2015). Amazon is able to deliver strong scores across a range of service metrics, from quality and efficiency over ease of doing business, timeliness and problem solving (Institute of Customer Service, 2015). This also highlights Amazon's focus on the whole customer experience for sustained business growth.

Practical aspects of their customer care include the informative FAQs section which explains all the main issues, such as ordering process, delivery charges and returns policy. The return handling can be done quickly and with little hassle, to create a lasting positive impact on customers.

### Customer franchise

Amazon's brand relationship is like someone who knows you, understands your preferences and tells you something new every time you make contact. This builds up a strong relationship as if dealing with human sales staff who have come to know customers in the course of many shopping trips.

## Ansoff matrix

The Ansoff matrix is illustrated in Figure 2.13 and can be applied to Amazon.

## Market penetration

Market penetration means seeking to achieve growth with existing products in their current market segments, aiming to increase their share of the market. Amazon has increased market penetration through value-added service. For example, as mentioned previously, they take on the responsibility to

| Product / Market | Present | New |
|---|---|---|
| Present | Market Penetration | Product Development |
| New | Market Development | Diversification |

**Figure 2.13** Ansoff Matrix

Source: Adapted from Ansoff (1957)

order items that they do not have at present and let the users know as soon as they become available. They allow users to sell used products and prices for used items appear alongside the selling price for a new product. The extended service and options translate into greater sales. The Look Inside program allows customers to search through and view pages from inside a book. This gives the reader a chance to read the book partly before actually buying it. The more services offered, the more chances there are it will lead to a sale.

## Product development

Successful retailers need to constantly challenge and innovate the product range in order to appeal to the increasing demands of today's customer. New technology paved the way for Amazon to remain competitive and reduced the risk of becoming a part of a bigger online marketplace with the inevitable brand, relationship and margin impact (IRUK, 2016).

Amazon stayed on top with compelling promotions, time limited offers, 1-hour delivery and user profiling, as well as investment in long-term innovation (e.g. drone delivery and delivery to an individual at any location) (Internet Retailing, 2016b).

New product offerings are developed to market to existing customers. Amazon also offers secondhand books to its product range, giving their customers the opportunity to sell their used books. Amazon also distributes its e-reader Kindle and e-books via its Amazon Kindle store (www. Amazon.co.uk/kindle-store).

## Market development

Market development concerns marketing existing products to a new audience. For example, Amazon signed an agreement with book retailer Waterstones, who would be selling the Amazon Kindle in the company's branches and on its website, with an intention to "make the Kindle experience better". Other retailers to stock the e-reading device include Staples and Tesco. These retailers will either receive a commission, or will be able to buy the devices below retail price, which greatly broadens the market range for Amazon.

## Diversification

Diversification refers to entering new markets with new products. Amazon has previously broken into new markets by offering travel services, software, electronics and toys.

Amazon Fresh has been introduced as a convenient grocery delivery service, as has the Amazon Dash button or Amazon Echo, a device to add items to your Amazon shopping list by voice recognition.

Amazon Fire TV adds to the Amazon Prime Membership by offering customers a streaming service, including Amazon Prime Instant Video, streaming movies and television, but also apps-based games, and provides an interface to Amazon's own retail products.

This is known as unrelated diversification as Amazon had no previous market experience in these areas. Nevertheless, having built up a successful brand name with a large number of loyal customers, the company is well placed to extend the franchise.

## Conclusion

Amazon has become one of the world's largest online retailers through constant innovation and embracing change in the market. Amazon currently invests almost its entire profit into innovation and new business lines to create a sustainable business model (Jarow, 2014). It has reinforced its market position through careful customer focus. All of its innovations are driven by the desire to enhance customer experience. Despite not always offering the cheapest prices, Amazon has few substantial competitors.

> The Internet store of the future should be able to guess what the customer wants to buy before the customer knows. – Jeff Bezos

## QUESTIONS

*Brief feedback to these questions is included at the back of the book.*

**Question 2.1** – Why are home electronics particularly suitable for online shopping?

**Question 2.2** – Why is it surprising that groceries are among the biggest selling e-retail products in the UK?

**Question 2.3** – Why are groceries one of the main UK e-shopping categories?

**Question 2.4** – How can online retailers reduce or avoid cart abandonment?

# NOTES

1 Including computer and IT accessories, TVs, music systems, home cinema systems, mobile phones and accessories, and electrical household appliances.
2 UK-based survey with 2,000 Internet users aged 16+.

# GLOSSARY

**'4G'** Fourth-generation mobile phone technology that allows fast data transmission, e.g. for Internet connections. It also enables increased download speed and provides the opportunity to stream and to access social media sites.

**Atmospherics** In the 'bricks' retail store, the deliberate design of sensory stimuli such as visual, aural, touch and smell to produce subconscious emotional effects in shoppers aimed at increasing sales. See also *Web atmospherics*.

**Blu-Ray** The name refers to the blue laser which reads the disc and allows information to be stored at a greater density than a DVD with high-definition video resolution (1080p). The main application of Blu-Ray is as a medium for video material such as feature films and physical distribution of video games.

**Broadband** A high-capacity transmission technique with the ability to simultaneously transport multiple signals and traffic types. In the context of Internet access it refers to high-speed Internet access which saves time in downloading large files such as audio and video and is necessary to obtain quality streamed material. There is no accepted definition of speed.

**Click-through** A measure of effectiveness of links to one site from another. For example, www.bettyinthesky.com (podcasts from a flight attendant) has links to books that Betty recommends, available from www.amazon.com. The monthly report from Amazon lists the number of times the link has been used, i.e. clicked through.

**DVD** Digital versatile disc. A type of CD format for greater storage of digital data. DVD movies play video and audio close to cinema quality (but need a good amplifier and speakers). You can burn your own home movie discs through a PC.

**'FAQs'** Frequently asked questions.

**Mobile shopping** The purchase of goods and services *via* mobile communications channels such as mobile broadband for personal or household use by consumers.

**P2P** Peer-to-peer data sharing between individual users, where individual users connect to each other rather than through a central server, e.g. swapping music files. This is frequently carried out by means of file-swapping software that can be downloaded.

**Shopbot (shopping robot)** Amazon may stock the CD that you want – but is the price the lowest possible? What about delivery charges? Shopbots address these questions. These are software agents that automate traditional search for the best prices or shortest delivery times, e.g. www.pricespy.co.uk

**Spam (sending persistent annoying messages)** Unsolicited junk e-mail, or, as a verb, the sending of such messages. Spamming is the opposite of permission marketing, whereby unsolicited messages are sent out in bulk to an entire database of addresses. The word is usually said to originate from a Monty Python sketch about a lodging house where you get Spam (processed meat) whether you like it or not.

**Streaming**  Playing audio or video live *via* the Internet (like radio or TV) as opposed to downloading files to be played later.

**Virus**  A computer code that attaches itself to another program, replicating by using that program's resources to make copies of itself and attach them to other programs, causing damage to the operation of networked computers.

**Web atmospherics**  The equivalent atmospheric stimuli for the 'clicks' store including sound; personalisation/customisation; visuals and video clips; 3D; navigation and usability of the website.

**Worm**  A self-replicating program that exists on its own, travelling through and damaging computer networks.

## FURTHER READING

Dave Chaffey and Fiona Ellis Chadwick (2015) *Digital Marketing*, London: Pearson. Practical guidance on how companies can get the most out of digital media and technology to meet their marketing goals.

Lisa Harris and Charles Dennis (2008) *Marketing the E-business*, London: Routledge. This is one of few books on Marketing written especially for e-commerce. Written in a student-friendly style and fully enhanced with pedagogical features such as topic maps, boxed examples and discussion questions, the book is ideal for use by students.

Tim Kitchen and Yvonne Ivanescu (2015) *Profitable Social Media Marketing: How to Grow Your Business Using Facebook, Twitter, Instagram, LinkedIn and More*, London, CreateSpace Independent Publishing Platform. Digital marketing bestseller – includes in-depth instructions for marketing using the main social media platforms.

Bernadette Tiernan (2000) *E-tailing*, Chicago, Dearborn. This is one of the few texts on e-retailing, written for a US audience.

## REFERENCES

AbeBooks (2016) *The AbeBooks Timeline*, [Online] Available at AbeBooks: https://www.abebooks.co.uk/docs/CompanyInformation/Timeline/ [Accessed 5 January 2016].

Aguiar L, Claussen J and Peuker C. (2015) *Online Copyright Enforcement, Consumer Behavior, and Market Structure*, [Online] Available at JRC Technical Reports: https://ec.europa.eu/jrc/sites/jrcsh/files/JRC93492_Online_Copyright.pdf [Accessed 26 January 2016].

Aguiar L and Martens B. (2013) *Digital Music Consumption on the Internet: Evidence from Clickstream Data*, [Online] Available at Ecommerce News JRC Technical Reports: http://ipts.jrc.ec.europa.eu/publications/pub.cfm?id=6084 [Accessed 17 January 2016].

Amazon.com, Inc. (2011) Form10-K for fiscal year ending 31st December 2011, [Online] Available at United States Securities and Exchange Commission: https://www.sec.gov/Archives/edgar/data/1018724/000119312512032846/d269317d10k.htm [Accessed 25 February 2016].

Belleflamme P and Peitz M. (2010) *Digital Piracy: Theory*, [Online] Available at Center for Operations Research: http://www.uclouvain.be/cps/ucl/doc/core/documents/coredp2010_60web.pdf [Accessed 17 January 2016].

Brynjolfsson E and Smith M. (2000) 'Frictionless commerce? A comparison of Internet and conventional retailers', *Management Science*, 46 (4): 563–585.

Burt R, Chandra V, Silverman S and Tortora G. (2015) *Capturing the Online Grocery Opportunity*, [Online] Available at ATKearny: http://www.atkearney.co.uk/documents/10192/6603479/Capturing+the+Online+Grocery+Opportunity.pdf/65385cfe-b3a9-482b-a24c-6260a272f0f7 [Accessed 19 January 2016].

Campaign (2016). *Amazon UK's Annual Sales Hit £6.3billion*, [Online] Available at Campaign: http://www.campaignlive.co.uk/article/amazon-uks-annual-sales-hit-63-billion/1381647# [Accessed 15 September 2016].

Chicksand L and Knowles R. (2002) 'Selling "look and feel goods" online', *IBM E-Business Conference*, Birmingham University, UK.

Childers T L, Carr C L, Peck J and Carson S (2001) 'Hedonic and utilitarian motivations for online retail shopping behavior', *Journal of Retailing*, 77: 511–535.

de Kare-Silver M. (2001) *e-Shock: The New Rules*, Basingstoke, UK: Palgrave.

Dilmperi A, King T and Dennis C. (2011) 'Pirates of the web: The curse of illegal downloading', *Journal of Retail and Consumer Services*, 18: 132–140.

Euromonitior International. (2015) *Internet Retailing in the United Kingdom*, [Online] Available at Marketline: http://www.euromonitor.com/internet-retailing-in-the-united-kingdom/report [Accessed 26 February 2016].

Farfetch (2016) *About Us*, [Online] Available at Farfetch: http://www.farfetch.com/uk/pag1988.aspx?ffref=ftr [Accessed 6 February 2016].

Guardian (2015). *Amazon Loses UK Market Share in Non-digital Entertainment to High Street*, [Online] Available at *The Guardian*: https://www.theguardian.com/technology/2015/nov/02/amazon-loses-uk-market-share-non-digital-entertainment-high-street-cds-games-dvds [Accessed 15 September 2016].

Henderson K V and Kunz M B. (2002) 'The convergence of brick and click retail atmospherics: Delivering similar worth utility online and on-land', *9th International Conference on Recent Advances in Retailing and Services Science*, Heidelberg, EIRASS.

Hunter R and Mukerji B. (2011) 'The role of atmospherics in influencing consumer behaviour in the online environment', *International Journal of Business and Social Science Special Issue*, 2 (9): 118–125.

Interbrand. (2015) *Rankings*, [Online] Available at Interbrand: http://interbrand.com/best-brands/best-global-brands/2015/ranking/ [Accessed 5 January 2016].

Internet Retailing. (2016) *Internet Retailing UK Top500*, [Online] Available at Internet Retailing: http://internetretailing.net/iruk/ [Accessed 25 February 2016].

Internet Retailing. (2016b) *Can Your Business Support Global Omni-Channel Commerce Alone?* [Online] Available at Internet Retailing: http://internetretailing.net/iruk/ [Accessed 25 February 2016].

IRUK. (2016) 'Amazon to open 13th UK warehouse as it expands its range and meets customer demand', [Online] Available at Internet Retailing: http://internetretailing.

net/2016/08/amazon-opens-13th-uk-fulfilment-centre/ [Accessed 15 September 2016].

iTunes. (2016) *iTunes Preview – Amazon App,* [Online] Available at iTunes: https://itunes.apple.com/us/app/amazon-app-shop-browse-scan/id297606951?mt=8 [Accessed 25 February 2016].

Jarow J. (2014) *Here's How Amazon Can Get Away with Never Earning a Profit,* [Online] Available at Business Insider UK: http://uk.businessinsider.com/jeff-bezos-on-profits-2014-12?r=US&IR=T [Accessed 26 February 2016].

Kim J H, Kim M and Lennon S J. (2009) 'Effects of web site atmospherics on consumer responses: Music and product presentation', *Direct Marketing: An International Journal,* 3 (1): 4–19.

Kotha, S. (April 1998). "Competing on the Internet: The Case of Amazon.com", *European Management Journal,* 16 (2): 212–222.

Marketline. (2015) *Changing Customer Behaviour in the UK – The Rise of the Smart Consumer,* [Online] Available at Marketline: http://advantage.marketline.com [Accessed 6 December 2015].

Marketline. (2015d) *Music and Video in Europe,* [Online] Available at Marketline: http://advantage.marketline.com [Accessed 5 January 2016].

Marketline. (2015e) *Online Music Streaming in the United Kingdom,* [Online] Available at Marketline: http://advantage.marketline.com [Accessed 5 January 2016].

Marketline. (2015f) *Amazon.com, Inc.,* [Online] Available at Marketline: http://advantage.marketline.com [Accessed 25 February 2016].

McKinsey. (2013) *The Future of Online Grocery in Europe,* [Online] Available at McKinsey: www.mckinsey.com [Accessed 20 January 2016].

Mintel Reports. (2014) *Will Digital Video Streaming Wipe Out DVD and Blu-ray Discs?* [Online] Available at Mintel Reports: www.mintel.com [Accessed 11 January 2016].

Mintel Reports. (2015) *Online Grocery Retailing UK,* [Online] Available at Mintel Reports: www.mintel.com [Accessed 7 December 2015].

Mintel Reports. (2015b) *Electrical Goods Retailing UK,* [Online] Available at Mintel Reports: www.mintel.com [Accessed 7 December 2015].

Mintel Reports. (2015c) *Try-Before-You-Buy: Is Online Fashion Retail Ready for Change?* [Online] Available at Mintel Reports: www.mintel.com [Accessed 12 February 2016].

Music Business Worldwide. (2014) Why Does the RIAA Hate Torrent Sites So Much, [Online] Available at Music Business Worldwide: http://www.musicbusinessworldwide.com/why-does-the-riaa-hate-torrent-sites-so-much/ [Accessed 6 January 2016].

Nagpal M. (2014) eCommerce Survey 2014, [Online] Available at Visual Website Optimiser: http://resources.vwo.com/ecommerce-survey-2014 [Accessed 26 January 2016].

Nielsen. (2014) *E-commerce: Evolution or Revolution in the Fast-Moving Consumer Goods World?* [Online] Available at Nielsen: http://www.nielsen.com [Accessed 6 December 2015].

Nielsen. (2015) *Music 360 Report – 2015 Highlights,* [Online] Available at Nielsen: http://www.nielsen.com [Accessed 10 January 2016].

Nielsen. (2015b) *Home Entertainment Consumer Trends – Digital Transition Tracker Report,* [Online] Available at Nielsen: http://www.nielsen.com [Accessed 10 January 2016].

Nielsen. (2015c) *The Future of Grocery – E-commerce, Digital Technology and Changing Shopping Preferences around the World*, [Online] Available at Nielsen: http://www.nielsen.com [Accessed 19 January 2016].

Palo Alto Networks. (2016) *Application Usage and Threat Report*, [Online] Available at Palo Alto Networks: http://researchcenter.paloaltonetworks.com/app-usage-risk-report-visualization/#sthash.IJICeurD.dpbs [Accessed 16 January 2016].

Porter M E. (1985). *The Competitive Advantage: Creating and Sustaining Superior Performance.* New York: Free Press.

Postnord. (2014) *E-Commerce in Europe 2014*, [Online] Available at Postnord: http://www.postnord.com/globalassets/global/english/document/publications/2014/e-commerce-in-europe-2014.pdf [Accessed 5 February 2016].

PricewaterhouseCooper. (2015) *Global Entertainment and Media Outlook 2015–2019*, [Online] Available at PricewaterhouseCooper: https://www.pwc.com/gx/en/global-entertainment-media-outlook/assets/2015/take-a-tour.pdf [Accessed 12 January 2016].

Scrapehero. (2015) *Amazon Top 10 Categories November 2015 Infographic*, [Online] Available at Scrapehero: https://learn.scrapehero.com/amazon-top-10-categories-november-2015-infographic/ [Accessed 25 February 2016].

Smith M D. (2016) *The Truth about Piracy*, [Online] Available at Technology Policy Institute: https://techpolicyinstitute.org/2016/02/02/the-truth-about-piracy/ [Accessed 26 January 2016].

Spaulding E and Perry C. (2013) *Making It Personal: Rules for Success in Product Customization*, London: Bain and Company. Available at: http://www.bain.com/publications/articles/making-it-personal-rules-for-success-in-product-customization.aspx [Accessed 16 September 2016].

Statista. (2015) *Commerce Websites Ranked by Visitors in the United Kingdom in May 2014.* [Online] Available at Statista: http://www.statista.com/statistics/286489/uk-visitors-to-mass-merchandiser-websites/ [Accessed 26 February 2016].

Statista. (2015b) *Importance of Delivery and Return Services in Online Retail in the UK 2015.* [Online] Available at Statista: http://www.statista.com/statistics/489858/importance-of-delivery-and-return-services-in-online-retail-in-the-uk/ [Accessed 26 February 2016].

Syndy. (2015) *The State of Online Grocery Retail in Europe*, [Online] Available at Syndy [Accessed 19 January 2016].

The Institute of Customer Service. (2015) *The UK Customer Satisfaction Index*, [Online] Available at The Institute of Customer Service: https://www.instituteofcustomerservice.com/research-insight/uk-customer-satisfaction-index [Accessed 25 February 2016].

The Institute of Grocery Distribution. (2013) *Spotlight on Click and Collect Grocery Shoppers*, [Online] Available at the Institute of Grocery Distribution: http://collectec.com/wp-content/uploads/2014/04/Click-and-Collect-grocery-shoppers-IGD-Guide-2013.pdf [Accessed 19 January 2016].

Tradedoubler. (2015) *Fashion and Trends in Online Retailing*, [Online] Available at Tradedoubler: http://docplayer.net/18999030-Fashion-trends-in-online-retailing-a-new-catwalk-for-fashion-brands-tradedoubler-com.html [Accessed 22 February 2016].

Waldfogel J. (2011) *Copyright Protection, Technological Change, and the Quality of New Products: Evidence from Recorded Music since Napster*, [Online] Available at Social Science Research Network: http://papers.ssrn.com/sol3/papers.cfm?abstract_id=1944001 [Accessed 17 January 2015].

E-RETAILING IN PRACTICE

 **WEB LINKS**

Amazon: www.amazon.co.uk – busy, friendly and informative; the market leader for books plus music, DVD movies and much more.

eBay: www.ebay.co.uk – buy or sell anything by auction; the UK's top e-retailer measured by audience numbers (see case study in Chapter 4).

Nike: www.nike.com – for customised shoes and clothing.

Marks & Spencer: www.marksandspencer.com – for a good selection of mass-market clothing, underwear and much more.

Tesco: www.tesco.com – top grocery supermarket online as well as in-store.

*Auctions*

In the US and the UK, e-auctions are one of the most active and popular ways of e-shopping, with eBay the leader for fun (and risk?). The UK site is www.ebay.co.uk (see case study in Chapter 4).

# Chapter 3

# Integration of e-retailing into an organisation

### LINKS TO OTHER CHAPTERS

- Chapter 1 – The world of e-retailing
- Chapter 6 – E-store design, navigability, interactivity and web atmospherics
- Chapter 8 – Branding on the web
- Chapter 9 – E-malls
- Chapter 10 – E-retailing models
- Chapter 11 – M-shopping
- Chapter 13 – Multi-channel success and the future of e-retailing

### KEY LEARNING POINTS

*After completing this chapter you will have an understanding of*

- Why traditional retailers integrate e-retail
- Strategies for e-retail integration
- Resource and change management implications

### ORDERED LIST OF SUBTOPICS

- Why traditional retailers adopt e-retail
- Strategies for integration
- Loyalty-based integration strategies
- Switching barriers and switching costs
- Implementation: change management and resource implications

INTEGRATION OF E-RETAILING

- Conclusions
- Chapter summary
- Case study
- Questions
- Glossary
- Further reading
- References
- Web links

## INTRODUCTION

The commercialisation of the Internet is an integral part of business conduct today, providing an essential channel for the sale of products and services. However, during the early days of online commercialisation, there was common speculation that traditional retail was dead and that all retailers would go virtual. Investors flocked towards dot.com stocks on the premise that a new economy was emerging where established organisations, with their inherent structural rigidity and reluctance to embrace change, could not compete with more nimble Internet startups, founded on embracing e-commerce.

This notion of 'either/or', 'bricks vs clicks' paradigm was, however, short-lived, as there were many reports of dot.com successes that became spectacular failures (see, for example, Cellan-Jones, 2003). Today, it has become clear that tremendously successful companies such as eBay and Amazon and other star retailers have been hybrids, and most often, established retailers who have successfully integrated e-commerce.

This chapter looks at the integration of B2C e-commerce, namely e-retail, into established businesses, and begins by examining the reasons for traditional retailers to incorporate e-retail into their business model, and considers some recent examples. It then goes on to review some frameworks that have been proposed to encompass strategies for integrating online and offline activities, and ends with consideration of the operational implications of such activities for the retailer.

## WHY TRADITIONAL RETAILERS ADOPT E-RETAIL

The number of customers shopping online has increased markedly each year since the beginning of e-commerce in the mid-1990s. In the UK during January 2015 for example, online shopping was up 16% on the previous year, reaching £52.25bn, and equating to 15.2% of all retail sales in the UK (Econsultancy, 2015). This alone might be a reason for a traditional retailer to look at e-retail, but the influences on such decisions have varied with time and understanding of e-commerce.

## Out of necessity versus fashion: commerciality

Today, all types of retail businesses are found online, spanning across all sectors. E-retailing is not only adopted out of fashion, but rather out of necessity to compete and to provide a service that consumers expect.

In the past, being online was more of a fashion statement and fashion alone was sufficient to drive most traditional businesses to consider moving into e-commerce, even if the boardroom rationale was to protect shareholder value. The word 'Internet' was associated with what seemed pervasive optimism for a new era. It meant youth, new possibilities, and an opportunity to break with traditional business and create new rules. The media and daily articles on achieved or projected IPO success and the restructuring of companies and creation of new opportunities to complement other resources made that the Internet and e-retailing could not be ignored.

While the shakeout of 2000 left fashion with the debris of countless failed startups, in its place came valuable lessons across e-commerce, and evidence for incumbent retailers that factors such as having an established brand was essential. The lessons over the past two decades have provided significant advantages in a-retail and play a part in developing better customer loyalty programmes and increased profit. These developments create the e-retail environment of today.

## Advantages of being established

Analysis of companies that failed online and a comparison with traditional retailers in the same industry, for example eToys (www.etoys.com) that folded in 2000 and was subsequently bought by an established toy retailer, versus Toys-R-Us (www.toys-r-us.com), which successfully opened an e-retail channel through collaboration with Amazon (www.amazon.com), has revealed several advantages for the established retailer.

Newcomers have to attract customers, and much of their cash-burn and early debt are usually caused by brand-building and promotion. Established businesses however, have an existing customer base and can build on brand values that are already in place. They also have existing marketing budgets usually able to furnish new online activity, and are experienced in the market they serve, unlike many startups.

Further advantages, such as having an existing value network including suppliers, buying, fulfilment and the teams to support these functions, have been shown to be generous compensation for being late to market.

## Benefits of e-retail

As discussed later, there are many strategic options for the adoption of e-retail and the level of involvement a business can choose in online activity, but clearly, as outlined in Chapter 1 (advantages and disadvantages of e-retailing for retailers), e-retail at the very least represents an alternative or additional channel for traditional retailers. While opening new physical retail outlets can expand the geographical reach of a business and add convenience for consumers, retailing online not only carries these benefits, but also offers further returns that are more specific to online trading.

The Internet has global reach, and provides the opportunity to trade internationally. Of course, this is not necessarily an advantage for a number of reasons, such as having to deal with multiple languages, currencies, laws and even cultures, and managing far-flung logistics including returns and toll and other tax issues also often prove to be an issue, but with foreign competition able to enjoy the potential of international trade online, businesses do need to consider their competitive position should they ignore e-retail.

Other broad benefits include the ability to trade 24×7 and operate with lower overheads in terms of staff and space, while more particular advantages include the ability to increase the number of customer 'touch points' and build more personalised customer experiences, products and relationships.

However, these e-retail advantages should not imply that an online presence is a recipe in itself for success; that kind of thinking was tried and failed with the dot.com boom and bust. Instead, if there is a recipe for successful integration, it is found in variants of established business practices, such as an understanding of the strengths and weaknesses of the business, for example in relation to technology awareness, which is a good indicator of e-commerce success. Most importantly, the adoption of e-retail relies on the competent formulation of an integration strategy of e-retailing, social media and online branding.

## STRATEGIES FOR INTEGRATION

Online retail shopping in the UK continues to grow and is expected to grow by 44.9% in the coming years to reach £62.7bn in 2020, accounting for 17.1% of total retail sales (Ormrod, 2015). Such predictions can be somewhat self-fulfilling and help fuel enthusiasm for continued research and development, providing a constantly changing environment for any integration strategy. It is necessary to keep abreast of these developments as they all impinge on strategic decisions.

## Overview of current developments

While the common e-retail interface remains the web browser running on a personal computer, many companies have investigated alternative methods of interfacing with the customer. T-commerce, that is e-commerce over a (smart) digital TV or instigated by TV commercials, is an important e-retail alternative, not least because 97% of UK homes have one or more televisions, and take-up of interactive TV continues to rise. Dominos Pizza had early success in T-commerce using satellite, cable and the web to achieve 98% brand recognition in multi-channel homes, and other retailers including Dixons and WH Smiths have followed. The medium has also been particularly popular with the finance industry and drawn several banks and building societies. This development is expected to grow further with the popularity of smart TVs that are becoming more interactive.

An important development that strengthens opportunities for e-retail exists in advances in smart mobile phone and tablet technology (considered in more detail in Chapter 11). According to Ofcom (2015) smartphones have overtaken laptops as the most popular device for getting online with record ownership and use. Two thirds of people now own a smartphone, using it for nearly 2 hours every day to browse the Internet, access social media, bank and shop online. With superfast 4G subscription, smartphones are changing the way consumers shop, bank, watch TV and communicate.

The growing deployment of Wi-Fi networks coupled with widespread subscription of 4G mobile broadband service will fundamentally change Internet access. As the mobile operators continue to expand their 4G networks, it is expected that 98% of premises will have an indoor 4G signal from at least one operator by 2017 (Ofcom, 2015). With more reliabile and fast Internet access, millions of consumers and businesses can do everything from weekly shopping to catching up with friends with face-to-face video calls.

The UK has its own significant developments. Ofcom will publish maps that make it easier for consumers to compare operators' mobile coverage throughout the UK, enabling users to zoom to a specific location, or simply enter a place name or postcode, and receive information on coverage for the Wi-Fi network down to 100 square metres. Other developments in the UK include the advanced retail communications network at Birmingham's Bullring shopping centre. As part of a dynamic retail environment, incorporating an intelligent buildings system and a multi-Gigabit cabling infrastructure, the 130 new shops are supplemented in the mall by 27 touchscreen interactive kiosks, 25 plasma screens and 155 thin client terminals linked to one of the largest Wi-Fi networks in Europe.

Also of interest to current developments, multi-device shopping has become the dominant method of shopping online, with 52% of consumers using more than one device to make online purchases in 2014, compared to 30% in 2012 (Ormrod, 2015).

Worth noting is that click and collect will outperform the overall online market, with expenditure estimated to grow by 78.8% between 2015 and 2020. Sixty-eight percent of online shoppers have used click and collect, compared to 51% in 2012, with many shoppers planning to start using the service. For online shoppers, click and collect has become a mainstream fulfilment option due to the convenience and control it offers, as shoppers using the service want to avoid or reduce home delivery charges (Ormrod, 2015).

Among the large traditional retailers, Argos (www.argos.co.uk), a UK catalogue company with streamlined ordering and collection at high street stores, has been prominent in developing alternative ordering and reservation methods as well as full online retail. The company has had success with in-store kiosks that provide fast track ordering and credit card payment, and was among the first to trial a text messaging 'Text and take home' system for product reservation. Using the system, customers can text the catalogue number of an item to check its availability at a particular store, and then in response to the text that confirms the item's price and stock position, can place a reservation on the product. The system reduces queuing and is part of the company's continuous innovation in ideas to increase customer convenience.

E-retail is getting smarter and recent predictions about the Internet of Things (IoT) suggest an integrated system where the smart fridge virtually orders food, automating the shopping experience (Steele, 2016). Such IoT e-retail platforms are now becoming available, and people in the industry are getting more experienced. However, no matter how accessible the technology of e-retail systems becomes, or how successful the big players have already been, companies that want to adopt e-retail need to understand what it offers and pursue an integration strategy that is appropriate to their business.

## Strategic options

A company's strategy towards e-retailing will be influenced by a number of factors, including its market sector and prospects for online and offline retail, in-house technical knowledge and experience of outsourcing, reengineering, and development projects, as well as its overall vision, desire and ability to operate in a very fast-changing and possibly unfamiliar commercial environment.

In order to recognise the additional complexity that e-commerce is likely to introduce, it is useful to consider the digital and physical dimensions of a business in relation to the type of product, process and delivery agent involved, as shown in Figure 3.1.

This model, developed by Choi et al., maintains currency, and conveys the prospect of choices and issues for a business contemplating e-commerce from a background of traditional commerce.

For a traditional retailer, the first questions regard how readily its products and services lend themselves to e-retailing, and then, the degree to which the business can exploit electronic processes. One method for approaching these questions is described by the ES Test and involves consideration of product attributes in terms of the five human senses and looking at consumer type and the familiarity of the consumer in purchasing the product. This method is discussed in Chapter 10.

Once a retailer has evaluated the potential of its products or services for e-retailing, it must then decide its position for e-retail adoption, and

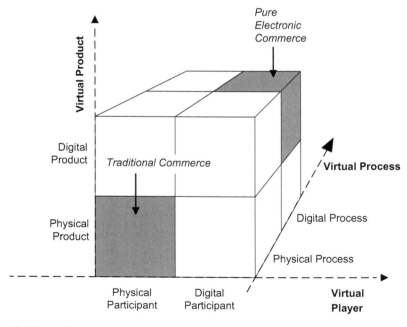

**Figure 3.1** E-commerce digitisation
Source: Adapted from Choi et al. (1997)

## INTEGRATION OF E-RETAILING

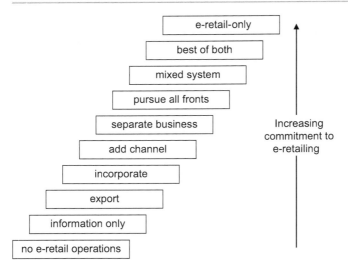

**Figure 3.2** Strategic options for retailers
Source: Adapted from de Kare-Silver (2001)

determine a course of action. de Kare-Silver (2001) lists 10 options that can be arranged on a scale from 'no e-retail operations' to 'e-retail only', in order of increasing e-shopping responsiveness, paralleled with increasing commitment to e-retailing as shown in Figure 3.2.

**No e-retail operations.** This is the defensive option, based on revitalising the 'experience' and social aspects of shopping based in towns and shopping centres. However, consumers now expect every organisation to have at least an information website, an e-mail address and possibly a social media presence such as a Facebook page.

**Information only.** Reluctance to tackle the disadvantages of e-retailing leads some high street retailers to use the Internet purely as a marketing communication channel rather than for online sales. In the UK, it is becoming increasingly difficult to find anyone using this option.

**Export.** This approach is aimed at protecting the business of the high street stores while widening the potential customer base with e-channels. de Kare-Silver cites the example of bookseller Blackwells (bookshop.blackwell.co.uk), which has 45 outlets (2012) in university towns and campuses across the UK, but its listing of several millions of specialist and academic titles is now available worldwide on the web.

**Incorporate into existing business.** This option seeks to protect the existing stores by using an 'order online and collect' system. The thinking is that by coming to the store to collect the order, the shopper does not have to wait for the postman's delivery at home and is more likely to think of extra purchases, or to pick up impulse buys. As noted earlier, this click-and-collect system is a popular way to go shopping, with the large retailers like John Lewis (www.johnlewis.com), Tesco (www.tesco.com), Sainsburys (www.sainsburys.co.uk), and so on, enjoying great success. Amazon has gone a step further by installing lockers in some shopping centres and in Co-op supermarkets, which consumers can then unlock by using a code sent to their smartphone (Wallop, 2013).

**Add another channel**. With this approach, retailers such as Next (www.next.co.uk) use e-retailing as an extra route to reach more of their target customers. Retailers in this category may be represented on an e-mall (see Chapter 9), saving much of the setting-up cost of a dedicated e-retailing operation.

**Set up a separate business**. The idea of the separate business is to offer competitive e-shopping benefits without alienating the existing customers for the high street operation, who probably pay higher prices. The separately branded direct operation has been popular for financial services, for example, Abbey National's e-bank 'Cahoot' (www.cahoot.co.uk).

**Pursue all fronts**. This is, for example, the National Westminster Bank multi-channel system, based on making every possible channel open to the customer: high street branches, direct mail, ATMs, mobile phone apps, interactive TV and Internet (www.natwest.co.uk).

**Mixed system**. This approach recognises that strong brands are essential to successful e-retailing. Brand strength is showcased in flagship stores in major cities, for example, Apple (www.apple.com).

**Best of both worlds**. Is it possible to retain all the high street operations while at the same time being state-of-the-art in e-retailing? This is probably only practicable for a clear market leader in a sector, and represents a high-investment strategy, making it more difficult for competitors to catch up—the Tesco approach.

**E-retail only (pure-play)**. Few retailers are brave enough to close all high street outlets and operate only virtual shops. A number of e-retail–only operations exist, the best known and most successful being Amazon (www.amazon.com). However, even Amazon sees benefits in some 'real' presence, given its joint venture with Toys "R" Us (www.toys-r-us.com). Only those operations high in e-shopping potential, such as travel, and with big budgets to build the brand (e.g. Lastminute.com—www.lastminute.com), are likely to be leaders with Internet-only operations.

INTEGRATION OF E-RETAILING

> **THINK POINT**
>
> Would you purchase goods from an 'unknown' company on the Internet? What features of the company's website would encourage you to do so?

Of course, a chosen course of action need not prohibit changes in future strategy. By monitoring the outcome of such decisions in terms of turnover, profit, customer acquisition, satisfaction or other determinant metrics, a business can develop a dynamic strategy that best reflects the successful aspects of its e-retail adoption. It is quite possible for a business to start by adding an e-retail channel, and then find that this new addition begins to outperform the company's traditional retail business. This is especially true say, for catalogue and mail-order businesses, where their operations are already suited to selling online. For example, outdoor recreation equipment company L.L.Bean has been a pioneer of mail order since the nineteenth century and is now a world e-retail leader in this market (see case study in Chapter 5).

### Mini case 3.1
### NETSHOP (www.netshop.co.uk)

Netshop Ltd is a privately owned company specialising in the online retail of computer networking products to end consumers. Evolving out of Homestead Electronics Ltd, a mail-order electronics company founded in 1983, Netshop now forms part of a multi-business e-retail portfolio with offerings in diverse market segments.

The technology and mail-order origins of the company, along with an established customer base and in-house knowledge of the networking market, assisted a smooth transition from mail-order retail to e-retail, since much of the order processing and fulfilment infrastructure was already in place and the company possessed the necessary skills to develop its own transactional website, and start small alongside its traditional business. Once its e-commerce systems were proven, they provided a platform for further online activities.

The company's background as a family business, coupled with its attention to success factors in the e-retail marketplace, have helped it foster an appreciation of customer expectations, and the requirement to be competent at more than just the technical process behind the shopping experience.

Many new customers arrive at the Netshop website from results at search engines such as Google (www.google.co.uk), and not all of them are seasoned e-consumers. Netshop recognises this, and works to establish trust by giving prominent space to the company's physical address, the history of the company, and telephone numbers so that customers are not forced to pursue an online transaction if they do not want to. Instead, prospective customers can phone and place an order, and even arrange to collect it, obviating the need to make credit card transactions online or by phone, or disclose address details (of course, it's still possible to order online and have products delivered). Recognising that their specialty products may require assistance, the shop offers free advice and product support with free call-back or e-mail. This customer-oriented approach is augmented by several features that add value, such as extensive product information, news articles on new products and aspects of networking, FAQs and support pages, manufacturers' links, and free driver downloads, providing a multi-channel presence for a company that has chosen to move most of its operation online.

## LOYALTY-BASED INTEGRATION STRATEGIES

The emphasis to focus on people rather than products, coupled with the requirement for a business to align its strategy with its ability to operate in an e-retail environment, raises the question of how to formulate strategy for e-retail integration that takes these key requisites into account.

Research by Cuthbertson and Bridson (2003) proposes a framework to tackle this question and how the Internet changes the traditional store-based model of marketing, by setting it in the context of customer loyalty, which has long been acknowledged as an important factor in a firm's competitive position. Successful relationship marketing is underpinned by the ability to both acquire and retain customers over the long term, and the need to customise the relationship to the individual has been shown to be a critical factor.

### Modelling the online retail experience

Cuthbertson and Bridson (2003) suggest that the loyalty marketing strategy is dependent on the fundamental structure of the retailer–customer relationship, and put forward a categorisation of retailer–customer relationships in an Online Retail Relationship Matrix as shown in Figure 3.3.

This matrix uses the two principal components of the retailer–customer relationship: the retailer-led channel proposition to the customer and the customer-led channel access to the retailer, and divides these based on the focus of each party.

The retailer may configure its offer as pure-play (online) or multi-channel, while the customer can choose to access the retailer directly or

## INTEGRATION OF E-RETAILING

|  | Retail Offer | |
|---|---|---|
|  | Online | Multi-Channel |
| Retailer | *Digital* | *Ubiquitous* |
| Marketplace | *Focal* | |

*Customer Choice*

■ **Figure 3.3** *The Online Retail Relationship matrix*
Source: Cuthbertson and Bridson, 2003

through a marketplace. Examples of marketplaces include those that are online, such as DealTime (www.dealtime.co.uk) and Groupon (www.groupon.co.uk).

The usefulness of the classification is that each category carries a higher likelihood of success for particular types of retailers, depending on the retailer's product/service. By mapping its type onto the matrix, a business can determine whether success is likely in a given configuration, with implications for the loyalty strategy that is most likely to succeed.

The categories comprise:

- The digital retailer–customer relationship
- The ubiquitous retailer–customer relationship
- The focal retailer–customer relationship

Cuthbertson and Bridson (2003) outline the strengths of each category for particular retailer types.

### The digital retailer-customer relationship

The digital retailer–customer relationship appears to be most applicable where:

> The service element at the point of transaction is low and the product can be distributed digitally.

This could relate to the retail of software, and financial or travel services. For example, airlines that retail tickets direct are likely to be successful by adopting a digital retailer–customer relationship.

### The ubiquitous retailer-customer relationship

The ubiquitous retailer–customer relationship appears to be most applicable where:

# INTEGRATION OF E-RETAILING

The retailer is selling a wide range of goods to customers where the frequency of purchase is relatively high, or selling expensive, technical products where the frequency of purchase is relatively low but a high degree of consideration is given to the purchase decision.

A grocery retailer such as Tesco, or a car retailer such as Ford, are examples of where a ubiquitous retailer-customer relationship is likely to be most successful.

### The focal retailer-customer relationship

The focal retailer-customer relationship appears to be most applicable where:

The retailer is a third party to the product/service vendor, and is providing customers with digital access to a range of goods, based on convenience.

This applies to third-party convenience retailers such as Shopping.com (www.shopping.com) or to those offering customers specialist access to goods, such as eBay (www.ebay.com) or online communities.

Loyalty strategies for retailers with a focal retailer-customer relationship depend on closely understanding customer requirements and providing a selection of retail opportunities to easily convert to purchases, with a mechanism for the third party to benefit from the transaction.

### Using loyalty marketing strategies

Cuthbertson and Bridson (2003) expand their model to identify the relevant loyalty strategy by proposing a matrix called the Purchaser-Purveyor Loyalty Matrix, shown in Figure 3.4, with five distinct choices: Pure, Push, Pull, Purchase and Purge, each appropriate for different retailers, dependant on their particular marketing mix and competitive position. The definition of each loyalty strategy is as follows:

- A *pure* loyalty strategy is based on the existing or *pure* relationship between the retailer and its customers, and focuses on the retailer's product and service offer.
- A *push* loyalty strategy aims to push customers towards the retailer, and focuses on the retail location and channel.
- A *pull* loyalty strategy uses retailer promotion to pull the customer to the retailer or particular products.

## INTEGRATION OF E-RETAILING

|  | Purchaser: Customer Perceived Choice | |
|---|---|---|
|  | Single Retailer | Many Retailers |
| Focused Offer | *Pure* | *Push* |
| Extended Offer | *Pull* | *Purchase* |
| Price-Led Offer | *Purge* | |

*(Purveyor: Retailer Offer)*

■ **Figure 3.4** The Purchaser-Purveyor Loyalty matrix
Source: Cuthbertson and Bridson, 2003

- A *purchase* loyalty strategy concentrates on increasing the number and value of purchase transactions, irrespective of which particular retailer benefits.
- A *purge* loyalty strategy is used where a retailer attempts to purge all unnecessary cost and aims at providing all customers with the lowest price possible.

In general, it is observed that successful digital retailers follow a purge loyalty strategy, ubiquitous retailers follow a push and pull loyalty strategy and focal retailers pursue a purchase strategy. These findings help put forward the appropriate loyalty strategy for any business attempting to integrate e-retail, and when used within the complete retailer-customer relationship model, go some way towards dealing with the complexity suggested by the E-commerce Digitisation view, and finding the appropriate choice among the 10 strategic integration options that have been outlined in this chapter.

## SWITCHING BARRIERS AND SWITCHING COSTS

An important discussion when it comes to e-loyalty that has been raised among researchers is whether loyalty can be achieved at all in online environments given that the competing offer is just one click away. It has become apparent that even satisfied customers might not consider themselves as loyal to a particular e-store and will shop elsewhere if the price is right. In such cases with extensive switching behaviour among customers, e-retailers have several strategic options, notably to retain customers by improving the satisfaction rate even more, so that the customer wants to stay with the firm, or to increase the customers' perception of switching barriers and 'sunk costs', which often impedes customer switching due to the impracticality associated with the switching. In recent research conducted by Ghazali et al. (2016), the authors consider via a survey of 590 shoppers of online pure-play retailers in the UK whether developing such online switching barriers might have any effect on the customers' e-loyalty. Their results raised the question that satisfaction alone might not be able to control customer defection. This means that despite customers being happy with the e-retailer, many will still defect, which is in accordance to a previous study, suggesting that even up to 50% of the customers will generally defect (Reichheld, 1996; Reichheld and Schefter, 2000). Hence, retaining customers based on satisfaction alone is not a sensible strategy, often referred to as the 'satisfaction trap'. In the Ghazali et al. study, their results further provided conclusive evidence which indicated that online switching costs (as a form of barrier to switch) will induce e-loyalty, thereby suggesting that switching costs indeed are a very important factor to develop loyalty, even more so than satisfaction, among online pure-play retailers. It is thus clear that when developing loyalty strategies for e-retailers switching barriers need be to managed more systematically; however, the e-retailers must be careful not to 'lock-in' their customers, as such tactics may be seen as unfair (Nguyen and Klaus, 2013). The key is moderation and a continuous evaluation of the e-retailer-consumer relationship.

## IMPLEMENTATION: CHANGE MANAGEMENT AND RESOURCE IMPLICATIONS

Even for businesses that develop the right e-retailing strategy with the appropriate mix of e-retail and traditional retail, and mindful of the organisation's skill base, it is necessary to recognise that moving from theory to practice will have an impact across the organisation, affecting resources and business processes. A fundamental re-evaluation of company strategy may lead to a radical overhaul of existing ways of doing business, with company structure and culture becoming much more customer focused. Moving organisations towards such ways of working will have widespread consequences. Resistance at all company levels may need to be overcome, with a corresponding need to build commitment and consensus around e-retailing strategies. However, in doing this, as noted earlier, companies must also deal with a paradox. As previous failures showed, there are many strengths in 'bricks-and-mortar' companies, particularly their customer base and brand profile, and organisational capabilities in areas such as supply chain management. Evolving a new business model must therefore avoid throwing out the 'best of the old'. Only by recognising and rising to these challenges and dilemmas, and devoting sufficient time, resources and expertise to them, will companies make a success of their e-retailing ventures. In other words, they have to be prepared to reorganise and restructure themselves continuously, and therefore understanding how to manage change effectively becomes essential.

The central role played by technology in e-retailing will add a layer of technical complexity to what may already be a quite dynamic situation. However, the redesign of business processes and structures is far from a simple 'technical' matter, and involves significant social redesign, especially when the new IoT era arrives. Such changes are likely to be politically controversial and therefore will always be open to disturbances and threats. The interests of a wide range of stakeholders may be threatened, there may be a high degree of uncertainty regarding what to do and how to do it, objectives may be less clear than usual, and resource requirements will be less well known. In addition, it may be more difficult to create shared perceptions of goals and build and maintain necessary commitment. So, in practical terms, management will need to become change agents, spending considerable time ensuring effective communication to encourage flexibility, address perceptions and generate involvement.

There are of course technical challenges involved in integrating e-retailing, and moving from a physical or 'bricks-and-mortar' organisation to 'bricks-and-clicks'. Here, a more 'virtual' form of organisation may result, mixing traditional ways of working with electronic communications. One of the key problems for existing companies here is to integrate front- and back-end systems while mindful that their 'legacy infrastructure' might well still be essential to other aspects of the business. While start-up companies can leapfrog these problems, established ones face some difficult challenges. This was one of the reasons why it was originally speculated that Internet pure-plays would become the dominant business model in the B2C e-commerce market place. This means that when customers interact *via* the web, placing orders and purchasing goods, the stock control and financial systems need to 'speak the same language' and carry out their part of the transactions. The problem is that many such back-end systems are unlikely to be based on open Internet protocols and may even have been custom-built. Nonetheless, these systems are usually critical to a company's business, and include such details as bank account data and stock rotation information. As Conway (2000) points out:

> IT managers are loath to replace them with something new and untested. They may not even fully understand how their legacies work any longer. The people who built the systems may well have left the company, leaving present IT experts reluctant to tinker. (p. 62)

Replacing such systems also takes time and requires particular IT skills and staff training factors which may impede the developments that are critical to speedy innovation.

There is one general criticism of the change management literature, that it tends to place considerable emphasis on strategies for overcoming different barriers to change, assuming that the 'traditional' companies in question have destructive, dogmatic cultures with bureaucratic tendencies. This insinuates that at a basic level, such companies are almost by definition 'change-phobic'. Many early writers made the rather enthusiastic presumption that Internet retailing was so revolutionary, traditional retailers would become obsolete. Traditional companies were criticised for being slow to engage and for adopting cautious 'toe in the water' strategies. For example, Windham (2000) criticised traditional retailers for not finding 'the vision, commitment and guts to proceed', and interprets caution as 'e-denial'. In fact, it now seems that those companies that exercised a careful web integration strategy have been the ones with the most durable strategies. They have in fact not resisted change, but instead embraced it in an incremental way by creating successful and sustainable online channels as part of holistic multi-channel strategies.

### THINK POINT

What is your perception of a modern company that does *not* offer multi-channel services to its customers?

## CONCLUSIONS

Most businesses recognise that the minimum involvement with the Internet today is to have e-mail and an informational website. This is a step up from a decade ago, and with the pace of change, suggests that businesses already need to consider whether it is now imperative to adopt a transactional online presence.

Many traditional retailers have already taken significant steps towards e-retail, and some of them, including larger, familiar brands such as Tesco and Argos, are setting the pace for online innovation and have e-retail integration strategies that work.

INTEGRATION OF E-RETAILING

### CHAPTER SUMMARY

E-retail has matured to become an additional or alternative channel with a number of serious advantages such as 24×7 availability, lower overheads, greater geographical coverage, and potential for mass customisation and personalisation of the retailer–customer relationship.

Although traditional retailers were late to market in comparison with their online startup competitors, their e-retail efforts have often been more successful in the long term, because many important requirements are already in place. Advantages such as having an established customer base, recognised brand values, and the facilities to offer customers face-to-face contact if necessary, mean that traditional businesses usually enjoy greater trust than their pure-play online competition, often outweighing difficulties in implementing e-retail.

However, much has been learnt in recent years on how traditional businesses successfully adopt online retailing, which has led to methods for evaluating business readiness for e-retail, and the proposal of specific strategic options for e-retail integration. In particular, customer loyalty and the type of retailer–customer relationship may be used to help determine appropriate strategy when adopting e-retail.

In the following chapter we will consider how an e-retailer can start to understand and communicate with customers.

### Case study 3.1
### BOOTS (www.boots.com)

This case study was kindly contributed by Wayne Godfrey.

The case concerns the well-known bricks (and now also clicks) group, Boots the Chemist. Boots opened its first store in Nottingham in 1849, selling herbal remedies. Developing new products such as Ibuprofen (1969) and Nurofen (1983) has helped Boots become a leader in the pharmaceutical business. Boots is now in almost every high street, and is one of the largest pharmaceutical chains, selling medicines, toiletries, cosmetics, fragrances and photographic equipment. The launch of the Advantage loyalty card in 1997 helped Boots gain an insight into its customers and experience in data mining. The 'bricks' stores, though, are approaching maturity in the retail life cycle and profits have been below expectations.

Boots has experimented with T-commerce, launching a 'Wellbeing' interactive digital TV channel in March 2001. However due to the slow uptake, and the lack of consumer support, the service closed in December 2001. Boots still remains committed to the idea and intends to re-launch when the market is ready.

The Boots e-retailing site was launched in 2001. It is packed full of health and nutrition information content and is better stocked than most high street Boots, with 10,000 products available. As we will demonstrate in Chapter 5, providing useful information can act strongly to drive e-shopping traffic. In its first year it turned over £4.3 million in sales. Customers can track their order progress online and there is currently no charge for deliveries (when you spend £45 and over). Returns can be posted back free. There is also an 'Order and collect' option, where customers can order by 8 p.m. and collect at a chosen store from 12 p.m. the following day. For a multi-channel experience, the Boots App enables customers to buy on the go via their smartphone or tablets and to receive personalised offers. The Boots site is renowned for customer satisfaction. According to a recent survey, 95% of customers will shop at the site again. It is the only UK website authorised to sell Chanel and one of only two selling Esteé Lauder and Clinique. Boots has one of the largest customer bases of any UK e-retailer.

Promotion is largely via a targeted e-mail CRM/data mining system allowing personalisation and offers relevant to individual consumers. Boots experience with the loyalty card database is invaluable here. In addition, Boots uses 'link popularity engineering' (discussed in more depth in Chapter 5) to direct traffic to the site. The idea is to make the site a 'one-stop shop' for health and wellbeing information. This makes the site popular with users and attracts links from other sites—characteristics that search engines use in determining rankings. The result is that if a surfer types 'wellbeing' into one of the major search engines (e.g. Google) the first 'hits' will all be Boots—a mixture of sponsored and non-sponsored links.

*Sources*: Various, including Sunday Times Doors 'Webwatch' site test, Boots plc annual report and www.boots.com.

### Case study 3.2
### TESCO (www.tesco.com)

This case was kindly contributed by Omar Chaudhry. See also the Groceries section of Chapter 2.

Tesco is one of the UK's largest e-retailers and the world's biggest e-grocer, overturning the myth that shoppers will not buy fresh products because of the 'look and feel' factor.

Tesco has been active in telesales (at pilot locations) since 1995. The initial telesales pilot, at Ealing, West London, was developed from the home delivery service to less mobile consumers, subcontracted from the Local Authority. This low-tech operation was developed in 1996 into the pilot for e-retailing (rolled out nationally in 1999) built on the proven delivery system and hand-picking from the shelves of the grocery stores. Tesco still uses this tried and reliable system for groceries in preference to a heavy investment in warehouse picking centres, although many non-food items such as books, CDs and DVD movies are now handled from a non-store facility. While Tesco's larger stores may carry only the top 50 CDs, Tesco.com claims to offer every CD currently available in the UK. Not only leading in grocery e-retailing, Tesco is rapidly gaining share in electronics, entertainment and clothing.

Despite the low-key approach, Tesco has invested heavily in its e-retailing operation including the transaction system, based on the ShoppingMagic proprietary system from Unipower systems. The Tesco Grocery App for smartphones and tablets is also gaining traction. Customers can purchase any of the 40,000+ product lines for next-day delivery (for orders placed by 4 p.m.) for UK customers within delivery distance of a store (encompassing 97% of the UK population). In selected locations, a trial is running for same-day delivery for £5. A limited product range is available for delivery worldwide. As an alternative to shoppers composing their shopping list online, Tesco sends them regular information on special offers by e-mail. Using the data from previous shopping, customers can speed up and simplify the ordering process as suggestions are presented, making it possible to save shopping lists and minimising the effort in placing future orders. This is a significant 'convenience' benefit, since much of the grocery shopping is replenishment. Tesco follows the maxim 'make it easy for your customers to buy', accepting orders by web, fax, telephone, and offering home delivery or collection, click and collect, and of course, in-store shopping. In addition to groceries, consumers can buy books, music, clothes, PCs, Internet and mobile phone service.

Tesco make use of the ready-digitised sales data for data mining and segmented offers. Targeted offers (for example via e-mail or SMS) are not perceived as spam by Tesco customers if they add value. HTML e-mails to customers achieve 10% to 30% response rates. In one example, Tesco achieved a 28% click-through to Unilever for a Dove promotion from 35,000 premium shampoo users. Tesco can use the lifestyle data from promotion responses to help plan other marketing initiatives. Running such promotions for manufacturers such as Unilever provides a valuable extra revenue stream for Tesco. In addition, there are affiliate deals with major portals based on cost-per-click or cost-per-sale.

Tesco's e-retailing joint ventures in Ireland, Korea (the country with the world's highest Internet penetration) and particularly, the US, allow the costs of development to be spread. New international markets can be entered at a fraction of the cost of starting from scratch.

In its 2005 annual report, Tesco claimed to be able to serve 98% of the UK population from its 300 participating stores. In the financial year that ended

24 February 2007, Tesco recorded online sales up 29.2% to £1.2 billion and profit up 48.5% to £83 million, with over 250,000 orders per week. This success might well be attributed to Tesco's single-minded determination to provide customer satisfaction, using an easy-entry, cost-effective e-retailing system. In July 2009, Tesco became the first supermarket in the world to offer an API for its shopping service (Arthur, 2009). The API enables customers to access the data stored in Tesco's database, for example about what sort of bananas it has in stock, how many there are and in which stores. This feature will potentially pave the way for smart appliances such as networked fridges that can automatically order food. It seems that Tesco is already preparing for the next smart era with the IoT.

*Sources*: Various, including Arthur (2009), Fernie and McKinnon (2003), Jones (2001) and www.tesco.com.

## QUESTIONS

*Brief feedback to these questions is included at the back of the book.*

**Question 3.1** – What do you consider to be the advantages and disadvantages that traditional retailers have in comparison with Internet pure-plays, in terms of online trading?

**Question 3.2** – Why do you think online customers may not be loyal to a particular company?

**Question 3.3** – What are the dangers of multi-channel operations from a company's perspective?

## GLOSSARY

**24×7**  Used for activities (such as retailing) that run 24 hours a day, 7 days a week. In other words, they are operating all the time, as opposed to 9 a.m. to 5:30 p.m., say, and usually every day of the year.

**IPO**  In an 'Initial Public Offering', shares of a company are offered for the first time on the stock market, and a company obtains a stock market listing. The new issue provides the company with capital for the financing of its future development.

**Startup**  A startup company is one that is formed from scratch, often using private or borrowed funds. By definition, startups are new businesses, and may have the advantages as well as the risks of first-to-market innovators, or in other cases, perhaps lack of experience when compared to businesses already operating in the same sector.

**T-commerce**  E-commerce facilitated by interactive TV, or instigated by TV commercials.

## FURTHER READING

Nicholas Carr (ed.) (2001) *The Digital Enterprise: How to Reshape Your Business for a Connected World,* Boston: Harvard Business School Press.

David Chaffey (2002) *E-Business and E-Commerce Management,* Harlow: Pearson Education.

Michael de Kare-Silver (2001) *E-Shock: The New Rules—E-strategies for Retailers and Manufacturers,* Basingstoke, Palgrave.

Rosabeth Moss Kanter (2001) *Evolve! Succeeding in the Digital Culture of Tomorrow,* Boston: Harvard Business School Press.

Mary Lou Roberts and Debra Zahay (2012) *Internet Marketing: Integrating Online and Offline Strategies* (3rd ed), Mason, OH: South-Western Cengage Learning.

Judy Strauss and Raymond D. Frost (2013) *E-marketing* (7th ed), New York: Routledge.

Peter Weill and Michael Vitale (2001) *Place to Space: Migrating to eBusiness Models,* Boston: Harvard Business School Press.

## REFERENCES

Arthur C. (2009) *Tesco Offers an API for Its Shopping. Now Start Thinking What to Use It for,* [Online] Available at *The Guardian* 14 July 2009: http://www.guardian.co.uk/technology/blog/2009/jul/14/tesco-api-programming-shopping [Accessed 7 March 2016].

Cellan-Jones R. (2003) *dot.bomb: The Strange Death of dot.com Britain,* London: Aurum Press.

Conway P. (2000) 'Lasting legacy?', *eBusiness* June: 62–64.

Cuthbertson R and Bridson K. (2003) 'Online retail loyalty strategies', *IBM E-Business Conference,* Surrey University, UK.

de Kare-Silver M. (2001) *E-Shock: The New Rules—E-Strategies for Retailers and Manufacturers,* Basingstoke, UK: Palgrave.

Econsultancy. (2015) *UK Online Retail Sales to Reach £52.25bn in 2015: Report,* [Online] Available at Econsultancy: https://econsultancy.com/blog/66007-uk-online-retail-sales-to-reach-52-25bn-in-2015-report/ [Accessed 6 March 2016].

Fernie J and McKinnon A. (2003) 'Online shopping: The logistics issues', in Freathy P (ed.) *The Retailing Book: Principles and Applications,* Harlow, UK: FT Prentice Hall.

Ghazali E, Nguyen B, Mutum D S and Mohd-Any A A. (2016) 'Constructing online switching barriers: Examining the effects of switching costs and alternative attractiveness on e-store loyalty in online pure-play retailers', *Electronic Markets—The International Journal on Networked Business,* doi:10.1007/s12525-016-0218-1.

Jones D T. (2001) 'Tesco.com: Delivering home shopping', *ECR Journal,* 1 (1): 37–43.

Nguyen B and Klaus P. (2013) 'Retail fairness: Exploring consumer perceptions of fairness in retailers' marketing tactics', *Journal of Retailing and Consumer Services,* 20 (3), 311–324.

Ofcom. (2015) *The UK Is Now a Smartphone Society,* [Online] Available at: http://media.ofcom.org.uk/news/2015/cmr-uk-2015/ [Accessed 13 September 2016].

Ormrod K. (2015) *UK Online Retail Sales to Reach £62.7bn in 2020*, [Online] Available at Verdict Retail: http://www.verdictretail.com/uk-online-retail-sales-to-reach-62-7bn-in-2020/ [Accessed 6 March 2016].

Reichheld F F. (1996) *The Loyalty Effect: The Hidden Force Behind Growth, Profits, and Lasting Value*, Boston: Harvard Business School Press.

Reichheld F F and Schefter P. (2000) 'E-loyalty: Your secret weapon on the web', *Harvard Business Review*, 78 (4), 105–113.

Steele B. (2016) *You Can Order Groceries from the Door of Samsung's New Fridge*, [Online] Available at Engadget: http://www.engadget.com/2016/01/08/samsung-family-hub-smart-fridge-hands-on/ [Accessed 6 March 2016].

Wallop H. (2013) *Click and Collect—The New Way to Go Shopping*, [Online] Available at *The Telegraph*: http://www.telegraph.co.uk/finance/newsbysector/retailandconsumer/9785532/Click-and-collect-the-new-way-to-go-shopping.html [Accessed 13 September 2016].

Windham L. (2000) 'Overcome e-business barriers', *e-Business Advisor* 18: 10.

 **WEB LINKS**

Information on e-retailing from many bricks-and-clicks high street names from **IMRG**: www.imrg.org/

# Chapter 4

# Understanding and communicating with the e-consumer

### LINKS TO OTHER CHAPTERS

- Chapter 1 – The world of e-retailing
- Chapter 2 – The business of e-retailing in practice
- Chapter 5 – Information search on the web
- Chapter 6 – E-store design: navigability, interactivity and web atmospherics
- Chapter 11 – M-shopping

### KEY LEARNING POINTS

*After completing this chapter you will have an understanding of*

- Why consumers e-shop (or do not e-shop)
- How consumers achieve satisfaction (or not) from e-shopping
- How consumer satisfaction from e-retailing compares with satisfaction from in-store shopping
- What factors are inhibiting the growth of e-shopping?

### ORDERED LIST OF SUBTOPICS

- Understanding e-consumer behaviour
- The perceived risk of e-shopping
- Introducing e-shoppers
- What does e-shopping offer the e-shopper?
- Disadvantages and advantages of e-shopping for consumers

- Social and experiential aspects of e-shopping
- Differences between male and female shopping styles
- Electronic word-of-mouth (eWOM) and e-reviews
- Consumer satisfaction: 'bricks' and 'clicks' shopping compared
- The communications mix for the e-retailer
- Conclusions
- Chapter summary
- Case study
- Questions
- Glossary
- Further reading
- References
- Web links

## INTRODUCTION

According to Charlton (2015) from eConsultancy, 61% of e-consumers read online reviews before making a purchase decision. User reviews reduce consumers' risk perceptions associated with a purchase; they are proven sales drivers and they are now essential for e-retail sites, as the majority of customers will want to see before deciding to make a purchase.

In this chapter we examine the issue of risk as it pertains to online shopping, present the evolving profile of the e-customer, reflect on consumer e-reviews and consider both the advantages and disadvantages of an e-tailing experience.

## UNDERSTANDING E-CONSUMER BEHAVIOUR

The study of e-consumer behaviour has been incredibly important over the past decades due to the explosion of online shopping. Consumer-oriented research in the online context has examined a myriad of topics, notably consumers' psychological characteristics, demographics, consumers' perceptions of risks and benefits, shopping motivation and shopping orientation, and so on (e.g. Dennis et al., 2009). The predominant reason for exploring these issues is to understand the way in which e-consumers make purchasing decisions, so that the e-retailer can cater to and satisfy their needs and wants.

The consumer purchase decision-making process consists of a series of interlinked stages that include information collection, evaluation of alternatives, the purchase itself and post-purchase evaluation (Engel et al., 1991). Many factors influence these decision-making processes such as consumers' attitudes, motivations and social factors, and a tremendous amount of research is dedicated to understand these factors. With social factors, for instance, understanding whether our best friends or family members influence the way in which we make a particular purchase is of great interest. Because although social influences and social interaction are important for e-shopping, e-retailers have oftentimes found it difficult to satisfy these needs in the online environment. Parsons (2002) suggested that social motives such as membership of peer groups, social experiences outside home, communication with others with similar interests and like-minded people and status and authority can be important motivators that influence intention. The closest thing to such a grouping is found on social networking sites and social interactions on online communities, both of which influence e-consumer behavior and e-shopping. Thus, with the rise of social media, e-retailers have become more and more interested in learning about their customers' personal behavior and preferences via such channels. For example, people with a specific, specialist fascination for athletic footwear may be members of SneakerPlay (www.sneakerplay.com) or consumers with a more general interest in social e-shopping are catered to by Osoyou (www.osoyou.com); both of these brands exist on social media, notably Facebook.

## THE PERCEIVED RISK OF E-SHOPPING

As online shopping grows exponentially, online purchases are still perceived as riskier than terrestrial ones (Laroche et al., 2005) and an online shopping consumer therefore relies heavily on experience qualities, which can be acquired only through prior purchase (Lee and Tan, 2003) or via peers and online reviews (Chen et al., 2015).

> 'Do ya' feel lucky, well do da, punk'? - Clint Eastwood's immortal character, Detective Harry Callahan, Movie 'Dirty Harry'
>
> (Fink et al., 1971)

It is one of the most quoted movie lines of all time and is very suitable to how potential consumers have felt about venturing into e-retailing. 'Do ya' feel luck?', or more specifically in this context, 'do you still trust online shopping after all that you have seen and heard about the dangers of e-retailing and do the benefits to you outweigh the fears?'

Shoppers often feel apprehension or risk when considering a purchase, especially from a new vendor. Perceived risk is a function of the uncertainty when making a purchase that may have unpleasant outcomes

(Forsythe and Shi, 2003). Such risk is linked to both the type of merchandise being acquired and the channel or method of acquiring that merchandise (Hisrich et al., 1972). The reasons why non-store purchases fuel a shopper's perceived risk relate to the touch and accessibility issues (Gillett, 1970; Spence et al., 1970; Phau and Poon, 2000), specifically:

- Not being able to touch merchandise before making a purchase.
- Barriers to returning merchandise.

Initial Internet adoption research identified risk as a significant barrier to e-retailing (GVU, 1998; Salam et al., 1998) and this has continued in more recent studies (Mortimer et al., 2016). Yet, simply identifying this phenomenon under the single concept of 'risk' is to miss the complexity of the issue. Risk is a multidimensional construct for e-shopping (Fenech, 2003) with the economic, social, performance, personal and privacy dimensions (Vijayasarathy and Jones, 2000; Miyazaki and Fernandez, 2001). These initial risk dimensions are summarized as:

- *Economic risk* – the probability of making poor purchase decisions.
- *Social risk* – the possibility of incurring societal disapproval for engaging in shopping using a particular medium.
- *Performance risk* – the chance of product/service performing less than expected.
- *Personal risk* – the potential for theft and abuse of credit card information.
- *Privacy risk* – the danger of compromising personal information.

(Vijayasarathy and Jones, 2000)

The first three Vijayasarathy and Jones risk dimensions (*economic, social* and *performance*) were an integral component of retailing prior to the Internet. A shopper in a bricks store can make a poorly researched purchase decision or select merchandise that fails to deliver its performance promise as easily as it could be done online, whereas the remaining risk dimensions (*personal* and *privacy*) are more frequently attributed to e-shopping and receive greater media attention.

## INTRODUCING E-SHOPPERS

The Internet did not create the non-store shopper or even the electronic shopper. An early characterisation of non-store shoppers was by Gillett (1970) who was looking at what he described as in-home shoppers. Such buyers were reported as being:

- More willing to buy without handling items and like shopping but not crowds.
- Greater need of convenience and product assortment.
- More price conscious and seeking a price advantage.
- Infrequent shoppers that make unplanned purchases.

Improvements in communications offered potential retail shoppers new avenues to make non-store purchases and become e-shoppers. One such facility was videotex. Videotex is a generic name for an interactive mass medium that transmits text and visual information between suppliers and consumers of these services usually through an adapted television set (Sauer et al., 1989). The reason most cited by retailers for moving to videotex in the late 1960s was to achieve a competitive advantage over retailers that have not adopted videotex and allowing small business to compete against larger competitors. The popularity of videotex, especially in France (referred to as Minitel), came before the common home ownership of computers and allowed the first true overseas Internet commerce when linked to the US Infonet (predecessor to today's Internet) system (English, 1990).

Shim and Mahoney (1991) identified impressions and characteristics that were applicable to videotex adopters, the first true e-shoppers, to be:

- A belief that it is easy to use electronic shopping;
- Less concern with convenience for shopping;
- Recreational shoppers;
- Shopping innovators.

The advent of the World Wide Web and online shopping through the Internet gave rise to a consumer with similarities and contrasts from the earlier non-store shoppers. Based upon the work of Donthu and Garcia (1999), the evolving web e-shoppers were then characterised as:

- More innovative in their shopping activities;
- Convenience oriented;
- More impulsive in purchases;
- Less brand conscious;
- Less price conscious.

As will be described in greater detail in Chapter 11, e-retailing did not finish with the cabled (wired) versions of the Internet and World Wide Web. The latest incarnation of the e-shopper is not restricted to a desktop or notebook computer with cable-linked modem or broadband connection. Quite the opposite, the new e-shopper is mobile with smartphones and tablets and may use e-retailing anywhere a wireless network is being broadcast. The mobile e-shoppers or m-shoppers share the characteristics of earlier non-store shoppers in that they are innovative shoppers likely to be impulsive in their purchases as they seek shopping convenience (Fenech, 2002). What distinguishes m-shoppers from other e-shoppers is how they look for variety in their shopping activities. The m-shopper is a consumer wanting diversity in the shopping offerings of retailers, a seeker and adopter of new retailing channels, and who if offered the right balance in the retail offering will make an unplanned purchase because an item is attractive and is perceived to be good value.

## WHAT DOES E-SHOPPING OFFER THE E-SHOPPER?

Shopper research by Tauber (1972, 1995) suggests the existence of personal and social consumer motives of shopping behaviour. Personal motives for shopping include role-playing, diversion, self-gratification, physical activity and sensory stimulation; social motives include meeting with others, peer group, status and bargaining (Tauber, 1972; Midgley and Dowling, 1993; Tauber, 1995). For some individuals the shopping experience is enjoyable and treated as a leisure activity or for amusement (Westbrook and Black, 1985). Work by Reynolds (1974) and Berkowitz, Walton and Walker (1979) established that while non-store shoppers may enjoy shopping, they have a negative attitude towards the traditional store-based shopping environment because of such issues as overcrowding and a lack of parking. Later research included work on catalogue shopping by Gehrt and Carter (1992) and cable television shopping by Eastlick and Liu (1997). Those authors found that the shopping enjoyment motivation is a positive influence for adoption of non-store shopping environments such as e-shopping through the Internet.

Whatever the shopping motivation of an individual, the result is not inevitable *shopping enjoyment* or purchase behaviour (Fenech and O'Cass, 2001). For some individuals there is a feeling of apathy or reluctance towards shopping and this compels them to minimise the amount of time spent shopping. As part of a larger research project on multi-channel retailing, data was collected by the authors on the benefits expected from using the web by customers of both business-to-consumer (B2C) and business-to-business (B2B) e-commerce. The results in Tables 4.1 and 4.2 show that despite the variation in recipient profiles (personal versus business), the principal advantages sought from, and given by the web are principally the same. That is, the web provides speedier ordering process, faster usage, an effective search facility and up-to-date product-related information.

**Table 4.1** The principal benefits expected by consumers from e-shopping

|  | Percent (%) |
| --- | --- |
| Faster – direct ordering process | 19 |
| Quicker to use | 13 |
| Efficient search facility | 12 |
| Web has most up-to-date information | 10 |
| Can do at own pace anywhere with web | 6 |
| Order accuray – ability to check stock availability | 6 |
| Easier to compare products and prices | 6 |
| Able to seek more information | 4 |
| Saves time | 4 |
| Environmentally friendly – no paper wasted on orders, invoices or promotional material | 4 |
| Available to place orders 24 hours a day | 4 |
| Ease of use | 2 |
| Web-only specials | 2 |
| Ability to track account details or order progress | 2 |
| No paperwork to type or fill in | 2 |
| Overall convenience | 2 |
| All products in range are shown in one place | 2 |
| Able to recall previously ordered items | 2 |
| Total | 100 |

*Source*: Author's published study of 650 personal shoppers (B2C) on the web

## DISADVANTAGES AND ADVANTAGES OF E-SHOPPING FOR CONSUMERS

### Disadvantages

Many disadvantages with e-shopping exist and remained persistent over the years. Back in 1996, the UK's largest e-consultancy, Cap Gemini, carried out an employee survey. The main disadvantages for shoppers, in ranked order were: 'Availability'; 'Can't be in to receive delivery'; 'Premium charged for delivery' and 'Can't see or feel the merchandise'. With years more experience, many e-retailers still do not have satisfactory

**Table 4.2** The principal benefits expected by business customers from e-purchasing

| | Percent (%) |
|---|---|
| Faster – Direct ordering process | 11 |
| Quicker to use | 10 |
| Efficient search faility | 9 |
| Web has most up-to-date information | 8 |
| No paperwork to type | 7 |
| Available to place orders 24 hours a day | 6 |
| Can do at own pace anywhere with Internet | 6 |
| Saves time | 5 |
| Overall convenience | 5 |
| No catalogues to store and retrieve | 5 |
| Able to seek more information | 3 |
| Environmentally friendly – no paper wasted on orders, invoices or promotional material | 3 |
| Web-only specials | 3 |
| No human seller interference with order | 3 |
| Ease of use | 3 |
| Order accuracy – ability to check stock availability | 3 |
| All products in range are shown in one place | 2 |
| Able to recall previously ordered items | 2 |
| To get a better look at the products | 1 |
| Enjoyment of using online systems | 1 |
| Track account details or order progress | 1 |
| Easier to compare products and prices | 1 |
| Ease of changing order | 1 |
| Can minimise webpage order if interrupted | 1 |
| Total | 100 |

Source: Author's published study of 978 occupation related shoppers (B2B) on the web

# UNDERSTANDING AND COMMUNICATING

answers to these problems. Typical shopper comments have included: 'They left it in the garden and didn't tell me'; 'It's a 24 hour shopping service but only a 6 hour delivery service' and 'Returning unwanted products is when it all goes low-tech' (Consumer surveys from Vincent and colleagues, 2000). Another survey reported, in ranked order, reasons why Internet-connected shoppers do not e-shop: 'Prefer personal shopping, seeing goods'; 'Credit card worries' and 'Don't know how' (Doidge and Higgins, 2000). In 2001, Verdict confirmed security fears as the number one barrier to more consumers shopping online. Our own surveys (e.g. Dennis et al., 2002 – discussed more fully below) have indicated that sixth form pupils are avid e-shoppers using their parents' credit cards. This is an obvious security worry for parents, but also a nuisance for young people, restricting their e-shopping activities. Credit cards are only offered to those of 18 years of age and above, although alternative 'plastic cash' is available for children, with transactions authorised (in the example of the Solo card www.solocard.co.uk) only up to what is in the bank account. The disadvantage is that so far these cards are accepted by only a tiny fraction of e-retailers. At the time of writing, the major credit card companies are developing a 'pay-as-you-go' system for e-shopping that should overcome these problems.

Nowadays, the disadvantages of e-shopping remain similar to the above points and include among other things: 'shipping rates and hidden costs', 'waiting', 'refunds/returns disputes', 'no bargaining', 'intangibility (no product feel)', 'asocial experience', 'tricky terms and conditions', 'no sales assistance', 'credit card hoaxes', 'unreliable pictures and size charts' (e.g. Listovative, 2015).

### Box 4.1
### DISADVANTAGES OF E-SHOPPING FOR CONSUMERS

- Credit card and security worries
- Lack of personal and social interaction
- Can't see or feel the merchandise
- Don't know how
- Can't be in to receive delivery
- Premium charged for delivery
- Difficulties with returning goods for refund
- Waiting

UNDERSTANDING AND COMMUNICATING

The disadvantages are typical of those that faced mail-order traders a few decades ago. Given time, as sales grow, sellers work to overcome the customers' concerns, and consumers become more confident. In the US, L.L.Bean (www.llbean.com) could claim to be the pioneer of mail order, selling goods to rural farmers since way back in the mid-1800s. Today the company has put their reputation for customer responsiveness, helpfulness, cheerfulness and reliability to use in becoming world leader in e-retailing outdoor equipment and clothing, with an efficient, award-winning site. See Chapter 5 for more on L.L.Bean. Recently, Amazon (www.amazon.com) has been investing heavily in their drone delivery service of their products with Amazon Prime Air. This futuristic delivery system aims to safely get packages to customers in 30 minutes or less using small unmanned aerial vehicles, also called drones. At the time of writing, Amazon is still waiting for regulatory support before the vision can be realised.

## Advantages

Counterbalancing the disadvantages and the slow responses of many UK e-retailers to addressing them, there are a number of advantages for shoppers. First in ranked order from the Cap Gemini survey: 'Convenient/easy'; 'Saves time' and 'Fits in with other activities'. Other commonly cited advantages, typified by responses to our own survey include 'Breadth and depth of products'; 'Prices favourable' and 'Convenient' (Dennis et al., 2002). According to Verdict, 'cost effectiveness' (rather than just low prices) is the key reason for shoppers to buy online, followed by convenience and ease of purchase.

**Box 4.2**
**ADVANTAGES OF E-SHOPPING FOR CONSUMERS**

- Cost effective
- Convenient
- Easy
- Saves time
- Fits in with other activities
- Breadth and depth of products
- Easy search of many alternatives
- Personalisation of presentation and merchandise
- Prices favourable
- Discreet shopping

## SOCIAL AND EXPERIENTIAL ASPECTS OF E-SHOPPING

Research has drawn attention to the importance of the social aspects of shopping (e.g. Dennis et al., 2001; Dholakia, 1999; Lunt, 2000; Shim and Eastlick, 1998; Westbrook and Black, 1985). Shopping has even been found to be central to loving relationships within the family (Miller, 1998). Similarly, enjoyment and entertainment have been demonstrated to be important benefits of shopping, increased by a pleasant atmosphere and reflected in spending (e.g. Ang, Leong and Lim, 1997; Babin et al., 1994; Donovan et al., 1994; Jones, 1999; Machleit and Mantel, 2001; Smith and Sherman, 1993; Sit et al., 2003; Spies et al., 1997).

In the case of e-shopping, social influences are also important but e-retailers have difficulty in satisfying these needs (Kolesar and Galbraith, 2000; Shim and associates, 2000). Rohm and Swaminathan (2003), in a study comparing a sample of e-shoppers with non-e-shoppers, found that social interaction, variety seeking and convenience were all significant motivators for e-shopping. Childers and colleagues (2001) found enjoyment to be strongly associated with attitude to e-shopping, particularly for examples that the authors described as 'hedonic' or pleasure related: e.g. Amazon (www.amazon.com) or Hot Hot Hot (sauces – www.hothothot.com). Similarly, Parsons (2002) found that social motives such as social experiences outside home; communication with others with similar interests; membership of peer groups; and status and authority were valid for e-shopping. Social and pleasure motives, important for bricks shopping, are, despite some qualification, also significant for e-shopping.

Two of our own studies emphasise the importance of the experiential aspects of e-shopping, as outlined briefly below. These studies are reported in more detail in *'E-business: Reality or Rhetoric'*, in the same series as this book (Dennis and Richardson, 2004).

**Box 4.3**
**MOTIVES FOR E-SHOPPING**

- Social
- Enjoyment
- Usefulness
- Ease of use
- Convenience

# UNDERSTANDING AND COMMUNICATING

- Navigation
- Knowledge and ability to make a purchase
- Influence of friends and family

*Sources*: Dennis and Papamatthaiou (2003); Parsons (2002)

## Study 1

We have already referred to this first study (initial results in Dennis et al., 2002) in the sections above. The method used was a questionnaire survey that compared shoppers' opinions of Internet shopping versus 'bricks' shopping centres. The 308 respondents were sixth form and university undergraduate students – the shoppers of tomorrow. One of the main themes from the qualitative part of the study was a preference for shopping in shopping centres as more enjoyable and sociable. Shoppers who both e-shopped and shopped in shopping centres commented typically:

> 'Internet shopping is not a personal experience. You cannot try and see what you're buying.... Shopping ... [should] be very sociable'.

Results from the questionnaire indicated that shoppers rated e-shopping higher than shopping centres for *favourable prices* and *convenience*. On the other hand, shopping centres were preferred for *positive image* and more emphatically for *customer service*. Box 4.4 illustrates the results for the sixth form students, but the results for undergraduates were similar.

**Box 4.4**
**SOCIAL MOTIVES FOR E-SHOPPING**

- Social experiences outside the home
- Communications with others having a similar interest
- Peer group attraction
- Status and authority – raising the standing of the shopper in the eyes of friends and colleagues
- Virtual communities

*Source*: Parsons (2002)

UNDERSTANDING AND COMMUNICATING

**Study 2**

Our second study concerned motivations for e-shopping and is discussed in more detail in Chapter 5 (preliminary results reported in Dennis and Papamatthaiou, 2003). Enjoyment, usefulness, ease of use, convenience, navigation, knowledge and ability to make a purchase, and the influence of friends and family were found to be important motivations.

Our results apply to students and are not representative of the average population. Indeed, these are people who within a few years are likely to be earning and spending significantly more than the national average. Bearing in mind this income effect and the high computer literacy of graduates, these are shoppers who will account for a disproportionately high percentage of discretionary income and comparison shopping. Our results, and those of other researchers, show a consistent picture of the importance of the social and experiential aspects of e-shopping. These motivators are being satisfied to good effect by the most successful e-retailers such as, for example, eBay – one of the most successful sites in terms of sales, time spent on the site and providing enjoyment (Nielsen NetRatings, 2016; Reynolds, 2000 – see case study at the end of this chapter).

**Box 4.5**
**ENJOYMENT AND E-SHOPPING**

**Enjoyment motives for e-shopping**

- Involvement
- Not boring
- Fun for its own sake

**Enjoyment and social features of e-retailing sites**

- Chat rooms
- Bulletin boards
- Customer written stories
- Product reviews
- Suggestion boxes
- Personalisation of offers

112

**The most popular 'enjoyment' e-shopping sites (in ranked order)**

- Amazon (www.amazon.co.uk)
- eBay (auction, www.ebay.co.uk)
- Ticketmaster (show tickets, www.ticketmaster.co.uk)
- Ryanair (www.ryanair.co.uk)
- Easy Jet (www.easyjet.co.uk)
- Opodo (air tickets, www.opodo.co.uk)

*Source*: Dennis and Papamatthaiou (2003)

## DIFFERENCES BETWEEN MALE AND FEMALE SHOPPING STYLES

Differences between male and female shopping styles may go back a long way. In hunter-gatherer societies, females tend to carry babies, are based around the camp and do the gathering. Males on the other hand are more likely to protect the group and do the hunting. Humans may have evolved in such a way that those best at their respective roles have been more likely to find a mate and to survive. For females, this meant excelling in gathering: finding the best food and other materials for the family. For males, it entailed being good hunters: fast, strong and decisive. Both sexes would look for those respective qualities in a potential mate, resulting in persistent traits. These differences in mate-seeking behaviour have survived into a wide cross section of modern cultures (Buss, 1989). In Western consumer societies, gathering may have translated into comparison shopping, hunting into earning money to support the family. Even in the US, where gender equality in the workplace is greater than most countries, differences in shopping styles can be clearly observed. The female style involves searching, comparing, weighing the advantages and disadvantages of alternatives, finding the best value and taking pride in the shopping activity (Underhill, 1999). This pride is justified as on average women make a 10% better cost saving than men do, making women the 'better shoppers' (Denison, 2003). Women see the activity of shopping as a satisfying experience in itself – i.e. a leisure activity. On the other hand, men see shopping as a mission and tend to go straight for what they want in a purposeful way (Underhill, 1999). For men, the focus is on 'the kill' – the actual moment of purchase when their heart rate quickens.

Evolutionary psychology has been founded on research demonstrating consistency of mating behaviour across widely different cultures. Accordingly, our own study has sought empirical evidence for an evolutionary basis to shopping sex differences by comparing shopping styles across cultures (reported in more detail in Dennis and Richardson, 2004). Thirteen 'mini focus groups' wrote shopping scenarios about the national culture(s) that they were most familiar with. Fourteen cultural nationalities were represented: five judge participants represented the UK national culture, eight continental European and 23 Asian, i.e. 36 judge participants in total. In general, there were some differences in shopping styles between the national cultures, but the differences between males and females were much more striking, reflecting the hunter and gather roles and providing support for the evolutionary hypothesis.

The stereotypes are not 100% accurate but the styles have been found to be equally valid for e-shopping (Lindquist and Kaufman-Scarborough, 2000). As with bricks shopping, the stereotype reverses when the product purchased is technical and expensive (Dholakia and Chiang, 2003).

### Box 4.6
### SHOPPERS IN CYBERSPACE: ARE THEY FROM VENUS OR MARS?

**Female shopping style – the gatherer**

- Women have a ritual of seeking and comparing
- Women imagine and envision the merchandise in use
- They tally up the pros and cons
- They take (justified) pride in their ability as shoppers
- The total shopping process (not just buying) is a leisure activity
- Women like to spend longer shopping than men do
- Social interaction is an important part of shopping
- Women favour sites designed for women – e.g. sites with horoscopes, health, beauty and diet
- Women are more likely to browse online, and then buy in-store

**Male shopping styles – the hunter**

- Men are incisive, decisive and determined shoppers
- Men's excitement with shopping is at the moment of 'kill' (purchase)

# UNDERSTANDING AND COMMUNICATING

- Men try to complete the shopping activity in the shortest possible time
- Men's lack of patience means they often miss the best buy
- But the stereotype reverses when the product is technical and expensive Men do take pride in shopping for (e.g.) cars and computers (and women are purposeful for those products)
- Men's favourite sites tend to include games, gambling and pornography
- Male e-shoppers are heavier Internet users and are more likely to shop via smart mobile devices

*Sources*: Dennison (2003); Dholakia (1999); Dholakia and Chiang (2003); eTypes (2001); Lindquist and Kaufman-Scarborough (2000); Lindquist and Kaufman-Scarborough (2000); Underhill (1999); Zorzini (2015)

### Box 4.7
### MALE AND FEMALE SHOPPING STEREOTYPES?

Is this cultural stereotyping? Or is there any truth in this research? BBC News (2003) ran a story on the Dennison (2003) research asking readers to post their own answers to these questions. Of 64 replies posted, 19 asked further questions or made different points ('*Louise [who hates shopping] – will you marry me?*' *Debt-ridden husband*). Of the remainder, 22% disagreed with the stereotypes, and 78% agreed.

Perhaps reflecting the greater attention given to the selection process, more women than men shop online (68% versus 72%), both women (82%) and men (85%) tend to do most of the shopping from their laptops although men are more likely to use their smartphones for a purchase (45% versus 34%). Women are bargain hunters (74% versus 54%) and love apps (install 40% more apps than men). The use of social media to compare products is used more by men (62% versus 50%). On social media, women are more likely to recommend a brand to others over social network (35% versus 28%).

Women are more likely to use coupons (74% versus 57%) and more responsive to marketing e-mails and sales while men are less interested in discounts, deals or out-of-season sales. For more about how to understand how people use the Internet the Consumer Barometer is a great tool (see Mini Case 4.1) – for example, heavy Internet users are also heavier than average in usage of mobile Internet devices and smart mobile phones. See Chapter 11 for more on m-shopping.

UNDERSTANDING AND COMMUNICATING

## Mini case 4.1
## CONSUMER BAROMETER (www.consumerbarometer.com/en/)

The Consumer Barometer is a tool to help marketers understand how people use the Internet across the world. It features extensive information on how consumers behave and transact online. CB has been constructed by combining demographic and lifestyle datasets from profiling companies and with data from Google, the leading Internet search organisation. The system offers the ability to (1) dive into the data with a graph builder and create a custom analysis to understand how people use the Internet; (2) compare digital trended data over time and see how Internet usage and device usage have evolved; (3) learn about the Internet's role in the lives of key audience segments; and (4) discover curated insights and create charts for quick viewing.

CB aims to tell e-retailers about the characteristics of e-shoppers and what they use the Internet for – whether it's finding holidays, buying CDs, managing their stocks and shares or just chatting. CB claims that this means e-retailers can get more from their e-shopper data – and a higher return on website investment.

*Source*: www.consumerbarometer.com/en/

### Box 4.8
### E-SHOPPING LIFE CYCLE STAGES

- **Stage 1 – Virtual virgins** These Internet users may not have bought online, or if they have, it is very seldom. Age tends to be the youngest and oldest
- **Stage 2 – Chatters and gamers** These are avid Internet users, spending more time online than the average. Twenty-five percent are e-shoppers. This group tends to be more worried about security than average
- **Stage 3 – Dot.com dabblers** Forty percent of these Internet users are e-shoppers. They are heavy users of entertainment and scientific sites
- **Stage 4 – Surfing suits** These are heavy e-shoppers, but spend less time online – only 60% of the average. They tend to be professional and financially aware
- **Stage 5 – Wired 4 life** The heaviest e-shoppers – 70% have purchased online. Many are graduates or cosmopolitan. These users tend to be in the mid-range age groups

*Source*: www.etypes.info

Earlier in this section we drew attention to the importance of shopping as a social activity. In line with the evolutionary psychology approach, these interpersonal aspects are particularly important for female shoppers (e.g. see Dholakia, 1999; Elliot, 1994). Women tend to want more interpersonal contact from e-shopping than men do, preferring chat and women's sites (Zorzini, 2015). 'Women want ease of navigation and sense of personalised relationship' – helped by 'community' or 'chat' rooms (Harris, 1998). An example of the more female and 'community' orientated approach is the e-mall and social networks (Karr, 2014). Women tend to be later adopters of e-shopping and are more likely to be in the first of the eTypes e-shopping life-cycle stages, 'Virtual virgins' (eTypes, 2001).

## ELECTRONIC WORD-OF-MOUTH (eWOM) AND E-REVIEWS

As noted in the introductory paragraph of this chapter, e-consumers of today are proactive readers of online reviews or e-reviews prior to making a purchase decision (Chen et al., 2015). Such e-reviews may be found on blogs, forums and rating websites. For example, consumers will frequently share experiences directly with others through Facebook or Instagram and each time, an opinion or feeling is developed, some times about a product, service offering or the e-retailer's brand. Such electronic word of mouth (eWOM) happens when e-consumers express their views to a vast number of potential consumers and in various forms, such as peer ranking and positive or negative reviews. E-retailers need to evaluate these influences as part of their overall online strategy as the insights from these e-reviews may provide a picture of their overall services.

Indeed, the use of social networks, smartphones, and tablets has changed the way e-consumers process information and make decisions. Proactively reading e-reviews is often to reduce the risk of a purchase. For example, Swarbrooke and Homer (2007) point out that, given the considerable monetary and emotion involvement of purchasing a holiday, consumers are very much influenced by others' experiences and opinions. In the past, this social group might have been family and close friends, but with the Internet, a shift has happened towards online sources as a resource to make decisions.

E-WOM is more trustworthy and more credible than other forms of marketing communication, such as advertising, because it is not influenced by the organisation itself. It has also the potential to reach a larger group of audience and it does not vanish once it has been published. Rather because it has been published online it can be both accessed globally and will be stored indefinitely and the information can be accessed any time and with ease. Whether or not the firm should intervene in such e-reviews has been a topic of considerate debate, as some scholars suggest that a more active role should be done to monitor and control the content, while others believe in a more interactive relationship between an e-retailer and its consumers to communicate any issues that may arise and otherwise remain passive in order to keep that credibility of the forum (Hallier-Willi et al., 2014). It is a case where the individual e-retailer would have to consider the audience, the platform as well as part of their online strategy. More research is needed to establish this important case.

## CONSUMER SATISFACTION: 'BRICKS' AND 'CLICKS' SHOPPING COMPARED

As outlined in Chapter 1, even at modest projections, e-retail will soon take a share approaching 17% of total retail sales (Ormrod, 2015). This may seem a small percentage, but it represents around £62.7 billion in sales. High street banks, other financial services and travel agents are most at risk. Some forecasters predict the eventual disappearance from the high street of any businesses that work better as e-businesses: banks, travel agents, book, music and electronics shops. 'Clothes shops will persist because the experience of shopping for clothes is too deeply ingrained, especially in women, to be abandoned'. Also specialist, up-market retailers that require expertise and offer the consumer a specific experience will flourish. The winners in the high street are likely to be well-branded retailers offering service and added value. Indications so far are that most e-retail success too is going to existing, well-branded retailers – likely to have efficient supply chain and fulfilment systems – a trend likely to continue for several years.

Researchers attempting to answer why people e-shop have tended to look to various components of the 'image' of e-retailing and specific e-retailers, in a similar way to measurements of the image of a bricks store (Wolfinbarger and Gilly, 2002). This may be a valid approach for two reasons. First, 'image' is a concept used to mean our overall evaluation or rating of something in such a way as to guide our actions (Boulding, 1956). For example, we are more likely to buy from a store that we consider has a positive image on considerations that we may consider important, such as price or customer service. Second this is an approach that has been demonstrated to work for bricks stores over many years (e.g. Berry, 1969; Lindquist, 1974) and it is largely the bricks retailers with strong images that are making the running in e-retail. According to Kimber (2001), shopper loyalty in-store and online are linked. For example, Tesco's customers using both online and offline shopping channels spend 20% more on average than customers who only use the store. Tesco is well known as having a very positive image both in-store and online, being the UK grocery market leader in both channels.

E-retail image measurements that have been used by commercial marketing research studies include ease of use, product selection, product information, price, on-time delivery, product representation, customer support, and privacy. There is empirical support for some of these dimensions of image, for example 'product selection' and 'ease of use' (Dennis et al., 2002; Dennis and Pappamattaiou, 2003, respectively) but in general the connection between the components of image and e-shopping spending behaviour remains an under-researched area. Perhaps the most extensive investigation to date has come from Wolfinbarger and Gilly (2003) who carried out focus groups and quantitative surveys to determine the components of e-retail quality. The qualitative analysis identified four factors: (1) fulfilment/reliability, (2) website design, (3) customer service and (4) security/privacy. *Fulfilment/reliability* includes both the description of a product and efficient delivery. *Website design* includes navigation, search and ordering. *Customer service* means responsive and helpful service, responding to customer enquiries quickly. The quantitative surveys indicated that these three factors were all significantly related to e-shoppers' understanding of e-retail quality.

*Security/privacy* refers to credit card payments and privacy. As mentioned earlier in this chapter, security worries have often been reported as one of the most important reasons for not e-shopping. It is surprising, therefore, that the survey did not find this factor to be significantly associated with e-retail quality. Other studies have shown that as e-shoppers become more experienced, they tend to shop more and become less concerned about security. In the case of the Wolfinbarger and Gilly study, those e-shoppers who were satisfied with e-retailers' reliability, website design and service may well have been more confident e-shoppers and therefore suffered less security worries, resulting in 'security/privacy' being swamped by the other factors in the analysis.

### Box 4.9
### COMPONENTS OF E-RETAIL QUALITY

**Fulfilment/reliability**

- Accurate display and description of a product so that what customers receive is what they thought they ordered
- Delivery of the right product within the time frame promised

UNDERSTANDING AND COMMUNICATING

**Website design** – all elements of the consumer's experience at the website:

- Navigation
- Information search
- Order processing
- Personalization
- Product selection

**Customer service**

- Responsive, helpful, willing service that responds to customer inquiries quickly

**Security/privacy**

- Security of credit card payments
- Privacy of shared information

*Source*: Wolfinbarger and Gilly (2003).

The balance of the evidence available is that a wide range of image and other attributes is important in consumer satisfaction and behaviour for e-shopping. Many attributes that are important for bricks shopping are also important for e-shopping. Some e-retailers have often paid less attention to elements such as the social and enjoyment aspects of e-shopping, but the best and most successful e-retailers are deliberately and successfully satisfying e-shoppers on motivators such as these. Emphasising the importance of addressing the overall experience of e-shopping, one survey indicated that if the worst-rated e-grocery were to improve the online experience to match the best competitor, online sales could be improved by 480%. For the average e-retailer, improved user experience could result in a 33% to 54% sales increase (Meekings et al., 2003).

**Mini case 4.2**
**CUSTOMER SERVICE FROM SCREWFIX**
**(www.screwfix.com – see Chapter 1)**

Screwfix's approach to customer service can be illustrated by our experience with a concrete mixer. After a few weeks' use, the electrical contactor start button failed, meaning the mixer would only run if the 'start' button was held in by hand. We informed Screwfix, explaining that the machine had already had

# UNDERSTANDING AND COMMUNICATING

some use, expecting to be offered a replacement electrical contactor. With such a large item of equipment, and the length of time it had been used, we did not realistically expect a replacement mixer. Nevertheless, the Screwfix help desk could not have been more helpful, and did authorise the replacement mixer – asking us just to pack up the old one in the original packaging and hand it over to the delivery driver who brought the new one. The problem was that the (very bulky!) packaging had been disposed of some time ago. No problem for Screwfix: 'we'll send you the new one. Unpack it over the next few days, then dismantle the old one and put it into the new packaging. We'll send another lorry to pick it up next week.'

### THINK POINT

Why do you think Screwfix offered to replace the item, despite the heavy extra carriage requirements, when a simple replacement of the contactor would have been acceptable?

## Mini case 4.3
### CUSTOMER SERVICE FROM MCWILLIES (NOT IT'S REAL NAME!)

A contrasting approach to that of Mini Case 4.2 can be illustrated by our customer service experience from McWillies. We used the shopbot Kelcoo to identify the best deal for a photo printer – which turned out to be from McWillies. Not only was McWillies cheapest for the printer but also there was a special offer including a free pack of photo print paper. McWillies sent an e-mail confirmation showing the price and the two items, printer and paper. The printer arrived within a few days, but without the paper. Some weeks later, despite an (unanswered) e-mail, the paper had still not arrived, so we phoned the 'customer service' line. Here is a summarised extract from the conversation:

McWillies (D): 'The paper was sent with the printer.'
Customer (C): 'But we didn't receive it.'
D: 'You must have received it because it was sent in the same box.'
C: 'There was only one box, the original packaging, and it was completely full with the printer.'

## UNDERSTANDING AND COMMUNICATING

D: 'Well we sent it.'
C: 'Well we haven't received it' [and so on for a few minutes], until:
C: 'Can I speak to a supervisor?'
D: 'The supervisor's busy'
C: 'Well, can I speak to someone at head office?'
D: 'I'll speak to head office, please hold.' [Long wait]
D: 'I've checked with head office and they say it's too late to do anything about it now.'
C: 'I would still like to speak to a supervisor' [audible click mid-sentence]:
D: 'Supervisor speaking. We can PROVE that we sent the paper, because we weigh all the parcels, so all we have to do is to check the weight on the docket and we'll prove that we sent it.'
C: 'That's great! What a good idea. Could you check it now, please, as it will prove that the paper wasn't in the box.'
D: '*NO!* We will not be doing that because *YOU* should've sent us an e-mail to let us know that the paper had not arrived.'
C: 'As I've already explained, we did send an e-mail.'
D: 'Well we have no record of it so the matter ends here.'
C: 'Can you check with head office before you refuse to confirm the weight of the parcel as that will prove that we didn't receive the paper?'
D: '*NO!* We can't check the weight and I'm not going to discuss this any further.' (Line went dead).

*Postscript*: We still have not received the paper and have given up trying to get it.

---

### THINK POINT

Why do you think McWillies suggested checking the package weights, but decided against this course of action when the customer said it was a good idea?

---

## THE COMMUNICATIONS MIX FOR THE E-RETAILER

All elements of the e-retail mix can actually form part of the communications mix. For example, '*Convenience*' can include the ease of finding the site, say by paid links from other sites or search engines, communicating the existence of the site to the potential customer. '*Customer value and benefit*' can be reflected in the width and depth of product offered and ease of navigating around this large range, communicating a benefit of buying online rather than in-store. '*Cost to the customer*' can communicate price positioning in the case of a cost leadership strategy. Alternatively, high prices with 'round' figures can communicate quality and prestige. '*Computing and category management*' can communicate added value from the availability of a wide range of products on short delivery times. '*Customer franchise*' is largely a communications and branding issue. For example, improving the information value of an e-retailing site can improve image and branding. Similarly, '*Customer care and service*' can communicate a positive image. Although many of the critical aspects of service are not visible until the order is fulfilled, a generous returns policy can act as a proxy in communicating an image of good service. Finally, '*Communication and customer relationships*' describes the communications mix proper, which can have a huge variety of elements from marketing research surveys to e-mail, and from advertising to sponsorship. Rather than try to cover everything (which would need another book), we will illustrate the elements outlined in Chapter 1 with some examples.

### Mini case 4.4
### THE E-RETAIL MIX COMMUNICATES WITH THE CUSTOMER

#### Compass24 boat chandlery and accessories (www.compass24.com)

Compass24 is Europe's largest direct sales boating equipment company. A brief illustration of how the Compass24 e-retail mix is utilised to communicate positively with customers follows.

*Convenience*

Entering '*boating equipment uk*' in the Google search engine (www.google.co.uk) brings up Force 4 (www.force4.co.uk) close to the top of the non-sponsored links. This is because many boating information sites are linked *to* the Force 4 site. Many boat equipment sites are linked by paid links *from* Force 4 precisely because it is near the top of the Google (unpaid link) search results. There is a link to Compass24 (www.compass24.com) in the 'Chandlers' section. Links from Force 4 and other popular sites related to the product category represent added convenience for the customer and greatly increase exposure to surfers interested in the specific product types.

## UNDERSTANDING AND COMMUNICATING

### Customer value and benefit

The huge range of 8,000 products is clearly available and easy to find. Navigation is by a close approach to 'free grid' (Vrechopoulos, 2001). This is a combination of a grid hierarchical tree structure with a free-flow navigation capability. Shoppers can either move through the e-store in a logical progression through departments or obtain direct access to end products using a search engine. Product categories are displayed in a 'left-frame'. The ease of finding products and the huge amount of boating equipment that can be supplied communicate the site's ability to satisfy wide-ranging customer requirements.

### Cost to the customer

The Compass online shop page does not offer 'bargain' positioning, but rather, promises 'good value'. With a separate search facility for 'brands', there is an emphasis on differentiation rather than price leadership. The pricing therefore communicates value, for example 'a Simrad [a top brand] RS12 VHF Navigation top value offer'. Nevertheless, the value pricing is strongly emphasised by using 'psychological pricing'. For example the RS12 is priced at £799.90, i.e. psychologically below the price point of £800.00 – emphasising the communication of good value. There are often premium-based rather than price-based special offers. For example 'spend £20.00 or more and we'll give you a free vacuum flask'. Promotions such as this communicate extra value for the customer without risking damage to the customers' perceptions of quality and the price goods are worth, as can be the case with price-based promotions like '£10 off'.

### Computing and category management

Compass is based on established and efficient supply chain arrangements with suppliers. Thus, there is a huge range of products available either from stock or drop shipped directly from suppliers on short delivery times. Compass delivers 'Just-in-Time': tell Compass when you want the goods (for example when you expect to return from your boating cruise), and for a small extra fee they will deliver that exact day. Supply chain efficiency is used to communicate the site's ability and desire to satisfy customers' particular needs.

### Customer franchise

The Compass site communicates established branding and image by links to bodies such as the Royal Yachting Association, weather forecasts from the Met. Office and tides data from Yachting and Boating World (www.ybw.com, Europe's top marine website). When the site was launched in the UK (it is German based), added credibility as endorsement from Sir Robin Knox-Johnston, the famous, record-breaking ocean rower and Yachtsman communicated an established brand.

## Customer care and service

Compass offers a 14-day 'no questions asked' return policy. Deliveries are fast and reliable. Fast and easy e-mail help is available, with the e-mail pages also showing telephone numbers. The telephone help line is courteous, knowledgeable and helpful. Some months after we got our 'free' vacuum flask (the offer mentioned above), the top started to leak. We contacted Compass24 to ask if we could buy a replacement top but they were unable to supply one as they were no longer selling that flask. Compass24 quickly sent a replacement, better quality flask – free. Such surprisingly good service communicates a commitment to putting the customer's interests first, despite the costs to the company.

## Communication and customer relationships

In addition to the communication tools mentioned above, Compass24 uses a wide range of communication mix elements, including

**Advertising** – In specialist paper-based yachting magazines in addition to web-based such as Force 4
**Direct Mail** – Catalogues, mini catalogues and special offers
**Word of mouth** – E.g. recommend Compass24 to a friend and get a free tool set
**Customer relationships** – Customers can opt in to the e-mail newsletter for tip-offs on special offers and other news.
**Web atmospherics** – Good illustrations and snappy animation that do not take too long to load

# Marketing research surveys

When we bought a new digital camera from Samsung, we had to register the software online. The registration process entailed uploading basic information on the use of the product that the supplier can use, for example to inform us of updates or new products that may be of interest. Other suppliers use a huge lifestyle questionnaire that gives the impression of being the guarantee registration. The lifestyle data can be used for profiling, but also may be rented for a highly selectable mailing list by other companies. To comply with data protection legislation, there is an 'opt out' box that can be checked, but the 'if you don't want this service, please tick' message is sometimes in very small print almost hidden among many pages of conditions. Most e-shoppers just click 'accept' and never even know.

## Offline advertising[1]

The scope of offline advertising is too wide to cover in detail here. Suffice it to say that an e-retailer should naturally include the web address not only in TV, radio and press ads, but also on all brochures, stationery, plus the label and packaging of the product (whether sold on or offline). Advertisements in specialist targeted publications are often more cost-effective than the mass media, especially for smaller niche markets. For example, for boat insurance, craftinsure (www.craftinsure.com) advertises in publications like *All at Sea*, a monthly newspaper distributed partly by subscription but mainly distributed free at boating shops and marinas. For a product of general interest to most people, like the department (e-) store John Lewis (www.johnlewis.com), e-retailers can advertise in Internet magazines such as. Net (www.netmag.co.uk), one of the biggest selling UK Internet magazines, whose readers are likely to e-shop. Another tip for the e-retailer is to advertise in the 'click here' sections of the general press (e.g. *Sunday Times*, *Daily Mail*), which are a lot cheaper and likely to be more cost-effective than large colour advertisements.

## Public relations (PR), sponsorship and publicity

PR and publicity aim to communicate positive messages without paying directly for the media space as advertising. PR activity includes press releases and press conferences, which can contribute towards positive press coverage. Publicity and PR opportunities are not limited to the official sponsors of such stunts.

The car e-retailer Edmunds (www.edmunds.com) illustrates PR in action. The website has a dedicated media area providing easy contact with the PR department, and press releases (such as forecasts of changes on the levels of car prices).

## Direct mail

Many of the most successful e-retailers communicate regularly with customers by post. Tesco (www.tesco.com) is a well-known example, mailing news, vouchers and special offers every 3 months. Tesco has found that expenditure on direct and database marketing can be far more cost effective than traditional above-the-line advertising. This cost effectiveness also leads niche marketers in particular to use direct mail. For example,

Screwfix (www.screwfix.com – trade and DIY supplies – see Chapter 1) posts regular catalogues, mini catalogues and special offers.

## E-mail permission marketing

Permission marketing via e-mail is increasing. The response rates to opt-in e-mail campaigns are significantly higher than other online ads; the cost per acquisition is lower; turnaround time is faster; and results can be accurately tracked. More companies are moving greater proportions of budget from postal direct mailings and conventional advertising to e-mail. Unfortunately, spam has also increased dramatically. More aggressive spam filters have been developed, but even so, most e-mail users are experiencing unacceptably high levels of unwanted e-mail messages. Responsible marketers use opt-in or even double-opt-in permission marketing and also make it easy for customers who have opted-in to opt-out again.

### Box 4.10
### THE PRINCIPLES OF AN E-MAIL MARKETING CAMPAIGN

- Acquire e-mail addresses (e.g. of people who have registered to receive information)
- Obtain permission to use the e-mail address for marketing. This is best done at the time of collection, e.g. registration or free samples may only be possible if the respondent checks the 'yes' box
- Select the addresses to target for the particular message
- Execute the campaign (possibly in conjunction with other communications channels)
- Respond to customer replies
- Correct and clean the e-mail list
- Track and measure the campaign performance

*Source*: Adapted from Harris and Dennis (2002).

## Short message systems (SMSs) and multimedia messaging services (MMSs)

While mobile phones and other mobile devices can be useful for 'distress' purchases such as paying a congestion charge (to drive into a city), the growth of m-commerce has been slow, even since the introduction of 4G. Nevertheless, even though it represents a small proportion of marketing budgets, advertising via SMSs and MMSs achieves high response rates. Because of this, spending on mobile advertising has been predicted to rocket. Mobile advertising is growing in popularity not just because of the high response, but also because smartphone web users represent an attractive demographic. These users are well segmented as a target for games, gambling and travel services – currently the biggest mobile advertising categories. See Chapter 11 for more on m-marketing.

## Social media

Social media is a new battlefront for e-tailing and plays a big part in the daily lives and business practices of the users (Okazaki, 2009). It allows the creation and exchange of user-generated content (Kaplan and Haenlein, 2010), which takes a variety of forms, including weblogs, social blogs, microblogging, wikis, podcasts, pictures, video, rating and social bookmarking. In January 2014, 74% of online adults use social networking sites (Duggan et al., 2015). Moreover, social media networks such as Facebook (www.facebook.com) and Twitter (www.twitter.com) allow users to connect with peers by adding them to networks of friends, which facilitates communication and word of mouth, particularly among peer groups (Zhang and Daugherty, 2009). More than 50% of social media users follow brands on social media and 29% follow trends and find product reviews and information, and 20% to comment on what's hot or new or to review products (Gallup, 2014). Such popularity makes social networks an ideal platform for e-tailers to interact with their customers.

As social media becomes the new battleground to interact with the e-consumer, e-tailers are joining and using social media to actively perform integrated marketing activities with much less effort and cost than before. Social media is currently being used as a marketing tool mainly for four purposes: (1) market research and feedback generation; (2) customer service and customer relationship management; (3) business networking; and (4) publicity, branding and reputation management (Thoring, 2011). An overwhelming majority of marketers 97% are participating in social media marketing to market their business (Stelzner, 2014). Facebook, Twitter, LinkedIn, YouTube, blogging, Google+ and Pinterest are the top seven platforms used by marketers (Stelzner, 2014).

## Viral marketing

Viral marketing is growing as more companies use it to promote and brand their products and services. Viral campaigns are becoming more

## UNDERSTANDING AND COMMUNICATING

sophisticated with social media and the culture of content sharing as well as the tracking of open, click-through and success rates. A potential problem with viral marketing campaigns is that the company is reliant on each individual in the chain to have permission to send such messages to each recipient. In many cases this is not done: viral marketing spreads much spam. The responsible marketer will be using tracking systems that can be used for follow-up of sample recipients to ensure that they do not object to such communications. As an example of opt-out viral marketing, consider the hypothetical way that this book could be promoted. Prospects may initially receive an information-only message, for example an invitation to a Marketing conference, ending with something along the lines of:

> Please forward this message to anyone else who may be interested. In the future we may want to inform you of other services and products (for example books) in which we think you may be interested. If you do not wish to receive such messages, please contact the sender to be removed from the list.

### Banners, pop-ups and interstitials[2]

Online advertising expenditure on media such as banners and pop-ups is growing vastly and in much greater numbers than cinema advertising, for example. The interstitial, a pop-up that interrupts browsing to show an ad, is a much more active form of advertising than banners. Some people using the web for a specific purpose find these irritating, though. Online advertising company RealMedia (www.uk.realmedia.com) is using a less-intrusive system called adPointer. This generates an ad when the cursor has not moved for a specific time.

Schemes that incentivise users to look at advertisements have been around for some years; on one occasion, in the UK, Bananalotto.com (www.bananalotto.com) raised the stakes by offering the chance to win one million pounds as you click the banner ad. KPE, the media and entertainment consultancy, has developed around 10 games for its clients. Managing Director Paul Zwillberg says: 'So much of the Internet has been characterised by repurposing things that worked well in print or TV. "Advergaming" is ... a new combination that's made for the medium ... . You take one of the most popular uses of interactive content and marry it with tried and tested advertising models like brand association, trial or data capture and you get something really wonderful'.

### Customer relationships

The direct mail and e-mail activities described above are part of the management of customer relationships. Building on these basic communication tools, the most successful e-retailers such as Amazon (www.amazon.co.uk) and Tesco (www.tesco.com) use various techniques of data mining, personalisation and customisation (explored in more detail in Chapter 2). For example, Amazon customises the webpage, making offers for new books, music or movies that are likely to be of interest based on past purchase patterns. Tesco likewise personalises its communications and special offers almost down to the level of the individual. These e-retailers are thus able to satisfy customers more specifically and therefore better using the customer relationship and data mining tools.

### Web atmospherics

Web atmospherics is too important and complex a topic for this single section, but is explored in Chapter 6 in greater depth. Briefly, atmospherics includes *visual* (e.g. text, design, colour management, video clips, 3D), *aural* (e.g. music or sound effects) and *olfactory* (e.g. perfume and samples). Mercedes Benz (www.mercedes-benz.com) car site is a good example of the use of exciting downloads of video and sound effects to illustrate their cars in action. With effects like this, the customers will get a feel of the luxurious brand and what it stands for in terms of quality and lifestyle. Atmospherics, even when fairly low tech, have much to offer in communications mix design.

### Link popularity

Search engines use 'link popularity' in locating and ranking sites. Improving link popularity by persuading other sites to link to yours raises a site in search engine rankings and is therefore a critical aspect of the communications mix.

### Customer experience

The creation of a compelling online customer experience has numerous positive impacts for e-retailers and should be part of any online strategy. When consumers immerse themselves in the shopping experience, it is easier for managers to induce consumer satisfaction and e-loyalty. It is particularly important in this respect to understand that consumers should not only be regarded as a target for products and services but also as a co-creator of experiences. E-retailers thus need to develop effective strategies that involve communicating and interacting with consumers in order to deliver increased brand value. This paradigm has been increasingly popular with the rise of Customer Experience Management practices (Klaus and Nguyen, 2013).

## CONCLUSIONS

E-shopping is growing and e-consumers are showing great diversity in their behaviours when it comes to shopping online. Although both disadvantages and advantages exist of e-shopping for consumers, retailers and shoppers are overcoming the problems as time goes by. Shopping online today provides not just functional goods but also real social and enjoyment benefits. Although originally thought of only in mechanistic terms, e-shopping can also provide social interaction and enjoyment, especially in this social media era. Even though in some aspects such as recreation, e-shopping trails behind bricks shopping, it is often the e-retailers that are good at satisfying these non-tangible benefits that are having most success. While the stereotypes cannot be generalised with certainty, there are differences between the sexes in shopping styles. Men tend to be more purposeful and faster shoppers. Women take more care, and want more social interaction than men do. In the past, e-shopping has been more suited to the male style, but women are now heavy users of e-shopping and female-orientated sites. For technical products such as cars and computers, the gender stereotypes tend to be reversed. There is a wide range of potential communications channels available to the e-retailer. Many successful e-retailers use a broad, integrated range of offline and online communications, but there is a trend towards the use of more permission and database marketing techniques.

### CHAPTER SUMMARY

The chapter started with an overview of the different areas and vast research within the e-consumer behavior literature. It became clear that much of the online shopping involves reducing the perceived risk of e-shopping, since consumers are not able to touch and feel the merchandise before making a purchase and numerous stories exist of dishonest e-retailers that do not deliver the promised goods. Hence, a list of different risk perceptions was introduced. This was followed by presenting an in-depth overview of the electronic consumer, which previously had been known as non-store shoppers. As the Internet evolved,

UNDERSTANDING AND COMMUNICATING

this group shares some similar traits, as discussed. Subsequently, the chapter presented the advantages and disadvantages of e-shopping, analysing the criteria, which consumers find most important for engaging in online shopping, of which, the advantages notably include factors such as convenience, saves time, cost effective, while the disadvantages include delivery issues and credit card worries. What is really lacking with online shopping is the missing element of social and experiential aspects and not being able to share the shopping experiences with family and friends. However, based on our own studies (as presented in Study 1 and 2), social features for e-shopping do exist, which include product reviews, social media and bulletin boards, to mention some. It also became clear that male and female shoppers have different shopping styles. To this end, Box 4.6 highlights the main differences. The importance of risk and social features is, to some extent, diminished with the presence of e-reviews, as the opinions and word-of-mouth of other shoppers have a great influence on one's own online shopping intentions. This is certainly something that the e-retailers should take note of when developing their communications mix, which is the focus in the final sections of the chapter. In particular, social media has become a powerful tool to add more value to the e-consumers, as interaction and dialogue can take place. In turn, such interaction is said to create more trustworthy and greater customer relationships.

In the following chapter we will explore the relevance to e-retailing of consumers' needs for information.

### Case study 4.1
### eBay (www.ebay.co.uk – see also the comparison with Amazon in Chapter 8)

eBay was founded in the US in 1995, originally under the name Auctionweb. The UK site was launched in 1999, growing after a slow start to become one of the UK's top e-commerce sites measured by monthly audience numbers. In the fourth quarter of 2015, the worldwide eBay site reached 162 million active users after surpassing 154 million active users at the end of 2014. The figures are a significant sign of the potential of the most profitable and successful Internet players to sell to consumers. Cheap though most individual products may be, eBay still sells for billions of pounds every year. There are a total of 25 million sellers on eBay, listing more than 800 million items. Each day, around 20,000 packages are sent globally, of which 80% are new items. The total number of global eBay app downloads is 279 million, with 40% of eBay sales by mobile devices. In the fourth quarter of 2015, eBay's revenue was $2.32bn (above facts provided by Craig Smith from DMR, 2016).

Visitors to eBay spend an average of 2 hours and 30 minutes per month on the site – one of the longest of any UK site. Visitors return to the site to check the status of items they are bidding for or selling. eBay.co.uk is one of very few e-retailers to achieve over a billion pages views per month.

Many UK users are earning a healthy living as 'power sellers' taking advantage of the worldwide market to offer everything from sports utility vehicles (SUVs) to comics, records and oddments like garden gnomes, T-shirts and kettles. In the same way as the major 'bricks' retailers are suffering increasing competition from charity shops and car boot sales, so the established e-retailers face growing competition from online auctions.

Most sellers are private individuals. For example, Pat Austin makes £30,000 per year selling an assortment of bric-a-brac that she finds in charity shops, car boot sales and physical auctions. She sells 1,000 plus items per year and 99.9% of her transactions have been positive. It is a full-time job, though, with correspondence and despatch taking up the mornings and sourcing goods the afternoons. Rosie English has a turnover of £100,000 plus selling high-class women's fashion for prices of £100 plus to £1000 plus. She reads the fashion press to identify what editors recommend and what celebrities are wearing, then buys from sample and factory sales or direct from designers. eBay is not all one-person businesses, though, as the 'big boys' are seeing the opportunities and joining in with companies like Dell, Dixons and Sears using eBay to shift excess stock.

It's a case of 'buyer beware' as auction sites do not take responsibility for deals that go wrong and offer only low insurance cover for losses. The way for buyers to identify the most reliable sellers is from feedback ratings – many regular sellers have hundreds of positive ratings.

### Box 4.11
### HOW EBAY WORKS

- Signing up is free
- Buyers bid online and the highest wins
- Sellers and buyers rate each other
- Listing fees vary in the approximate range £0.15 to £2.00
- eBay also charges a percentage of the sale price, between approximately 1.75% and 5.25% – the more valuable the item, the lower the percentage

UNDERSTANDING AND COMMUNICATING

### Box 4.12

**Tips for auction sellers**

- **Provide a detailed description** Include a photograph if possible. Be honest about any faults in order to avoid negative feedback
- **Choose a suitable category** The categories help bidders to find goods quickly. Fees are higher in some categories than others
- **Sell internationally** This is how to reach a bigger audience – but always get the payment cleared before sending the goods
- **Provide a 'little extra' customer service** Rosie English gift wraps everything. She has 500 positive feedback messages and 100% feedback rating

**Tips for auction buyers**

- **Read the description carefully** Make sure that you know what you are getting. For example, one buyer bid for a rug, then found out that it was from a doll's house!
- **If in doubt, contact the seller** The relationship may be important if things go wrong
- **Think whether it is too good to be true** In-demand items like home theatre, plasma screens and digital cameras can attract the dodgy deal at very low prices
- **Check for spelling mistakes** For example the 'Stradivarious' violin offered at a fraction of the price you would expect
- **Bid high, then stop** Research shows that the final price can be up to 30% higher when bids arrive fast (Haubl and Popkowski Leszeczyc, 2003). Limit spending from the outset in order to avoid bidding frenzy

*Sources*: Adapted from *Sunday Times* 6 July 2003 and *Sunday Times Doors*, 10 August 2003, with additional material from *Marketing Business*, June 2003

## QUESTIONS

*Brief feedback on these questions is included at the back of the book.*

**Question 4.1** – Why do people shop?

**Question 4.2** – Can e-shopping satisfy shoppers as much as bricks shopping does?

# UNDERSTANDING AND COMMUNICATING

**Question 4.3** – How can the mechanistic process of e-shopping satisfy shoppers' social motives?

**Question 4.4** – What can e-retailers do to provide enjoyment and social benefits for e-shoppers?

## NOTES

1. This section adapted from Lundquist, 1998.
2. This section summarised and adapted from Marketing Business 'e-Business' supplement.

## GLOSSARY

**Ad**  Short for 'advertisement'.

**Double-opt-in**  After customers have opted-in to a mailing list, a message is sent asking them to confirm that that is what they want. This ensures the correct identity of the recipient.

**E-zine**  A magazine published only in electronic format.

**Multimedia Messaging Services (MMSs)**  Message services for 3G mobile devices, incorporating graphics and/or sound.

**Opt-in**  Opt-in lists are based on obtaining permission for future mailing, e.g. by checking a box for 'yes, please send me future communications'. A potential problem is that people can sign others up for services that they do not want (see 'double-opt-in').

**Opt-out**  Opt-out lists assume permission by requiring the recipients to take action to remove themselves from mailings. An individual may be automatically added to a mailing list if he or she fails to notice the 'Check here if you do not want to receive future mailings'.

**Permission marketing**  Marketing addressed only to individuals who have specifically requested contact, and limited to the extent of the permission granted by the customer. It is designed to build up trust.

**Personal Digital Assistant (PDA)**  A mobile device incorporating diary facilities, word processing, e-mail and web Internet access.

**Short Message Systems (SMSs)**  An increasingly popular text messaging system.

**Videotex**  is an early, television-based, data transmission system; while its use has diminished, its legacy is the ability of television sets to be able to show closed captions for the hearing impaired. France's videotex industry came to be called Minitel under the marketing umbrella of the nation's telecommunications organisation.

**Viral marketing**  Taking advantage of the network effects of the Internet to spread messages widely by customer endorsement.

## FURTHER READING

Ian Chaston (2001) *E-marketing Strategy,* Maidenhead, UK: McGraw-Hill. This is a comprehensive textbook on Internet marketing.

Charles Dennis, Lisa Harris and Balraj Sandhu (2002) 'From bricks to clicks: Understanding the e-consumer', *Qualitative Market Research – An International Journal,* 5 (4): 281–290.

Lisa Harris and Charles Dennis (2002) *Marketing the E-business,* London: Routledge. This is one of the few Marketing texts written specifically for the e-business. It has useful chapters for communicating with the e-consumer on relationship and multi-channel marketing.

Leslie Heeter Lundquist (1998) *Selling Online for Dummies,* Hoboken, NJ: Wiley. Written for US readers, this is a simple guide to promotion and all aspects of selling online.

Mary Lou Roberts and Debra Zahay (2012) *Internet Marketing: Integrating Online and Offline Strategies* (3rd ed), Mason, OH: South-Western Cengage Learning.

Bernadette Tiernan (2000) *E-tailing,* Chicago: Dearborn. This is one of the few texts on e-retailing, written for a US audience, with useful material for communicating with the e-consumer.

Ralph Wilson (2001) *Planning Your Internet Marketing Strategy: A Doctor Ebiz Guide,* New York: John Wiley and Sons. Written for US readers, this is a practical guide to Internet marketing strategy.

## REFERENCES

Ang S H, Leong S M and Lim J. (1997) 'The mediating influence of pleasure and arousal on layout and signage effects: Comparing more and less customized retail service', *Journal of Retailing and Consumer Services,* 4 (1): 13–24.

Babin B J, Darden W R and Griffin M. (1994) 'Work and/or fun: Measuring hedonic and utilitarian shopping value', *Journal of Consumer Research,* 20: 644–656.

BBC News. (2003) *Primeval Shopping Instincts Revealed,* [Online] Available at: http://news.bbc.co.uk [Accessed 17 September 2003].

Berkowitz E N, Walton J R and Walker O C. (1979) 'In-home shoppers: The market for innovative distribution systems', *Journal of Retailing,* 55, Summer: 15–33.

Berry L L. (1969) 'The components of department store image: A theoretical and empirical analysis', *Journal of Retailing,* 45 (1): 3–20.

Boulding K E. (1956) *The Image,* Ann Arbor: University of Michigan.

Buss D N. (1989) 'Sex differences in human mate preferences: Evolutionary hypotheses tested in 37 cultures', *Behavioural and Brain Sciences,* 12: 1–14.

Charlton, G. (2015) *Ecommerce Consumer Reviews: Why You Need Them and How to Use Them,* [Online] Available at Econsultancy: https://econsultancy.com/blog/9366-ecommerce-consumer-reviews-why-you-need-them-and-how-to-use-them/ [Accessed 8 March 2016].

Chen C H S, Nguyen B, Klaus P and Wu M S. (2015) 'Exploring electronic word-of-mouth (eWOM) in the consumer purchase decision making process: The case of online holidays – evidence from United Kingdom (UK) consumers', *Journal of Travel and Tourism Marketing,* 32 (8): 953–970.

Childers T L, Carr C L, Peck J and Carson S. (2001) 'Hedonic and utilitarian motivations for online retail shopping behaviour', *Journal of Retailing*, 77: 511–535.

Denison T. (2003) *Men and Women Arguing When Shopping Is Genetic*, [Online] Available at *News Shop*, Exeter University: www.ex.ac.uk/news/newsshop.htm [Accessed 22 September 2003].

Dennis C, Merrilees B, Jayawardhena C and Wright L T. (2009) 'E-consumer behaviour', *European Journal of Marketing*, 43 (9/10): 1121–1139.

Dennis C and Pappamatthaiou E-K. (2003) 'Shoppers motivations for e-shopping', *Recent Advances in Retailing and Services Science, 6th International Conference*, The European Institute of Retailing and Services Studies, Portland, Oregon, August 7–10.

Dennis C E, Harris L and Sandhu B. (2002) 'From bricks to clicks: Understanding the e-consumer', *Qualitative Market Research – An International Journal*, 5 (4): 281–290.

Dennis C E and Hilton J. (2001) 'Shoppers' motivations in choices of shopping centres', *8th International Conference on Recent Advances in Retailing and Services Science*, Vancouver, EIRASS.

Dennis C E and Richardson O. (2004) 'E-retail: Paradoxes for suppliers and consumers', in Harris L and Budd L. (eds.) *E-Business: Reality or Rhetoric*, London: Routledge.

Dholakia R R. (1999) 'Going shopping: Key determinants of shopping behaviour and motivations', *International Journal of Retail and Distribution Management*, 27 (4-5): 154.

Dholakia R R and Chiang K-P. (2003) 'Shoppers in cyberspace: Are they from Venus or Mars and does it matter?', *Journal of Consumer Psychology*, 13 (1/2): 171–176.

Doidge R and Higgins C. (2000) *The Big Dot.com Con*, London: Colliers Conrad Ritblat Erdman.

Donovan R J, Rossiter J R, Marcoolyn G and Nesdale A. (1994) 'Store atmosphere and purchasing behavior', *Journal of Retailing*, 70 (3): 283–294.

Donthu N and Garcia A. (1999) 'The Internet Shopper', *Journal of Advertising Research*, 39 (2): 52–58.

Duggan M, Ellison N B, Lampe C, Lenhart A and Madden M. (2015) *Social Media Update 2014*, [Online] Available at Pew Research Center: http://www.pewinternet.org/2015/01/09/social-media-update-2014/ [Accessed 13 September 2016].

Eastlick M A and Liu M. (1997) 'The influence of store attitudes and other nonstore shopping patterns on patronage of television shopping programs', *Journal of Direct Marketing*, 11 (3): 14–24.

Elliot R. (1994) 'Addictive consumption: Function and fragmentation in postmodernity', *Journal of Consumer Policy*, 17: 159–179.

Engel J F, Kollat D T and Blackwell R D. (1991) *Consumer Behavior*. New York: Holt Rinehart and Winston.

English W D. (1990) 'Videotex: Pandora's Box for retailers', *Journal of Direct Marketing*, 4 (2): 7–18.

eTypes. (2001) *Who's Buying Online? UK Online 2001*, London: eTypes/CACI.

Fenech T. (2002) 'Exploratory study into WAP (Wireless Application Protocol) shopping', *International Journal of Retail and Distribution Management*, 30 (10): 482–497.

Fenech T. (2003) 'Factors influencing intention to adopt wireless shopping', in Lewin J E (ed.) *Proceedings of World Marketing Congress*, Perth, Western Australia: Academy of Marketing Science: 729.

Fenech T and O'Cass A. (2001) 'Internet users' adoption of Web retailing: User and product dimensions', *Journal of Product and Brand Management,* 10 (6): 361–381.

Fink H J, Fink R M and Riesner D. (1971) *Dirty Harry* (Movie) (Siegel D, ed./producer/director), Hollywood, CA: Warner Bros.

Forsythe S M and Shi B. (2003) 'Consumer patronage and risk perceptions in Internet shopping', *Journal of Business Research,* 56: 867–875.

Gallup. (2014) *The Myth of Social Media: A Majority of Consumers Say They Are Not Influenced by Facebook or Twitter,* [Online] Available at: http://online.wsj.com/public/resources/documents/sac_report_11_socialmedia_061114.pdf [Accessed 13 September 2016].

Gehrt K C and Carter K. (1992) 'An exploratory assessment of catalog shopping orientations', *Journal of Direct Marketing,* 6 (1): 29–39.

Gillett P L. (1970) 'A profile of urban in-home shoppers', *Journal of Marketing,* 34, July: 40–45.

GVU. (1998) *8th WWW User Survey,* [Online] Available at Graphic, Visualization, and Usability Center: www.gvu.gatech.edu/user.surveys/survey_1998 [Accessed 7 October 1998].

Hallier-Willi C, Melewar T C, Dennis C, and Nguyen B. (2014) 'Corporate impression formation in online communities – A qualitative study', *Qualitative Market Research: An International Journal,* 17 (4): 410–440.

Harris K. (1998) 'Women on the Net II: The female-friendly site', *Sporting Goods Business,* 31 (13): 16.

Harris L and Dennis C E. (2002) *Marketing the e-Business,* London: Routledge.

Haubl G and Poplowski Leszeczye P T L. (2003) 'Bidding frenzy and product valuation in ascending-bid auctions', *10th International Conference on Recent Advances in Retailing and Services Science,* Portland, OR: EIRASS.

Hisrich R D, Dornoff R J and Kernan J B. (1972) 'Perceived risk in store selection', *Journal of Marketing Research,* 9: 435–439.

Jones M A. (1999) 'Entertaining shopping experiences: An exploratory investigation', *Journal of Retailing and Consumer Services,* 6: 129–139.

Kaplan A M and Haenlein M. (2010) 'Users of the world, unite! The challenges and opportunities of social media', *Business Horizons,* 53 (1): 59–68.

Karr D. (2014) *Men vs. Women Online Shopping,* [Online] Available at Marketing Tech Blog: https://www.marketingtechblog.com/men-vs-women-online-shopping/ [Accessed 8 March 2016].

Kimber C. (2001) *Researching Online Buying's Offline Impact,* London: CACI.

Klaus P and Nguyen B. (2013) 'Exploring the role of the online customer experience in the firm's multichannel strategy – An empirical analysis of the retail banking sector', *Journal of Strategic Marketing,* 21 (5): 429–442.

Kolesar M B and Galbraith R W. (2000) 'A services-marketing perspective on e-retailing: Implications for e-retailers and directions for further research', *Internet Research: Electronic Networking Applications and Policy,* 10 (5): 424–438.

Laroche M, Papadopoulos N, Heslop L A and Mourali M. (2005) 'The influence of country image structure on consumer evaluations of foreign products', *International Marketing Review,* 22 (1): 96–115.

Lee K S and Tan S J. (2003) 'E-retailing versus physical retailing: A theoretical model and empirical test of consumer choice', *Journal of Business Research,* 56 (11): 877–885.

Lindquist J D. (1974) 'Meaning of image: A survey of empirical and hypothetical evidence', *Journal of Retailing,* 50 (4): 29–38, 116.

Lindquist J D and Kaufman-Scarborough C. (2000) 'Browsing and purchasing activity in selected non-store settings: A contrast between female and male shoppers', in *Retailing 2000: Launching the New Millennium, Proceedings of the 6th Triennial National Retailing Conference, the Academy of Marketing Science and the American Collegiate Retailing Association,* Hofstra University, Columbus, OH.

Listovative. (2015) *Top 10 Major Disadvantages of Online Shoppping,* [Online] Available at Listovative: http://listovative.com/top-10-major-disadvantages-of-online-shopping/ [Accessed 13 September 2016].

Lundquist L H. (1998) *Selling Online for Dummies,* Hoboken, NJ: Wiley.

Lunt P. (2000) 'The virtual consumer', *Virtual Society? Delivering the Virtual Promise? From Access to Use in the Virtual Society,* ESRC presentation led by Brunel University, London, June 19.

Machleit K A and Mantel S P. (2001) 'Emotional response and shopping satisfaction: Moderating effects of shopper attributions', *Journal of Business Research,* 54: 97–106.

Meekings A, Russell C, Fuller M and Hewson W. (2003) *Profit or Pain from Your User Experience,* London: Hewson Consulting Group.

Midgley D F and Dowling G R. (1993) 'A longitudinal study of product form innovation: The interaction between predispositions and social messages', *Journal of Consumer Research,* 19: 611–625.

Miller D. (1998) *A Theory of Shopping,* London: Polity.

Miyazaki A D and Fernandez A. (2001) 'Consumer perceptions of privacy and security risks for online shopping', *Journal of Consumer Affairs,* 35 (1): 27–44.

Mortimer G, Hasan S F E, Andrews L and Martin J. (2016) 'Online grocery shopping: The impact of shopping frequency on perceived risk', *International Review of Retail, Distribution and Consumer Research.* doi:10.1080/09593969.2015.1130737.

Nielsen NetRatings. (2016) [Online] Available at: www.nielsen-netratings.com [Accessed 13 September 2016].

Okazaki S. (2009) 'The tactical use of mobile marketing: How adolescents' social networking can best shape brand extensions', *Journal of Advertising Research,* 49 (1): 12–26.

Ormrod K. (2015) *UK Online Retail Sales to Reach £62.7bn in 2020,* [Online] Available at Verdict Retail: http://www.verdictretail.com/uk-online-retail-sales-to-reach-62-7bn-in-2020/ [Accessed 13 September 2016].

Parsons A G. (2002) 'Non-functional motives for online shoppers: Why we click', *Journal of Consumer Marketing,* 19 (5): 380–392.

Phau I and Poon S M. (2000) 'Factors influencing the types of products and services purchased over the Internet', *Internet Research: Electronic Networking Applications and Policy,* 10 (2): 102–113.

Reynolds F D. (1974) 'An analysis of catalog buying behavior', *Journal of Marketing,* 38 (July): 47–51.

Reynolds J. (2000) 'Pricing dynamics and European retailing: Direct and indirect impacts of eCommerce', in *Proceedings of the International EARCD Conference on Retail Innovation* (CD-ROM), ESADE, Barcelona, European Association for Education and Research in Commercial Distribution.

Rohm A J and Swaminathan V. (2003) 'A typology of online shoppers based on shopping motivations,' *Journal of Business Research*, 57 (7): 748–757.

Salam A F, Rao H R and Pegels C C. (1998) 'An investigation of consumer-perceived risk on electronic commerce transactions: The role of institutional trust and economic incentive in a social exchange framework', in *Proceedings of Conference for the Association of Information Systems (AIS)*, Baltimore, MD.

Sauer P, Young M and Talarzyk W W. (1989) 'The potential impact of emerging communication technologies on distribution channel', *Journal of Direct Marketing*, 3 (4): 28–37.

Shim S and Eastlick M A. (1998) 'The hierarchical influence of personal values on mall shopping attitude and behaviour', *Journal of Retailing*, 74 (1, Spring): 139–160.

Shim S, Eastlick M A and Lotz S. (2000) 'Assessing the impact of Internet shopping on store shopping among mall shoppers and Internet users', *Journal of Shopping Center Research*, 7 (2): 7–43.

Shim S and Mahoney M Y. (1991) 'Electronic shoppers and nonshoppers among videotex users', *Journal of Direct Marketing*, 5 (3): 29–38.

Sit J, Merrilees W and Birch D. (2003) 'Entertainment-seeking shopping centre patrons: The missing segments', *International Journal of Retail and Distribution Management*, 31 (2): 80–94.

Smith C. (2016) *By the Numbers: 24 Amazing eBay Statistics*, [Online] Available at DMR Digital Stats/Gadgets: http://expandedramblings.com/index.php/ebay-stats/2/ [Accessed 13 September 2016].

Smith R B and Sherman E. (1993) 'Effects of store image and mood on consumer behaviour: A theoretical and empirical analysis', *Advances in Consumer Research*, 20 (1): 631.

Spence H E, Engel J F and Blackwell R D. (1970) 'Perceived risk in mail-order and retail store buying', *Journal of Marketing Research*, 7: 364–369.

Spies K, Hesse F and Loesch K. (1997) 'Store atmosphere, mood and purchasing behaviour', *International Journal of Research in Marketing*, 14: 1–17.

Stelzner A M. (2014) *Social Media Marketing Industry Report*, [Online] Available at: http://www.socialmediaexaminer.com/report2014/ [Accessed 13 September 2016].

Swarbrooke J and Horner S. (2007) *Consumer Behaviour in Tourism* (2nd ed.), Oxford: Butterworth-Heinemann.

Tauber E M. (1972) 'Why do people shop?' *Journal of Marketing*, 36 (October): 46–59.

Tauber E M. (1995) 'Why do people shop?' *Marketing Management*, 4 (2): 58–60.

Thoring A. (2011) 'Corporate tweeting: Analysing the use of Twitter as a marketing tool by UK trade publishers', *Publishing Research Quarterly*, 27(2): 141–158.

Underhill P. (1999) *Why We Buy*, London: Orion.

Verdict. (2001) *Verdict on Electronic Shopping, 2001*, London: Verdict.

Vijayasarathy L R and Jones J M. (2000) 'Print and Internet catalog shopping: Assessing attitudes and intentions', *Internet Research*, 10 (3): 191–202.

Vincent A, Clark H and English A. (2000) 'Retail distribution: A multi-channel traffic jam', *International Journal of New Product Development and Innovation Management*, 2 (2): 179–196.

Vrechopoulos. (2001) *Virtual Store Atmosphere in Internet Retailing: Measuring Virtual Retail Store Layout Effects on Consumer Buying Behaviour*, Brunel University, unpublished PhD thesis.

Westbrook R A and Black W C. (1985) 'A motivation-based shopper typology', *Journal of Retailing,* 61 (Spring): 78–103.

Wolfinbarger M and Gilly M C. (2002) *.comQ: Dimensionalizing, Measuring and Predicting Quality of the E-Tail Experience,* Working Paper No. 02–100. Marketing Science Institute, Cambridge, MA.

Wolfinbarger M and Gilly M C. (2003) 'eTailQ: Dimensionalizing, measuring and predicting etail quality', *Journal of Retailing,* 79 (3): 183–198.

Zhang J and Daugherty T. (2009) 'Third-person effect and social networking: Implications for online marketing and word-of-mouth communication', *American Journal of Business,* 24 (2): 53–63.

Zorzini C. (2015) *Infographic: Online Shopping Habits Men vs. Women,* [Online] Available at Ecommerce Platforms: http://ecommerce-platforms.com/ecommerce-news/infographic-online-shopping-habits-men-vs-women [Accessed 8 March 2016].

# WEB LINKS

**E-marketer:** www.emarketer.com – e-marketing statistics and reports.

**eTypes:** www.e-types.com – demographics, classifications and consumer e-shopping behaviour.

**Forrester:** www.forrester.com – Internet usage data.

**New Media Age:** www.nma.co.uk – new media news items.

**Nielsen/NetRatings:** www.nielsen-netratings.com – performance and viewing ratings for Internet sites and advertisers.

**NUA:** www.nua.com/surveys – Internet statistics.

# Chapter 5

# Information search on the web

### LINKS TO OTHER CHAPTERS

- Chapter 2 – The business of e-retailing in practice
- Chapter 3 – Integration of e-retailing into an organisation
- Chapter 4 – Understanding and communicating with the e-consumer
- Chapter 8 – Branding on the web
- Chapter 9 – E-malls

### KEY LEARNING POINTS

*After completing this chapter you will have an understanding of*

- The difference between the 'clicks' and 'bricks' experience
- Shoppers' search behaviour on the web
- Search engines
- Directories
- Ways to improve your web 'visibility' and monitor the use of your pages

### ORDERED LIST OF SUBTOPICS

- 'Clicks' and 'bricks'
- The background to searching the Internet and the web
- Surveys on what people do and where people 'go' on the web
- Searching and finding on the web
- The average web session

# INFORMATION SEARCH ON THE WEB

- Focus
- Directories
- Search engines
- Monitoring the use of your webpages
- Conclusions
- Chapter summary
- ❖ Case study 5.1
- ❖ Case study 5.2
- ❖ Questions
- ❖ Glossary
- ❖ Further reading
- ❖ References
- ❖ Web links

## 'CLICKS' AND 'BRICKS'

In the e-retail literature, much is made of the *similarities* between the new electronic ways ('clicks') to sell goods to consumers and the traditional ways ('bricks'). One can talk about e-stores, e-shop fronts, e-shoppers, e-malls and so on. In this chapter, we highlight some of the *differences* between 'clicks' and 'bricks'. These differences arise from the totally different technologies which are used in a clicks store compared with a bricks store, and the totally different approach used by e-shoppers to find goods and services, compare prices and generally browse around. The essential concept is *search*, the process by which e-shoppers find information about products and services.

## THE BACKGROUND TO SEARCHING THE INTERNET AND THE WEB

The Internet is a worldwide network of servers and machines, originally set up (as the ARPAnet) to facilitate information exchange between US government contractors and university researchers (Wolinsky, 1999). From the earliest days of the Internet, a major activity has been *searching* for information. As the Internet grew, a variety of tools were set up to help users perform searching to find the required information.

Nowadays, the focus of activity is the World Wide Web, which uses Internet technology with an improved user interface, making huge amounts of information available to the end-user, often a home computer user. Much of this information is about products and services for mass distribution, provided by e-retailers.

**143**

The interface employed by most users is a graphical web browser (i.e. Microsoft Internet Explorer, Mozilla, Safari, Google Chrome, etc.). In practice much of the information is textual in nature, with graphical layout (such as the use of lists) to provide structure and additional graphics to provide other information and 'decoration'. Although much has been made of the idea of e-malls (see Chapter 9), where a group of e-shops congregate together like a conventional shopping mall, the typical user experience involves focussing on a specific website often linked to one company's offerings.

## SURVEYS ON WHAT PEOPLE DO AND WHERE PEOPLE 'GO' ON THE WEB

A computer scientist would say that what e-shoppers actually do is to use a web browser to examine data from the web rendered into graphical images. A typical user would say something rather different – the experience is that you explore a virtual world and that at any moment you are at one 'place' in that world. From then you might explore the place more deeply or move on to other places which are linked.

Many surveys have been done to help us understand the nature of what people use the web for. According to Rodgers and Sheldon (2002), there are four primary motives for Internet use: researching (in the most general sense), shopping, socialising and generalised surfing (for enjoyment).

Shehan (2002) carried out a cluster analysis of types of Internet sessions, finding that 'I need to find some information' was a significantly stronger motivation than all others. Visiting news sites, using search engines, searching for product information and using online databases together accounted for 34% of users' online time. Searching for product information alone accounted for 7% of online time, compared with only 1.7% spent e-shopping. Eighty-five percent of all Internet traffic comes from 13 major search engines (Gehan, 2003). Information search is important for consumers and it is important for e-retailers too: in a US study, the use of the Internet to search for information was the strongest predictor of e-shopping intention (Shim et al., 2001). In addition, information search improved shoppers' attitudes towards e-retailing and helped overcome the perceived barriers to e-shopping. Similarly, Fink and Laupase (2000) carried out an experiment with 30 Australian and 30 Malaysian participants who evaluated selected websites. They found evidence of a relationship between products and services and news stories. The authors argued that the impact of products and services displayed could be maximised through the presence of news stories providing information about recent developments.

In Chapter 4 we referred briefly to our study investigating shoppers' motivations in e-shopping (Dennis and Pappamatthaiou, 2003; discussed in more detail in *'E-business: Reality or Rhetoric'*, in the same series as this book, Dennis and Richardson, 2004). The respondents were a sample of 150 undergraduate students. Enjoyment was one of the main motivations and 'Involvement' was one of the most important enjoyment dimensions. In addition to Amazon (www.amazon.co.uk) and eBay (auction, www.ebay.co.uk) as the the most popular sites to 'variety seeking' (Rohm and Swaminathan, 2004), recently Facebook (www.facebook.com) and Pinterest (www.pinterest.com) have acquired a huge attention especially among youth (Harris and Dennis, 2011; Phillips et al., 2014; Duffet, 2015 forthcoming).

Amazon and eBay are the top two retail sites in the US in terms of audience numbers (Nielsen NetRatings 2010 – see case studies in Chapters 2 and 3, respectively, and the comparison in Chapter 8). eBay is particularly strong on involvement, with visitors spending on average 1 hour and 11 minutes on the site, one of the longest of UK e-retailers (see case study at the end of Chapter 4). Visitors return to the site frequently to check on items they are buying or selling. There is also a feedback feature on sellers that helps to build trust. eBay is one of few UK e-retailers to achieve over one billion page views per month. These sites enthusiastically embrace the 'involvement' aspect of enjoyment with features such as chat rooms, bulletin boards, customer written stories and product reviews, suggestion boxes and personalisation of the website offers. In short, many of the features that make these sites involving, enjoyable and successful are based on satisfying shoppers' needs for information in one form or another. Some e-retailers use surfers' needs for information as a successful method of directing traffic to their sites. For example, outdoor equipment supplier L.L.Bean (www.llbean.com) provide information on national parks and chemist/drugstore Boots specialises in nutrition and health information. See the case studies at the end of this chapter and Chapter 3, respectively.

## SEARCHING AND FINDING ON THE WEB

Shoppers, then, spend a lot of time *searching*. E-retailers are, of course, most interested in what they *find* ('Seek, and ye shall find!'). They would like shoppers to find information on their products and services at their virtual store, and to find (and execute) ordering and payment processes. E-retailers thus need to understand what technologies the shoppers use, and how they use these technologies, in order to improve the chance of sales and services on the web. E-retailers that can help satisfy surfers' wants for information have a head start in selling to those customers.

## INFORMATION SEARCH ON THE WEB

### THE AVERAGE WEB SESSION

Let us consider what average users do in an average web session:

- The users sit down and start their web browser, often set up so that the initial screen (the Home Page) points to some major website, and it displays a list of links to other sites and services. For example, the Home Page might be set to the Yahoo! main page (www.yahoo.com). Possibly they might decide to *focus* immediately on some site they know about and type in the web address (URL) or use 'favorites' or 'bookmarks' to access that site.
- Otherwise, they look through the Home Page visually and *evaluate* the list, and make some decision based on what they are interested in.
- They might then decide to access a *search engine*, for example Google, (www.google.com) and by entering suitable search phrases and hitting the Search button, instruct the engine to produce a list of relevant webpages with a brief summary of their contents. Having got that list, it is then scanned and evaluated.
- They might decide to examine a *directory system* related to their search goals, and scan through that and evaluate items.
- The process of scanning through lists for relevant items and/or using search engines is repeated until the relevant items are found. If nothing suitable is found, the search is re-focussed or *abandoned* at any point, the search goals may be re-focussed from information retrieved, deliberately or not (some advertisement might pop up). The users might even go directly to some site, even if it does not come up on a directory or search engine list, if they know the web address (URL).

Several important concepts arise from the above consideration. Let us now examine these in more detail. They are:

- Focus;
- Directories;
- Search engines.

### FOCUS

Suppose you want to purchase some hair conditioner. If you go down to the local town centre and locate a major shopping mall or high street area, you have expectations as to what you might find there and the ways you can quickly locate items of interest. For example, you would expect to be able to find a chain pharmacy store in a few minutes – in the UK, a branch of Boots or Superdrug. Having found such a store, you would expect to quickly locate a section with hair products and to soon locate a range of shampoos and conditioners. What you might also do is use some sort of directory (possibly the Yellow Pages) to locate stores of interest.

Compared with the bricks experience, an e-shopper on the web operates in a rather different way. On the web, a user starts up a web browser with some initial page, perhaps that of their Internet service provider. They then start searching for the item required, following appropriate links. Almost certainly they will use some sort of web search engine.

Obviously, we need to design webpages so that they are useable and attractive to the user. Nielsen (2000) has written extensively on website useability, and has pointed out a number of important considerations. A prime component of making sites useable is clarity and focus. If the user finds the site difficult to use, and the design messy and unfocussed, the user will abandon the site and turn to searching elsewhere. Nielsen suggests some standards to create user consistency, good design and relevance, leading to a unified user experience across the site. As we discuss in detail later, we also need to make automatic web search systems (search engines) 'notice' our pages and rank them highly.

## DIRECTORIES

People like lists, from the Seven Wonders of the Ancient World to the Top 20 pop songs. Directories are lists compiled around some specific topic, such as the telephone directory and trade directories. In the early days of the web, people (editors) compiled lists of the most popular sites. As the number of sites grew, the lists became rather long. To improve accessibility, they were split into categories and sub-categories. Well-known web directories include Yahoo! (www.yahoo.com).

Let us consider Yahoo! in a little detail. Yahoo is compiled by human editors who also create a short description that is shown alongside the link to the web address. The editors categorise the topics logically, in a way a search engine does not. For example, a category listed on the Yahoo! main page might be *Shopping*. This might lead to *Electronics*, which might lead to *Cell Phones*. This might point to a list of cell phone items e-shoppers might be interested in.

This hierarchical arrangement ensures that shoppers can fairly quickly get to items in which they are interested.

Improvements in search engines mean that directories are losing some value, but they are still useful for locating groups of relevant websites on a similar topic. It should be noted that directories of this nature can be very wide in scope, or they could be more focused, in the nature of a trade directory. E-retailers might consider something much more focussed to ensure contact with potential customers.

One point: note that Yahoo!, for example, is rather more than just a directory. It includes a search engine (confusingly, the Google engine), and a range of services such as mail and instant messaging. Such a service, which acts as a 'port' to many other web and Internet services, is known as a *portal*. Portal owners hope that users will use their portal as their homepage and point of departure, hence making them targets for selective advertising and other delights. This does make portal sites attractive (if expensive) places to place web banners and other advertising material. The big portals are hard at work implementing a 'Search, Find and Obtain' model across information, shopping and entertainment channels. The effectiveness can be demonstrated by usage figures: Yahoo! Is the most popular portal worldwide with more than 700 million people every month.

## SEARCH ENGINES

Search engines on the Internet have been around some time. The first ones actually did a 'live' search of remote file systems holding documents (FTP servers), looking for filenames which matched search terms. When the web became popular, researchers built web search engines to try out new software and hardware on the huge amounts of data that became available. Later on, these experimental systems were commercialised. The most used commercial search engine system is actually Google (www.google.com).

First, programs called 'crawlers' gather information about websites. This is done by starting with a list of 'well-known sites' and from there searching the sites they reference. This is an automatic process. The HTML (HyperText Markup Language) code corresponding to each webpage is scanned for links to other sites. In the HTML, such a link will appear like this:

<a href='http://www.gre.ac.uk/schools/index.html'>

If this link is followed, the corresponding webpage will also have links, and these too are followed. This process is continued, until millions of webpages are accessed. Each page is analysed for content. What this means is all the information in the page HTML – the title, the text of the body of the page and any additional information tagged on to the page (meta-information) is extracted and examined for relevance, according to rules set up by the owner of the crawler. All this information is then put into a database (also called a catalogue or index). This process is repeated at regular intervals, possibly every 2 weeks.

The database is indexed on content, and is made available to the e-shopper via a web interface. Given some search term, such as 'shampoo', the database is searched for matching terms and the corresponding page URLs are retrieved, together with the page titles and summaries of the page contents. This information is then formatted into a webpage which is returned to the e-shopper. So the user inputs the word 'shampoo' and obtains a page of references to websites involving that term.

The following are a few technical points:

- Following of links from any one page is only done to a certain 'depth', which means that it is important to put significant information on the Home Page or just a little 'below'.
- Web crawlers see a webpage split into 'frames' as a number of pages, and therefore explore these less deeply than pages without frames. Frames are best avoided if you want web crawlers to extract as much information as possible from your pages.
- Web crawlers are not clever enough to deal with databases (for example, catalogues) which might be accessed from your pages. Really significant information should be able to be accessed as plain HTML pages, rather than by using some catalogue systems. Catalogues are really meant for human users.

Note that the process of database construction is automatic, but guided by concepts such as *well-known sites* and *relevance*. It is also possible to notify a search engine system of a site for inclusion, which again guides the crawler. Websites that meet the criteria are added to the index whether they have been submitted for inclusion or not.

## Popular search engines

Google (www.google.com) is the world's most popular search site, accounting for 60% of all searches (Nielsen, 2010). Google compiles its catalogue of over four billion webpages every week or so. Despite being faster, larger and more efficient than competitors, even Google indexes only a fraction of the total webpages available. However, the coverage is very wide.

Although most e-shoppers use search engines, the typical user is usually not willing to spend much time formulating search terms, and often gets rather frustrated if the information required is not returned. They might abandon the search, or perhaps try another search engine. Many systems offer Boolean search, which means that search terms and phrases can be linked. For example:

'Digital camera' and Canon and inexpensive

Some systems also offer the option of fine-tuning the results by allowing the user to input terms used to rank (put in some order of precedence) the returned results. The average e-shopper is not usually willing to learn how to set up these more sophisticated queries. They want a reasonable set of results with as little work formulating the query as possible. Otherwise, they tend to give up and try some other method.

They might use *meta-crawlers*, which bring together results from various search engines and directories. Coverage is wide but operation can be cumbersome, with little fine-tuning possible, so these are not that popular.

The most useful systems as far as many e-shoppers are concerned are systems that allow natural language, for example a query such as:

Tell me where I can buy inexpensive Canon digital cameras?

Systems such as *AskJeeeves* (www.ask.com) specialise in such natural language queries. Observation by the authors shows that users often pose their questions in natural language whatever the system! They do this because no-one has ever told them that they cannot, and because reasonable results are often returned, since many search engine systems filter *noise words* (such as 'the', 'and' and 'but') and use the remaining words as search terms and for ranking the results. Systems such as Google also make suggestions in an attempt to correct spelling results.

## Growth in search engine activity

Most of the growth in e-shopping is being driven by search engines like Google and the link for purchase on social networks like Facebook (Dou et al., 2010; Harris and Dennis, 2011). Improved search quality, pioneered by Google, has made search engines an easy and efficient way for people to find things online – and for advertisers to find customers. At the same time, eBay, a haven for small businesses, has become the fastest-growing major shopping site, and much of Amazon's growth has come from serving as an intermediary for independent retailers. Another example is that of Visa, which noted that online sales, including travel, have increased considerably, much more than sales using Visa cards with traditional retailers.

According to eMarketer, a firm that compiles Internet research, online sales are rising by nearly 30% per year, and soon 100 million people a year are expected to make online purchases. Recent studies on consumer search behavior in online shopping environments show that while on the one hand the search cost in this market is reduced to zero as consumers exploit several search tools free of charge, on the other hand the cost for searching is much higher in terms of time and effort spent finding significant results (Kumar et al., 2005). In fact, subsequent studies demonstrated the large effect of search engine rankings on consumers' behavior, since they reduce consumers' effort and time in searching (Ghose et al., 2014). This means that consumers pay more attention to the results listed at the first, and having a good rank within the search results represents an emerging challenge for e-marketers.

## Search engine marketing and search engine optimization (SEO)

Marketers have two main ways to exploit search engines in order to promote their websites: place their websites in a top position within the search engine results (see SEO techniques) and provide a link to their websites in the "sponsored section" of a search engine. These elements, even if they do not effectively increase the number of visitors to the page, enhance the brand awareness (Dou et al., 2010), thus they have a critical role in the e-marketing strategies. Hence, search engine marketing (SEM) allows firms to create brand positioning online through search engine results pages (SERPs).

As anticipated, the visibility of a website to the prospective audience very often depends on how well the website ranks in a certain search engine's results pages, which is perceived by users as a sort of popularity index (Killoran, 2013). In fact, users usually pay attention only to a limited number of results (such as the first five of the list) (Killoran, 2013). Content creators orient their website both to attract and maintain existing audience, and to accommodate and take advantage (where possible) of search engines and related raking rules. The practice of orienting a site to search engines in order to obtain better search rankings in search engine results pages has been defined as search engine optimization (SEO). The goal is to place the website on the top position, or at least within a reasonable number of positions based on specific keywords targeted to have better chances to catch users' attention and visitors (Lukito et al., 2015). SEO experts suggest a list of steps to follows to successfully achieve this goal:

- Selection of an appropriate domain name, which relies on the prediction of the number of words (or keywords) a user will type or click. Thus, the domain name should be as close as possible to the keywords search in order to be displayed by the search engine at the top positions.
- Selection of keywords. Google provides tools for predicting the number of users typing a certain keyword, for a realistic estimation of the number of possible visitors. After choosing the first keywords, it is possible to identify the derivatives of this keyword from the keyword planner, having in mind to consider other keywords able

to correspond to products/services already present or that will be presented later.
- Definition of meta-tags. Meta-tags consist of a few main keywords coming from the description of the website. Providing descriptive meta-tags for each webpage of the site increases the likelihood of appropriate hits on the website.
- SEO on page. This consists of the maximal optimization technique for the website, which could be based on some criteria such as the selection of SEO templates (either free or paid, preferably fast loading); use of meta-tags (if meta-tag and related meta-description are placed, search engines like Google make a better description of the website), fix unique permalink in posts (each post/article might be reached directly by using number, which can be changed to keywords according to the suggestions of keyword planner, in order to distinguish the website offer from competitors; use keywords in the pace or article (each page should include at least one keyword from keyword planner in order to improve the visibility of the page within the search engine results); keyword placement (within the title of article, article link, meta-tag and meta-description, first paragraph, the unique image through the tag); unique images (add new and unique images to enrich the quality of contents and tag keywords within the image surface); check existing indexes (i.e. Google provides indexes by typing the command "site: xyz.com").
- Place. This guarantees web access to the page, which emerges as listed in certain engines according to the previous identified keywords.

### Mini case 5.1
### HILTON NORDICS

Hilton Hotels is one of the most famous brands in the hotel industry, with more than 540 hotels around the world. In 2014 Hilton wanted to create a new website for better reaching Scandinavian consumers (Danish, Norwegian, Swedish and Finnish), by focusing on their search behavior. Therefore, Hilton found a local partner, Marketing Lion, for optimizing the website according to this target. The agency proposed a keywords analysis with a mother tongue from each country to identify the relevant search queries in the native language and proposed new title tags, meta-descriptions and headlines based on the results. In particular, Marketing Lion developed a comprehensive keywords analysis in Danish, Norwegian, Swedish and Suomi (Finnish). In this way, Hilton Nordic website increased visibility and rankings in Google's search results list.

# INFORMATION SEARCH ON THE WEB

The site is an example of how also large and international recognized companies need to develop local e-marketing strategies to achieve international visibility by using the main SEO techniques.

*Source*: Summarised and adapted from Marketing Lion case study, 21 April 2015

### Mini case 5.2
### DAVID STEAD ORCHIDS

David Stead Orchids (www.orchid-guide.co.uk/~davidstead) is a small to medium size supplier of orchid plants and orchid-related sundries, based in Leeds, UK. Its website was created by a local web developer.

### *Focus*

The firm has a (fairly) memorable URL, which they quote in their advertisements in the *Orchid Press*. The site has an internal database, which the e-shopper can use to home down on what they require.

### *Directories*

The firm appears in a number of directories, for example The Wedding Network (www.wsn-uk.co.uk/England/West_Yorkshire/Flowers), Easy Exotics (www.easy-exotics.co.uk) and the Stephen H Smith Garden Centre (www.shrubs.co.uk).

### *Search engines*

All pages are correctly titled, and meta-information is used (description and keywords). Searches on the phrase 'David Stead Orchids' gave 39 hits on Google and 39 hits on AltaVista. Using the meta-crawler Dogpile (www.dogpile.com) gave 49 hits!

The site is an example of how a small, local company can achieve international visibility by using the three main techniques mentioned.

## MONITORING THE USE OF YOUR WEBPAGES

Having set up your site, you need to monitor what use is made of it. The simplest approach is to add a page counter to each major page. The information from this can be rather limited, but at least you can find out how many visits ('hits') have been made over a given period.

Every time a webpage is accessed, information is recorded in a log file on the web server. These logs can be provided to you by either your IT personnel or by the company that 'hosts' your pages (sometimes at an additional cost). The log stores information about the page URL, the time and date of access, the type of browsers used for access, (possibly) the location of the user and so on. By themselves, the logs are quite difficult to process, but there are log analysis programs which can produce useful tables and charts which summarise activity. By examining the logs, it is even possible to see what web crawlers are accessing your system! You might get a few surprises here, and read information about visits from experimental crawlers at universities, and from web crawlers run by institutions like the US Defence Department.

## CONCLUSIONS

A number of things can be done to make your website more visible.

First, encourage shoppers to *focus* on your site. There are a number of aspects of the concept of focus that have arisen from the above discussion. Nielsen (2000) considers focus in the context of webpage design and suggests retaining the attention of users by building consistent style ad pages, built to good design standards, and with relevant content.

Advertisements, which can be added on to directory and web search engine webpages are a means of changing the focus of a user's search towards your pages.

Make it easy for users to get to your site by choosing a memorable URL, for example www.gardentplants.com (not www.somesite.com/gardens/).

Advertise your website URL in your conventional advertising (magazines, flyers and so on). Wine makers have printed the URL on their bottles in order to bring the site to the attention of users.

Make shoppers want to look at your website by constantly changing the information. One way to do this is to link the site to a product catalogue database, so that shoppers can search for the latest up-to-date product information.

Ensure your website is well designed. Use a professional website designer. Do *not* use your computing staff – they can build you a site but are (probably) not professionals in human-computer interaction.

Submit your website URL to major web directory systems. But be careful of offers you may receive to list your webpage URLs in directories. Some of these are like offers to list your profile in a directory of 'World Business Leaders'. It might be that the only people who ever access these directories are the subscribers who have paid a substantial fee!

INFORMATION SEARCH ON THE WEB

**CHAPTER SUMMARY**

- E-shoppers are avid users of the web and use web search engines and directories to guide their search
- E-retailers can set up the webpages on their site to make them more attractive to e-shoppers – to focus their search
- It can be arranged that the webpage addresses appear in relevant directories
- It can also be arranged that the webpage addresses are picked up by the search engines used by the majority of e-shoppers
- Use web logs and other systems to determine how often your webpages get accessed

In the following chapter we consider what happens when potential e-shoppers find the e-retail site – the design and interactivity issues.

### Case study 5.1
### BENVENGUDO

Benvengudo Hotel was a family business managed close to the Les Baux in the Provence region (Southern France). Due to the new generation of family managers and the changes in the market, the property needed to be repositioned as a premium hotel and restaurant. Managers started being aware of the possibility to increase the hotel image and visibility starting from a search engine. Hence, they commissioned to develop a new website using the SEO techniques. According to a hotel website designer, the hotel achieved a good position in the top google.com results (i.e. the first page of SERPs) if clicking on: provence hotel, provence hotel deals, provence restaurants, provence holidays, provence cooking classes, les Baux, Les Baux hotel, Les Baux restaurants, etc. In addition, website designers stated that the results are still increasing.

*Source*: Summarised and adapted from the seoWORKS.com case studies, 21 April 2015.

### Case study 5.2

In the US, L.L.Bean (www.llbean.com) has been a pioneer of mail order, selling goods to rural farmers since way back in the mid-1800s. Today the company has

**155**

put a reputation for customer responsiveness, helpfulness, cheerfulness and reliability to use in becoming world leader in e-retailing outdoor equipment and clothing, with an efficient, award-winning site. But the L.L.Bean site is not just about selling – it is packed with useful information about the outdoors. For example, when someone searches for a campground (or camp site in UK parlance), say in British Columbia (Canada), L.L.Bean comes high up the listings. The link will go immediately to a huge, easily accessible amount of information not just on camping, but also trails (walks) and activities in national parks all over the world. For instance, the 'Park search' link is ideal to 'Plan your next adventure with ... 2200 worldwide park listings'.

The home page links easily to clothing, maps, books, camping and outdoor equipment and outdoor information is always high on the agenda, with for example, 'Preserving Acadia: L.L.Bean helps protect Maine's National Park.'.

The morale seems to be that a good site does not necessarily do 'hard' selling, and that useful related information can lead surfers to shop from an e-retail site.

## QUESTIONS

*Brief feedback to these questions is included at the back of the book.*

**Question 5.1** – What is the *one* thing I can do to get my website noticed?

**Question 5.2** – I've put up a good webpage some months ago, but nobody is accessing it much nowadays. What can I do?

## GLOSSARY

**Directory**   Webpage with a list of website URLs, usually arranged in some hierarchical manner, arranged by subject matter. Example: Yahoo!

**Meta-crawler engine**   A search engine that submits search terms or words to several other search engines, produces a webpage that combines the results and sends this to the e-shopper.

**Search engine**   System used by e-shoppers to obtain lists of URLs related to search terms or words they input.

**Search Engine Marketing**   Groups marketing strategies for creating brand positioning online through SERPs.

**Search Engine Optimization**   Includes practices to optimize the place of a certain website within the top results of the SERPs.

**Search engine page results (SERPs)**   Consist of the list of results returning by a search engine.

**Search term/word**   Something that describes what an e-shopper might be interested in and which is to be submitted to a search engine, such as 'shampoo' or 'dendrobium orchids'.

**Web crawler**   A program used to set up the database used by a search engine.

## FURTHER READING

Chaffey D, Mayer R, Johnston K and Ellis-Chadwick F. (2003) *Internet Marketing: Strategy, Implementation and Practice*, Harlow, UK: Pearson Education.

Ray E and Ray D. (1998) *The AltaVista Search Revolution*, New York: Osborne-McGraw-Hill.

## REFERENCES

Dennis C and Pappamatthaiou E-K. (2003) 'Shoppers motivations for e-shopping', *Recent Advances in Retailing and Services Science, 6th International Conference*, The European Institute of Retailing and Services Studies, Portland, OR, August 7–10.

Dennis C E and Richardson O. (2004) 'E-retail: Paradoxes for suppliers and consumers', in Budd L and Harris L (eds.), *E-business: Reality or Rhetoric,* London: Routledge.

Dou W, Lim KH, Su C, Zhou N and Cui N. (2010) 'Brand positioning strategy using search engine marketing', *MIS Quarterly*, 34 (2): 261–279.

Duffet R G. (2015) 'The influence of Facebook advertising on cognitive attitudes amid Generation Y', *Electronic Commerce Research,* 15 (2): 243–267.

eMarketer. (2003) *Portal Plays: Strategies and Developments of the 'Big Three',* New York: eMarketer.

Fink D and Laupase R. (2000) 'Perceptions of Web site design characteristics: A Malaysian/Australian comparison', *Internet Research: Electronic Networking Applications and Theory,* 10 (1): 44–55.

Gehan M. (2003) *Search Engine Marketing – The Essential Best Practice Guide,* [Online] Available at: www.search-engine-book.co.uk. [Accessed 15 May 2016].

Ghose A, Ipeirotis PG and Li B. (2014) 'Examining the impact of ranking on consumer behavior and search engine revenue', *Management Science,* 60 (7): 1632–1654.

Harris L and Dennis C. (2011) 'Engaging customers on facebook: Challenges for e-retailers', *Journal of Consumer Behaviour,* 10 (6): 338–346.

Killoran J B. (2013) ' How to use search engine optimization techniques to increase website visibility', *IEEE Transactions on Professional Communication,* 56 (1): 50–66.

Knight J. (2003) 'Unleash the magic of searching', *Sunday Times* 15 (June), 51–52.

Kumar N, Lang KR and Peng Q. (2005) 'Consumer search behaviour in online shopping environments', in *Proceedings of the 38th Hawaii International Conference on System Sciences*, New York: IEEE: 1–10.

Lukito R B, Lukito C and Arifin D. (2015) 'Implementation techniques for search engine optimization in marketing strategies through the Internet', *Journal of Computer Science,* 11 (1): 1–6.

Murphy D. (2003) 'Putting your website on the map', *Marketing Business,* 117 (March): 21–25.

NAMNEWS. (2003) 'US: eBay tells analysts growth can be sustained', *NAMNEWS The Original Newsletter for Key Account Managers,* [Online] Available at EMR-NAMNEWS, London: www.kamcity.com/namnews [Accessed 15 May 2016].

Nielsen J. (2000) *Web Usability: The Practice of Simplicity,* Thousand Oaks, CA: New Riders.

Nielsen NetRatings. (2010) [Online] Available at: www.nielsen-netratings.com [Accessed 15 May 2016].

Phillips B J, Mille J and McQuarrie E F. (2014) 'Dreaming out loud on Pinterest: New forms of indirect persuasion', *International Journal of Advertising*, 33 (4): 633–655.

Rodgers S and Sheldon K M. (2002) 'An improved way to characterise Internet users', *Journal of Advertising Research*, 42 (5): 85–94.

Rohm A J and Swaminathan V. (2004) 'A typology of online shoppers based on shopping motivations', *Journal of Business Research*, 57 (7): 748–757.

Shehan K B. (2002) 'A typology of Internet users' online sessions', *Journal of Advertising Research*, 42 (5): 62–71.

Shim S, Eastlick M A, Lotz S L and Warrington P. (2001) 'An online prepurchase intentions model: The role of intention to search', *Journal of Retailing*, (77): 397–416.

Wolinsky A. (1999) *The History of the Internet and the World Wide Web*, Berkeley Heights, NJ: Enslow.

# WEB LINKS

**Pandia:** www.pandia.com – for a European perspective on search engines, lots of information and a helpful free search engine tutorial.

**Putting your website on the map:** www.communicationsteam.com/mb/archive/march2003/main2.htm – David Murphy looks at the fine art of making sure that your website is search engine friendly (see Bibliography).

**Search engine book:** www.search-engine-book.co.uk – download a free report, rankings test, e-marketing newsletter and more.

**Search engine watch:** www.searchenginewatch.com – offers a free daily newsletter, SearchDay, to keep you up to date with developments.

**Sample search tools** (recommended by *Sunday Times Doors*, 15 June 2003):

**Engines:** www.google.co.uk, www.alltheweb.com

**Directories:** www.search.yahoo.com, www.excite.co.uk

**Meta-crawlers:** www.dogpile.co.uk, www.vivisimo.com.

Chapter 6

# E-store design navigability, interactivity and web atmospherics

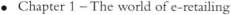

### LINKS TO OTHER CHAPTERS

- Chapter 1 – The world of e-retailing
- Chapter 7 – E-service

### KEY LEARNING POINTS

*After completing this chapter you will have an understanding of*

- The overall nature, purpose and scope of e-store design
- Navigability as a fundamental design issue
- Interactivity as a higher level e-store design issue
- Design enhancement through web atmospherics
- An integrated approach to e-store design
- To understand the importance of clarifying the objectives and strategy of the e-retailer *before starting* to create or re-develop an e-store design
- To understand the possibility to integrate augmented reality technologies to improve e-store

### ORDERED LIST OF SUBTOPICS

- What is e-store design?
- The purpose and scope of e-store design
- Why is store design more important for e-retailers?
- Start e-store design with navigability
- Progress to interactivity

**159**

- Building e-relationships through interactivity
- Enhancements through web atmospherics
- All together for an integrated approach to e-store design
- The role of objectives and strategy in guiding e-store design
- Conclusions
- Chapter summary
- Case study
- Questions
- Glossary
- Further reading
- References
- Web links

## WHAT IS E-STORE DESIGN?

E-store design refers to the purposeful design of the e-retailer's site. This includes listing products or services for sale, providing product information including a product description and price for each item, enabling users to move about the site, providing a method of ordering and paying for merchandise, and generally listing broader company policies, such as security, privacy and guarantees if given. Apart from providing information, it is also necessary to design in other features, such as graphics, and in some cases, audio.

## THE PURPOSE AND SCOPE OF E-STORE DESIGN

Simply put, e-store design is part of the retail mix that helps the e-retailer market their business generally, and more specifically, to sell merchandise. All elements of the retail mix have a role to play, but clearly having a place to buy the merchandise is a fundamental part of the process.

There are some similarities to traditional (offline) retailing in which the shop and the way it is designed (including infrastructure, layout and visual presentation) are a necessary part of the shopping (buying) process. Another similarity to offline retailing is that store design plays a *broader* purpose than just a place to buy. Store design plays a bigger marketing role in that different designs create different images. The store design might convey an image that really reinforces the merchandise in a particular store, which makes it more likely that customers seeking that type of merchandise will purchase something from that particular store.

So it pays both offline and online stores to invest in choosing the right store design that fits the image they want as well as making it easy for

# E-STORE DESIGN NAVIGABILITY

customers to buy what they want. The e-retailer and the traditional retailer have to think carefully about basic functional activities like layout movement and checkout, as well as more symbolic issues like creating the right look and feel of the store.

Scope of e-store design includes layout, visuals, interactivity, information search engines, checkout facilities and the posting of policies. Each of these elements needs to be specified and coded and made operational.

### Mini case 6.1
### CLOTHING ONLINE SEARCHES

Click onto www.gap.com/home_gap

This is a typical e-retail site that offers catalogue products for consumers to buy. The home page has a menu selection for gender and age for a range of clothing covering uses and seasons. The catalogue items include scanned photographs of garments with a description and price. The site includes a basket for collecting items and functions for purchasing and delivery details.

These direct purchase sites are less popular for consumers than was first thought. It would seem that people prefer to touch and examine certain products before making a decision.

## WHY IS STORE DESIGN MORE IMPORTANT FOR E-RETAILERS?

We have already established that store design is important to both traditional retailers and online retailers. The reader may have already guessed that e-store design is relatively more important for online retailers and might even be considered the most important part of their retail mix. Why?

The main reason is that store design has bigger scope with e-retailers. Store design in traditional offline retailing is generally confined to the physical aspects of the store, such as the infrastructure and layout. The online scope of store design is greater because it also includes what used to be covered by interaction with the salesperson. Almost everything has to be covered by what is on the computer screen, so the e-store design is clearly a very important domain. Additionally, areas like customer service and after-sales service that were separate departments in offline retailing, now have to be incorporated into the e-store design. This further increases the scope and importance of e-store design.

E-STORE DESIGN NAVIGABILITY

**Mini case 6.2**
**ONLINE CAR SEARCHES**

Click onto http://autos.msn.com/home/new_research.aspx

This site provides information on new cars and includes data on make, model, dealership, specification, photogallery, quotes, prices and insurance. It is a typical site in this retail category, but additionally offers a link to multimedia presentations that provide 360-degree views of the exterior and interior of the motor vehicle. The function can be controlled for both speed and vertical views directly by the user.

The site is typical to others such as boats, motorcycles, caravans, etc. and includes new and secondhand cars. This is useful for searching for unique or hard-to-find items such as collectables and is convenient for consumers and sellers alike and providers a greater market reach.

## START E-STORE DESIGN WITH NAVIGABILITY

Navigability is the most fundamental building block of e-store site design. By navigability we mean the ability of the user to move around the site easily and efficiently, that is, without getting lost. If users have to travel through several topics or layers to find information, they will get frustrated or lost, possibly causing them to exit the site prematurely. Thus a key objective of good navigation design is to minimise travel, depth and redundancy when travelling within a site (see Wixom and Todd, 2005).

Another way of thinking about navigation design is to ask three basic questions in terms of a user at a point in time on an e-site:

1 Where am I at the moment?
2 Can I get back to where I have been?
3 How can I go forward to a particular location?

For well-designed sites, these three questions are readily answered for most users. If a user struggles, then the site is badly designed.

> **Exercise 6.1:** Go to an e-retailer site and make a couple of moves around the site. Now answer the three basic questions above. Write down on a piece of paper how well this particular site answers these three basic questions. If the answers are not good, what could the e-retailer do to improve their e-store design? Can you find a site that is really good at this function?

Another study has developed a checklist to assist with evaluating the navigability of a site. Merrilees and Fry (2002) have come up with the following points:

- Is navigation easy?
- Is navigation efficient?
- Is navigation fast?
- Does layout of the site make it easy to use?
- Does the site have a good menu system?
- Overall, is the design simple and user friendly?

**Exercise 6.2:** Briefly go back to the site that you did exercise 6.1 with. Now answer the six new questions about site design. Do you get more or less the same answers as to how well the site performs? Would you agree that you need both lists to get the right answer?

Although navigation design might be seen as a technical function, it nonetheless needs to address fundamental requirements that create a user-friendly experience. Two checklists have been presented here to help the reader evaluate existing sites or alternatively, to guide the development of a new site or a new e-store design for an existing site.

Different devices can be used to facilitate this process, including links that can take the user back to the home page from any page, or have clear menu signposts of how to proceed. The reader can learn from experience of which sites do a good job on this fundamental process. As an example, one site (an online secondhand bookstore used several times by one of the authors) has a good recovery system if a user accidentally double-clicks on the ORDER button. The instructions enable an e-mail to be sent or offer suggestions of another way of proceeding without re-keying in everything again. However, while these suggestions for recovery are good, would it not be better to re-design the site so that it does not collapse if someone does inadvertently double click instead of single click?

## PROGRESS TO INTERACTIVITY

Interactivity is another fundamental aspect of e-store design. In simple terms, it refers to the interaction between the user of an e-site and the site itself. Thus this refers to a *person-machine interaction*. However, this relationship has more depth than say the relationship that you have with an ATM or even your home computer doing desktop work. The extra depth comes about because the '*machine*' in the e-retailer context is an ongoing '*entity*', with a capacity to provide service, sell goods, transact money, be cheerful or grumpy, be there tomorrow for you, and so on. Such extra depth makes this particular person-machine interaction *virtually* (but not quite fully) that of a person-to-person interaction.

Another way of saying this is to compare the *user to e-retailer interaction* in the e-world to that of the *consumer-salesperson interaction* in the 'brick-and-mortar' world. With a traditional offline retailer, if as a customer you have a question about a product it is common to ask a salesperson. Salespeople are also important if you want to pay for merchandise, or alternatively, if you want to return goods. Instead of a salesperson, these functions are handled by a computer interface. Usually the answers are built into the program, such as a description of the product or a mechanism to order and pay for the merchandise. Discrete questions can be asked, but are usually handled as part of a Frequently Asked Questions (FAQ) routine. If FAQ does not provide an answer then a separate e-mail might be called for, though most e-retailers do not encourage this option because it is deemed too time-consuming.

Thus the user–e-retailer interaction has to anticipate the sorts of questions that might be normally asked of a salesperson and, where possible, to automate these procedures into the design of the e-store. Obviously it is important to convey the right tone and mood. It is better to have a friendly and helpful 'sales assistant' and similarly the same for the user–e-retailer interface.

The difference between the online, e-retailer and the offline, 'bricks-and-mortar' retailer can be exaggerated. Traditional offline retailers have increasingly become more self-service in their orientation with less personal service from sales assistants, through the introduction of new technologies (i.e. interactive touch screens, self-service cash/desks, etc.). To some extent this trend is even true with normal department stores that used to be very labour intensive. The move to more reliance on self-service has been achieved through more effective layout of the store and visual merchandising, such as more helpful product tags. In other words, it has become necessary for offline retailers to improve their skills in selling merchandise with less or no help from salespeople. This is exactly what an e-retailer does, so in a sense it is really an extension of existing offline trends rather than a radically different way of selling.

We can take a closer look at interactivity in the e-retail sense by examining how the academic literature views it. Most of the interpretations of interactivity have a strong communication element, which builds on the analogy with the salesperson interaction in the offline world. Five major impressions or dimensions of online interactivity can be highlighted. The most common impression of interactivity from the literature is that it is primarily *communication* based. Infrequently, other activities, such as downloading software or making a purchase, are noted as forms of interactivity that seem to have something else other than communication as the driving force. In such cases, we would wish to highlight the communication or information aspects of those activities. *Second*, interactivity is about *two-way communication*. This spans communication from the viewer to the firm and from the firm to the viewer, as well as simultaneous interaction between the two parties. All three aspects of two-way communication need to be addressed in better understanding the meaning of interactivity. *Third*, a special feature of Internet interactivity is the ability to *personalise* and possibly customise the situation for an individual. *Fourth*, a number of writers have emphasized the ability of the individual to *control* the communication and *learn* as a noteworthy feature of the interactive process. *Fifth* and finally, a broader more holistic role of interactivity has been noted as an important contributor to building up the total *shopping experience* on the Internet.

Based on a wide body of Internet-related literature, Merrilees (2002) developed the following checklist of aspects of interactivity:

- The site helps the viewer participate, learn and act.
- There is good two-way communication.
- The site facilitates feedback from the viewer to the retailer (directly via the web and/or e-mail).
- The overall shopping experience is very pleasant and enjoyable.
- The site develops a close, personalised relationship with the viewer.
- Any query or question that you have can be answered quickly and efficiently.
- The site has good interactivity (capstone item).

The reader interested in following through with more reading on interactivity can see the references in Merrilees (2002), with some of the key ones given at the end of the chapter.

## BUILDING E-RELATIONSHIPS THROUGH INTERACTIVITY

Given the importance of communication in developing *offline* quality relationships, it seems likely that the same may be true in the e-commerce context. Kolesar and Galbraith (2000) suggest that establishing a relationship with customers is harder to achieve in an e-retail context because alienation makes it harder to create the kind of bond that is often enjoyed between other service providers and their customers. They argue that because the Internet as a medium is less personal than other retail channels, surrogates for direct personal interaction must be provided in an e-retail transaction.

The issue of managing customer relations in e-commerce begs the question as to what the strategic drivers of effective e-relationships are. Some writers (Lindstrom and Anderson, 1999) argue that e-relationships are critical for developing strong e-retail sites. One of the few empirical papers demonstrating the importance of interactivity in developing quality e-relationships is Merrilees (2002), who studied www.amazon.com for books and an Australian online grocer, www.coles.com.au.

The relationship between interactivity and higher quality relationships between users and the e-retailer (as perceived by the user) was very strong.

**Box 6.1**
**PIONEERING MAJOR ARTICLE ON WEB ATMOSPHERICS**

One of the first major journal academic studies of web atmospherics was that of Eroglu, Machleit and Davis (2001). The paper supports the idea that various online cues could influence outcomes like satisfaction, amount purchased and time spent online. Their emphasis is on the process by which these cues work and begin by adopting two types of atmospheric qualities, namely high task-relevant environment and low task-relevant environment. The high-task cues include product description, price, terms of sale, delivery, product reviews and return policies, product pictures and navigation aids. Low-task cues include unrelated special offers, colours, borders and background patterns, icons and image maps and affiliations. Sites are likely to have a different mix of high-task and low-task cues, so there is a need to get the balance right. The authors argue that there is a greater need for high-task cues for segments of customers who are either high-involvement or very sensitive to their environment's atmosphere.

## ENHANCEMENTS THROUGH WEB ATMOSPHERICS

Web atmospherics have an analogy to traditional offline retailing. Retailers in the latter environment have long added to the atmosphere of the store, in the belief that the feel and look of the store would encourage shoppers to spend more time in the store and to buy something or something extra. To a certain extent, atmosphere is strongly influenced by visual merchandising – that is the way the merchandise is presented to the customer. The patterns of the displays and the use of colour and textures are sometimes set in a real-life setting, like a bedroom to sell beds. Such displays can take on various tones, such as sophistication, stylish or economic, depending on the target market of the retailer. Music and other audio can reinforce the mood that the retailer is attempting to create.

# E-STORE DESIGN NAVIGABILITY

The same principles apply to e-store design. The visual look of the e-store can change the perception that viewers have of the store. If controlled properly and if they are aligned to the profile of the target market, then web atmospherics can stimulate an increase in sales.

## Mini case 6.3
## BELLS AND WHISTLES ADDED FOR SPECIAL EFFECTS

The website for Denbigh Farm Bed and Breakfast in the Lockier Valley, Australia, illustrates a site that has 'bells and whistles' with an interesting presentation. The home page has contemporary music while the menu bars make a typewriter tap and school bell ring when selected. The site includes the normal array of menus with links to other tourist sites, bookings, queries and e-mails.

The gallery displays a number of smaller photographs that are magnified onto a centre screen when the cursor is passed over them. Bordering the pages are merging pictures superimposed by the menus. The site is interesting with the original design, colours, sounds and displays.

---

Although it makes sense that the use of visuals might help, caution is needed in the extent to which they are used by the e-retailer. Some visuals are a good thing, but there are two major caveats if they are overused. Over-use of visuals applies when it results in slow downloading time. So even if all users really liked visuals, they would get frustrated if there were long delays until each visual fully appeared. This is a clear case where the e-store design should be pilot tested before fully launched. Second, not all e-retail users want a lot of visuals. There is a big segment of users that primarily want product and price information, and want it quickly and efficiently, in order to buy well-specified products like dry groceries, books or CDs. This segment may be bigger than for offline shopping, where there is a segment of shopper that wants to get into a supermarket quickly and get out quickly. Notwithstanding such a large segment, there might be an opportunity to show a realistic colouring of say fruit in the store, as an aid to online fruit purchases as part of an online grocery store. Most online grocery stores have a very limited fresh food department.

E-retailers can create web atmosphere using music and visuals, such as 3D displays and downloadable video clips. One way of tackling the

**167**

problem is to provide a 'click here for broadband' (for a more sophisticated, high memory requirement version).

A number of detailed studies by Vrechopoulos, including Magnanari, Siomkos and Vrechopoulos (2009), Vrechopoulos (2010) and Krasonikolakis, Vrechopoulos et al. (2013), and Vrechopoulos et al. (2004) have provided considerable insights into e-store layout design. His approach essentially combines layout (which we discuss under the heading of navigation) and web atmospherics, in that some forms of layout have enhanced atmospherics. Much of the work by Vrechopolous is based on experimental study with online grocery shopping, but it has wider implications. Vrechopoulous et al. (2004) identified three types of layout constant in both offline and online retail environment. The three layouts were the grid approach (rows and columns of shelves; a very hierarchical way of selecting goods, dominating brick supermarkets), the freeform approach (more chaotic but exciting approach, common in fashion stores) and the racetrack approach (circular route to selecting goods). It is argued that the grid approach dominates conventional supermarket design, which it does, though in Australia there is a big swing to combining a large grid section for dry grocery products with a large free flow section for fresh fruit and vegetables, so it is a qualified agreement that the grid dominates conventional supermarket layout design.

## Augmented reality and virtual try-on on e-stores

Recent progress in information and communication technologies supports the creation of new retail environments enriched with digital technologies (Rese et al., 2014). Papagiannidis, Pantano, See-To, Dennis and Bourlakis (2016) found that an immersive 3D environment has the potential to rival traditional shopping in terms of experience, resulting in higher sales for retailers and satisfaction for consumers. These results suggest the potential for augmented reality, a real-time view of the physical world enhanced (augmented) with virtual elements generated by computer, such as digital images or video stream, etc. (Azuma, 1997; Carmigniani et al., 2011).

Recently, marketers started to be aware of the advantages of augmented reality also in Internet retailing, as a tool for enhancing consumers' shopping experience within the online scenario (Rese et al., 2014). In fact, augmented reality enriches visual elements (digital and interactive images, videos, etc.), texts, audio, simulated experiences, etc. Thus, if compared to traditional e-commerce scenarios, augmented reality applications offer more dynamic 3D animation through high realistic interfaces (Lee and Park, 2014). Meaningful application of augmented reality for Internet retailing consists of the virtual try-on, which would be able to overcome a crucial limit of e-stores, by enhancing interactions with the product through the possibility to virtually *experience* or *try* the product in terms of scent, texture, appearance, fit or sound (Lu and Smith, 2007). In this way, consumers have the possibility to virtually touch the favoured items. For these reasons, famous brands such as Ray-Ban introduced this kind of technology for supporting online purchase.

The results of Vrechoupolos' study quickly eliminated the racetrack design, making it a two-horse race for which layout design was best for online grocery shopping. Although not unanimous, it was nonetheless found that the free flow was superior to the grid method in terms of satisfaction with users. The grid and free flow e-retail layouts are illustrated in Figures 6.1 and 6.2, respectively. Vrechoupolos argues that this is a good argument for being cautious about simply adopting the conventional retailing principles and applying them to an e-retailing context. One might challenge, at least slightly, the conclusion that free flow is a better layout design than grid for online grocery shopping. This might depend on whether it was regular users of online grocery sites or non-users, because the latter might have liked the 'variety' and interesting aspects of free flow design compared to a possible greater need for a grid design by regular users. In any case, the study does highlight the need for e-retail sites that service frequent, routine, regular purchases to recognize the need to go beyond simple linear models of layout design and as well incorporate more interesting atmospherics in layout via the free flow. Perhaps the best solution of all comes when Vrechopolous proposes a new layout design that he calls the 'freegrid', which is a hybrid of the grid and free flow designs. See Figure 6.3 for a schematic representation of the freegrid e-retail layout.

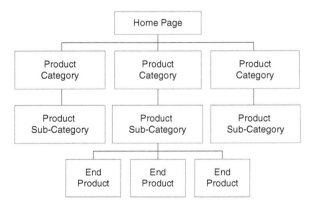

■ *Figure 6.1* Simplified representation of a grid layout e-retail store

Source: The authors, based on Vrechoupolos et al. (2004)

FREE FLOW LAYOUT ONLINE

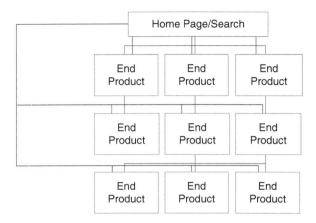

**Figure 6.2** Simplified representation of a free flow layout e-retail store
Source: The authors, based on Vrechoupolos et al. (2004)

FREEGRID LAYOUT ONLINE

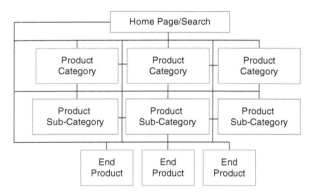

**Figure 6.3** Simplified representation of a free grid layout e-retail store
Source: The authors, based on Vrechoupolos et al. (2004)

Exercise 6.3: As a follow-up to the Vrechoupolos' study just discussed, look up two or three online grocery e-retailers and compare and evaluate the layout design in them. Does this reinforce your thinking or change your thinking about this issue?

## Engaging consumers on social networks

The Internet scenario offers the possibility to spread and collect information in several formats (e.g. blogs, podcasts, social networks, wikis, instant pictures, etc.); most of them are user (consumer) generated, referring to digital reviews or comments created by customers, involving limited inferences by firms while providing also a measure of the *popularity* of each product/firm (De Vries et al. 2012). The large presence of consumers on social networks like Facebook pushed firms and organizations to consider the power of these media for marketing purposes. In particular, these media support the knowledge sharing among firms, stakeholders and consumers, through the large amount of free user-generated contents and interactive and ease-of-use tools. Hence, several authors have started recognizing the influence of social networks on consumers' purchase behavior, especially for youth, by positing new challenges for retailers (Harris and Dennis, 2011; Pantano and Di Pietro, 2013). In fact, consumers might access social networks like Facebook to collect information on products and past experiences from consumers for supporting their decision-making process.

These virtual places offer also several tools giving firms the possibility to offer customers more "social" purchase experiences by operating directly with them within social media. For instance, in early 2015 Facebook launched the possibility to add the "buy" and "book" tools to the traditional pages. These tools might be linked to internal or external Facebook page and should support consumers to buy goods easily and rapidly from the page on Facebook. A meaningful example is the Shangri-la Hotel (Paris, France) that allows booking a room directly from Facebook; clicking on the "book now" tool, the consumer goes directly to the official online booking of the hotel. Similarly, the tool "buy now" on the Facebook page of the famous Italian singer Eros Ramazzotti is linked to another page where users can choose to buy his works through iTunes, Amazon, etc.

**Box 6.2**
**WEBSITE DESIGN FEATURES TO SELL 'LOOK AND FEEL' GOODS ONLINE**

Chicksand and Knowles (2002) present a paper counter to much common opinion and argue instead that look and feel sites, such as clothing, beauty products and furniture, do have a potentially important role to play in e-retailing. In a study of 45 such e-retailers they found a clear majority did have a good design in terms of the basics: layout, navigation, information and image. In contrast, only a small minority seemed to make strong use of web atmospherics, such as customization, colour management, technology and chat communication lines. Thus they argue that part of the reason why these types of sites have not spread at the same rate as other e-retail sites may be due to the under-utilisation of web atmospheric cues in these sites.

> Chicksand and Knowles (2002) refer to a number of 'good practices' that might be relevant for 'look and feel' (and potentially any e-retailer) e-retailers to go further with their web atmospherics. Examples using technological advances include the 'My Virtual Model' option on the Lands' End site, allowing shoppers to create virtual models of them online. Thomasville Furniture uses Zoom View technology, allowing shoppers to view home furnishings in minute detail, down to wood grain and moulding detail.
>
> Personalisation and customisation examples include Eddie Bauer's virtual closet whereby a customer can choose items of clothing and see how they match by viewing them on a 'Style Builder' program. Beauty product e-retailer, www.EZFace.com allows consumers to download a photo of themselves and preview makeup products that will be added to the photo. Online apparel firm www.Fanbuzz.com customises styles, colours, graphics and sizes, though charges a 10% to 20% premium for doing so.
>
> Smell can be enhanced through peripheral devices that can be plugged into a computer. DigiScent has designed a product called the iSmell Personal Scent Synthesizer, which receives code from the website and emits the relevant smell.
>
> Online colour can be improved through technology that, for example, downloads a cookie, which then reads the monitor's colour output. This issue is important because colours can be difficult to gauge when looking at a computer screen, with each monitor displaying colours differently. Retail support companies, such as E-Color, Imation, Pantone and WayTech, are targeting e-retailers selling goods such as clothing that rely on colour presentation.

## ALL TOGETHER FOR AN INTEGRATED APPROACH TO E-STORE DESIGN

This chapter has focused on three important concepts that influence e-store design, namely navigability, interactivity and web atmospherics. Designers of e-stores should pay a lot of attention to each of these concepts if they are to really satisfy users of e-retailing. Checklists have been given in each section to guide students, designers and e-retailers themselves on ways of achieving higher standards of performance with respect of navigability, interactivity and web atmospherics, considered separately.

In this section we show how the three key concepts fit together in the total design of the e-store. That is, rather than treating navigability, interactivity and web atmospherics as three separate pieces of an e-store design, we want to show how they interface with each other. The inter-relationships between the three concepts provide greater insight into e-store design, enabling the designer to incorporate synergies across the components.

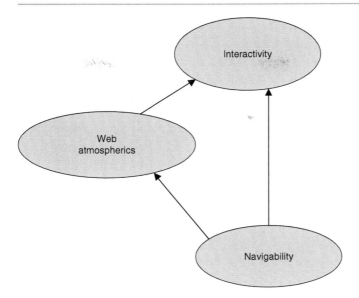

**Figure 6.4** *An integrated framework for e-store design*

Figure 6.4 shows graphically how the concepts interface with each other. Navigability is really the base of the system because it (twice) influences other things but is not in turn influenced by them. Thus it should be seen as the base building block in an e-store design.

The first influence that navigability has is on web atmospherics. If you think about what this says it makes sense. The more freely, easily and efficiently that a user can move around an e-store site, then the more readily can the user enjoy the web atmospherics, be it nice visuals, special deal offers, book reviews, audio or whatever. Alternatively, if the site is slow and frustrating, then the viewer is less likely to appreciate the web atmospherics and indeed the atmospheric effects could even be counter-productive.

The second influence that navigability has is on interactivity. Again this makes sense for broadly similar reasons. The more freely, easily and efficiently that a user can move around an e-store site, then the more readily and willingly can the user interact with the e-retailer. Alternatively, if the site is slow and frustrating, then the viewer is less likely to stay longer on the site, even less likely to engage in a more deep and meaningful way, and probably not wanting to make a revisit in the future.

Figure 6.4 also depicts another inter-relationship, that is, from web atmospherics to interactivity. This is likely to be a very strong relationship. What it says is as follows: users who enjoy the web atmospherics are more likely to seek interactivity with the e-retailer. So if the nice visuals, the book reviews, the audio, the special deals or whatever the particular web atmospherics are positively perceived, then more interactivity will be sought in the future. In such a case, the user will engage more with the e-retailer and a stronger, communication-based relationship will be formed.

In summary, this section augments the insight that the separate key concepts of navigability, interactivity and web atmospherics provided for e-store design. Figure 6.4 helps us see how the three key design concepts fit together and thus provide a more powerful and holistic way of seeing the big picture.

## THE ROLE OF OBJECTIVES AND STRATEGY IN GUIDING E-STORE DESIGN

The integrated model presented in the previous section is a good way to pull your thoughts together in terms of designing the components and linkages across the components of an e-store site. Helpful information has been given to assist in this design, or redesign, task. However, although we have mentioned it in passing, there is one missing piece of critical information, namely the objectives and strategy of the e-retailer.

Most likely a common objective of e-retailers is to sell as much as possible online, or at least enough (critical mass) to make the online operation viable. If this is the case then it is necessary to make the e-store experience a positive one, with easy and efficient navigation, relevant interactivity to solve any problems and sufficient web atmospherics to make it interesting and enjoyable. If navigability and interactivity are deficient, then online users will get frustrated and abandon their trolley. It is therefore important to have a good understanding of online consumer behaviour in designing the ideal e-store site.

Another objective, but not a generic one, is to create the appropriate image for the e-store. An e-retailer might wish to convey an image of high quality, another that of a discounter, while others might build a unique image. Each of these objectives would require an entirely different e-store design, so clearly it is necessary to be clear about the specific e-retail objectives *before* designing the e-store.

## CONCLUSIONS

E-store design is about creating desirable features on the e-store website, particularly the technical components of navigability and interactivity. Although such features can be considered to be technical in the first instance, in the final analysis they are more about the human-machine interface. That is, what sort of e-store design is going to appeal to the type of customer that the e-retailer is targeting? Thus it is important to have a good profile of the typical customer and to be clear about the strategic objectives of the e-retailer.

The question of optimal e-store design is a challenge for all e-retailers and all students or designers inputting into this process. Part of our approach in this chapter has been to provide conceptual tools (such as concepts like navigability and interactivity; checklists; and maps like Figure 6.4) to help answer the question. It is up to the reader to follow through with this challenge, partly by evaluating existing sites and partly by leveraging this learning into a blueprint for success.

## CHAPTER SUMMARY

E-store design is about creating desirable features on the e-store website, particularly technical components of navigability and interactivity.

The main components of e-store design that we have focused on include:

- Navigability
- Interactivity
- Impact on e-relationships
- Web atmospherics

We have also provided an overall framework (Figure 6.4) that graphically integrates these various components and shows the interrelationships between them. Another integrating device is the need to underpin the e-store design with explicit objectives that need to be achieved by the e-retailer and which closely reflect the strategy of the e-retailer.

In the next chapter we will consider the emphasis that e-retailers need to place on providing service to customers.

### Case study 6.1
### RAY-BAN (www.ray-ban.com)

### Introduction

Ray-Ban was formed in 1937 by American company Bausch & Lomb through Lester Belisario with the creation of the model "Aviator" (which aimed at celebrating the

US Airforce). In 1999, Baush & Lomb sold the brand to the Italian Luxottica Group, which is now the sole owner of Ray-Ban. Luxottica has over 77,000 employees and new sales of more than 7.6 billion euros.

## E-store

Ray-Ban.com was launched in the US in 2009 in order to guarantee a new e-store where exclusive services could be found. In 2013, Ray-Ban also launched customized services through the e-store for improving the offer for consumers. However, allowing customers to customise their glasses in terms of colors and lens does not overcome the problem of personalisation such as not actually being able to physically try on the products. Therefore, in 2014 Ray-Ban launched the innovative virtual technology of try-on (available also for smartphone and tablets): the "smart mirror" to encourage consumers to try the favored glasses before buying.

## Virtual try-on

The Ray-Ban virtual mirror represents a meaningful example of augmented reality technology for supporting the online shopping experience. The virtual mirror accesses the consumer's camera and takes a picture of his/her face (while providing some suggestions for the correct position to take the best picture for the system's right functioning). Using key points on the face, pairs of augmented reality shadows are mapped on the face. Afterwards, the consumer is able to choose the favourite items among the available glasses and virtually try them. The system further adds the glasses to the picture and simulates the final results.

**Figure 6.5** *User interacting with Ray-Ban virtual mirror*

## Usability

Web usability looks at the design of the interface and navigation of the site. Usability is often the most neglected aspect of websites, yet in many respects it is the most important. If visitors can't use the site, they leave and may never become customers. Moreover, the average user is impatient and has approximately a 5 second attention span on the web.

Ray-Ban clearly indicates the system functioning, supported by the usage of consistent icons, graphic identity schemes, and graphic or text-based overview and summary screens. These give users confidence with the tools, and allows them to find what they are looking for without wasting time.

Creating a website with creative elements such as the virtual try-on system helps depict a flamboyant and expensive brand design, but importantly it also helps portray an innovative organization and allows consumers to relate back to the offline store. Furthermore, creativity and ease of use help keep the site in the memories of the user. This is known as making the site 'Sticky'.

A good online customer experience can also lead to higher off-line sales depending on the firm's strategy. In fact, the most of online retailers have created on their retail site a 'Store locator' that gives information on the local brick-and-mortar store nearest to the customers' location. Therefore, consumers can buy online and collect at the nearest physical point of sale, or even if customers do not want to purchase online, they can check in advance the availability of a certain item in the favoured physical store and they are able to visit one of the stores where they can enjoy the physical atmospherics and maybe induce them into purchasing products. A meaningful example is Nespresso (famous coffee and coffee machine retailer) who give consumers the possibility to order and buy online and collect the purchases to any of the stores or corner in any department mall partner.

## Navigation aids

Many web gurus list web navigation to be a key driver of online purchases. The majority of web users are mainly concerned with accomplishing their goal of locating the correct product efficiently, and purchasing the product quickly. In a physical retail store context, consumers navigate for desired products by identifying representations of the store layout and by understanding the logic used to organise, categorise and merchandise goods. Most user interactions with webpages involve navigating hypertext links between documents. The main problem in websites is that 'you don't know where you are' within the organisation of information, thus it is essential that clear navigational aids are provided to inform consumers of where they are and where they have to go. Such a procedure is facilitated by 'progress icons'.

*Progress Icons tell you where you are in the process, and where you still have to go.*

Ray-Ban uses progress pages to inform users of progress in the customisations process of their glasses, from the choice of the model to the choice of the chase. This allows the customers to visually see how long the process will take. It also encourages repeat online sales.

## Navigation schemes

The navigation scheme uses a broad and shallow approach, requiring fewer clicks to reach the same pieces of information than would a narrower, deeper one. The disadvantage can be that the design of the screen potentially becomes cluttered. The Ray-Ban site allows users to switch from differing regions with just one click, e.g. from the US to the UK site.

## Visual

Visual elements in web atmospherics study the colour, text style and design attributes of the site. A major goal is to look at the quality of images used, text fonts and whether the site downloads quickly, say within 10 seconds. Ray-Ban has developed the site using Macromedia Flash, which is a dynamic web application tool that allows cross-platform implementation and interactive development that normal stand-alone HTML cannot create. However, a major issue with Flash is that not all users have Macromedia Flash or Flash plug-ins installed on their machines and thus, would not be able to view the site to its full potential. This would not adhere to usability heuristics, as it would rule out users with less computational power. A method around this would be to provide an alternative HTML site with reduced graphics and images. Though it would not deliver the same graphical impact, it would enable transactions for users with less computing power.

## Images

The Ray-Ban site uses quality images and graphics, essential in portraying a quality brand image online. Furthermore, high quality images have been used to show the product in as much detail as possible. However, as stated earlier this may cause problems with downloading, as consumers are not patient enough to wait while graphics download.

## Text

The product information provided is in-depth, but uses short concise sentences that should be clear to any reader. The font is Verdana which is the industry standard for webpages. This font is useful as the characters are spaced and have good readability.

## Conclusion

Ray-Ban has produced a dynamic website which uses high quality images along with a good font structure so that the website is user friendly and can be read easily. Furthermore, Ray-Ban has allowed customisation of the products and made the site interactive in the form of game. Navigation aids inform the user of where they are in the design process of customised glasses (either eyeglasses or sunglasses), again increasing user friendliness.

However, while the full e-commerce transactions can take place on all the sites, the virtual mirror does not run similarly. In fact, the local website of some countries does not support the system, which should check the international website to access the virtual try-on. Similarly, the virtual mirror does not support all the products or the customized products.

The Ray-Ban site might be improved by

- Allowing trying virtual mirror on all sites
- Increasing customization products online through the virtual mirror
- Increasing interactivity by offering the possibility to share both the customized product and the one tested virtually through the smart mirror through social networks (including Facebook, Twitter, Pinterest, etc.)

## QUESTIONS

*Brief feedback to these questions is included at the back of the book.*

**Question 6.1** – Why do you think design issues are more important for e-retailers than offline (brick) retailers?

**Question 6.2** – Two checklists have been presented in this chapter (a three-point list and a six-point list) to assist in the evaluation of the navigability of an e-retail site. How would you develop these two lists into a 'metric' that quantifies these points?

**Question 6.3** – How could an e-retailer use the metrics developed in question 6.2 to help improve its navigability performance?

**Question 6.4** – What is e-interactivity and how would you measure it?

**Question 6.5** – How does interactivity help an e-retailer build a stronger relationship with its customers?

**Question 6.6** – Consider two different types of e-retailers. Name them. What sort of web atmospherics would be best for each of them, not necessarily what they are currently using?

## GLOSSARY

**E-store design**  Refers to the purposeful design of the e-retailer's site. This covers text, graphics and audio. It includes listing products, product information including price, method of payment, navigation, policies, interaction and web atmospherics.

**Interactivity**  Refers to the interactivity between the user of an e-site and the site itself. The site is not simply a machine but rather an ongoing entity, with a capacity to provide service, sell goods, transact money, be cheerful or grumpy, be there tomorrow for you and so on.

**Model of e-store design**  Is a way of integrating the main components of design, recognising that one component might be an influence (causation) on another. Figure 6.4 is a three-component model of e-store design that reflects navigability influencing web atmospherics, while both web atmospherics and navigability combine to influence e-interactivity.

**Navigability**  Means the ability of the user to move around the site easily, efficiently and effectively – that is, without getting lost. A key objective of good navigation design is to minimize travel, depth and redundancy when traveling within a site.

**Virtual try-on**  Includes new technologies that allow consumers to virtually try products from the desk computer. They allow overlapping the virtual reconstruction of the product with the human face/body (through the computer camera).

**Web atmospherics**  Refer to the sum of the cues to stimulate the senses of the online user or consumer. Graphics, visuals, audio, colour, product presentation at different levels of resolution, 3D displays are among the more common examples.

## FURTHER READING

Moran M and Hunt B. (2015) *Search Engine Marketing*, 3rd edition. Indianapolis, IN: IBM Press.

## REFERENCES

### Navigability

Merrilees B and Fry M-L. (2002) 'Corporate branding: A framework for e-retailers', *Corporate Reputation Review,* 5 (2,3): 213–225.

### Interactivity

Azuma RT. (1997). 'A survey of augmented reality', *Presence: Teleoperators and Virtual Environments*, 6 (4): 355–385.

Carmigniani J, Furht B, Anisetti M, Ceravolo P, Damiani E, and Ivkovic M. (2011). 'Augmented reality technologies, systems and applications', *Multimedia Tools and Applications*, 51 (1): 341–377.

De Vries L, Gensler S, and Leeflang P S H. (2012) 'Popularity of brand posts on brand fan pages: An investigation of the effects of social media marketing', *Journal of Interactive Marketing*, 26 (2): 83–91.
Harris L and Dennis C. (2011) 'Engaging customers on Facebook: Challenges for e-retailers', *Journal of Consumer Behaviour*, 10: 338–346.
Kolesar M B and Galbraith R W. (2000) 'A services-marketing perspective on e-retailing: Implications for e-retailers and directions for further research', *Internet Research*, 10 (5): 424–438.
Lee E-J and Park J. (2014) 'Enhancing virtual presence in e-tail: Dynamics of cue multiplicity', *International Journal of Electronic Commerce*, 18 (4): 117–146.
Lindstrom M and Anderson T. (1999) *Brand Building on the Internet*, South Yarra, Australia: Hardie Grant Books.
Lu Y and Smith S. (2007) 'Augmented reality e-commerce assistant system: Trying while shopping', *Lecture Notes in Computer Science*, 4551: 643–652.
Merrilees B. (2002) 'Interactivity design as the key to managing customer relations in e-commerce', *Journal of Relationship Marketing*, 1 (3/4): 111–125.
Pantano E and Di Pietro L. (2013) 'From e-tourism to f-tourism: Emerging issues from negative tourists' online reviews', *Journal of Hospitality and Tourism Technology*, 4 (3): 211–227.
Papagiannidis S, Pantano E, See-To E, Dennis C and Bourlakis M. (2016 forthcoming) 'To immerse or not? Experimenting with two virtual retail environments', *Information Technology and People*.
Rese A, Schreiber S and Baier D. (2014) 'Technology acceptance modelling of augmented reality at the point of sale: Can surveys be replaced by an analysis of online reviews?' *Journal of Retailing and Consumer Services*, 21 (5): 869–876.
Wixom B H and Todd P A A. (2005) 'Theoretical integration of user satisfaction and technology acceptance', *Information Systems Research*, 16 (1): 85–102.

## Web atmospherics

Chicksand L and Knowles R. (2002) 'Overcoming the difficulties of selling "look and feel" goods online: Implications for Website design', *IBM E-Business Conference*, Birmingham University, UK.
Eroglu S, Machleit K and Davis L. (2001) 'Atmospheric qualities of online retailing: A conceptual model and implication', *Journal of Business Research*, 54 (2): 177–184.
Krasonikolakis I, Vrechopoulos A, Pouloudi N and Goula K. (2013) 'Design visual examplars of 3D online store layouts types', *IFIP Advances in Information and Communication Technology*, 399: 311–324.
Manganari E E, Siomkos G J and Vrechopoulos A P. (2009) 'Store atmosphere in web retailing', *European Journal of Marketing*, 43 (9): 1140–1153.
Merrilees B and Fry M-L. (2002) 'Corporate branding: A framework for e-retailers', *Corporate Reputation Review*, 5 (2,3): 213–225.
Vrechoupolos A P. (2010) 'Who controls store atmosphere customization in electronic retailing?' *International Journal of Retail and Distribution Management*, 38 (7): 518–537.
Vrechoupolos A P, O'Keefe R M, Doukidis G I and Siomkos G J. (2004) 'Virtual store layout: An experimental comparison in the context of grocery retail', *Journal of Retailing*, 80 (1): 13–22.

## Overall model of e-store design

Merrilees B and Fry M-L. (2002) 'Corporate branding: A framework for e-retailers', *Corporate Reputation Review*, 5 (2,3): 213–225.

 **WEB LINKS**

www.macromedia.com – Usability White Paper

www.creativegood.com – White paper on creativity

# Chapter 7

# E-service

### LINKS TO OTHER CHAPTERS

- This chapter builds on Chapter 6 E-store design: Navigability, interactivity and web atmospherics in particular.

### KEY LEARNING POINTS

*After completing this chapter you will have an understanding of*

- The overall nature, purpose and scope of online service
- The many facets of e-service
- Different classifications of e-service
- The importance of measuring e-service performance
- Two different ways of developing metrics for evaluating e-service
- The concept of e-retail service quality

### ORDERED LIST OF SUBTOPICS

- E-service as the fourth stage of e-commerce development
- Three approaches to e-services
- A second taxonomy of e-services
- The self-service myth
- E-service performance
- A critical incident approach to e-service performance
- E-service metrics: a management tool
- E-retail service quality: an alternative performance metric

183

# E-SERVICE

- Additional guidance on practical e-service provision
- Conclusions
- Chapter summary
- Case study 7.1
- Case study 7.2
- Questions
- Glossary
- Further reading
- References

## E-SERVICE AS THE FOURTH STAGE OF E-COMMERCE DEVELOPMENT

The literature on e-service has by and large followed the commercial thrust of Internet marketing development. Initially the most common application by firms and use by users was through the website itself, often a basic overview of the company and more in keeping with having a public relations 'presence' in the e-commerce world. The next most common application was to post more detailed information about products, and conversely this was the second most common use by users. The third wave of application is the now dominant interest in e-selling – that is the use of the web to sell or buy goods. This takes us to the fourth and emerging wave, one that is still greatly under-utilised, namely e-services.

E-services offer the potential for some of the more advanced applications of Internet technology. For example, firms could use intelligent agents to provide extraordinary service, by tracking and data mining previous histories through Internet sites and developing known patterns of user's requirements. Customer relationships can be developed, based on prior 'modelled' understanding of which offers a consumer is likely to respond (see Cravens, Merrilees and Walker, 2000; Nguyen and Mutum, 2012). This is a special case of market segmentation to a market of one. As another application of work, a manufacturer of washing machines could include in its warranty agreement the electronic capability of monitoring the ongoing usage of the machine via the Internet of Things (IoT). Suppose that after the machine has been bought, the household has a new baby. If detergent dosage or load patterns place strain on the motor, the machine could have the built-in communication capability to automatically page the manufacturer's service depot. The depot receives a message for a service representative to visit the household and adjust the washing machine before it becomes a problem. In this way, while both the information technologies and the servicing component are largely unobtrusive to the household, they are nonetheless essential to maintaining customer satisfaction and potential loyalty. Such scenario is no longer considered as science fiction with the rise of the IoT, and accordingly, the use of smart objects such as smart thermostat systems and washer/dryer that use Wi-Fi for remote monitoring have become widespread.

While the literature has discussed e-services, it is somewhat unstructured. For this reason, a review of the literature plays a particularly important front-end role in this chapter and we provide a simple classification of the literature to assist. We have included a separate section debating whether self-service is a myth for e-services. Our own position on this matter is made clear. We follow the literature review with a proposed more systematic typology of e-services, which could be useful to readers beyond this chapter.

> **THINK POINT**
>
> Try and anticipate the difference between service that is offline on one hand and online on the other hand. Are they different? Are they the same? Is it just a few slight differences or nuances between them?

## THREE APPROACHES TO E-SERVICES

We have identified three types of e-service literature. The first is what we call the *macro or very broad view* of e-service, namely that e-service is effectively synonymous with e-commerce. The second, an *intermediate view* of e-service, is that we can study the provision of *specialist services* made available by *specialist service providers* that help service Internet users (both individuals and companies). The third perspective on e-service is what we term a *micro perspective*, namely the provision of particular and varied detailed customer services within a site as *part* of the website-to-user interface.

At the broadest level is the view that e-commerce *per se* is an electronic service to customers, one that provides greater convenience. This view places e-commerce as an option available to customers, providing another channel of distribution or information channel. For example, instead of spending say an hour to physically access and purchase from a bookstore, the customer has the option to purchase the same electronically. As a further example, a company may use the web to provide information about the company's offering to assist consumers in their product search, without necessarily enabling the consumer to purchase through the web.

A related macro view of e-service is the *services marketing* perspective on e-retailing (Kolesar and Galbraith, 2000). Kolesar and Galbraith (2000) argue that e-retail offerings are service offerings and exhibit many of the same characteristics as other non-Internet-based services. They further argue that Internet services can be evaluated by similar criteria, such as responsiveness, empathy and the establishment of trust through courtesy and competency. The principal service provided by e-retailers is a search and evaluation facility that potentially saves time and effort for the consumer. The task of the e-retailer is to provide a website design that caters to different shopping styles, provides evidence to reduce risk and also educates the user in a shopping mode that may differ to what they are used to in conventional retail shopping.

There are now a considerable number of papers that have applied the macro perspective of e-service to a specific industry. For example, Muir and Douglas (2001) have studied how service delivery has changed in legal services with the rise of e-commerce. They argue that the quality of service is potentially improved with the web. A web presence allows legal practices to be more transparent and to offer greater access to information to customers by way of improving their services. It is suggested that this improved communication may lead to a reduction in complaints against solicitors.

An *intermediate perspective* of e-service is the provision of *electronic services* from *specialist providers* to users of the Internet and Intranet. Thus we have a market (external or internal) in which key electronic services are similar to products and sold or exchanged in a market to general users of the web. There are a huge variety of specialist-firms that offer their services (products) to web users. Web-designers is a stereo-typical group in this category, but also included are all types of suppliers of a wide range of Internet services, such as portal-providers or providers of any specific link in the Internet network. For example, consider the commercial services offered by America Online (AOL) and Google. The pages of the national financial newspapers are filled with the advertisements of companies offering such web-enabling services, some claiming to offer an integrated service.

Electronic trust services are specialist e-services that provide re-assurance and trust to the financial and privacy security of Internet information flow. There are a number of third-party commercial service providers that guarantee protection of either the financial security or the personal confidentiality of information flows. A special case of this situation is the role of the electronic signature, an issue discussed by Travers (2001). He argues that electronic signatures can be considered within a knowledge management framework and proposes a six-part system that incorporates people, clients, knowledge, matters, business development and training. Travers notes that the legislation around this area would provide:

- An approvals scheme for businesses providing cryptography services such as electronic signature services and confidentiality services;
- The legal recognition of electronic signatures and the process under which they are verified;
- The removal of obstacles in other legislation to the use of electronic communications and storage in place of paper.

A somewhat unusual example of a specialist e-service is the provision of electronic money (Buck, 1997), which could be redefined as a trust-service, but Buck did not do so in his paper. Buck (1997) notes that there is a range of online payment systems, including credit systems (e.g. *Payflow Pro*), debit systems (e.g. *BankNet*), token-based mechanisms (e.g. *Digicash*) and electronic cash schemes (e.g. *Mondex*). Such mechanisms vary considerably in terms of safety, privacy protection and trustworthiness. A recent example of digital money is Bitcoin, which has gained huge support from merchants and users because users can transact directly without an intermediary. Transactions are incredibly safe, as they are verified by network nodes and recorded in a public distributed ledger called the block chain. However, despite a large increase in the number of merchants accepting Bitcoin, the cryptocurrency have not yet gained much momentum in retail transactions (Orcutt, 2015).

An example of a specialist e-service within an internal market is that of an e-mail–mediated help service (Hahn, 1998). Hahn (1998) analysed 265 help service responses from service logs and found, among other things, that users and help-service staff held different internal models for ideal e-mail communication. Users desired a fairly simple exchange of communication – that is, a clear question followed by a quick simple response. Staff, on the other hand, envisaged the need for a more complex inter-relationship, over several messages.

This takes us to the *third perspective of e-service*, namely the micro approach. Perhaps the dominant element in this field is the role of information. Some authors see information-based marketing as a potential competitive advantage (Rintamäki and Mitronen, 2014; Weiber and Kollmann, 1998). Other scholars see the web as important for tracking and gathering customer feedback (Garrigos-Simon et al., 2015; Sampson, 1998; Sen et al., 1998). Still other writers focus on the role of e-information as an aid in facilitating consumer search (Chen et al., 2015; Ratchford, Talukdar and Lee, 2001; Ward and Lee, 2000).

A second significant micro area of e-service is that of interactivity. Despite the importance of interactivity for websites, there is still not consensus as to what should be included by this phenomenon. For example, Hoffman and Novak (1996), Schloerb (1995), Shih (1998), Steuer (1992) and Welch et al. (1996) interpret interactivity very narrowly, as relating to speed of feedback and control. See also the related studies by Ghose and Dou (1998), Ha and James (1998) and Wu (1999). It is particularly in Merrilees (2001) that a broader perspective is given to interactivity. He embraces a more multi-dimensional approach to the concept of interactivity. Included factors are two-way communication between the e-retailer and the user; the ability of each party to communicate with the other including through e-mail; the ability to personalise the situation for the individual user; and the ability of the individual to control the communication and learn from it. This broader approach to interactivity is what is frequently seen today on social media and virtual communities and the approach taken in the current chapter (see also Chapter 5). Interactivity is especially widespread on Facebook pages with communication and interaction between the peers as well as with the e-retailer itself. Other interactive sites include Apple's Mac Forum, Swissmom and so on (see for example, Hallier-Willi et al., 2014).

Finally, there are numerous other Internet studies that emphasise particular aspects of e-service besides information or interactivity. For example Mols (2000) in his study of Danish retail banking examined the role of more individualised services for consumers and their need for a close relationship with the bank. As a final example of a difficult to classify study of providing services on the Internet see Mathur (1998) who takes a financial accounting approach to the topic.

In summary, we have used our three-part classification of macro, intermediate and micro as an initial way of structuring the literature, as it exists. This is not to say that we endorse all perspectives of the literature. In particular we have reservations about the macro perspective. In a sense, the use of the World Wide Web by a retailer to market their organization as an online e-retailer is no more a services marketing exercise than the use of catalogues make Lands' End a services marketer. The service component for an e-retailer is the sum total of the ancillary support mechanisms provided by the retailer and the channel intermediaries to aid the web prospective buyer to select, pay for and receive the merchandise. The e-retailer may provide services for the consumption of the prospective buyer through the web channel, but this still does not make the channel a service unto itself. Thus we prefer the intermediate and micro perspectives

E-SERVICE

of initial classification and our empirical research design is more in keeping with the micro perspective. A more refined taxonomy of e-services is developed below.

### Mini case 7.1
### BRITISH LIBRARY (www.bl.uk)

This is a free service provided by the British Library in London that includes a 'turn the page' function. The home page offers a range of services provided by the library and is easy to use with simple menu selection and navigation.

Of interest is the 'turn the pages' of Leonardo da Vinci notebook. This technology displays a scanned image of the original notebook and allows the user to turn pages using the cursor with similar characteristics as a real book. To enter this site, select 'turn the pages' on the home page and follow the instruction. This is an interesting site for those who are interested in history.

## A SECOND TAXONOMY OF E-SERVICES

We initially used a three-way classification of the e-service literature, namely macro, intermediate and micro, as a way of sorting the literature in this fragmented domain.

Our thinking on this topic has progressed to another proposed taxonomy of e-services, as given in Figure 7.1. Not all of the aspects covered in this taxonomy are addressed in the empirical part of our chapter that follows in the next section. However the Figure 7.1 taxonomy is put forward as an initial framework that can be debated by interested academics or practitioners.

## THE SELF-SERVICE MYTH

Before leaving the literature, it is useful to discuss a crucial issue in the e-service area referred to by Moon and Frei (2000). They give the example of customers visiting a typical airline website and being confronted by a self-service search engine. If they know exactly when and where they want to travel, the website will generate a list of feasible flights. However the search process becomes more complex if they are flexible on the dates and destinations. Moon and Frei (2000) remain sceptical of the self-service approach to e-service and suggest that the customer is likely to

**189**

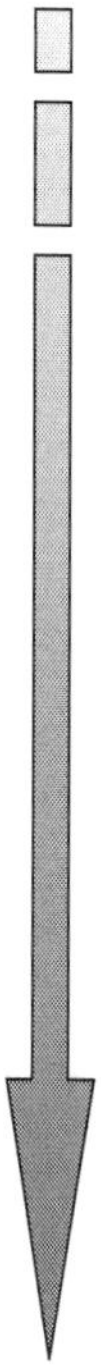

# E-SERVICE

**Consumer awareness of site existence**

- Search engines i.e. www.google.com
- Portals, i.e. www.yahoo.com
- Print media stories
- Broadcast media stories
- Website banner advertising
- Web links from channel partners
- Social media

**Consumer awareness of faults and risks in using certain websites**

- Print media stories
- Broadcast media stories
- Website banner advertising
- Web links from channel partners
- Alerts issued by consumer groups and government agencies e.g. www.bbb.org

**Consumer confidence in products and/or the website**

- Written and tabled comparisons provided by portal sites or journals, e.g. www.pcmag.com
- Comparisons and recommendations from consumer groups, e.g. www.choice.com.au
- Third-party rankings of sites and products, e.g. 'Top 100 (undiscovered) Web Sites' from www.pcmag.com

**Payment options**

- Credit card provider indemnities, e.g. Citibank iCard (www.citigroup.com.au)
- Online credit systems, e.g. Payflow Pro (www.verisign.com)

**Confidence in privacy and security**

- Third-party verification of a site's policies, e.g. www.verisign.com
- Use of secured document systems, e.g. www.microsoft.com/Windows/ie/using/howto/digitalcert/using.asp
- Site is part of a well-known online group or cybermall, e.g. www.jumbomall.com

■ *Figure 7.1* Web ancillary services that influence e-retail trust

have a much more satisfying experience if they call the airline's call centre for handling more complex situations.

Co-production is proposed by Moon and Frei (2000, p. 26) as a better model than self-service for e-commerce. In the co-production model the company undertakes many of the tasks in shopping and buying, relieving the burden on the customer. The new model recognises that although customers like having choices, they do not want too many and appreciate pre-screened alternatives geared to their needs. Co-production also understands that customers want to state their preferences only once. Moon and Frei (2000) conclude that e-commerce firms should focus on customer service *not* self-service and give illustrative examples of companies like Dell Computer Corporation. Dell performs a host of back-end transactions that are invisible to customers, such as grouping products by customer segments and displaying only in-stock items. The literature has also more recently used the term service co-creation, which is the idea that value arises in the form of personalized, unique experiences for the customer when they take part on the process of service co-creation with the e-retailer. The e-retailer in turn derives greater value from its investment in the form of new knowledge and superior brand loyalty. An example is Nike giving customers online tools to design their own sneakers and Converse persuading its most passionate customers to create their own video advertisements for their products (for a deeper discussion, see also Vargo et al., 2008; Grönroos and Voima, 2013).

The current authors tend to endorse the sentiment of Moon and Frei (2000) and Vargo et al. (2008) in that we agree that it would be foolish for owners of e-sites to provide a minimalist infrastructure and to simply let users do their own thing. Our only objection is what to call the 'co-production model'. We are content to keep calling it a *self-service model*, but one that is designed appropriately and optimally. Indeed we believe that the challenge is for e-commerce firms to strive for an optimal self-service design capability. The current chapter will shed light on this question, but much more research is needed on this topic. Dabholkar (2000) studies what consumers want from technologically based self-service options, and suggests that speed, control and privacy are generally required. However two additional attributes that positively influence the attitude of consumers towards computer technology are ease of use and fun or enjoyment. Web designers searching for the most effective design are advised to consult Dabholkar (2000) and Parasuraman et al. (2005).

We should point out that the same issue has been debated with conventional retailing. Some *weak* retailers have taken the view that *self-service* equals *no service* and have provided very little help to consumers, using the opportunity to reduce their costs (in particular less sales staff). This approach will only leave consumers frustrated and unable to find what they want and so they are likely leave the store very unhappy. In contrast, as Merrilees and Miller (1996) note, for better performing stores 'self-service' does *not* mean 'no service'. The best self-service stores, like IKEA, Wal-Mart and many superstores, appreciate that self-service needs to be designed in such a way that it delivers good service, albeit of a kind other than personalised service. Thus *good self-service design* in *conventional retailing* includes a well-organized store, with good layout, good signage, helpful visual displays and ready access to product information. Merrilees and Miller (2001) have argued that the approach taken by superstores represents a new self-service paradigm of retail service. Broadly speaking, the same good self-service design principles readily transfer from conventional retailing to e-retailing.

## E-SERVICE PERFORMANCE

Knowing what is meant by e-service is an important first step in managing an e-retail business. However it is necessary to take another step, namely the measurement of how well an organization is performing in each e-service activity. At this point it is clear that we only have a limited understanding of which e-service functions are important to consumers and how well e-retailers deliver these services. For this reason, this chapter in the next section introduces some much-needed research, namely a study of critical incidents in e-service delivery. Our critical incident analysis is followed by an examination of the role of e-service metrics as a management tool. In turn we discuss an alternative measure of e-service performance, namely e-retail service quality.

## A CRITICAL INCIDENT APPROACH TO E-SERVICE PERFORMANCE

This section outlines the results of a research study initiated especially for this book. A content analysis of 138 e-retail sites was undertaken by four judges in order to assess the nature and effectiveness of e-service across those sites. It was suggested that a good way of getting started might be with book, music, gift and department store sites, because these represent a high share of the e-selling transaction activity. The final discretion of sites chosen was left to the individual judges. The main criterion for selection as a judge was expertise in analysing e-retailer websites. Notwithstanding each judge's expertise, further controls were built into the evaluation process through careful briefing and training of the judges. This briefing included careful instruction to make sure that all items were fully understood by each judge and that all judges had the same meaning for each. Another instruction was that each judge was to spend about 10 to 15 minutes moving through the site to understand its features and its content before answering the various set questions. Each site was analysed in the same way.

A survey instrument (protocol) was designed for each judge to use with each site. A wide number of site attributes were assessed on a Likert scale of 1 to 7, depending on whether the judge agreed or not that the site performed well on a particular attribute. There was also an open-ended section of the survey instrument where the focus was made of the overall level of e-service for the site, based on a 1 to 7 Likert scale. On the same page the judge was asked to describe up to three important critical incidents/areas (if any) that positively contributed to their assessment of the overall level of e-service. Additionally, up to three important critical incidents (if any) could be listed that detracted from the level of e-service.

## Results

### Positive critical incidents

Initially we present the incidents that positively contributed to e-service. We do this in two ways. First we can note those positive facilitators to e-service across the *total* sample of 138 sites. We also break the results into *high-service sites* and *low-service sites*. High-service sites are those sites that were rated highly on the basis of the perceived overall level of e-service — that is, those sites that scored a 5, 6 or 7 out of 7. Those sites that scored 1 to 4 were called low-service sites.

As Table 7.1 shows, across the total 138 sites, the three most positive incidents that contributed to e-service were:

- Interactivity and communication (56% of all sites);
- Special offers (33%);
- Information (20%).

**Table 7.1** Positive critical incidents affecting e-service (percentage)

| E-service element | Overall sites [n = 138] | High-service sites [n = 89] | Low-service sites [n = 49] |
|---|---|---|---|
| Interactivity | 56 | 72 | 27 |
| Special offers | 33 | 39 | 20 |
| Information | 20 | 26 | 10 |
| Variety of items for sale | 14 | 16 | 12 |
| FAQ | 12 | 17 | 2 |
| Ease of use of site | 12 | 13 | 10 |
| Security/privacy | 8 | 11 | 2 |
| Delivery | 7 | 9 | 4 |
| Returns | 4 | 4 | 0 |

*Note*: Figures may add to more than 100% because of multiple incidents.

The next most important batch included:

- Variety of items for sale (14%);
- Frequently asked questions (FAQ) (a separate type of interactivity) (12%);
- Ease of use (12%).

Other less important facilitators of e-service included security and privacy references (8%), good delivery (7%) and returns policy (4%).

If we compare high-service and low-service sites, we more or less get a similar picture of what is important. One key difference shown in Table 7.1 is that the number of positive incidents of good e-service is a lot less in low-service sites. Thus interactivity and special offers remain the highest two facilitators of good e-service, but the rate of incidence is about twice as much in high-service sites. For example, in low-service sites there is a 27% incidence of interactivity (compared to 72% in high-service sites) and a 20% incidence of special offers (compared to 39% in high-service sites). A number of key determinants of e-service in high-service sites are downgraded in low-service sites. These include information, FAQ, security/privacy and returns.

### Negative critical incidents

Apart from coding those elements of e-service that contribute to the overall level of e-service of a site, we have also analysed those elements that have reduced the overall level of e-service. We have retained the same classification of elements, but now we refer to negative critical incidents. That is, interactivity now refers to a lack of interactivity or a low level of service from this element. The same applies to the other eight elements of e-service.

Table 7.2 now shows the pecking order of negative critical incidents that affect overall e-service. The two most important negative incidents are a narrow variety of goods for sale (15% of sites had this problem) and poor delivery service (14% of sites). Other problem areas of e-service included interactivity (11%), information (10%), ease of use (8%) and returns policy (8%). The other three elements, FAQ, security/privacy and special offers, were rarely mentioned as a negative incident.

We have extended this analysis to a comparison of high-service and low-service sites. As we would expect, the number of negative incidents is almost thrice as great in the low-service sites. Variety and delivery were the top biggest problem areas for both types of sites, but had an incidence rate of less than 10% in the high-service sites (compared to more than a quarter of the low-service sites). For the rest of the e-service elements, the most

# E-SERVICE

**Table 7.2** Negative critical incidents affecting e-service (percentage)

| E-service element | Overall sites (n = 138) | High-service sites (n = 89) | Low-service sites (n = 49) |
| --- | --- | --- | --- |
| Variety of items for sale | 15 | 8 | 29 |
| Delivery | 14 | 8 | 27 |
| Interactivity | 11 | 6 | 20 |
| Information | 10 | 4 | 20 |
| Ease of use | 8 | 1 | 20 |
| Returns | 8 | 4 | 14 |
| FAQ | 4 | 2 | 8 |
| Security/privacy | 4 | 3 | 6 |
| Special offers | 3 | 3 | 4 |

*Note*: That figures may add to more than 100%.

notable difference in the rankings is that of ease of use. It was the equal third highest problem area among high-service sites, but the lowest (and almost non-existent with a 1% incidence) among the high-service sites.

## Logistic regression of high-low service sites

We can extend our analysis from an enumeration of the critical incident elements (as a form of Pareto analysis), to a binary logistic regression analysis in which we can predict which sites fall into the high-service or low-service categories. The dependent variable is binary (either one type of site or the other). The independent variables are the nine dummy variables denoting positive critical incidents and the nine dummy variables denoting negative critical incidents.

The results are shown in Table 7.3. Overall the degree of explanation is high, with an adjusted coefficient of determination of 0.53. Nine of the dummy variables were significant at the 5% level. The model predicts very well, with an 88% hit rate.

The six major e-service elements that shunt a firm into either a high-service or low-service category were:

- Positive interactivity incidents
- Negative information incidents
- Negative delivery incidents

**195**

E-SERVICE

**Table 7.3** Logit regression differentiating high-service and low-service sites

| Dependent variable<br>Binary variable<br>0 = low-service site<br>1 = high-service site | Beta coefficient<br>(standardised) | t-Value<br>(absolute) |
| --- | --- | --- |
| Positive interactivity incident | 0.37 | 5.69 |
| Negative information incident | −0.27 | 4.36 |
| Negative delivery incident | −0.23 | 3.76 |
| Negative interactivity incident | −0.23 | 3.74 |
| Negative ease of use incident | −0.22 | 3.50 |
| Positive FAQ incident | 0.21 | 3.40 |
| Positive information incident | 0.17 | 2.80 |
| Positive special deals | 0.17 | 2.72 |
| Negative variety of items | −0.15 | 2.35 |

- Negative interactivity incidents
- Negative ease of use experiences
- Positive FAQ incidents.

In addition, less important influences were positive information incidents, positive deals and negative variety of items for sale incidents.

*Multiple regression analysis of overall service rating*

Given that we have recorded the actual overall service rating of the site, on a 1 to 7 scale, we can also analyse the data with conventional multiple regression analysis, with the overall service rating as the dependent variable and the same independent variables as before. This is another way of testing the robustness of our results, although the logistic regression and the multiple Ordinary Least Squares (OLS) are testing slightly different models and therefore we would not expect exactly the same results to be produced.

Table 7.4 summarises the results. The adjusted coefficient of determination is good, at 0.56. Eight variables were significant. The six most important e-service elements explaining the overall service rating were:

- Positive interactivity incidents
- Negative delivery incidents

# E-SERVICE

**Table 7.4** OLS regression determining overall site e-service rating

| Dependent variable<br>Overall e-service rating | Beta coefficient<br>(standardised) | t-Value<br>(absolute) |
| --- | --- | --- |
| Positive interactivity incident | 0.39 | 6.19 |
| Negative delivery incident | −0.28 | 4.76 |
| Negative ease of use incident | −0.26 | 4.38 |
| Negative information incident | −0.25 | 4.27 |
| Positive information incident | 0.24 | 4.03 |
| Negative interactivity incident | −0.22 | 3.76 |
| Positive variety of items incident | 0.13 | 2.16 |
| Positive special deals | 0.11 | 1.85 (n.s.) |
| Negative variety of items | −0.11 | 1.76 (n.s.) |

*Note*: n.s. denotes not significant at the 0.05 level

- Negative ease of use incidents
- Negative information incidents
- Positive information incidents
- Negative interactivity incidents.

Additionally, positive variety of the offerings had a marginal influence on overall service rating, while positive deals and negative variety of items were not quite significant.

If we compare Table 7.3 and Table 7.4, we see that essentially the same elements are at work. However there are slight differences, with some elements appearing in one table only and the pecking order changes marginally. For example, a positive FAQ service might elevate an e-retailer into the high-service category Table 7.3, but did not have any discernible influence on the overall rating regression (Table 7.4).

## E-SERVICE METRICS: A MANAGEMENT TOOL

Our research in the previous section revealed that interactivity was overwhelmingly important for achieving a perception of high e-service. This finding is even stronger when we add social media communication, live chatbots and frequently asked questions (FAQ) to its role because these are different forms of interactivity. In a sense the emphasis on interactivity is akin to the importance of personal service in the conventional literature. Interestingly, personal service was found to be the most important type of customer service in conventional retailing (see Merrilees and Miller, 1996, Chapter 14). Interactivity in the e-context includes two-way communication, the ability of the e-retailer to communicate to the user and the ability of the user to communicate with the e-retailer, responsiveness in answering questions (including the special case of FAQ) and personalisation of the process (see also Merrilees, 2001; Hallier-Willi et al., 2015; and Chapter 6).

Even without measurement, interactivity is clearly a good candidate as a capstone element in a powerful e-service program. With social media, like Facebook, interactivity between customer and brand has gained popularity as an e-service channel. Customers have now an immediate channel to ask questions about their orders, delivery or any other issues that they might come across, oftentimes with an immediate response. Chapter 6 provides guidance on how an e-retailer could effectively use interactivity as an online strategy. Similarly, we recommend that an e-retailer should audit its interactivity every year or so, along the lines suggested in the previous section (using say a critical incident analysis). If interactivity is found to be too low or not as high as desired, then steps can be undertaken to increase it, through for example, increased customisation, or other means.

A second key finding of our research study is that interactivity needs to be supported by special offers, information, variety of items for sale and ease of use, as part of an integrated approach to e-service. An e-service audit of an e-retail site should incorporate all components of e-service.

A third key finding of our research is also very important for the practice of good e-service. We have shown that it is not sufficient to create and manage *positive e-service experiences.* Equally the firm's e-commerce strategy needs to be able to handle *negative critical incidents.* The first point is that *even high-service sites* experience periodic problems in e-service. For example, Table 7.2 shows that high-service sites, while generally having a very high (72%) positive incidence of interactivity, nonetheless had a 6% (that is, non-zero) incidence of negative interactivity. The same pattern occurs in the areas of product variety and delivery. Firms need to take steps to continuously improve (that is, lower) the rate of negative incidents. Ideally, more interactivity may need to be built in if all other aspects of interactivity fail – this is the ultimate approach to service-failure recovery. Perhaps it is a toll free phone service that is needed as a service in the last resort?

A fourth key finding of our research that needs to be carefully considered by websites is that the solution for sites attempting to increase their e-service capability is not simply *to add* more information, an FAQ service or similar facility. Such actions are a necessary, though insufficient condition to becoming a high-service site. Take information for example.

Information incidents, both positive and negative, were important in determining membership of the e-retailer into a high-service or low-service category and the overall level of e-service of the site. Yet there was only a slight difference (and one that was *not* statistically significant) in the quantity of information across high-service and low-service sites. This suggests that the problem for some sites is not the *quantity* of information, but rather he *quality* and *relevance* of information. Thus the high rate (20%) of negative incidents about information on the low-service sites (see Table 7.2) may be due to overemphasis on the wrong information, that is, the wrong details, rather than the lack of information in general.

In summary, we suggest that e-retailers should regularly monitor or audit all of their e-services, at least as frequently as annually. The critical incident approach is a simple way of doing this and the method is robust because it captures both positive and negative incidents in e-service. Notwithstanding the merit of this approach, there are alternative ways of evaluating e-services and we turn to one of those in the next section.

## E-RETAIL SERVICE QUALITY: AN ALTERNATIVE PERFORMANCE METRIC

Retail service quality entails the application of service quality as both a concept and measure to retailing. The landmark study in this respect is Dabholkar, Thorpe and Rentz (1996). One advantage of using a measure of (retail) service quality is that it represents a composite measure, pulling together a number of components of service, such as personal service, store design and problem solving. So instead of having to say that six or seven or whatever components of service are performing at the individual service level, we can combine our assessment into a composite service quality measure.

More recently, researchers have extended their scope of retail service quality from conventional retailing to also include Internet or e-retailing. These studies include Zeithaml, Parasuraman and Malhotra (2000), Wolfinbarger and Gilly (2002), Janda, Trocchia and Gwinner (2002), Francis and White (2002a; 2002b) and Parasuraman et al. (2005). Each study uses slightly different dimensions (or items under each heading) of e-retail service quality, but generally the dimensions include:

- Website design
- Security
- Ordering system
- Delivery system
- Communication.

The five dimensions of e-retail service quality provide an umbrella approach for e-retailers wishing to use an alternative measure of e-service performance. We offer no view as to whether this approach or the critical incident approach is better. Indeed, e-retailers could quite easily use both sets of metrics to evaluate their e-service, as they complement each other.

Wolfinbarger and Gilly (2003) highlight four components of e-retail quality based on a comprehensive and sound methodology among many of the articles in this field. They identified:

- Website design (navigation, order processing, personalisation)
- Fulfillment/reliability (receipt of correct goods, delivery on time)
- Privacy/security (security of credit card payments and privacy of shared information)
- Customer service (responsive to customer inquiries).

In terms of the predictive power of these four components, two of them (website design and fulfilment) were found to be the most important in contributing to overall quality, satisfaction and return purchases.

Some technology-enabled retail services such as call centres, digital kiosks and self-service equipment make some conventional service quality measurements irrelevant. For example, Li et al. (2003) demonstrated that technology-enabled services made the measurement of tangibles superfluous. Assessing e-service technology now requires new e-service quality dimensions, such as customer to customer communication, automated search, information acquisition, content, ease of use mass and customization (Doll and Torkzadeh, 1988; Peterson et al., 1997; Roy et al., 2016). Parasuraman et al. (2005) developed a four-dimensional multi-item scale called E-S-QUAL to assess electronic service quality. This scale consists of the dimensions of efficiency, fulfilment, system availability and privacy. Many other measurement scales exist. For example, Van Riel et al. (2001) identified four e-service quality dimensions for Internet-enabled businesses, namely, user interface, core service and supplementary services. Collier and Bienstock (2006) found that e-service quality consists of process, outcome and recovery quality, whereas Cristobal et al. (2007) identified web design, customer service, assurance and order management, as representative of e-service quality.

As a way to measure customers' perceptions of e-service quality and their willingness to embrace new technologies, Parasuraman (2000) developed the Technology Readiness Index, which consists of four dimensions: optimism, innovativeness, discomfort and insecurity. Fassnacht and

Koese (2006) have advanced a hierarchical model of e-service quality that incorporates environment quality, delivery quality and outcome quality. In their case, graphic quality and layout clarity were considered as sub-dimensions of *environment quality*; attractiveness of selection, information and technical qualities and ease of use were sub-dimensions of *delivery quality,* and finally; reliability, functional and emotional benefits were sub-dimensions of *outcome quality.* It is clear that many e-service quality measures depend on the context and a single measure may have difficulty capturing the overall e-service quality.

In online settings, Wolfinbarger and Gilly's (2003) eTailQ scale suggests that four factors, namely website design, fulfilment/reliability, security/privacy and customer service, are strong predictors of customers' judgments of quality, customer loyalty and attitudes toward the website. For automated banking services, Al-Hawari et al. (2005) used ATM quality, telephone banking quality, Internet banking quality, core service and price as the key quality dimensions. Equally, Joseph et al.'s (1999) study on e-banking employed its categories and dimensions in the forms of convenience/accuracy, feedback/complaint management, efficiency, queue management, accessibility and customization. For online banking, Herington and Weaven (2009) focused on four factors: personal needs, site organization, user-friendliness and efficiency of website, while Ho and Lin (2010) found customer service, web design, assurance, preferential treatment and information provision to be of relevance.

Both self-service technology and call centres have garnered attention in e-quality research. For example, for self-service technology, the quality dimensions consist of a wide range of factors, such as use, fun, usefulness, saving time and money, performance, solving intense need, avoiding service persons, technology anxiety and robustness (Curran and Meuter, 2005; Dabholkar and Bagozzi, 2002; Meuter et al., 2000, 2003). For call centre services, the categories include adaptiveness, assurance, authority, empathy, anticipating customer requests, customer orientation, offering explanations/justifications, educating customers and offering personalized information (Burgers et al., 2000; Dean, 2002, 2004). Svensson (2006), focusing on the interactions between customers and self-service technologies, recommends that incorporating interactivity in e-service quality models would help with a more accurate assessment of its quality. This is very much like our own view on the matter relating to e-retail service quality measurement, as having clear evaluation criteria enables an e-retailer to commit more or less to a specific dimension and thereby improve its overall service.

## ADDITIONAL GUIDANCE ON PRACTICAL E-SERVICE PROVISION

The chapter already provides a number of practical tools that could help the improved delivery of e-services for e-retailers. First, key concepts, such as interactivity and delivery, have been highlighted as having special importance. Second, the idea of e-service metrics is another practical tool ready for actual use by e-retailers. In addition to these ideas and tools, the reader might wish to consult a number of 'how to' books, including Sterne (1996), Cusack (1998), Zemke and Connellan (2001) and Brooks (2006).

## CONCLUSIONS

This chapter has provided two taxonomies of e-service as a contribution to an otherwise indistinct field. The chapter has also made a statement about the self-service myth in e-service, suggesting a semantic resolution of the debate. Indeed, the challenge to web-designers and web-marketers is to find the *optimal self-service* design for interactive marketing. In part, the fieldwork conducted in this study helps to make a contribution to this pursuit.

The research part of the chapter has evaluated critical incidents in a sample of 138 e-retailer sites. We have analysed the total number of websites in the sample as well as sub-samples of *high-service* and *low-service* websites. We have also contrasted *positive* critical incidents from *negative* critical incidents. Perhaps an unexpected result, we found that the main e-service elements that drive positive e-service are *not* the same as the elements that cause negative critical incidents in e-service. Interactivity in particular, strongly supported by special offers and information about the product and firm, were the key components of positive e-service. In contrast, negative e-service experiences were most often associated with a lack of variety of items for sale and poor delivery arrangements.

We have suggested that interactivity could be the key capstone element for e-retailers trying to build a powerful e-service program, with support from information, ease of use, variety and special offers. This is now more prevalent than ever with the social media platforms. There is also a need to manage *service-failure recovery*, that is, the myriad of negative critical incidents. This may lead to the ultimate form of interactivity − namely an interactive service that handles the collective failure in all the other interactive mechanisms.

# E-SERVICE

## CHAPTER SUMMARY

The service component for an e-retailer is the sum total of the ancillary support mechanisms provided by the e-retailer and the channel intermediaries to aid the web prospective buyers to select, pay for and receive the merchandise. Two different taxonomies or classifications were used to explore the nature of e-services. We also argued that self-service is not a myth for e-services and should not be taken for granted. It needs to be properly designed to genuinely help the e-customer.

E-service performance is important for e-retailers, if they are to fully understand what attributes are needed by customers. Two different ways of measuring e-service performance were given, namely a critical incident approach and an e-retail service quality approach.

In the following chapter, we draw together the issues of site design, products and e-service with a consideration of branding for the e-retailer.

### Case study 7.1
### LEGAL SERVICES: BELL LEGAL GROUP
### (www.belllegal.com.au)

This is a legal services site of the Bell Legal Group on the Gold Coast, Australia, that offers a full range of legal services from corporate to individual issues. The site is typical of a service provider with a professional appearance and an abundance of information on the services that they provide. This site differs from many others due to the very detailed information sheets (free downloads) on the home page.

The menu offers: our people, a group that lists employee's qualifications and experience with portrait photographs. It has the usual menu selection for contacts and queries with linked pages to a large range of predominantly Government websites related to legal matters ranging from privacy codes to taxation issues. The notion of providing an extra service through linkages to established sites is a fairly easy and cost-effective way of adding value to customers. Essentially it is a public service that is an option available to any e-commerce firm.

**203**

E-SERVICE

## Case study 7.2
## MOTORING ORGANIZATION: RAC (www.rac.co.uk)

This is a motoring organization that offers a range of services from breakdown to insurance coverage. The site is representative of a large organization that offers a multitude of services and requires careful navigation to locate particular information. This is made even more difficult with the amount of linked advertising and special deals scattered over the pages. If followed carefully the menu items on each page are self-explanatory and will lead to the desired location. The site is typical of similar motoring organizations worldwide that offer online services and information on their core and related products. While some of the site is intended to gain customers, there are some that could be seen as public service, such as traffic conditions.

The home page includes connection to localities, insurance for vehicles, property and holidays, motoring information for breakdown, technical reports and car care, holiday information, accommodation deals, vehicle hire, ship/airline bookings and tours. It also covers a range of finances for loans and insurances as well as legal matters. The site is interesting enough, with standout colours and complemented with related photographs, coupled with an abundance of graphic deals.

## QUESTIONS

*Brief feedback to these questions is included at the back of the book.*

**Question 7.1** – What is the difference between the macro and the micro view of e-services?

**Question 7.2** – Why do Moon and Frei (2000) prefer the co-production model (or co-creation) of e-service rather than the self-service model?

**Question 7.3** – Do you agree that the factors that contribute to *good* e-service are different from the factors that contribute to *bad* e-service? Why?

**Question 7.4** – Explain how e-service metrics can help an e-retailer better manage their business.

## GLOSSARY

**E-service** The micro perspective involves the provision of particular and varied detailed customer services within a site as part of the website to user interface.

**Service component for an e-retailer** The sum total of the ancillary support mechanisms provided by the retailer and channel intermediaries to aid the web prospective buyer in selecting, paying for and receiving the merchandise.

## FURTHER READING

Lusch R F and Spohrer J C. (2012) 'Evolving service for a complex, resilient, and sustainable world', *Journal of Marketing Management*, 28 (13–14): 1491–1503.

Zwass V. (2010) 'Co-creation: Towards a taxonomy and an integrated research perspective', *International Journal of Electronic Commerce*, 15 (1): 11–48.

## REFERENCES

Al-Hawari M, Hartley N and Ward T. (2005) 'Measuring banks' automated service quality: A confirmatory factor analysis approach', *Marketing Bulletin*, 16: 1–19.

Brooks P. (2006) *Metrics for IT Service Management*, Wilco, Amersfoort, the Netherlands: Van Haren Publishing.

Buck, S. (1997) 'From electronic money to electronic cash: Payment on the net', *Logistics Information Management*, 10 (6): 289–299.

Burgers A, Ruyter K D, Keen C and Streukens S. (2000) 'Customer expectation dimensions of voice-to-voice service encounters: A scale-development study', *International Journal of Service Industry Management*, 11: 142–161.

Chen C H S, Nguyen B, Klaus P and Wu M S. (2015) 'Exploring electronic word-of-mouth (eWOM) in the consumer purchase decision making process: The case of online holidays – Evidence from United Kingdom (UK) consumers', *Journal of Travel and Tourism Marketing*, 32 (8): 953–970.

Collier J E and Bienstock C C. (2006) 'Measuring service quality in e-retailing', *Journal of Service Research*, 8: 260–275.

Cravens D, Merrilees B and Walker R. (2000) *Strategic Marketing Management for the Pacific Region*, Sydney, Australia: McGraw-Hill.

Cristobal E, Flavian C and Guinaliu M. (2007) 'Perceived e-service quality (PeSQ) – Measurement validation and effects on consumer satisfaction and web site loyalty', *Managing Service Quality*, 17: 317–340.

Curran J M and Meuter M L. (2005) 'Self-service technology adoption: Comparing three technologies', *Journal of Services Marketing*, 19: 103–113.

Cusack M. (1998) *Online Customer Care: Applying Today's Technology to Achieve World-Class Customer Interaction*, Milwaukee, WI: ASQ Quality Press.

Dabholkar P. (2000) 'Technology in service delivery: Implications for self-service and service support', in Swartz T and Iacobucci D (eds.) *Handbook of Services Marketing and Management*, Thousand Oaks, CA: Sage.

Dabholkar P A and Bagozzi R P. (2002) 'An attitudinal model of technology-based self-service: Moderating effects of consumer traits and situational factors', *Journal of the Academy of Marketing Science*, 30: 184–201.

Dabholkar P, Thorpe D and Rentz J. (1996) 'A measure of service quality for retail stores: Scale development and validation', *Journal of the Academy of Marketing Science*, 24 (1): 3–16.

Dean A M. (2002) 'Service quality in call centres: Implications for customer loyalty', *Managing Service Quality*, 12: 414–423.

Dean A M. (2004) 'Rethinking customer expectations of service quality: Are call centres different', *Journal of Services Marketing*, 18: 60–77.

Doll W J and Torkzadeh G. (1988) 'The measurement of end-user computing satisfaction', *MIS Quarterly*, 12: 259–274.

Fassnacht M and Koese I. (2006) 'Quality of electronic services – Conceptualizing and testing a hierarchical model', *Journal of Service Research*, 9: 19–37.

Francis J and White L. (2002a) 'A model of quality determinants in Internet retailing', *Proceedings of 2001 ServSIG Services Research Conference*: New Horizons in Services Marketing, AMA: 59–67.

Francis J and White L. (2002b) 'Exploratory and confirmatory factor analysis of the Perceived Internet Retailing Quality (PIRQ) Model, in Shaw R N, Adam S and McDonald H (ed.) *Proceedings of ANZMAC* [CD-Rom].

Garrigos-Simon F J, Llorente R and Morant M. (2015) 'Pervasive information gathering and data mining for efficient business administration', *Journal of Vacation Marketing*, doi:10.1177/1356766715617219.

Ghose S and Dou W. (1998) 'Interactive functions and their impacts on the appeal of Internet presence sites', *Journal of Advertising Research*, 38 (2): 29–43.

Grönroos C and Voima P. (2013) 'Critical service logic: Making sense of value creation and co-creation', *Journal of the Academy of Marketing Science*, 41 (2): 133–150.

Ha L and James E. (1998) 'Interactivity reexamined: A baseline analysis of early business Web sites', *Journal of Broadcasting and Electronic Media*, 42 (4): 457–470.

Hahn K. (1998) 'Qualitative investigation of an e-mail mediated help service', *Internet Research: Electronic Applications and Policy*, 8 (2): 123–135.

Hallier-Willi C, Melewar T C, Dennis C and Nguyen B. (2014) 'Corporate impression formation in online communities – A qualitative study', *Qualitative Market Research: An International Journal*, 17 (4): 410–440.

Herington C and Weaven S. (2009) 'E-retailing by banks: E-service quality and its importance to customer satisfaction', *European Journal of Marketing*, 43: 1220–1231.

Ho C B and Lin W. (2010) 'Measuring the service quality of internet banking: Scale development and validation', *European Business Review*, 22: 5–24.

Hoffman D L and Novak T P. (1996) 'Marketing in hypermedia computer-mediated environments: Conceptual foundations', *Journal of Marketing*, 60 (July): 50–68.

Janda S, Trocchia P and Gwinner K. (2002) 'Consumer perceptions of Internet retail service quality', *International Journal of Service Industry Management*, 13 (5): 412–431.

Joseph M, McClure C and Joseph B. (1999) 'Service quality in the banking sector: The impact of technology on service delivery', *International Journal of Bank Marketing,* 17: 182–191.

Kolesar M and Galbraith R. (2000) 'A services-marketing perspective on e-retailing: Implications for e-retailers and directions for further research', *Internet Research: Electronic Networking Application and Policy*, 10 (5): 428–438.

Li Y N, Tan K C and Xie M. (2003) 'Factor analysis of service quality dimension shifts in the information age', *Managerial Auditing Journal*, 18: 297–302.

Mathur L. (1998) 'Services advertising and providing services on the Internet', *Journal of Services Marketing*, 12 (5): 334–345.

Merrilees B and Miller D. (1996) *Retailing Management: A Best Practice Approach*, Melbourne: RMIT Press.

Merrilees B and Miller D. (2001) 'Superstore interactivity: A new self-service paradigm of retail service', *International Journal of Retail and Distribution Management*, 29 (8): 379–389.

Merrilees B. (2001) 'Interactivity design as the key to developing Internet relationships', *Journal of Relationship Marketing*, 1 (3&4): 111–125.

Meuter M L, Ostrom A L, Roundtree R I and Bitner M J. (2000) 'Self-service technologies: Understanding customer satisfaction with technology-based service encounters', *Journal of Marketing*, 64: 50–64.

Meuter M L, Ostrom A L, Bitner M J and Roundtree R. (2003) 'The influence of technology anxiety on consumer use and experiences with self-service technologies', *Journal of Business Research*, 56: 899–906.

Mols N. (2000) 'The Internet and services marketing – The case of Danish retail banking', *Internet Research: Electronic Networking Applications and Policy*, 10 (1): 7–18.

Moon Y and Frei F. (2000) 'Exploding the self-service myth', *Harvard Business Review*, 78 (3, May-June): 26–27.

Muir L and Douglas A. (2001) 'Advent of e-business concepts in legal services and its impact on the quality of service', *Managing Service Quality*, 11 (3): 175–181.

Nguyen B and Mutum D S. (2012) 'A review of customer relationship management: Successes, advances, pitfalls and futures', *Business Process Management*, 18 (3): 400–419.

Orcutt M. (2015) *Is Bitcoin Stalling?*, [Online] Available at MIT Technology Review: https://www.technologyreview.com/s/535221/is-bitcoin-stalling/ [Accessed 13 March 2016].

Parasuraman A. (2000) 'Technology Readiness Index (TRI) – A multiple-item scale to measure readiness to embrace new technologies', *Journal of Service Research*, 2: 307–320.

Parasuraman A, Zeithaml V A and Malhotra A. (2005) 'E-S-QUAL: A multiple-item scale for assessing electronic service quality', *Journal of Service Research*, 7: 213–233.

Peterson R A, Balasubramania S and Bronnenberg B J. (1997) 'Exploring the implications of the Internet for consumer marketing', *Journal of the Academy of Marketing Science*, 25: 329–346.

Ratchford B, Talukdar D and Lee M. (2001) 'A model of consumer choice of the Internet as an information source', *International Journal of Electronic Commerce*, 5 (3): 7–21.

Rintamäki T and Mitronen L. (2014) 'Creating information-based customer value with service systems in retailing', in Kyoichi Kijima (ed.) *Service Systems Science, Translational Systems Sciences,* Japan: Springer, pp. 145–162.

Roy S K, Lassar W M, Ganguli S, Nguyen B and Yu X. (2016) 'Measuring service quality: A systematic review of the literature', *International Journal of Services, Economics and Management,* 7 (1): 24–52.

Sampson S. (1998) 'Gathering customer feedback via the Internet: Instruments and prospects', *Industrial Management and Data Systems,* 98 (2): 71–82.

Schloerb D. (1995) 'A quantitative measure of telepresence', *Presence: Teleoperators and Virtual Environments,* 4 (1): 64–80.

Sen S, Padmanabhan B, Tuzhilin A, White N and Stein R. (1998) 'The identification and satisfaction of consumer analysis-driven information needs of marketers on the WWW', *European Journal of Marketing,* 32 (7/8): 688–702.

Shih C. (1998) 'Conceptualizing consumer experiences in cyberspace', *European Journal of Marketing,* 32 (7/8): 655–663.

Steuer J. (1992) 'Defining virtual reality: Dimensions determining telepresence', *Journal of Communication,* 42 (4): 73–93.

Sterne J. (1996) *Customer Service on the Internet: Building Relationships, Increasing Loyalty and Staying Competitive,* New York: Wiley.

Svensson G. (2006) 'New aspects of research into service encounters and service quality', *International Journal of Service Industry Management,* 17: 245–257.

Travers T. (2001) 'Electronic trust services will inspire the next chapter of e-commerce in 2002', *Business Information Review,* 18 (4): 24–33.

Van Riel A C R, Liljander V and Jurriens P. (2001) 'Exploring consumer evaluations of e-services: A portal site', *International Journal of Service Industry Management,* 12: 359–377.

Vargo S L, Maglio P P and Akaka M A. (2008) 'On value and value co-creation: A service systems and service logic perspective', *European Management Journal,* 26 (3): 145–152.

Walsh J and Godfrey S. (2000) 'The Internet: A new era in customer service', *European Management Journal,* 18 (1): 85–92.

Ward M and Lee M. (2000) 'Internet shopping, consumer search and product branding', *Journal of Product and Brand Management,* 9 (1): 6–20.

Weiber R and Kollmann T. (1998) 'Competitive advantages in virtual markets – Perspectives of "information-based marketing" in cyberspace', *European Journal of Marketing,* 32 (7/8): 603–615.

Welch R, Blackman T, Liu A, Mellers B and Stark L. (1996) 'The effects of pictorial realism, delay and visual feedback, and observer interactivity on the subjective sense of presence', *Presence: Teleoperators and Virtual Environments,* 5 (3): 263–273.

Wolfinbarger M and Gilly M. (2002) '.comQ: Dimensionalising, measuring and predicting quality of the e-tail experience', *Marketing Science Institute Working Paper Series,* Number 02.100.

Wolfinbarger M and Gilly M. (2003) 'eTailQ: Dimensionalising, measuring and predicting etail quality', *Journal of Retailing,* 79 (3): 183–198.

Wu G. (1999) 'Perceived interactivity and attitude toward website', Paper presented at 1999 *Annual Conference of American Academy of Advertising,* Albuquerque, NM.

Zeithaml V, Parasuraman A and Malhorta A. (2000) 'A conceptual framework for understanding e-service quality: Implications for future research and managerial practice', *Marketing Science Institute Working Paper Series*, Number 00.115.

Zemke R and Connellan T. (2001) *E-Service: 24 Ways to Keep Your Customers – When the Competition Is Just a Click Away*, New York: AMACOM.

# Chapter 8

# Branding on the web

### LINKS TO OTHER CHAPTERS

*This chapter builds on the following chapters in particular:*

- Chapter 1 – The world of e-retailing
- Chapter 6 – E-store design: navigability, interactivity and web atmospherics
- Chapter 7 – E-service

### KEY LEARNING POINTS

*After completing this chapter you will have an understanding of*

- The nature of branding on the web
- The role of interactivity and trust in building strong e-brands
- Re-iterating the nature of the e-retail mix
- The notion of the overall e-retail offer
- How to choose an appropriate e-retail offer for an e-retailer
- E-branding and how to use this concept to strengthen the overall e-retail offer

### ORDERED LIST OF SUBTOPICS

- Branding in conventional retailing
- Different approaches to branding on the web
- Branding as hype: the narrow meaning
- E-brand development I: start with the brand concept

- E-brand development II: build the brand platform
- E-brand development III: implement through the brand elements
- E-brand development IV: the special role of interactivity and trust in building strong e-brands
- The role of the e-retail mix in branding
- What is the overall e-retail offer?
- A framework for choosing an optimal e-retail offering
- Brand innovation on social media
- Conclusions
- Chapter summary
- ❖ Case study
- ❖ Questions
- ❖ Glossary
- ❖ Further reading
- ❖ References

## INTRODUCTION

Branding on the web is by far one of the most important aspects of any successful online marketing strategy. With endless choices of products and services online, having a recognisable brand that stands out not only attracts customers but also makes them stay with the brand. The brand is the face of the e-retailer and reveals the characteristics – a certain personality or identity – that differentiate it from competitors. A brand provides a 'promise' to the customer that what it offers is reliable and trustworthy. While a brand can be a logo, URL, name, trademark and other external symbols, it is also an evolving entity that brings added value, emotional benefits, associations and assists in the development of a customer's self-expression. For example, many e-retailers now provide a social value as a means to represent a consumer's identity via social status and group membership. With the rise of social media, brands have ample opportunities to develop brand communities, for example, on Facebook pages, in which videos, messages, posts and other activities are innovatively promoted to their consumers. Online interactivity between a brand and its customers has increased substantially and in return, e-retailers are now learning more and more about their consumers' profiles and behavior (Nguyen et al., 2015).

Before going further, we need to clarify that by the term *retailer brand* we are referring to the overall brand of the retailer across all of their business. The Body Shop is a brand that increases in value whenever that retailer improves their overall retailing performance. In a sense a retailer brand is a *corporate brand* or an *organizational brand*. In contrast, there is also something called a store brand or an own brand or a private brand and is one that attaches to certain *products* within the store. In the United Kingdom the use of own or private brands is very high, up to 30% of all products in some retail categories. For the purpose of this chapter we mainly refer to branding in the *corporate/organizational* sense rather than in terms of particular *products*.

## BRANDING IN CONVENTIONAL RETAILING

Branding has become one of the most striking developments of conventional ('bricks') retailing over the past decade. This has become a worldwide trend, led to some extent by well-known American retailers like The Gap, Home Depot, Toys "R" Us and Wal-Mart. The same is true in the United Kingdom, led by the Body Shop, Tesco, Sainsbury's and Marks and Spencer. In Australia brand leaders include Woolworths, Coles, Big W, Flight Centre and David Jones. In the Australian case, retailers occupy six of the twenty largest and most valuable brands. So branding has become a big business in its own right and good retailers can add value to the organization through clever brand management. We thus have a good reason to see how we can apply branding principles to the e-retailing context.

Maintaining a brand is essential in today's competitive online environment, and a primary objective of having a brand is to increase its overall value, which is often referred to as brand equity (Han et al., 2015). Increasing an e-retailer's brand equity means that the outcome of all its branding activity investments has improved, including all consumers' combined associations, quality perceptions, awareness and so on, and this is important because brand equity enables the measurement of a brand's value, so that evaluation can be done to improve the overall brand.

## DIFFERENT APPROACHES TO BRANDING ON THE WEB

Branding is a major consideration in developing an e-retail business. However what we mean by branding and how it should be implemented vary according to different perspectives. Some people see branding in a fairly narrow sense, essentially part of the product decision. In this sense it is basically a logo or symbol or slogan. So an e-retailer might add the slogan *'serving you better'* to its home page website. Of course, in the example given, there could be a presumption that the e-retailer really does serve you better, but the reality might be otherwise. In other words, a consultant or someone has advised the e-retailer to add a slogan and may even have supplied the words, without necessarily establishing that the policies and design of the e-retail site really do make a difference in the service. If this were the case, then consumers using such a site would get cynical and possibly angry and may eventually deliberately boycott such a site as soon as service gets bad or even ordinary. Branding yourself as something that you are not is worse than no branding at all because you raise consumers' *expectations* about the quality of what they will get.

An alternative, almost opposite approach to branding is not to diminish it to a *small part* (the symbolism) of the product offer, but to suggest that it represents *everything* about the e-retailer. For this meaning the

> *e-brand* is a summary of the unique package of benefits offered by and distinctively associated with the e-retailer.

The above definition of a brand for an e-retailer is a very powerful way of looking at branding. It also means that to understand branding you have to look at what lies behind the brand name. The brand name is just the tip of the iceberg. One has to look deeper and ascertain the *substance* and *essence* of the brand. Nike is not just a name or a swish; additionally there is meaning associated with the quality and performance of the products and the associated uses of those products, together referred to as the substance and essence of the brand.

We begin by reviewing the notion of branding as hype – that is the narrow meaning of branding as simply a symbol, logo or slogan. Although we have already argued that this is too superficial, it nonetheless is an approach taken by many marketers and e-retailers. We then move to the definition of an e-brand used by this book, namely one that takes a broad approach to branding. Next we ask how we can build a *specific e-brand* to suit a particular e-retailer and market. We focus on the special role of interactivity, that is, relationships, in building a strong e-brand. This takes us into related issues about the nature of the e-retail mix and how to develop a market position in cyberspace.

## BRANDING AS HYPE: THE NARROW MEANING

We have referred to the narrow meaning of branding as a sign, symbol or slogan. Another way of expressing this is to view branding as part of web atmospherics. One can inject slogans, visuals, pop-ups and colours to create a particular 'branding' impact. A good example is Sanity, the Australian DVD/Blu-Ray store. The physical store is relatively cool and hip, with lots of metal, ducting and exposed ceilings creating a very industrial look. The online site is similar, with an extreme use of colour to convey the same cool and hip image.

There are many e-retailer sites that have a high image/personality impact as soon as you click on. Good examples would include the websites for fashion clothes, watches and jewelry sites, where it is quickly obvious what the mood of each site is. Personality plays a big part in these sites. For some e-retailers, the high impact, strong personality is the main approach to branding. The reader might try to identify examples of e-retailers that have a *primarily* narrow-hype approach to branding.

There is nothing absolutely negative with this approach, *but it misses opportunities* to use branding in a more powerful way. For example, in the case of Sanity online, the cool and hip web atmospherics can be reinforced through more personalised selection of the product range of DVDs offered. The other danger with the narrow, hype approach to branding is that in some cases it could be misleading, for example when 'serving you better' is not fulfilled in the experience of the customer, as discussed in an example above.

## E-BRAND DEVELOPMENT I: START WITH THE BRAND CONCEPT

Our broader approach to e-branding is one that taps into all of the basic principles of branding used in the offline world. We begin with our new definition of branding that puts an emphasis on the distinctive package of benefits offered to customers (see above).

So a useful way of starting the process of brand development is to appreciate that the brand name is only a part of the story and the *essence* of the brand has to be built. The central aspect of a brand is something called *brand identity*. What exactly is the meaning of the brand? What does the brand stand for? What sort of things or attributes do you (as a consumer) associate with the brand? Fundamentally this is the first step in building a brand. It is not enough to say that 'we are an e-retailer selling Blu-Rays' because that is too general and does not uniquely identify a particular e-retailer. Brands require a degree of focus and selectivity. For example, you could aim to be *the* Blu-Ray e-retailer with the fastest delivery in a particular region (as far as logistics will allow) or a specialist in 1960s movies or indie movies or whatever. This process needs to be continued until a unique package of benefits is created. As can be seen already though, uniqueness is not necessarily based purely on product differentiation; it could equally be based on service or image differentiation.

Although an image can be based on a variety of attributes, the end result has to be a simple, clear brand image that is very quickly comprehended by the consumer. If this is not the case then there is need to further clarify and simply. The authors propose the 1-second test. Mention the word 'McDonald's' and within 1 second most consumers have a very good impression of what is conveyed by that brand. Within a second most people can conjure up the image of fast food, quick service, clean floors and Ronald McDonald. This is not to say that everyone has the same positive image of McDonald's – far from it; even if there is a majority with a positive image there could also be a large minority with a negative image. The same is true for most brands. In summary, the first step in brand development is to develop a clear and strong brand identity (*brand concept*), one that gives the company a competitive advantage in the market.

In the context of e-retailing, Lindstrom and Andersen (1999), discuss the development of a web concept briefing. They suggest two sections for the web concept, first outlining the market position of the brand and second developing the brand platform. The first of these sections concentrates on being clear about how your brand is perceived in the market, including such things as budget or premier brand, degree of quality, degree of service, etc. The second section covers the core values of the brand, its personality, target audience profile and their experience with the Internet.

## E-BRAND DEVELOPMENT II: BUILD THE BRAND PLATFORM

After the brand identity or brand concept is decided, the next step is to elaborate on this concept in terms of developing a solid brand platform foundation. The four key aspects of a brand platform (see Lindstrom and Andersen, 1999, p. 146) include role, personality, achievement and brand backup.

The e-retailer needs to ascertain the purpose of the brand, how it can help people's lifestyle and the functional and emotional benefits being offered. This view links into the very nature of the brand, that is, what is the brand concept? What are the core values of the brand? For example, the predominant values of the Libra site (www.lovelibra.com.au), associated with the feminine hygiene product, Libra pads, are feminine, cool and confident. The personality of the brand includes the look and feel of the brand. A helpful way the e-retailer can approach this issue is to associate the brand with an animal; for example, a cheetah is fast. Another approach is for the e-retailer to think in terms of the personality of the typical user and to build that into the e-retail site.

Achievement, the third aspect of the brand platform, refers to the realized differentiation of the e-retailer brand compared to competitors.

Brand backup, the fourth aspect of the brand platform, asks whether the site is authentic. Can the claims or promises be backed up? Is the brand trustworthy?

Before leaving this section, we return to the suggestion made above that the e-retailer could establish what the personality of the typical user was and then use that to guide the development of a personality for the e-retail site. Notwithstanding, e-retailers need to be careful not to stereotype personalities. For example, it has been shown that there is not a single 'teenage personality', though there are some common needs such as high expectations, speed and a need to be entertained and diverted constantly (Lindstrom, 2001, p. 258). There is also a fascinating question about whether people adopt a 'mask' when interacting with a computer, so that the screen social self is different from the real social self (Hallier-Willi et al., 2014; Wallace, 1999). More research is needed on these sorts of issues, as they are important in terms of what ideal personality benchmark is needed when designing an e-brand and e-store in general.

## E-BRAND DEVELOPMENT III: IMPLEMENT THROUGH THE BRAND ELEMENTS

Brand elements are the points of contact between the brand and the consumer. Banner advertisements are an example. Other examples include the myriad of signals sent from the e-retailer site to the consumer. The price of a product and the quality of the service are examples. Web atmospherics are another brand element that needs to be designed to reflect the desired look and feel of the brand and its personality. Communication and interactivity could also be considered branding elements.

In broad terms, the brand elements are all of the elements of the e-retail mix or the marketing mix. These brand elements need to be controlled and adjusted correctly if the design of the brand concept and the brand platform are to be successfully applied. Designing the right brand is really important and needs to be carefully thought out. But this will not come to much unless the brand elements are properly aligned to the brand platform. In other words, formulating a good brand is very important, but equally important is the execution or implementation of the brand through the brand elements.

## E-BRAND DEVELOPMENT IV: THE SPECIAL ROLE OF INTERACTIVITY AND TRUST IN BUILDING STRONG E-BRANDS

The previous three sections represent the essential features of a three-stage framework, comprising brand concept, brand platform and brand elements, on how to develop an e-brand.

More detailed information on how to progress the three-stage e-brand development process can be found from either conventional books on brand building (see Aaker, 1991, 1996; Kapferer, 1997; Keller, 2003; Lindstrom and Andersen, 1999; Moon and Millison, 2000; Carpenter, 2000;

Lindstrom, 2001; Braunstein and Levine, 2000; Accenture, 2001) or from the increasing number of new books that are explicitly devoted to branding on the web. Some of the better books include Greenberg and Kates (2013) and Rowles (2014).

In one way or other we have already covered the potential role of trust and interactivity. Trust was referred to as 'backup' as the fourth aspect of the brand platform (the need for credibility), while interactivity was mentioned as one of several brand elements to be used to help implement the brand platform. Notwithstanding the fact that we have mentioned these two factors, we now wish to highlight the extraordinary role that they might make to the power of an e-brand.

We have referred to the increasing number of books explicitly devoted to e-branding. Interactivity and trust are two of the more common themes running through all of these books. The predominance of the interactivity and trust themes in all of the major published works on e-branding is unlikely to be coincidental. At face value it makes sense – e-retailers are experiential brands. That is, consumers' perceptions of e-brands are driven by their total experience on the website, with interactivity being a central aspect of the experience. Such interactivity is now commonly the case with the widespread use of Facebook pages and other social media platforms.

The views that interactivity and trust are the key to e-branding come across as very strong by the authors of the e-branding books, although we need to remind ourselves that the views are based on the *opinions* of the authors. It is true that these opinions are very informed because the authors tend to be experts, often with a lot of e-brand consulting experience. However, more and more *empirical* academic works have also explicitly tested the proposition that interactivity and trust are the key determinants of successful e-branding. Such work is found in Merrilees and Fry (2002), Ha (2004), Yadav and Varadarajan (2005), and Wu et al. (2010), to mention a few, and as a result, we can now make it clear that positive brand attitudes towards e-retailers are shaped by key elements such as interactivity trust.

To see these connections more clearly we can further develop the model presented in Chapter 6, namely Figure 6.1. Figure 6.1 represented a schematic way to guide e-store design, namely by developing interactivity through web atmospherics and navigability. The three components of navigability, web atmospherics and interactivity can now be extended to three more components, namely trust, brand attitudes and brand loyalty. We show this as Figure 8.1.

Figure 6.1 previously had shown an e-retailer how to develop interactivity, namely through a combination of navigability and web atmospherics.

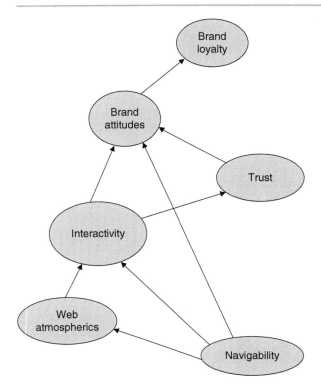

**Figure 8.1** An integrated framework for e-branding
Source: Adapted from Merrilees and Fry (2002, p. 216)

Having developed interactivity, this can be used by the e-retailer to build trust with the consumer. In other words, the more contact/communication between the two players and the more willing the e-retailer is to answer questions and solve problems, then the greater the trust. Trust is built on a solid relationship between the e-retailer and the consumer.

The next stage in the process is critical for brand building. Figure 8.1 shows that strong brands are driven by three elements that (according to Merrilees and Fry, 2002) are interactivity, trust and navigability. This model still holds today in the digital era of social media. Importantly, the stronger the dialogue between the two parties (interactivity), the more highly regarded is the e-retailer (brand attitude). Trust reinforces this relationship and can be enhanced through appropriate cues, including privacy and security policies.

The final step in the Figure 8.1 framework is the link from brand attitudes to brand loyalty. Users with a more positive brand attitude to the e-retailer are more likely to return to the site and to repeat purchase. Such a final link is the clincher that it is worthwhile for the e-retailer to nurture

# BRANDING ON THE WEB

a strong brand, with a fundamental requirement to pay close attention to interactivity and trust.

We conclude by saying that from the point of view of both e-brand experts and academic research, e-retailers wishing to build strong e-brands need to invest in both interactivity and trust.

So far in this chapter we have used a traditional brand-building framework, starting with the brand concept, moving to brand platform and then to brand elements, with a special look at interactivity and trust. An even more traditional way of approaching these issues is through the notion of the e-retail mix and market positioning. We now turn to this approach, which should reinforce some of the ideas already presented and further help the e-retailer get focus in their marketing activities.

### Mini case 8.1
### TWO OF THE GREATEST E-BRANDS: AMAZON AND EBAY

Click onto www.amazon.com and www.ebay.com
(See the case studies in Chapters 2 and 4, respectively, for more on these e-retailers)

There is little debate that Amazon and eBay are two of the greatest e-brands since e-retailing began. Neither company was the absolute pioneer in the book or auction categories, respectively. However, they were pioneering in the way they did e- business.

Amazon was the first online company to *explicitly* walk the customer through each step of the five-step purchasing process and essentially became the benchmark for most e-retailers. Indeed, the entire site was developed keeping the customer foremost in mind, to ensure a satisfactory customer online experience. The five-step approach was later upgraded to the 'one-click ordering technology' and the company was actually awarded a patent on this. Later Amazon sued Barnes and Noble for infringement, causing critics to argue that the patent office was too liberal in awarding e-commerce rights. Amazon's strong customer service begins with a very personalised greeting each time a customer clicks back on, using a first name basis coupled with memory of the categories of interest to the user. Amazon is also very strong in terms of security and fast delivery. In the Australian book e-retailing case below, Amazon generally outgunned the two local e-retailers in practically every aspect of the e-retail mix (see the Figure 8.2 snake diagram), demonstrating just how good the Amazon brand is in a competitive situation. Amazon generally appears as a case study in many best practice e-commerce books (see for example

Seybold, 1998, pp. 123–138). For a more in-depth story about the Amazon business model approach and how this has evolved over time see Spector (2000).

eBay as that name is slightly more recent than Amazon (ignoring its previous life as Auction Web), with the auction category closely following books and CDs as early popular areas. eBay is particularly well known for its feedback ratings and the way in which categories were laid out. The ratings method seems to be a major contributor to building trust that is really critical for an auction trader attempting to bring buyers and sellers together.

To give a brief snapshot of just some of the eBay happenings throughout just one year (namely 1997) we can draw on Cohen (2002). Up to mid-1997, eBay still had less than 40 employees. The new staff being added had to fit in with the culture of eBay which was itself changing. Marketing and business development were becoming more formalized. For example, rather than relying on organic growth, a pact was made with Netscape for ads that would drive traffic to eBay's site. eBay also launched a major public relations offensive. Further, CKS Interactive, a leading Silicon Valley branding expert, was called in to reposition the eBay brand and redesign its website. Customer surveys indicated some positive news, that the brand conveyed a crisp, clear message about what the company was trying to be, an online trading platform. Today, the eBay website still proclaims that its mission is '*to provide a global online marketplace where practically anyone can trade practically anything, enabling economic opportunity around the world*'. Later in 1997, eBay had to do battle with some tough competitors, Auction Universe and Onsale Exchange. For further installments on the history of eBay see Cohen (2002) and Wikipedia (https://en.wikipedia.org/wiki/EBay).

One of the real strengths of eBay is that it provides a sense of community, which is a higher-level form of interactivity. Revisit our discussion of interactivity in Chapter 6. The intention is to create a network that is more than just buying and selling. Additionally users can have fun, shop around, discuss topics of interest, share information, get to know one another and pitch in.

Auction sites require trust, safety and privacy if they are to succeed. Davis and Benamati (2003) argue that eBay has performed very highly in this respect, in terms of privacy and protecting users against fraud. eBay's rating system adds an important layer of trust based on other peers' experiences. Additionally, as discussed by Joines, Scherer and Scheufele (2003), one of the main reasons for using a site like eBay is to save time and money.

## THE ROLE OF THE E-RETAIL MIX IN BRANDING

Chapter 1 introduced the concept of the (e-) retail mix. Just as there are the Four Ps in the conventional marketing mix, there are various components of the (e-) retail mix. In Chapter 1, we used the memory aid 'Sale the 7 Cs' to simplify the components of the (e-) retail mix.

The retail mix is an important concept in conventional retailing. As we explained in Chapter 1, these components include personal service, advertising and in-store promotions, pricing, visual merchandising and other parts of store design and location, among others. The retail mix is a bit like the marketing mix in that the components represent the various marketing function activities that can be controlled by the retailer in order to influence the consumer. For example, if a retailer wants to sell more merchandise so as to reduce surplus inventory they can have a 'sale' using a combination of the price and promotion components of the retail mix. As another example, a retailer may upgrade their image by upgrading the tone and materials of the visual merchandise displays. In each example, a different combination and different direction of the retail mix are used, depending on the objectives of the retailer.

The same principles apply to the e-retail mix. In other words, the e-retail mix is an aid to the e-retailer to assist in the achievement of desired marketing objectives. Different e-retailing objectives require a different e-retail mix. As outlined in Chapter 1, price levels, price specials and advertising remain in the e-retail mix as per the marketing mix and the conventional retail mix. Sometimes there might be subtle differences in execution, such as banner ads, pop-up ads or pop-up special offers, but the essence of the component remains the same. In contrast, for some components of the retail mix, the e-retail mix counterpart takes on a radically different form. For example, the very important personal service in conventional retailing becomes 'interactivity' in the e-retail mix (see Chapter 6). Other types of customer service in conventional retailing become part of e-service in the e-retail mix (see Chapter 7). As another example, store design in conventional retailing becomes site design in the e-retail mix (see Chapter 6). A special part of store design, namely visual merchandising, becomes web atmospherics in the e-retail mix (see Chapter 6). Another important part of store design, layout, in conventional retailing becomes layout and navigability in the e-retail mix (see Chapter 6). Further, location in conventional retailing becomes global with universal access in the e-retail mix, instead of a fixed physical site, though supplemented by portal and e-mall alliances (see Chapter 9). Finally, although convenience was always indirectly represented in conventional retailing through the location component, it is now worth *explicit* consideration in the e-retail mix context because of the special significance of convenience for e-retailing consumers. Taken together, the elements of the e-retail mix can be seen as representing the package of benefits offered by the e-retail brand.

## WHAT IS THE OVERALL E-RETAIL OFFER?

The overall e-retail offer is the particular package of offerings made by the e-retailer to the consumer. For example, an e-retailer might specialise in secondhand books and offer a wide search capacity combined with a good deal on the books offered. The restriction to secondhand books is a speciality in the product area, while emphasis is primarily given to wide choice and fair prices. The overall e-retail offer therefore focuses on three elements of the e-retail mix, namely product specialisation, wide search and low prices, with less attention to other elements of the e-retail mix, such as e-service (transaction processing and delivery) and to web atmospherics.

The reader might now see the connection between the previous section (describing the e-retail mix) and this one (understanding the e-retail offer). The e-retail offer represents the value proposition made by the e-retailer to the consumer. It represents a particular package or combination of the e-retail elements. The e-retailer has an infinite number of combinations of the e-retail mix to choose from. The next section addresses how the e-retailer chooses the best package of offerings.

## A FRAMEWORK FOR CHOOSING AN OPTIMAL E-RETAIL OFFER

There are a number of issues that the e-retailer must work through before choosing what seems to be the best package of benefits to the consumer. First, the notion of *trade-offs* must be addressed. It is not possible for an e-retailer to offer the best of everything because sometimes attributes are opposites. It would not be possible or desirable for a company to offer the highest quality and the lowest price. Similarly a high-service, high-convenience e-retailer would require a lot of finances and resources to make that happen, so it would be very difficult to also present as the cheapest site. Thus there is a trade-off between convenience (service) and low price. An e-retailer needs to be clear up front and decide which of convenience or low price do they want to emphasise.

Second, the issue of trade-offs raises a related point about exactly what are the strengths of an organisation? In other words, the optimal e-retail offer (mix) should highlight those areas in which the e-retailer has a particular strength. For example, an e-retailer might decide that they are particularly effective in logistics and therefore might emphasise speedy and reliable delivery service as a key part of their value package to consumers. The same outcome might arise from an e-retailer who jointly has a large 'bricks' network of stores that might be used for e-retailer consumers to more easily return goods that are not satisfactory. As a different example, another organization might have strong web design skills helping it build user-friendly navigation links or clever forms of interactivity.

Third, the issue of trade-offs is not confined to extreme cases like high convenience versus low price. In fact it applies to all pairs of e-retail mix elements. Even if it had a lot of resources it would be too difficult for a company to try to move in all directions at the same time; it gets too confusing for all concerned. Ultimately it becomes necessary to focus scarce resources in a particular direction. Michael Porter developed a model sometime ago suggesting that companies needed to choose between differentiation and low cost (with niche business a third choice). Other approaches to strategy formulation come from Cravens, Merrilees and Walker (2000) who develop four alternative generic strategies for firms to choose from, namely *branding, innovation, channel management* and *price leadership*.

## BRAND INNOVATION ON SOCIAL MEDIA

An important aspect for brands today is to be present on social media and to innovate while being there. Being active on social media, which includes both websites and mobile platforms, requires that e-retailers be proactive in engaging with their customers and at the same time acquiring knowledge about their customers by tracking their conversations, questions, demographics and so on. Combined with an overall market-oriented strategy, meaning that the e-retailer aims to discover new market opportunities by either being reactive (satisfying existing customer needs) or proactive (addressing unexpressed needs), e-retailers can innovate successfully with new campaigns, services and ways to interact with the customers (Nguyen et al., 2015). For example, Coca-Cola has been very successful with their 'Share a Coke' campaign, where they created personalised bottle labels and created a buzz when their customers would share their labels online on Facebook and Instagram. Social media holds without a doubt many possibilities to enhance an e-retailer's operations. Customers are more interactive and brand communities can be built; products and experiences may be shared online and advertising can go viral; key employees may be identified and hired and operations may be more dynamic and expedient. A key to being successful on social media is to create content that is worth discussing and interacting with. With a brand innovation strategy around social media content, the possibilities and opportunities are endless. For those interested in this specialised topic, more reading can be done by reading the many social media branding books that have surfaced in recent years.

## CONCLUSIONS

Branding on the web is about selecting a unique or distinctive package of benefits to be offered to the consumer in a way that gives a competitive advantage to the e-retailer. From the outset we make it clear that branding is more than the name of the e-retailer (URL). It is about the essence and substance of the e-retailer and might relate to the products, services or image of the particular e-retailer.

Branding does not come naturally to many retailers or e-retailers, but rather presents quite a challenge as to how to do this well. To assist with this process the book presents a three-stage brand development framework for e-retailers. Critically it is clear that branding needs to start with a clear understanding of exactly what is the brand, in terms of its meaning and identity. The brand platform is the next stage and develops the detailed components of the brand concept, including core brand values, personality, point of difference and credibility. Finally, the third stage focuses on implementation, which requires alignment between the brand platform and the brand elements that are at the sharp (consumer) edge.

Special attention has been given to interactivity and trust as the key to building a strong e-brand. This position is supported by the literature, essentially that of e-brand consultants. However one particular academic study is also used to support the notion that interactivity and trust are the key drivers of strong e-brands. A diagram (Figure 8.1) is used to help reinforce how these components fit together to drive brand attitudes and brand loyalty.

### CHAPTER SUMMARY

There are different approaches to branding on the web, ranging from the very narrow approach focusing on web atmospherics to a more strategic approach. The strategic approach is akin to the methods used by branders in traditional settings and follows a three-stage process. Brand development goes through the following three stages:

- Start with the brand concept (brand identity);
- Then build the brand platform;
- Then implement through the brand elements (including interactivity and web atmospherics).

A related, though different, approach to web strategy is through manipulation of the e-retail mix. The e-retail offer represents a

BRANDING ON THE WEB

particular package or combination of the e-retail elements. This chapter provides guidance for the e-retailer into selecting the best package of benefits to offer to the consumer.

In the next chapter we consider the potential for expanding the audience for an e-retail offer by being represented with other e-retailers on an e-mall.

## Case study 8.1
## THREE AUSTRALIAN BOOK E-RETAILERS

Merrilees (2001) applies this new four-type generic strategy framework to three Australian book e-retailers. To see the three sites, click onto:

www.dymocks.com.au
www.bookworld.com.au
www.amazon.com

He concludes that *Amazon.com* is currently using the dual strategies of branding and channel management; *Dymocks* is using mainly a channel management strategy and *Angus & Robertson* is using a low price strategy. For example, the Dymocks channel management strategy is built around responsiveness to customer needs; a convenient returns policy; and a book club program to nurture their own loyal base of customers.

The generic strategy framework provides a guide to the selection of an optimal e-retail offer. Simply put, an e-retailer should choose from the four generic strategies, with the possibility (as in the Amazon.com case) that dual strategies could be chosen. Once the generic or dual generic strategies are chosen, it is still necessary for the e-retailer to shape the generic strategy in a distinctive way to reflect that particular e-retailer. Thus both Amazon and Dymocks use a channel management strategy, but each formulates this in a slightly different and unique way.

An alternative way of moving towards an optimal e-retail offer is to pinpoint a unique *market position* on a map, relative to other competitors. One limitation of most textbook maps is that they are two-dimensional, so we would be limited to two attributes, when in practice there are many elements in the e-retail mix as discussed above. A somewhat novel way to compare different e-retailers on a map when there are four or five or more key attributes (e-retail mix elements) entails the researcher to use a *snake diagram*. An example of this is Figure 8.2, which shows the three Australian book e-retailers assessed against seven e-retail mix elements, including low price, latest books, wide selection,

**225**

fast delivery, fair and easy returns policy and close personal relationship (see Merrilees, 2001). Based on a survey of users, readers can apply this technique to any e-retail category.

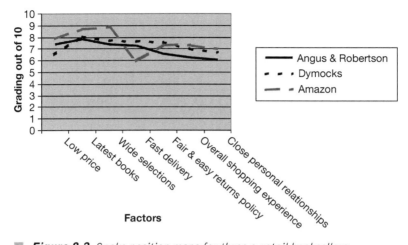

**Figure 8.2** *Snake position maps for three e-retail booksellers*
Source: Adapted from Merrilees (2001b, p. 179)

## QUESTIONS

*Brief feedback to these questions is included at the back of the book.*

**Question 8.1** – A common mistake in branding or the understanding of branding is to treat it very narrowly as a sign, symbol or slogan. What is wrong or limiting with this approach?

**Question 8.2** – Briefly summarise the three-stage approach for e-brand development outlined in Chapter 8.

**Question 8.3** – The brand platform stage of e-brand development includes the need to develop the personality of the e-brand. Select a particular e-retailer and show how you would use web atmospherics to develop the brand of this particular e-retailer.

**Question 8.4** – Chapter 8 has really highlighted the importance of interactivity and trust as necessary for building strong e-brands. Why have these two aspects been highlighted in this role?

**Question 8.5** – Why are Amazon.com and eBay regarded as such strong e-brands?

## GLOSSARY

**Brand development**   A three-stage process moving from brand identity, to the brand platform and then implemented through the brand elements.

**E-branding**   The application of branding principles to projecting a brand image of an e-retailer.

**Model of e-branding**   An integrated approach linking key concepts that eventually lead to brand value being created by the e-retailer. Figure 8.1 is a six-component model, including navigability, web atmospherics, interactivity, e-trust, brand attitudes and brand loyalty.

**Snake diagram**   A market-positioning map suitable for multi-attributes. That is, we can use the snake diagram to compare e-retailers across more than two dimensions, which is the limit of the traditional market position maps. In Figure 8.2 we are able to compare three e-retailers across seven attributes.

## FURTHER READING

Melewar T C and Syed Alwi S F. (2015) *Corporate Branding: Areas, Arenas and Approaches*, London: Routledge.

## REFERENCES

Aaker D. (1991) *Managing Brand Equity*, Free Press: New York.

Aaker D. (1996) *Building Strong Brands*, Free Press: New York.

Accenture. (2001) *Beyond the Blur: Correcting the Vision of Internet Brands*, [Online] Available at: http://www.cio.com/research/ec/cc_market.html.

Braunstein M and Levine E. (2000) *Deep Branding on the Internet*, Roseville, CA: Prima Venture.

Carpenter P. (2000) *E-Brands: Building an Internet Business at Bottleneck Speeds*, Boston: Harvard Business School.

Cohen A. (2002) *The Perfect Store: Inside E-Bay*, Boston: Little, Brown and Company.

Cravens D, Merrilees B and Walker R. (2000) *Strategic Marketing Management for the Pacific Region*, Sydney: McGraw-Hill.

Davis W and Benamati J. (2003) *E-Commerce Basics: Technology, Foundations and E-Business Applications*, New York: Addison-Wesley.

Greenberg E and Kates A. (2013) *Strategic Digital Marketing: Top Digital Experts Share the Formula for Tangible Returns on Your Marketing Investment*. New York: McGraw-Hill Education.

Ha H-Y. (2004) 'Factors influencing consumer perceptions of brand trust online', *Journal of Product and Brand Management*, 13 (5): 329–342.

Hallier-Willi C, Melewar T C, Dennis C and Nguyen B. (2014) 'Corporate impression formation in online communities – A qualitative study', *Qualitative Market Research: An International Journal*, 17 (4): 410–440.

Han S H, Nguyen B and Lee T. (2015) 'Consumer-based chain restaurant brand equity (CBCRBE), brand reputation, and brand trust', *International Journal of Hospitality Management*, 50: 84–93.

Joines J, Scherer C and Scheufele D. (2003) 'Exploring motivations for consumer Web use and their implications for e-commerce', *Journal of Consumer Marketing*, 20: 90–108.

Kapferer J. (1997) *Strategic Brand Management*, 2nd edition, London: Kogan Page.

Keller K. (2003) *Building, Measuring and Managing Brand Equity*, Upper Saddle River, NJ: Prentice Hall.

Lindstrom M. (2001) *Clicks, Bricks and Brands*, Melbourne: Hardie Grant.

Lindstrom M and Andersen T. (1999) *Brand Building on the Internet*, Melbourne: Hardie Grant.

Merrilees B. (2001) 'Do traditional strategic concepts apply in the e-marketing context?' *Journal of Business Strategies*, 18 (2): 177–190.

Merrilees B and Fry M. (2002) 'Corporate branding: A framework for e-retailers', *Corporate Reputation Review*, 5 (2,3): 213–225.

Moon M and Millison D. (2000) *Firebrands: Building Brand Loyalty in the Internet Age*, Berkeley, CA: Osborne McGraw-Hill.

Nguyen B, Yu X, Melewar T C and Chen J. (2015) 'Brand innovation and social media: Knowledge acquisition from social media, market orientation, and the moderating role of social media strategic capability', *Industrial Marketing Management*, 51: 11–25.

Rowles D. (2014) *Digital Branding: A Complete Step-by-Step Guide to Strategy, Tactics and Measurement*, London: Kogan Page.

Seybold P. (1998) *Customers.com*, New York: Random House.

Spector R. (2000) *Amazon.com*, New York: Harper Business.

Wallace P. (1999) *The Psychology of the Internet*, Cambridge: Cambridge University Press.

Wu G, Hu X and Wu Y. (2010) 'Effects of perceived interactivity, perceived web assurance and disposition to trust on initial online trust', *Journal of Computer-Mediated Communication*, 16: 1–26.

Yadav M S and Varadarajan R. (2005) 'Interactivity in the electronic marketplace: An exposition of the concept of implications for research', *Journal of the Academy of Marketing Science*, 33 (4): 585–603.

# Chapter 9
# E-malls

### LINKS TO OTHER CHAPTERS

*This chapter builds on the following chapters in particular:*

- Chapter 1 – The world of e-retailing
- Chapter 6 – E-store design: navigability, interactivity and web atmospherics
- Chapter 7 – E-service
- Chapter 8 – Branding on the web

### KEY LEARNING POINTS

*After completing this chapter you will have an understanding of*

- The nature of online malls
- How to transfer lessons from conventional malls to online malls
- The need to explore mall look-alikes, including ancillary malls
- The value of using case studies to get more insight
- The role of interactivity and trust in building strong e-brands
- The importance of interactivity in building e-mall trust
- The importance of mall design (navigability) and tenant mix (quality) in building interactivity

### ORDERED LIST OF SUBTOPICS

- Conventional (bricks) malls
- Lessons from conventional malls for online malls

- Multiple category e-retailers
- Shopping bots: intelligent shopper assistants or virtual mall?
- Virtual reality mall
- Portals and other quasi e-malls
- E-malls as ports of entry for newly started businesses: the tenant perspective
- Conclusions
- Chapter summary
- ❖ Case study
- ❖ Questions
- ❖ Glossary
- ❖ Further reading
- ❖ References

## INTRODUCTION

An e-mall is sometimes referred to as a cyber-mall or a virtual mall or an e-shopping centre. It brings together a number of separately owned e-retail sites to a single virtual location, with the individual e-retailers paying rent to the centre management, as in an offline mall. The e-mall term may be loosely used to include e-marketplaces or *online marketplaces*, which refers to an e-commerce site where product or service information is provided by multiple third parties. For example, Amazon, eBay, Craigslist, and price comparison websites for airfares or insurance all qualify as e-malls.

The e-mall should *not* be confused with a related system in which consumers can be guided to a particular offline (brick) shopping centre, where they can use special deal coupons downloaded from the central system. This is the case as some sites are provided by brick malls, with similar announcements of book signings, promotions and general information about the tenants in each of the malls in the multi-mall portfolio of the mall owner. See for example: Westfield (www.westfield.com.au).

As e-malls continue to evolve, recent examples have seen the development of Virtual Reality (VR) shopping centres – accessed via the use of Oculus headsets – that allow users to shop in digital environments alongside giraffes and zebras. According to Crank (2015): "The next form of the store or mall is no longer physical, but virtual, one where virtual reality and augmented reality will replace the physical mall or store". Truly an immersive virtual shopping experience, Crank believes that such e-malls will revolutionise store design and the shopping experience.

## CONVENTIONAL (BRICKS) MALLS

In most Western countries malls have gradually become the dominant shopping location for much of what we buy. At the same time malls have become more competitive with each other and now use a variety of extra methods including promotions and entertainment to capture the highest market share. As with other chapters, we continue to draw upon an understanding of conventional retailing in order to guide e-retailing businesses. So initially we need to identify the key principles that are important in conventional mall marketing and management. From this benchmark we can then draw lessons for e-malls.

> **THINK POINT**
>
> Before outlining the conventional mall principles it is interesting to reflect on a puzzle. How many e-malls does the reader know about, let alone use? One suspects that the typical reader does not know very many and perhaps a large number of you may not know any! Of itself your lack of information does not really matter, because by the end of the chapter you will know some and have visited them.

Conventional malls are not all the same, though some have been criticised for being too similar in terms of the retailer tenants in them. Each mall is different in some respect. Sometimes it is simply a size matter, with contrasts across jumbo malls, medium to large conventional malls, down to small, neighbourhood malls. In other cases it is special or unusual features, with extreme examples of the indoor skiing at Mall of the Emirates in Dubai or the Lego store and many rides at Mall of America. Malls differ as well in terms of their specialisation, with differences in the format. Many malls adopt the conventional format of having fashion, home and food components. But some are more specialised, such as *power centres* (a small number of large superstores, catering to bulky purchases like furniture, bedding, carpet or electrical goods) or *factory outlet centres* (opportunity to buy well-known brands like Wedgwood or Nike at discount prices). Another point of difference between malls is the different emphasis given to entertainment, with some malls putting on fashion and other shows or having electronic games parlours. Careful selection of tenants could also differentiate one mall from the others, for example by grouping a lot of trendy, independent fashion designers.

An Australian study (Sit, Merrilees and Birch, 2003) has pulled together the literature on conventional malls. The study has identified four main areas which shape the image of a mall, including:

- Merchandise (types of tenants, quality, assortment, pricing)
- Accessibility (ease of access to the centre and within the centre)
- Services (including signs, escalators, restrooms)
- Atmospherics (including ambience, music, décor).

These four broad areas tend to repeatedly appear in the growing number of studies of shopping malls. The four areas thus represent a starting point for any mall owner to define what sort of brand they want to be. Notwithstanding, Sit et al. (2003) note that the academic studies have neglected some factors that could be important in differentiating shopping centres, namely entertainment, food and security. These authors note that entertainment and food in particular seem to be increasingly used as a method of shopping mall differentiation.

A British study (Dennis, Murphy, Marsland, Cockett and Patel, 2002), based on a study of six British malls, has provided more detailed insight into the branding of conventional malls. An interesting finding by this study was that consumers were able to associate a personality to a particular shopping centre. One shopping centre studied was described as 'dull and boring and old-fashioned – lower working class or elderly'. As an animal it was like a cat or dog – not exciting, just O.K. In contrast, another centre was described as like a tiger, lion or peacock – strong, vibrant, big and colourful. Dennis et al. (2002) conclude with some advice about active brand management of malls: The first step is to focus on key attributes like quality, service, atmosphere and infrastructure. Second, choice of the right market positioning is important to create a point of difference. Third, internal marketing has potential to help. Finally, well-blended communication can develop credibility.

There is also a broad literature that focuses on how to build a good relationship between the shopping centre landlord and the retail tenant (see Howard, 1997; Roberts and Merrilees, 2003). Howard suggests that in the past too much attention has been placed by landlords on property as a financial investment, rather than investing in the relationship between the landlord and the tenant. Roberts and Merrilees (2003) empirically show that stronger cooperation between the landlord and the tenants (such as joint promotions or joint planning of tasks) can improve the performance of the mall. The same authors also show that trust is a precondition for tenants to be willing to cooperate.

> **THINK POINT**
>
> If we include small neighbourhood shopping centres, then the majority of Australian, British, American and other Western country shoppers would visit a mall or centre at least once every 2 weeks. For a sizeable minority, much of the shopping and even a lot of the social lifestyle are mall-based. *Why is there such a contrast between the role of the conventional mall and that of the e-mall?* Why is the e-mall not utilized to the same extent? Think about this issue yourself and work out what YOU regard as the main answer. We will return to the issue at the end of the chapter.

## LESSONS FROM CONVENTIONAL MALLS FOR ONLINE MALLS

One of the key lessons from conventional mall management that applies to online mall management is the need to manage the business-to-business relationship between the online mall landlord and the e-retailer tenants. There is a need for the online mall landlord to build a trusting relationship with its online tenants. Most likely interactivity or cross-communication may be the best way to do this, which is consistent with the Australian case evidence below (although this evidence only relates between the online mall and customer/users of the mall, and not tenants per se). Additional mall management issues include things like leasing arrangements and policies. The terms of the lease need to balance the needs of both the landlord and the tenant and to provide financial incentives to expand the online tenant business as much as possible.

Another lesson from conventional mall management is the need for the online mall landlord to provide appropriate and reliable services to the e-retailer tenants. In an online context, appropriate services might include a well-designed mall, referring to the architecture of the mall, including access entrances and layout. Deck (1997) highlights the importance of navigation and other architectural design issues for successful e-malls. Second, services might also include 'décor', which in this context might mean ensuring that each e-retailer has neat and clean premises, rather than a shabby, disorganized appearance. Décor might also include the appropriate 'atmosphere', an issue that most conventional mall studies highlight. Third, traditional mall management includes 'security' which in the online context might entail a third-party guarantee (from the online mall manager, who in turn might outsource this service to a regular third-party vetting firm) that each e-retailer tenant in the online mall has secure facilities for financial transactions online.

Yet another lesson from conventional mall practices is the need to market the online mall in various ways. One way this could be done is through advertising, possibly online. There could also be a co-ordinated mall-wide promotion for a limited time, say a 10% off deal. A further marketing tool relates to the selection of the tenant mix. Usually the tenant mix is not accidental, but rather is planned and designed to project a particular image (brand) of the mall. Malls can be upmarket, no frills, entertainment-based and so on. Some malls are very specialised, such as factory-outlet or power centres. An online mall owner can deliberately create a particular mall brand image and might be judged on how consistently they could execute this image. This is a fundamental aspect of mall marketing. Atmospherics can also be interpreted as a marketing tool, supporting the overall e-mall brand image.

Finally, *Chapter 8* provides a useful input into online branding, drawing on practical book references as well as recent academic research. The main finding from e-retailer branding is that interactivity and trust were very important influences in terms of creating online brands.

## MULTIPLE CATEGORY E-RETAILERS

Although not strictly an e-mall, it is interesting to consider multiple category e-retailers. Amazon.com is probably the best-known example in this situation, where a single site owner sells goods across multiple retail categories, including books and DVDs. In fact Amazon.com resembles an online department store in this respect. Perhaps surprisingly there are not many explicit online department stores. An Australian example was d-store, which had about 20 departments, though this has now ceased operating as an online department store.

Although multiple category e-retailers provide an interesting source of ideas and inspiration that may be useful for e-malls, to date there is very little academic research investigating such a format. Merrilees (2001), among other authors, has studied Amazon.com, but purely in terms of a single category (books) and not in terms of multiple categories. No doubt a lot of the well-known good properties of Amazon flow over to the multiple category situation, but there is still a need to ascertain how convenient and useful the site is to search and buy multiple categories of goods on a *single* shopping trip. Further, how many users actually buy more one than category of goods from Amazon in a single trip?

# E-MALLS

> **THINK POINT**
>
> The lack of academic studies on Amazon.com in terms of its potential usefulness to buy more than one category of goods in one shopping trip does not stop you the reader from simulating such a trip. Click on to Amazon and see how easy or not it would be to buy from say two categories of goods. Can you suggest any improvements in the design of the site to improve on the user friendliness of Amazon for consumers who might wish to use it as an online department store (that is, multiple categories rather than a single category of goods)?

## SHOPPING BOTS: INTELLIGENT SHOPPER ASSISTANTS OR VIRTUAL MALL?

Shopping bots are tools that help e-shoppers identify, locate and compare products available from e-retailers (Rowley, 2000, p. 298). There can be a consumer/shopper perspective or an e-retailer one. In the former sense shopping bots are another tool for searching the Internet and are not very different from an online directory or a search engine.

Alternatively, we can conceptualise a shopping bot from the perspective of the *e-retailer* who forms a contractual relation (like a tenant) with the *provider* of the shopping bot (like a landlord). It is in this sense that the shopping bot can be considered as a virtual mall, which helps e-retailers present and project their merchandise to the public (Rowley, 2000).

Bots tend to be either comprehensive or specialised (say books, music, DVDs, gifts) in terms of product categories carried. Some examples of shopping bots include Google Shopping (www.google.com/shopping), Shopzilla (www.shopzilla.com/), PriceGrapper (www.pricegrabber.com) and Become (www.become.com).

Category search is a common approach to move through a bot. As an example, Amazon invites shoppers to select a department; with the next screen displaying a series of product categories in that department; choosing one of these categories will display a number of merchants.

Rowley (2000) does address the difficulty of how the consumer might choose across shopping bots. Some shopping bots seem more suitable for certain products, but it is difficult to generalise. There are also a number of traps to watch out for, with a need for the correct level of specificity and specification. For example, a searcher might specify both the author and title of a book, but there might not be an exact match because of the way the shopping bot database is set up. Ironically, in this hypothetical case, a lower level of specification, such as only the author's name, might be more successful in locating the book. In another case, 'running shoes' might be more successful than 'shoes' or 'sports shoes'. It is hard to see how anything other than one's own experience or praise or complaints from friends can guide the selection of shopping bots. More academic research might help us on this matter.

## VIRTUAL REALITY MALL

While the Internet has taken customers beyond the traditional store and into a world where purchases are made by scrolling through product images on offer or via shopping bots, as indicated above, the future retail space could be experienced through virtual reality, thanks to several developments on the virtual store concept by companies such as Trillenium, who claims to be the leading builder of 3D and VR experiences for retailers. Their plan is to change the online shopping experience beyond the current 'drag and drop to your cart' style towards a real-time immersive shopping experience, where customers can walk though virtual shops, examine virtual versions of real-life products and make purchases like they would in the real world (Ingham, 2015). At the time of publication of this book, the company estimates that a publicly available VR platform, tested in collaboration with ASOS, should be completed by the end of 2016 (Hoang, 2015). Once completed, customers will be able to put on virtual goggles like Oculus Rift, and do everything they would normally do in the real retail stores, such as interacting with friends and shop assistants, trying on the clothes, walking around and so on – all this from their living room. This will be a major upgrade from clicking through images online to creating a truly immersive experience that enables customers to enjoy online shopping in the same way they would do in the real-life stores. There are certainly clear benefits associated with VR, such as personalised environment, convenience of 24/7 shopping and all the other benefits of online shopping, just more fun, adventurous and social. We will have to see what the VR concept brings, but with Facebook investing heavily in VR and with many recent developments in augmented reality, a new era may be upon e-retailing. While e-malls may not be as vital for an e-retailer compared to a physical mall for a traditional retailer, due to the fact that most e-retailers now have their own websites, which gives them more control and the need to be part of an e-mall has thus diminished, with the emergence of virtual reality, the e-retailer might just find it necessary to become part of the e-mall that provides the best virtual reality platform.

## PORTALS AND OTHER QUASI E-MALLS

We have just seen that shopping bots can be considered to be a type of virtual mall. We should also acknowledge that there are many additional Internet listing and search tools or intermediaries and other third-party sites that also contribute to the world of e-commerce. Google is probably the most famous site, but there are hundreds of sites that also contribute a similar or related linking of parties through the network. We simply acknowledge this component of the e-retail sector, leaving it to other researchers to elaborate on their role (see for example Dong and Su, 1997).

## E-MALLS AS PORTS OF ENTRY FOR NEWLY STARTED BUSINESSES: THE TENANT PERSPECTIVE

Before closing the chapter, it has been obvious that the main perspective that we have taken so far has been that of the e-mall owner. From this perspective we have questions like how should the e-mall be designed so as to be attractive to e-retailer tenants and to potential users or consumers of the e-mall. Although it has been implicit, another perspective is that of the tenant. This leads to a different set of questions. Do I need a presence in an e-mall for my business? If so, what would a suitable e-mall look like? Which one (s) should I become a tenant in?

An appropriate answer to some of these questions is almost certainly connected to the consumer evaluation of an e-mall. The two Australian case studies of e-malls were on the basis of users or consumers assessing an e-mall. If consumers or users rate an e-mall highly then that would be a positive cue to an e-retailer who is considering becoming a prospective tenant. However it is not a simple matter of a prospective tenant choosing the most popular e-mall site for consumers. The reason is that the best or most popular e-malls will also have the highest rents. A prospective tenant may like to have a high traffic, high selling e-mall presence, but may not be able to afford it. This lesson is derived from conventional retailing. McDonald's likes to have high traffic sites; but it has to pay a lot for them. Within a conventional mall, rents differ for different stalls (micro sites) depending on the traffic flows. The same principles apply in cyberspace.

Additional issues in how tenants might choose or use an e-mall are discussed in Hill (2000), O'Hara (2001) and Turban et al. (2015).

Moving on from the rent issue, the e-mall presents a great means for an upstart online organization to get a presence. Sometimes the upstarts become the main player. Huff (2000) describes the case of Indianapolis-based National Wine and Spirits Inc. wanting an online presence. Rather than potentially getting upstaged, the company formed its own e-mall (eSkye.com Inc) that was a national marketplace for beverage makers, distributors and retailers to buy and sell online. Hall (1998) and Strom (1998) also elaborate on the idea that e-malls are a useful means not only to help launch or grow e-retailers, but in some cases to totally create the e-retailer! So one of the services provided by some e-malls is to help create the e-retailer from scratch.

## CONCLUSIONS

The e-mall presents a challenge to e-retailers' aspiration to have full coverage on the web. Shopping in the conventional brick world is greatly facilitated by the presence of malls and in fact they tend to dominate the way we shop. Yet the two *think points* at the beginning of this chapter suggest that a completely different situation applies in the e-world, with a minimal role to date for the e-mall. Why is this the case? Perhaps one answer is that there is in fact a range of close substitute sites that resemble online malls. Such sites include portals, search engines and shopping bots. Similarly there are major category e-retailers that resemble a virtual department store, like Amazon or eBay, and these are also substitutes for an e-mall.

An alternative answer is that it is not entirely clear that there is a major need for a multi-category, multi-owner e-mall. Although there is a real and established need for a brick mall in which we can pick up the bread, milk, newspaper and a video from say three different vendors at a local mall, is there an equivalent situation where we need to go to an e-mall for the same type of experience? For the majority of consumers the answer is probably no, with a few exceptions.

On the other hand, there might be a high demand for a mega e-retailer in a particular category (e.g. Amazon) or one offering multiple categories (e.g. Amazon or eBay). There could also be a reasonably large demand for a specialised or single-category e-mall, such as fashion (see Hill, 2000) or defense (see O'Hara, 2001). With this view we speculate that the dominant current and probable future use of cyberspace is primarily a single or limited use shopping expedition, with a constrained view as to the type of e-malls needed. This future e-retail space seems to be moving towards virtual reality, where customers are able to go shopping from their couch. Our viewpoint is consistent with the immediate and instant gratification nature of e-retailing shopping, focused on *immediate needs* though not *immediate consumption*. We envisage a norm of limited online shopping expeditions, focused on gift buying, or fashion buying or e-grocery purchasing for example, but rarely a combination of all these tasks in the one 'trip'.

Having established that the most desirable type of e-mall is a highly focused and specialised one, what is the best way to design such an e-mall? This chapter has argued that there are lots of lessons to be drawn from conventional brick malls, in terms of choosing the right array of tenants, merchandise, quality, services and support. Relationship marketing and management is also likely to be a big issue. Specifically and drawing on the two Australian case studies, interactivity and trust were seen as the most crucial means of building the e-mall brand. Such a finding is consistent with what we found in Chapter 8 in terms of individual e-retailers wishing to build their brands.

The case studies were able to provide further understanding in terms of advice about how to develop trust in an e-mall site. This can be a big challenge for any e-mall, as it is necessary to convey not just the overall trustworthiness of the mall, but also each e-retailer tenant in it. Such a challenge is especially great for an e-mall with a large proportion of pure click retailers in it, such as the sofcom.com e-mall. The finding in Table 9.2 was that interactivity was the main way of building trust in an e-mall. However this was somewhat less effective in the sofcom e-mall, meaning that e-malls with a high proportion of pure click tenants have to work harder in building trust and ultimately a strong brand.

Finally, we can ask the question of how e-mall owners should develop interactivity, that is, a closer relationship between consumers and the overall e-mall site. The answer here is a combination of more effective navigability (site design) and retail mix quality (mix of tenants).

There still remain some unanswered questions, particularly for more developed e-malls, such as Craigslist.com. What is the role of web atmospherics for the value of such sites? What is the best way of handling the security and privacy guarantees? What is the best way of handling returned goods? What is the scope to internationalise such e-malls? Future research is needed to resolve these issues, though the reader might provisionally come up with his or her own solutions or approach.

**CHAPTER SUMMARY**

As in other chapters, we started by examining conventional (mall) retailing practices and principles as a basis for designing the appropriate e-retail (e-mall) system. The main finding from conventional mall marketing is the need to control the brand image through the tenant mix, merchandise quality, services and atmospherics, as well as building a good landlord-tenant relationship.

# E-MALLS

More or less the same principles, suitably adapted, apply in the case of e-malls. Careful selection of the tenants and the quality of merchandise was important, with a suggestion not to have too many pure click e-retailers as tenants. A healthy proportion of 'brick-and-click' e-retailers relative to 'click' e-retailers helps to build familiarity with the consumer and contributes to greater trust of the e-mall overall.

E-malls are not radically different from single-ownership e-retailers covered in other chapters, but there is a greater threshold in terms of 'acceptance' of (trust towards) an e-mall. Part of the problem with trust of an e-mall relates to the general lack of familiarity of e-malls and a lack of a norm or experience in how to use e-malls. Just as Amazon.com invented a simple five-step model for how e-shoppers could use an e-retailer, there is a need to do something similar for e-mall shopping. Not surprisingly, trust and interactivity were found to be the main influences on the strength of an e-mall brand.

In the following chapter we will investigate how business models may be useful to e-retailers.

## Case study 9.1
## AUSTRALIAN RESEARCH E-MALLS

This chapter is a little different to other chapters in that instead of several smaller case studies, we have one mega case study of two Australian malls. The details of the case study follow in the next section.

**Click onto:** www.ozeshopping.com.au

### An Australian research study of two e-malls

The authors have developed a questionnaire based on the literature, deriving issues important to Internet users/shoppers relevant to their attitudes towards purchasing from e-malls. Respondents were asked to familiarize themselves with two pre-determined Australian sites, namely *ozeshopping.com.au* and *sofcom.com.au*, and explore the two sites' features before answering a set of Likert scale–based questions.

By way of broad description, there was a difference in the overall image of the two sites. Ozeshopping.com.au was fairly close to what you might term or imagine a regular (online) shopping mall. It had an anchor store, that was an online department store (dstore) and more than 30 tenants, including many well-known Australian brick-and-click e-retailers (such as Sanity or Strathfield). The site was fairly organized and looked like a solid upper-middle market mall. In contrast, sofcom.com.au had an entirely different image. It came across as much more variable in the types of tenants, from sophisticated to somewhat 'seedy'. Most of the tenants could be said to have a strong tourist-Australiana image, making it more of a niche mall. It had an anchor store (e-store; an electrical goods store) and had a higher proportion of pure click retailers.

In constructing the survey items specific to this study, prior studies were reviewed to extrapolate items examining web usage and branding theory research, a survey was designed with items intended to capture the underlying multi-item constructs of e-brand attitudes, e-interactivity, e-trust, navigability and retailer-quality. Each survey item was measured on a seven-point scale of (1) disagree very strongly to (7) agree very strongly.

The current case focuses particularly on the potential roles of interactivity and e-trust inter alia, in influencing brand attitudes with respect to e-malls. Both *interactivity* and *e-trust* have previously been shown to be powerful and central determinants of brand attitudes with respect to a particular e-retail site (Merrilees and Fry, 2002) and the same might be expected with respect to e-malls.

The study consisted of 116 Australian undergraduate marketing students from a large regional area. The student sample *met the minimum conditions* needed for this study in that they (1) were familiar and experienced with the Internet for information search and (2) were of an age (mostly 18 to 25) that comprises a major segment in the Internet buying market. Importantly, as the study focuses on purchase intention rather than actual purchase, it was not critical that respondents had previously purchased via the Internet. All respondents had access to the Internet, either privately or through university facilities. The sample consisted of an equal number of males and females with a median age of 21 years.

## *Modelling the determinants of e-mall brand attitudes*

This entailed estimating the various paths of the model, with the emphasis on a multiple regression of the determinants of e-mall brand attitude, for each e-mall separately. Table 9.1 summarises the regression analysis that explains e-mall brand attitude. It should be noted that the statistical fit is good, with adjusted R-squares of 0.66 and 0.57.

**Table 9.1** Determinants of brand attitudes in two Australian e-malls

| Variable | Ozeshopping e-mall | Sofcom e-mall |
| --- | --- | --- |
| Constant | −0.37 | −0.20 |
|  | (1.1) | (0.6) |
| E-trust | 0.54 | 0.54 |
|  | (6.06)** | (6.69)** |
| Interactivity | 0.32 | 0.29 |
|  | (3.62)** | (3.62)** |
| Adjusted R-square | 0.66 | 0.57 |
| F-ratio | 106.3** | 71.8** |

*Notes:* * Denotes significant t or F value at 5% level;
\*\* Denotes significant t or F value at 1% level.

The main findings in Table 9.1 are that both e-trust and interactivity were key determinants of brand attitude for the sample of users of the two Australian e-malls. The standardized beta coefficient on the e-trust variable was 0.5, meaning that for every additional *two* points of e-trust (measured on a seven-point scale), there will be a *one*-point increase in positive brand attitude towards that e-mall. Similarly, the beta coefficient on the interactivity variable was approximately 0.33, that means for every *three* points of interactivity (measured on a seven-point scale), there will be a *one* point increase in positive brand attitude towards that e-mall. Both of these two variables were significant at the 1% level, with high *t*-values. No other variables had a statistically significant effect on brand attitude.

### Modelling the determinants of e-mall trust

The results of ascertaining the determinants of e-mall trust produced only one statistically significant variable, namely interactivity (see Table 9.2). There was a high beta coefficient of interactivity on e-trust for both of the e-mall sites. That is, the greater the level of interactivity, the greater the level of e-trust, that was significant at the 1% level.

### Modelling the determinants of e-interactivity

The regression results are shown in Table 9.3. The perceived interactivity of each e-malls can be largely explained by a combination of both the site navigability and the quality of the retail mix in the mall.

**Table 9.2** Determinants of e-trust in two Australian e-malls

| Variable | Ozeshopping e-mall | Sofcom e-mall |
|---|---|---|
| Constant | 1.30 (4.31)** | 1.81 (5.30)** |
| Interactivity | 0.78 (12.98)** | 0.62 (8.26)** |
| Adjusted R-square | 0.60 | 0.38 |
| F-ratio | 168.4** | 68.3** |

Notes: * Denotes significant t or F value at 5% level;
** Denotes significant t or F value at 1% level.

**Table 9.3** Determinants of interactivity in two Australian e-malls

| Variable | Ozeshopping e-mall | Sofcom e-mall |
|---|---|---|
| Constant | 1.25 (3.02)** | 1.28 (4.57)** |
| Navigability | 0.49 (5.15)** | 0.55 (6.88)** |
| Retail mix quality | 0.21 (2.21)* | 0.26 (3.23)** |
| Adjusted R-square | 0.42 | 0.50 |
| F-ratio | 40.5** | 55.8** |

Note: * Denotes significant t or F value at 5% level;
** Denotes significant t or F value at 1% level.

## LESSONS FROM AUSTRALIAN CASE STUDIES OF E-MALLS

The main finding of our empirical work is that both e-trust and interactivity were crucial in forming brand attitudes towards each of the two Australian e-mall sites studied. In broad terms this finding is similar to earlier research that had found the same two variables were also crucial in forming brand attitudes at the site of an individual e-retailer, CD Now (Amazon) (Merrilees and Fry, 2002). Thus these two variables seem fundamental in explaining brand attitudes of sites that use a variety of *business-to-consumer* business models.

However there are some subtle differences in comparing brand attitudes across e-retailers and e-malls. With the *e-retailer site*, interactivity was the most important determinant of brand attitudes, while with the two *e-mall sites*, e-trust was relatively more important. This suggests that with the more complex and multi-retailer site, trust seems to be a bigger issue. This makes sense in that trust is more difficult to assess if there are multiple retailers and doubts can arise if trustworthy retailers are juxtaposed with less trustworthy retailers.

Trust is most likely a key factor in *any* company's reputation, whether e-commerce or not. This seems likely because trust is akin to being reassured that the specific company will look after the interests of the user or consumer and protect them in all respects. It is a form of meta-guarantee, one that goes beyond just a product guarantee. Trust is likely to be even more important in the context of e-retailers and extremely important for e-mall owners. This is because major consumer concerns over the adequacy of credit card security or the way that privacy matters are handled could deter the completion of transactions; especially if different firms have different security and privacy policies.

The issue of e-trust can also be explored by comparing the Table 9.2 results across the two e-malls. The www.sofcom.com.au site is different to the www.ozeshopping.com.au site in that it has less of the large, well-known branded 'bricks' retailers and more smaller retailers and pure e-retailers. These characteristics make it harder for the sofcom e-mall to gain the trust of users. This may be why the constant term in the sofcom mall is larger and more significant than that for the ozeshopping mall; that is, 1.81 versus 1.30.

The case breaks new ground in explaining brand attitudes in the *e-mall* context. The two most important drivers of e-mall brand attitudes were *e-trust* and *e-interactivity*. These relationships were both large (that is, large regression beta coefficients) and highly statistically significant (at the 1% level). Thus the model suggests that e-trust and e-interactivity are two key elements in successful web branding of e-mall sites.

The results suggest that trust is relatively more important for e-malls compared to individual e-retailer sites in terms of developing Internet brand attitudes. This may be due to the diversity of retailers in the mall context and the inclusion of smaller retailers and pure e-retailers. Owners and prospective developers of future e-mall sites need to be cognizant of the need to develop an overall strategy of trust building. This includes the need to put in place various explicit policies and implement other mechanisms that help project confidence and trust to the consumer and other stakeholders. It also requires careful selection of on-line tenants, those that will instil trust among e-mall consumers. Finally and perhaps most importantly, e-mall sites need to develop interactivity, because this is fundamental to e-trust specifically and ongoing relationship more generally.

## QUESTIONS

*Brief feedback to these questions is included at the back of the book.*

**Question 9.1** – What is important in managing conventional malls?

**Question 9.2** – How do you *translate* the principles in managing conventional malls to e-malls?

**Question 9.3** – Do you regard a shopping bot as an intelligent agent or a virtual mall? Why?

**Question 9.4** – Why are e-malls less dominant in cyberspace than brick malls are in physical space?

## GLOSSARY

**E-mall**  An e-mall is sometimes referred to as a cyber-mall or a virtual mall or an e-shopping centre. It brings together a number of separately owned e-retail sites to a single virtual location, with the individual e-retailers paying rent to the centre management, as in an offline mall.

**Shopping bots**  Tools that help e-shoppers identify, locate and compare products available from e-retailers. The bots can be considered from either a consumer/shopper perspective or an e-retailer one.

## FURTHER READING

Bennett R and Savani S. (2011) 'Retailers preparedness for introduction of third wave (ubiquitous) computing applications: A survey of UK companies'. *International Journal of Retail and Distribution Management*, 39 (5): 306–325.

Calderwood E and Freathy P. (2014) 'Consumer mobility in the Scottish isles: The impact of Internet adoption upon retail travel patterns'. *Transportation Research A*, 59: 192–203.

## REFERENCES

Crank A. (2015) 'Virtual reality mall lets consumers shop alongside digital giraffes and zebras', [Online] Available at *de zeen magazine*: http://www.dezeen.com/

2015/11/11/virtual-reality-theatre-mall-allison-crank-design-academy-eindhoven-dutch-design-week-2015/ [Accessed 19 March 2016].

Deck S. (1997) 'Ease of navigation key to successful e-malls', *Computerworld*, July 14, p. 4.

Dennis C, Murphy J, Marsland D, Cockett W and Patel T. (2002) 'Measuring image: Shopping centre case studies', *International Review of Retail, Distribution and Consumer Research*, 12 (4): 353–373.

Dong X and Su L. (1997) 'Search engines on the World Wide Web and information retrieval from the Internet: A review and evaluation', *Online and CD-ROM Review*, 21 (2): 67–81.

Hall E. (1998) 'Viaweb Store 4.0 makes I-commerce setup simple', *InfoWorld*, February 2, p. 47.

Hill S. (2000) 'To de-mall or e-mall? Shaping Web shopping', *Apparel Industry Magazine*, February: 36–37.

Hoang L-M. (2015) 'Trillenium takes virtual reality into online shopping', [Online] Available at Reuters: http://www.reuters.com/article/us-britain-retail-trillenium-idUSKCN0RB1I220150912 [Accessed 26 March 2016].

Howard E. (1997) 'The management of shopping centres: Conflict or cooperation?' *The International Review of Retail, Distribution and Consumer Research*, 7 (3): 249–261.

Ingham L. (2015) 'Virtual reality shopping: VR stores to let you visit the mall from your sofa', [Online] Available at Factor Tech: http://factor-tech.com/connected-world/18872-virtual-reality-shopping-vr-stores-to-let-you-visit-the-mall-from-your-sofa/ [Accessed 26 March 2016].

Merrilees B. (2001) 'Do traditional strategic concepts apply in the e-marketing context?' *Journal of Business Strategies*, 18 (2): 177–190.

Merrilees B and Fry M. (2002) 'Corporate branding: A framework for e-retailers', *Corporate Reputation Review*, 5 (2,3): 213–225.

O'Hara C. (2001) 'Defense e-mall changes hands', *Federal Computer Week* (February 19), 15 (4): 1.

Roberts J and Merrilees B. (2003) 'Managing the mall relationship: Does trust lead to cooperation?' *ANZMAC Conference Proceedings*, Adelaide.

Rowley J. (2000) 'Shopping bots: Intelligent shopper or virtual department store?' *International Journal of Retail and Distribution Management*, 28 (7): 297–306.

Sit J, Merrilees B and Birch D. (2003) 'Entertainment-seeking shopping centre patrons: The missing segments', *International Journal of Retail and Distribution Management*, 32 (2): 80–94.

Strom D. (1998) 'Building your online storefront', *InfoWorld*, February 2: 45, 47.

Turban E, King D, Lee J K, Liang T-P and Turban D C. (2015) *E-Commerce: Mechanisms, Platforms, and Tools, Springer Texts in Business and Economics,* Switzerland: Springer International, pp. 51–99.

# Chapter 10

# E-retailing models

### LINKS TO OTHER CHAPTERS

- Chapter 4 – Understanding and communicating with the e-consumer
- Chapter 5 – Information search on the web
- Chapter 6 – E-store design: navigability, interactivity and web atmospherics
- Chapter 7 – E-service
- Chapter 8 – Branding on the web
- Chapter 9 – E-malls
- Chapter 11 – M-shopping

### KEY LEARNING POINTS

*After completing this chapter you will have an understanding of*

- The categorisation of e-retailing business models
- The electronic shopping test to assess a product's suitability for e-retailing
- Assessing the fit between an organisation's objectives and the available business models

### ORDERED LIST OF SUBTOPICS

- What is a business model
- The retail participant groups in a retailer's environment
- Distribution channels

247

- Revenue streams
- Assessment of the fit between organisational objectives and the business models
- Assessment of product suitability for e-retailing using the de Kare-Silver's electronic shopping ES test
- Chapter summary and conclusions
  ❖ Case study
  ❖ Questions
  ❖ Glossary
  ❖ References

## WHAT IS A BUSINESS MODEL?

Though often quoted in Internet and e-commerce literature, the term business model has no uniform definition. In this text, we will define an Internet business model as follows:

> An Internet business model is an organisation's strategic business system for producing a customer oriented value proposition. The business system is composed one or more targeted customer segments; hardware and software architecture, the organisation's product offering; the organisation's business partners and associated resources required to achieve the organisational objectives.

As suggested by Eduard (2001), many retailers carry out their business through five retail participant groups in their environment and the five Olympic rings in Figure 10.1 can simplify these elements.

■ *Figure 10.1* Five rings of influence in the business environment
Source: Eduard (2001)

# THE RETAIL PARTICIPANT GROUPS IN A RETAILER'S ENVIRONMENT

## Customers

Central to the retailer's marketing concept is the customer. To satisfy customer needs and wants an organisation must comprehend the nature of their relevant customer base. Useful for this purpose is the segmentation of the customers into logical groups, for example geographic regions or purchase frequency.

## Staff

Currently, frontline employees need to establish strong relationships with consumers, for maintaining market share and providing retailer information for increasing business profitability. The continuous progress in information and communication technologies allows transferring employees' skills to an automated technological process and firms' knowledge to a system that delivers enriched information, while staff might use these tools for improving their professional practice (Pantano and Migliarese, 2014). As a consequence, these new technologies affect relationships (Wagner et al., 2003; Sun et al., 2009; Gaur et al., 2012; Drollinger and Comer, 2013), as well as the way the information is shared between employee and consumer (Choe, 2008). For this reason, some studies consider the customer-employee relations in contrast with consumer-technology interaction emerging in the new retail environment (Keeling et al., 2013). For instance, self-service systems might reduce consumers' interactions with employees.

## Shareowners

Persons owning shares in a retailer require information on the operation and strategy of the organisation to be able to monitor the investments. In the pre-online era, the shareholder was restricted to information from printed annual reports, the annual general meeting, direct mail, and telephone enquiries made upon the retailer. Now with the web, the shareholder may interact with the retailer by monitoring the retailer's website for breaking news, the shareholder exchanging e-mail correspondence with retailing staff, and the shareholder exchanging comments with other shareholders through online channels (including social media), and through consumer analytics (i.e. Google analytics).

## Suppliers, partners and dealers

Operation of retail activities is not done in isolation. Retailers require business suppliers and stakeholders to provide merchandise supplies, financial systems, logistics, legal advice and ancillary services. Online architecture made up of the Internet and electronic data interchange (EDI) systems enable the business suppliers and partners to keep the stakeholders informed of activities with a minimum of delay and thereby permit quicker responses and feedback.

## Community

The community is composed not only of current and prospective shoppers but also individuals and groups that will exert influence upon others who will in turn determine the operating environment of the retailer. Growth in the community awareness of environmental, ethical, and social welfare issues has led to greater attention being paid to business operations. Members of the community seek to acquire information on the activities of retailers and any potential negative affects on the environment, such as the use and disposal of packaging waste. Organisations can use Internet information facilities (i.e. webpages or Facebook groups/pages) to provide public relations communications to emphasise positive corporate environmental issues and counter negative impressions held by the community.

From interactions with these five retail participant groups, the retail organisation may anticipate positive or negative outcomes that will be quantitative or qualitative. Quantitative outcomes in the business environment are most readily revealed as number of units sold, the revenue figures generated, returns on investment and company share price. Not as easy to measure, though still essential to the successful operation of a business are qualitative outcomes. Examples of qualitative outcomes include customer loyalty, client satisfaction, employee loyalty, corporate image and supplier confidence.

> **THINK POINT**
>
> With so many academic articles written on the significance of qualitative outcomes, i.e. customer loyalty, why aren't these issues as prominent in a published summaries of retailing activities as sales revenues and inventory costs?

# E-RETAILING MODELS

## Categorising e-retailing business models

For the e-retailer to integrate the needs of the five retail participant groups, adapt to the merchandise mix offered and still meet the business objectives, the e-retailer may select from a variety of business models. Initially, the e-retail business models are categorised by *Distribution Channel*, that is, how the customers will access the retailer's merchandise mix. Following this, the business models may be categorised by *Revenue Stream* used to maintain the sales activity for the retailer.

## DISTRIBUTION CHANNELS

The logistics for the retailer and prospective customer to establish contact and achieve an exchange of merchandise for payments have not always required a physical store. Apart from the physical *bricks-and-mortar* store, the retailing channel is also achievable through *direct retailing* and online through a *virtual retailer*.

## Virtual retailer

The increase of online commerce, also supported by the integration of e-commerce with social media with emphasis on companies' Facebook pages, strongly encouraged the development of *virtual retailers* or *pure-play* e-retailers. Perhaps the first best-known virtual retailer is Amazon.com, which started selling books over the web in 1995. The *virtual retailer* enables Internet users to conduct retailing activities previously restricted to store-based retailers (i.e. product and price comparisons and payment systems) but in a speedier and more convenient manner.

## Bricks-and-mortar retailers

With the establishment of the *virtual retailer* came a renaming of the traditional retailer to accommodate the e-commerce environment. Retailers retaining a physical store presence are now termed "*bricks-and-mortar*" retailers. A significant difference between the *virtual retailer* and the *bricks-and-mortar* retailer is the ability of the prospective *bricks-and-mortar* retail customer to physically inspect store merchandise before making a purchase and exiting the store.

## Direct retailers

*Direct retailers* have utilised a variety of distribution methods to provide a retail space for the customer. Examples of *direct retailers* have included

**251**

# E-RETAILING MODELS

catalogue marketing since the 1800s — that is, the Sears catalogue; door-to-door selling, e.g. Avon since the 1960s; telephone shopping since the 1970s, e.g. Lands' End (http://www.landsend.com); and 24-hour television shopping since the 1980s, e.g. QVC (http://www.qvc.com).

## Categorising hybrid retailers

Marketers today are not restricted to just *bricks-and-mortar, direct* and *virtual* categories of retailing. In-between these categories are the three hybrid forms of retailing: the *click-and-mortar retailer*, the *catalogue retailer* and the *digital retailer*.

The *click-and-mortar retailer* has a physical store for consumer shopping and also conducts web-based retail operations through the Internet. In the majority of cases, such a retailer originally transacted business as a *bricks-and-mortar* retailer. In fact, the actual trend is to support offline stores with online ones (e-shops), while many companies simultaneously provide the possibility to buy online or offline at the same price with the same service quality guarantee. In other cases, an established *direct marketer* or *virtual retailer*, such as Amazon in November 2015 (in Seattle, Washington), establishes a store-based retail outlet to provide potential customers the opportunity to physically examine merchandise. As such, the retailer counters one of the leading objections to online purchases, the inability to personally view and inspect items before making a purchase.

*Catalogue retailer*: Portal-based catalogue-marketing companies have been very successful in meeting their marketing and sales objectives. By developing websites that are online representations of printed brochures and catalogues, the catalogue companies are able to widen their distribution network without replacing or alienating their postal clients. The positive outcomes in this channel are reduced distribution costs; the expansion of the potential customer base; and speedier more convenient feedback to prospective clients.

*Digital retailer*: Consumer access to the Internet has provided a logical environment for the distribution and exchange of items that are deliverable in a digital form. Currently, popular digital items sold by retailers over the Internet include recorded music and computer software. While visiting a digital retailer's website, the Internet user may sample such items, e.g. hear the music or try the software, before making a purchase decision. Once happy with the sampled digital product, the Internet customer may download the complete digital product and arrange for payment.

## REVENUE STREAMS

Customer-centred e-retailing business models are often categorised by the revenue stream achieved by the online retailer. The four revenue business models are based on *advertising, merchandise sales, transaction fee* and *subscriptions*.

### Advertising-based e-retailing

The retailer generates revenues by selling adverting space on their website. As one of the original revenue models of the Internet, portals such as Yahoo have charged third parties a flat fee for placing an advertisement on their webpage or charged for each web visitor that clicks on the web advertisement, and this is known as the "click-through" rate to a third party's website. Consumer analytics such as Google analytics (basic analytics provided by Google Inc. free of charge for companies) can monitor the traffic coming to a web (from e-mails, banners, etc.) and provide this site traffic data to the e-retailer for marketing decisions. A few years ago this service led to complaints from web users about invasion of privacy to which Double Click responded with a revised Privacy Policy that has placated much of this criticism and maintained the organisation's competitive advantage.

### Merchandise sales e-retailing

As with the traditional bricks-and-mortar retailer, this revenue business model produces revenue from the sale of the retailer's merchandise over the web, i.e. Sanity (http://www.sanity.com.au) selling recorded music.

### Transaction fee e-retailing

Similar to the concept of brokerage, retailers may charge a third party for the marketing of merchandise to the retailer's customers. The most successful Internet example of transaction fee e-retailing is eBay.com (http://www.ebay.com) where the auction facilitator receives a fee once the successful bidder finalises an online auction using eBay's online technology.

### Subscription e-retailing

As an adaptation of direct marketing, the subscription-based e-retailing revenue model allows consumers to access merchandise facilities, usually

# E-RETAILING MODELS

in a digital form, and through a subscription, e.g. NYTimes.com (http://nytimes.com) for web-based archival news stories.

> **THINK POINT**
>
> Many sites provide free content or content at reduced cost through subsidies provided by adverting revenues. This revenue requires the site to monitor and record website traffic with such devices as cookie files. If site visitors get the advantages of such free or subsidized content, why are many people so against their web usage being monitored?

## ASSESSMENT OF THE FIT BETWEEN ORGANISATIONAL OBJECTIVES AND THE BUSINESS MODELS

In selecting the business model suited to a retail operation, the retailer will initially assess their marketing and sales objectives for the three principal retail channels: *bricks-and-mortar*, *direct retailers* and *virtual retailer*. Samples of these objectives are given below for the five retail participant groups using a five star scale; one star is given for low and five stars for high, representing the level of potential in each retail channel. Note that objectives are *samples* and not an exhaustive list. A retailer's unique environment may require the retailer to add or remove objectives from the following tabled samples.

### Scoring the retailer's objectives for customers

The potential for a retail channel to meet the individual objectives for customers is assessed out of a five (5). A retail channel with little potential to meet an objective scores one (1) increasing to five (5) for a retail channel with a high potential to meet the customer objectives. Using the series of objectives in Table 10.1 and totalling the scores for each retail channel, the maximum potential score is twenty-five (25).

The structure of each retail channel and the method of accessing the channel's target audience provide advantages for communicating certain information and appealing to certain human senses. For communicating information that appeals to the senses of sight, sound, touch, taste and smell of customers, there is currently no better medium than the face-to-face interaction possible in a physical retail store. This conclusion is reinforced by the 20/25 score for the *bricks-and-mortar* retailers in Table 10.1.

**Table 10.1** Assessment of retail channels in meeting a retailer's objectives for customers

| Retailer's objectives for customers | Bricks and mortar | Direct retailers | Virtual retailer |
|---|---|---|---|
| • Inform prospects of product details/features | 5 | 3 | 4 |
| • Demonstrate product features | 5 | 1 | 2 |
| • Stimulate prospect interest and customer demand by communicating details about the retailer's available and pending merchandise lines | 5 | 3 | 4 |
| • Advise prospects and customers of retailer's achievements (e.g. sales levels, awards) | 3 | 5 | 3 |
| • Provide merchandise access to potential customers in multiple geographic locations (domestic *and* international) | 2 | 4 | 5 |
| Total score for the retail channel | 20 | 16 | 18 |

Restricted to audio and static visual images, *direct retailers* cannot provide moving a tactile experience for a customer and this resulted in a score of 16/25. Encouragingly, research into direct retailing shows that such customers often retain the retailer's marketing correspondence to be re-read in the future. Such correspondence may include details (e.g. retailer achievements) often overlooked while browsing in a retail store or un-clicked on the retailer's website.

Though computer software and hardware facilities for the web are improving to encompass audio, video and tactile reproductions of the real world, the experience is still not a replacement for the communication facilities and immediate feedback of the store environment. As an advantage over the direct retailers, the virtual retailer's ability to include more realistic virtual experience (i.e. augmented reality tools) and online search facilities enables improved demonstration ability for merchandise offered, giving the *virtual retailer* a score of 18/25.

Globalisation created by the Internet means that many retail names formerly restricted to domestic markets have become internationally recognised brands. While some retailers have attempted to establish a physical bricks-and-mortar presence in overseas markets, the logistical costs and unique requirements of the overseas locations has for some retailers resulted in major losses and eventual withdrawal from the overseas market.

# E-RETAILING MODELS

*Direct retailers* have utilised the well-established international postal and courier systems for decades. With little more than a sales orientation, many direct retailers have accepted orders from overseas customers, packaged the orders and passed the distribution responsibility to transport groups such as DHL (http://www.dhl.com) or FedEx (http://www.fedex.com). The transport groups arrange pickup of the packaged merchandise, export documents, customs clearances, final delivery and in some cases payment clearances. For a small direct retailer, such international sales provide new market revenues without a major investment in logistics infrastructure, i.e. a specialised international shipping group. A drawback for the direct retailer is not being known by potential customers in other parts of the country and overseas. Many of us have turned to the phonebook to look for a supplier but what if you don't have every phonebook in the world? The answer is to turn to the World Wide Web and use search engines. The Internet has given every person with access to the web an access to every virtual retailer as testified by the meteoric growth of Amazon.com (http://www.amazon.com) from the sale of books to a few avid readers to become one of the largest book and video retailers in the world, and all this exclusively online. Worldwide access to the web is now so entrenched that successfully established direct retailers such as Lands' End (http://www.landsend.com) established sophisticated order taking websites and integrate sites into the retailer's marketing and distribution plans as an added retail channel.

## Scoring the retailer's objectives for staff

The potential for a retail channel to meet the retailer's objectives for staff is assessed out of a five (5). A retail channel with little potential scores one (1), increasing to five (5) for a retail channel with a high potential to meet the individual staff objectives. Using the series of objectives in Table 10.2 and totalling the scores for each retail channel, the maximum potential score is fifteen (15).

Why did each retail channel in Table 10.2 receive the same score of 15/15 for staff objectives? It is because no matter what retail channels a marketer uses, staff must be prepared to provide the finest service possible within the constraints and advantages of that channel. Consider the negative perception of a prospect should they ask a question concerning the exchange policy of the retailer's staff (face to face, by mail or through a website) only to receive the reply *"I don't know"* and without the follow up *"..but I will find out and get back to you by (x period)."* Quality support systems are also essential in all retail channels because it is the retailer's personnel that receive the ire of annoyed prospects when an electronic system (e.g. website or ordering facilities) fails.

# E-RETAILING MODELS

**Table 10.2** Assessment of retail channels in meeting a retailer's objectives for staff

| Retailer's objectives for staff | Retail channel | | |
|---|---|---|---|
| | Bricks and mortar | Direct retailers | Virtual retailer |
| ■ Training: For staff to provide prospective customers with information about the retailer's policies (e.g. returns and privacy) | 5 | 5 | 5 |
| ■ Training: For staff to respond to the queries of prospective customers about applicability of the retailer's policies and information about the suitability of the merchandise to the customer's needs/applications | 5 | 5 | 5 |
| ■ Support: Provide systems to enable staff to maintain the sales systems (store-based and web shopping cart procurement systems) which include a 24 hour, 7 days a week website and data collection methods | 5 | 5 | 5 |
| Total score for the retail channel | 15 | 15 | 15 |

## Scoring the retailer's objectives for shareholders

The potential for a retail channel to meet the retailer's objectives for shareholders is assessed out of a five (5). A retail channel with little potential scores one (1), increasing to five (5) for a retail channel with a high potential to meet the individual shareholder objectives. Using the series of objectives in Table 10.3 and totalling the scores for each retail channel, the maximum potential score is fifteen (15).

The immediacy of response and round-the-clock access of the Internet places the *virtual retailer* in an enviable position for providing shareholders with detailed information as demonstrated by the 15/15 score in Table 10.3. Unlike the brief summaries of financial and business information conventionally available in an annual report, web-based documents may incorporate interactive graphics and video to display information for more impact upon the shareholders.

Not all shareholders will be retail customers and therefore not exposed to the marketing communications provided by both *bricks-and-mortar* and *direct retailers*. To inform their shareholders these retailers traditionally use printed media and call centre responses to shareholder enquiries, therefore

# E-RETAILING MODELS

**Table 10.3** Assessment of retail channels in meeting a retailer's objectives for shareholders

| Retailer's objectives for shareholders | Bricks and mortar | Direct retailers | Virtual retailer |
|---|---|---|---|
| ■ The shareholders have access to the latest financial data pertaining to their retail investment | 3 | 3 | 5 |
| ■ Keep shareholders informed about upcoming matters that require their attention, i.e. meetings (annual and extraordinary) or changes in payment methods | 3 | 3 | 5 |
| ■ Advise shareholders of "news" which may include industry awards, new merchandise lines and responses to media reports | 3 | 3 | 5 |
| Total score for the retail channel | 9 | 9 | 15 |

giving both retail channels a score of 9/15 in Table 10.3. Though effective, such methods have high labour costs and are slower to update when compared to the information storage and retrieval available with web-based retailing.

## Scoring the retailer's objectives for suppliers, partners and dealers

The potential for a retail channel to meet the retailer's objectives for suppliers, partners and dealers is assessed out of a five (5). A retail channel with little potential scores one (1), increasing to five (5) for a retail channel with a high potential to meet the individual supplier, partner and dealer objectives. Using the series of objectives in Table 10.4 and totalling the scores for each retail channel, the maximum potential score is fifteen (15).

Synchronising data records between the retailer and their suppliers, partners and dealers is essential to avoid such errors as:

- Missed or duplication of orders;
- Misdirected correspondence to personnel or addresses that have changed;
- Non-compliance of legislation (e.g. government reporting schedules);
- Missed targets (e.g. end of month summaries or sale dates).

# E-RETAILING MODELS

**Table 10.4** Assessment of retail channels in meeting a retailer's objectives for suppliers, partners and dealers

|  | Retail channel |  |  |
| --- | --- | --- | --- |
| Retailer's objectives for suppliers, partners and dealers | Bricks and mortar | Direct retailers | Virtual retailer |
| • Maintain up-to-date contact information for both the retailer and their third-party providers | 2 | 3 | 4 |
| • Establish an audit trail to track financial transactions and exchanges of information | 4 | 4 | 5 |
| • Fast and accurate recovery of data (for both the retailer and their third-party providers) following a disaster | 3 | 3 | 4 |
| Total score for the retail channel | 9 | 10 | 13 |

*Direct retailers* have honed their record systems to finalise sales and associated records in the absence of physical customer to score a total of 10/15. When disputes with customers and suppliers do occur, it may take time for the direct retailers to consult and correlate the electronic and manual record systems. *Bricks-and-mortar* retailers also pay a great deal of attention to daily summarising of financial exchanges. Though important, third-party contact records (e.g. contact names at suppliers or shipping agents) may not be updated as regularly nor do they carry the same level of priority customer interactions and this lessens the overall score to 9/15. By the nature of their operational environment, *virtual retailers* depend upon efficient real-time data exchanges through the Internet network which itself depends upon detailed and automated record keeping of transmitted information. Such an improved information exchange with the relevant parties gave the virtual retailer a higher score of 13/15 assuming the e-retailer and their third-party partners regularly update and utilise the pertinent data over the Internet.

## Scoring the retailer's objectives for the community

The potential for a retail channel to meet the stated retailer's objectives for the community is assessed out of a five (5). A retail **channel** with little potential scores one (1), increasing to five (5) for a retail channel with a high potential to meet the individual community objectives. Using the series of objectives in Table 10.5 and totalling the scores for each retail channel, the maximum potential score is fifteen (15).

# E-RETAILING MODELS

**Table 10.5** Assessment of retail channels in meeting a retailer's objectives for the community

| Retailer's objectives for the community | Bricks and mortar | Direct retailers | Virtual retailer |
|---|---|---|---|
| ■ Keep the public informed of improvements in the retailer's social activities, e.g. increased recycling | 2 | 3 | 5 |
| ■ Promote the contributions to charitable instructions | 3 | 3 | 5 |
| ■ Promote training and employment programs | 3 | 3 | 5 |
| Total score for the retail channel | 8 | 9 | 15 |

An integral component of modern marketing plans is keeping the community informed about the direction and intentions of the retailer. For each retail channel, there are alternative communications mediums to carry messages to the relevant community. The previous communications mediums available to the *bricks-and-mortar* and *direct retailers* include print (e.g. newspapers), broadcast (e.g. television), while the current one might also include social media (e.g. Facebook), and mobile (e.g. ad hoc mobile apps). Though extensive, such mediums may not reach every community person that has a stake in a *bricks-and-mortar* and *direct retailer* channels and this restricts the total scores to 8/15 and 9/15, respectively, by pushing bricks-and-mortar to include also interactive channels (i.e. social media, website, mobile apps, etc.). In communications to the community, the *virtual retailers* have an interactive advantage over the other two retail channels. The e-retailer's website may incorporate a series of messages to support their objectives for the community in a more convincing manner. Helping to communicate these messages through the website and achieving a score of 15/15, the retailer may include any of these online facilities:

- Hyperlinks to relevant websites
- Live footage (web cameras streaming video)
- Storage of printable documents (e.g. Adobe Acrobat format)
- Interactive games
- E-mail exchanges
- Live chat and links to social media (i.e. Facebook, Twitter, etc.)
- Mobile version of the website
- Free mobile apps and the link for the direct download

As shown, each of the retail channels, *bricks-and-mortar*, *direct retailers* and *virtual retailer* have varying degrees of suitability to meet organisational objectives. By summing the scores for each objective and each channel, the retailer will identify the retail channel with the greatest opportunity for marketing plan success.

To reiterate, the objectives for the five retail participant groups are *samples* and *not* an exhaustive list for all retailers; the unique environments facing the retailers may require the retailer to add or remove objectives from samples in Tables 10.1 through 10.5. Taking the results for each set of *sample* objectives, the results are 59/85 for *direct* retailers, 61/85 for *bricks-and-mortar* retailers and 76/85 for virtual retailer, placing the *virtual retailer* in the most effective position to meet the sample of objectives for the five retail participant groups. This does not restrict the retailer to a single channel. The growing consumer acceptance of electronic shopping is allowing traditional retailers to expand into multiple retailing channels. To do this and provide the greater likelihood of meeting the retailer's multifaceted objectives, the channels chosen should be in order of their scores, which for this set of objectives is the *virtual retailing*, followed by *bricks-and-mortar* retailing and finally *direct retailing*.

Concentrating on the virtual retailer, the next stage is to gauge how suitable is merchandise for this particular retail channel.

## ASSESSMENT OF PRODUCT SUITABILITY FOR E-RETAILING USING DE KARE-SILVER'S ELECTRONIC SHOPPING ES TEST

In his book, de Kare-Silver (2000) provided a framework to assess products and services for online retailing suitability. The ES (Electronic Shopping) test simultaneously evaluates fit according to three factors: (1) product characteristics; (2) familiarity and confidence; and (3) consumer attributes as displayed in Figure 10.2.

### Product characteristics

Certain products appeal to one or more of the five human senses of sight, sound, smell, taste and touch. The store-based retail environment is most suitable where a consumer's purchase behaviour benefits from a physical interaction with a particular product. Conversely, products that primarily activate the sight and sound senses, i.e. music and movies, are most suited for an electronic retailing environment. In addition to the five senses, people assess certain products and services in an analytical manner using what de Kare-Silver describes as the intellect sense. Figure 10.3 maps the

# E-RETAILING MODELS

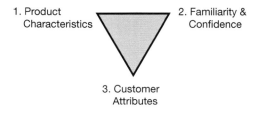

**Figure 10.2** *The Electronic Shopping ES test*
Source: Adapted from de Kare-Silver (2000)

fit between a selection of products and the six noted human senses. Based upon Figure 10.3, very few items are "pure" touch, taste or smell only products. A large group of products utilise the sight and touch senses, thereby making such products suitable for the store-based retail environment. Encouraging for the electronic retailer is the significant number of products that appeal to the senses of sight and sound and are therefore appropriate for online retailing.

*Scoring the electronic shopping with product characteristics*

Using a score out of ten (10), the more a physical a product's appeal, the closer the result is to zero (0). If a product has an appeal that lends itself to the virtual environment of the Internet then the product scores closer to the maximum ten (10). The scoring for product characteristics appears in Figure 10.4.

## Familiarity and confidence

The second component of the ES test examines a consumer's level of familiarity and confidence towards a product or service considered for purchase. Should a consumer have used or purchased a product line in the past and therefore be familiar with that product, that consumer is likely to have a higher level of confidence. As portrayed in Figure 10.5, this greater familiarity and confidence reduce the consumer's need to physically handle the product in a future purchase and improve the product's suitability for an online retailing environment.

The confidence that consumers attribute to a product is not always the result of personal usage. Individuals may develop a positive or negative attitude from communications with family and peer groups or from the reputation associated with a product's brand. On identifying a brand, a consumer will perceive various anticipated value dimensions

# E-RETAILING MODELS

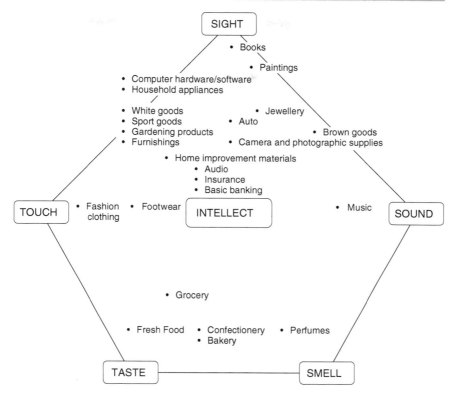

**Figure 10.3** *Product characteristics and the five senses*
Source: Adapted from de Kare-Silver (2000)

**Figure 10.4** *Scoring product characteristics*
Source: Adapted from de Kare-Silver (2000)

even if the consumer has not used a particular product from that brand. Depending upon the brand's reputation for social status and quality of finish, a consumer will depend upon a physical inspection that would usually be associated with trying something new. An electronic retailer that emphasises universally recognised brands will not only attract confident online shoppers but individuals that do little or no online shopping.

# E-RETAILING MODELS

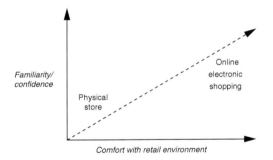

**Figure 10.5** Familiarity/confidence and electronic shopping
Source: Adapted from de Kare-Silver (2000)

*Scoring the electronic shopping with familiarity and confidence*

Using a score to a maximum of ten (10), the individual is given a higher score as his or her familiarity/confidence with a product environment also increases. This familiarity/confidence is gauged by three components: previous level of product usage; the satisfaction gained from using the product; and the familiarity with the reputation and branding of the organisation offering the product. The scoring for familiarity/confidence is displayed in Figure 10.6.

## Customer attributes

The influence and experience with a product or service are themselves not adequate determinants of the retail environment used by a shopper. The failures of many dot.com retailers might result from a misconception that being online was itself a sufficient attraction to Internet sites and sales. Just as traditional retailers try to understand their shoppers to secure sales, online retailers also need to identify consumer attributes, shopping motives and shopping triggers.

A number of researchers have attempted to profile and categorise individuals' online shopping behaviour (Childers et al., 2001;

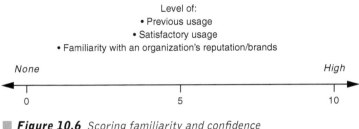

**Figure 10.6** Scoring familiarity and confidence
Source: Adapted from de Kare-Silver (2000)

Gefen et al., 2003; Kau et al., 2003), by proposing the following six categories:

- ***Social shopper:*** Such an individual enjoys the shopping experience. This person visits stores for a pleasurable social experience that may include meeting up with friends or family.
- ***Experimenter:*** As the name implies, this person is at ease with trying new stores and ways of shopping, e.g. the Internet or mobile phone shopping.
- ***Convenience shopper:*** This shopper seeks opportunities to save time when shopping and avoid the delays associated with traditional store shopping, i.e. finding parking or waiting in checkout lines. This shopper often welcomes retail opportunities such as Internet retailing that can remove these "inconvenient" steps to shopping.
- ***Habit die-hard:*** Such an individual is entrenched in a routine or system for doing activities and that includes shopping. They may not be a technophobe or dislike the use of computerisation but still not using electronic shopping because it is a departure from their status quo.
- ***Value shopper:*** This is not merely a seeker of cost savings. Such a shopper looks for the combination of product quality, effective service and monetary outlay that in totality equals good value for that person. Should electronic shopping offer cost savings while for the same quality of product and provide relatively equal service levels to a store alternative, the value shopper should utilise this new shopping channel.
- ***Ethical shopper:*** A small but growing segment, this shopper is less concerned with the shopping medium than the social and ethical issues associated with shopping. For example, is the seller socially responsible in their waste packaging or do they source products from child labour employers? Should the electronic retailer establish the credibility and ethical procedures, the ethical shopper will become a likely user of this retail channel.

Figure 10.7 demonstrates the potential for each of these consumer categories to use electronic shopping: the social shoppers have the lowest electronic shopping potential and convenience shoppers have the greater potential for the new retail channel.

### Scoring the electronic shopping with customer attributes

Owing to the significant influence of this electronic shopping factor, scoring for customer attributes is out of a maximum of thirty (30). This third step in the electronic shopping test begins with an assessment of the

# E-RETAILING MODELS

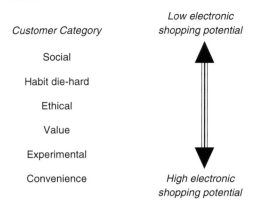

**Figure 10.7** Consumer categories and electronic shopping potential
Source: Adapted from de Kare-Silver (2000)

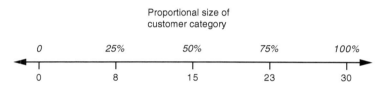

**Figure 10.8** Scoring customer attributes
Source: Adapted from de Kare-Silver (2000)

organisation's proportions for each of the customer categories (i.e. social, ethical, convenience). Next is the evaluation of which customer category dominates (the largest group) the organisation's market for the product in question. Finally, it must be decided if the dominating category is large enough to sustain a targeted marketing effort for electronic shopping, in other words, are the returns from this group worth the expenditure of marketing resources by this organisation? The scoring for customer attributes is shown in Figure 10.8.

The three de Kare-Silver tests for electronic shopping ("ES") are now added together to give a possible maximum ES test score of fifty (50) as shown below.

| | |
|---|---|
| Scoring Product Characteristics | 10 |
| Scoring Familiarity and Confidence | 10 |
| Scoring Customer Attributes | 30 |
| | 50 |

To further illustrate the ES test, a series of products and services are evaluated and displayed in Table 10.6.

# E-RETAILING MODELS

**Table 10.6** Examples of electronic shopping ES tests

| Product or service | 1. Product characteristics (0–10) | 2. Familiarity and confidence (0–10) | 3. Customer attributes (0–30) | Total (0–50) |
|---|---|---|---|---|
| Perfume (new youth oriented) | 1 | 8 | 20 | 29 |
| Perfume (long standing) | 1 | 9 | 5 | 15 |
| Acer Tablet PC | 5 | 6 | 21 | 32 |
| Domestic airline booking | 10 | 8 | 15 | 33 |
| Groceries | 4 | 8 | 15 | 27 |
| Books | 8 | 7 | 23 | 38 |
| DVD movies | 8 | 6 | 25 | 39 |
| Car insurance | 10 | 6 | 9 | 25 |

The results in Table 10.6 indicate that certain products and services have a greater potential for electronic shopping due. To highlight the process, a distinction is given between a new perfume produced for the youth market and a long-standing/traditional perfume. For both a new/youth-oriented perfume and a long-standing brand of perfume the product characteristics are similar and the sense of smell dominates the human assessment. The confidence with the product and brand will be slightly greater for the long-standing perfume as a result of longer exposure to the marketing communications for that brand. Nonetheless, the likely media saturation to promote the youth-oriented new perfume is likely to result in a familiarity level for that market that is not far behind the mature perfume. Where the two perfumes will differ significantly in the ES-test is in the customer attributes component. The target market for the newer perfume has a higher awareness of computer and Internet usage. This market will not feel a high aversion to the concept of electronic shopping for this new perfume, especially if it means price savings and easy access to stock levels that may be lower in retail stores following media promotions. In contrast, the long-standing perfume will have a more mature (older) market with less hands-on exposure to the Internet and not as comfortable with electronic shopping. In addition, while the youth market may congregate with peers at fashion venues, i.e. a mall for the social interaction, the mature market (female) may enjoy the pampering provided at retail

# E-RETAILING MODELS

store perfume counters and again lessen the propensity to shop for such a perfume online. In summary, the new youth-oriented perfume has a greater score (29 versus 15) in the electronic shopping test compared to the long-standing perfume brand.

## CHAPTER SUMMARY AND CONCLUSIONS

Retailing through the Internet requires more sophistication than setting up a website and offering merchandise for sale. The e-retailer needs to consider the business model that will most effectively meet their objectives and the expectations of their prospective customers. Participant groups that will help determine the e-retailer's business model will include the customers; staff; shareholders; suppliers, partners and dealers; and the community. Categorisation of the business model is initially done by type of distribution channel and then by the revenue stream the model derives. To assess the appropriateness of a particular e-retailing business model one may assign a score to the retailer's customer objectives; the retailer's staff objectives; the retailer's shareholder objectives; the retailer's supplier, partner and dealer objectives; and the objectives for retailer's community. The suggested technique in this chapter for scoring participant group objectives is the de Kare-Silver (2000) ES (Electronic Shopping) test.

Not every piece of merchandise will be successful in every channel of distribution and this includes the World Wide Web. We can increase the likelihood of achieving sales success in e-retailing by examining the elements that make up the retailer's market place and using devices such as the ES test to assign a suitability rating before the merchandise is offered online.

## Case study 10.1
## NORDSTROM (http://shop.nordstrom.com/)

The digital landscape is becoming extremely competitive and complex for luxury brands, as the industry witnessed an average 9% increase in online performance between the first and the second half of 2015 (Jones, 2016a). In this scenario, multi-brand retailers lead the luxury e-tailing market, representing four of the top five vendors in the environment (Jones, 2016b). The American firm Nordstrom

# E-RETAILING MODELS

(founded in 1901 in Seattle, Washington) operates in the luxury market with Nordstrom store chain, off-price outlet Nordstrom Rack, flash sale site Haute-Look and menswear service Trunk Club, for a total of 11.67% of market share (Jones, 2016b). This company has built upon its successful business model by expanding the e- and mobile retailing capabilities for its flagship with a new feature able to support shopping via text message: TextStyle. This feature allows consumers to interact via text with a trusted sales associate, performing a secure purchase in a traditional way at the first department store offering this service. Luxury Daily (Jones, 2015) reports the words of a representative of Nordstrom saying that they launched this new service because a third of their consumers told them they prefer to be contacted via text: "We felt enabling a text to buy option was the next step forward that lets customers shop how they want". With TextStyle, consumers might receive personalized private messages (recommendations) from a salesperson, including product information and a photo of the product. If the suggested product meets the consumer's requirements, he/she might purchase through replying to the message with the word "buy", along with his/her unique 10-digit code (for privacy concerns). Afterwards, Nordstrom fulfils the order through the Nordstrom.com account details, and the order is shipped via a standard free delivery.

Another recent innovation in early 2015 consists of the inclusion of a new feature for the Nordstrom iOS application providing consumers the possibility to interact with the catalogue through the new scanning function Scan & Shop. In particular, this allows consumers to bring up the products they prefer on the physical page of the catalogue and buy them through the smartphone (or tablet) through an innovative digital link between the catalogue and the e-commerce.

Moreover, Nordstrom also started a collaboration with social media agency Curalate to use its Like2Buy platform, which hosts Instagram pictures that link directly to a brand's existing e-commerce site, in order to provide another instant access to products.

From the analysis, a continuous need to innovate emerges into Nordstrom marketing strategies. Since the year of foundation, Nordstrom had to improve the retail strategies by innovating, with emphasis towards the digital channels, with consequences on the business models.

## QUESTIONS

*Brief feedback to these questions is included at the back of the book.*

**Question 10.1** – How would use of the retail participant groups in a retailer's environment help minimise channel disintermediation?

**Question 10.2** – If mobile apps are starting offering additional features to exploit the physical catalogues, why do many websites resist offering online catalogue?

**Question 10.3** – Can a customer be in more than one of the A.C. Nielsen electronic shopper categories?

## GLOSSARY

**Bricks-and-mortar retailers**  Retailers retaining a physical store presence are now termed "*bricks-and-mortar*" retailers. A significant difference between the *virtual retailer* and the *bricks-and-mortar* retailer is the ability of the prospective *bricks-and-mortar* retail customer to physically inspect store merchandise before making a purchase and exiting the store.

**Cookie files**  Small computer files that record a website user's site visits to personalize information to improve online sales/services, enable subscribers to access a site without a password, record popular links, record demographics and track visitor search preferences.

**Direct retailers**  *Direct retailers* have utilised a variety of distribution methods to provide a retail space for the customer. Examples of *direct retailers* have included catalogue marketing since the 1800s – i.e. the Sears catalogue; door-to-door selling, e.g. Avon since the 1960s; telephone shopping since the 1970s, e.g. Lands' End (http://www.landsend.com); and 24-hour television shopping since the 1980s, e.g. QVC (http://www.qvc.com).

**Disintermediation**  The elimination of supply chain members.

**Electronic shopping test (ES)**  A framework to assess products and services for online retailing suitability. The "ES" (Electronic Shopping) test simultaneously evaluates fit according to three factors: (1) product characteristics, (2) familiarity and confidence and (3) consumer attributes.

**Virtual retailer**  Enables Internet users to participate in conducting retailing activities previously restricted to store-based retailers, such as buying products.

## REFERENCES

Childers T L, Carr C L, Peck J and Carson S. (2001) Hedonic and utilitarian motivations for online retail shopping behaviour. *Journal of Retailing,* 77 (4): 511–535.

Choe J M. (2008) 'Inter-organizational relationships and the flow of information through valuechain', *Information and Management,* 45: 444–450.

de Kare-Silver M. (2000) *The Electronic Shopping Revolution: Strategies for Retailers and Manufactures*. London: Macmillan Press.

Drollinger T and Comer L B. (2013) 'Salesperson's listening ability as an antecedent to relationship selling', *Journal of Business and Industrial Marketing,* 28 (1): 50–59.

Eduard T. (2001) 'Adding clicks to bricks', *Consulting to Management,* 12 (4): 10–23.

Gaur S S, Herjanto H and Bathula H. (2012) 'Does buyer–seller similarity affect buyer satisfaction with the seller firm?' *International Review of Retail, Distribution and Consumer Research,* 22 (3): 315–335.

Gefen D, Karahanna E and Straub D W. (2003) 'Trust in online shopping: An integrated model', *MIS Quarterly: Management Information Systems,* 27 (1): 51–90.

Gillian C and Richard M S W. (2009) *Strategic Marketing Planning,* 2nd edition. London: Routledge.

Jones S. (2015) *Nordstrom Simplifies Mobile Commerce with Text Message Buying,* [Online] Available at Luxury Daily: http://www.luxurydaily.com/nordstrom-simplifies-mobile-commerce-with-text-message-buying/ [Accessed 17 March 2016].

Jones S. (2016a) *Luxury Brands Ramp Up Digital Efforts, Show Varied Priorities: Report.* [Online] Available at Luxury Daily: http://luxurydaily.com/luxury-brands-ramp-up-digital-efforts-show-varied-priorities-report/ [Accessed 28 June 2016].

Jones S. (2016b) *Luxury Online Retail Market to Reach $41.8B by 2019: Report.* [Online] Available at Luxury Daily: http://luxurydaily.com/luxury-online-retail-market-to-reach-41-8b-by-2019-report/ [Accessed 17 March 2016].

Kau A K, Tang Y E and Ghhose S. (2003) 'Typology of online shoppers', *Journal of Consumer Marketing,* 20 (2–3): 139–156.

Keeling K, Keeling D and McGoldrick P. (2013) 'Retail relationships in a digital age', *Journal of Business Research,* 66: 847–855.

Pantano E and Migliarese P. (2014) 'Exploiting consumer-employee interactions in technology-enriched retail environments through a relational lens', *Journal of Retailing and Consumer Services,* 21 (6): 958–965.

Sun T, Tai Z and Tsai K-C. (2009) 'The role of interdependent self-construal in consumers' susceptibility to retail salespersons' influence: A hierarchical approach', *Journal of Retailing and Consumer Services,* 16 (5): 360–366.

Wagner J A, Klein N M and Keith J E. (2003) 'Buyer–seller relationships and selling effectiveness: The moderating influence of buyer expertise and product competitive position', *Journal of Business Research,* 56: 295–302.

# Chapter 11

# M-shopping

### LINKS TO OTHER CHAPTERS

- Chapter 2 – The business of e-retailing in practice
- Chapter 4 – Understanding and communicating with the e-consumer
- Chapter 6 – E-store design: navigability, interactivity and web atmospherics
- Chapter 7 – E-service

### KEY LEARNING POINTS

*After completing this chapter you will have an understanding of*

- Identify shopper motivations for m-shopping
- Classify products and services into the main m-shopping categories
- Become aware of the developments in m-shopping

### ORDERED LIST OF SUBTOPICS

- Remote shopping continues to evolve, now into m-shopping
- How has m-shopping come about?
- What is needed to go m-shopping?
- Features that distinguish m-commerce from traditional e-commerce
- Contributors to the growth in m-commerce
- Mobile payments
- Profiling the m-shopper

- Chapter summary and conclusions
- Case study
- Question
- Glossary
- Further reading
- References

## REMOTE SHOPPING CONTINUES TO EVOLVE, NOW INTO M-SHOPPING

Retailing has seen many incarnations in the last two hundred years. The diffusion of the smartphone (more in general of mobile devices characterized by high connectivity to Internet) offers another channel for shopping based on mobile networks and applications, designed for an easier, faster, and funnier access to products (Pantano and Verteramo, 2015).

Moreover, mobile technologies can be integrated with additional tools, such as ad Quick Response codes (QR), Near Field Communication (NFC), image recognition, augmented reality, 3D functionalities, and contactless systems for increasing the functions and services. The ubiquitous retailing emerges as an evolution of mobile stores based on the adoption of ubiquitous computing, by creating a new ubiquitous scenario for shopping from mobiles (Pantano, 2013), which will be better detailed in the subsequent chapter. The rapid diffusion of Internet technologies among potential consumers provides new online platforms where clients can purchase directly at home 24/7 (recognized as I-commerce, e-commerce, e-tailing, or e-store), by offering the online easy access to shopping environment (e-store) also to that part of the population with limited mobility.

As the established usage of Internet and mobile devices for shopping, many terms are used to describe the emerging electronic shopping environment. Examples of such terms are mobile commerce, m-commerce, m-business, mobile shopping and m-shopping. For this text we shall use the term m-shopping to define:

> Any retail purchase made from a mobile electronic device, such as a cellular phone through a wireless network; in most cases these transactions are made through Internet mediated facility.

Where store retail meant shopping at the store's address and web shopping means shopping where the computer is wire connected to the Internet, m-shopping provides shopping access where the buyer is geographically located within a wireless network, in a sort of shopping anytime and anywhere.

## HOW HAS M-SHOPPING COME ABOUT?

In less than one decade the Internet has gone from a file transfer facility between academics around the world to a communications and entertainment medium for almost every person with a personal computer. Growth of smartphone usage and mobile Internet connectivy is growing fast.

For instance, recent studies revealed that nearly three-quarters (71%) of marketing e-mails were opened from mobile devices in the UK in the first months of 2015 (WARC, 2015a). This implies that marketers should reflect on developing new e-mail formats, which means both creating simpler messages easily readable from mobiles and creating new post-click experiences able to make the message included more effective. Similarly, consumers declared in recent surveys that around 25% of them had clicked on a mobile ad at least once within the last month to access more information about a product or service, and that of all those who had made a purchase as a result of clicking a mobile ad, 43% added that they had bought in a bricks-and-mortar store, while 82% had done so online (WARC, 2015b). Interviewed consumers further lead marketers to consider that engaging with 1 minute of advertising on mobile devices is equivalent to £6.80 per client for advertisers (WARC, 2015b). In fact, Adyen, the global payments technology company, published the quarterly Mobile Index, which stated that the online payments made through mobile devices continue growing globally, currently accounting for 27.2% of the total online payments made in the first quarter of 2015, up 39% on the corresponding period of the last year (Adyen, 2015). The same report indicates that the total amount of goods purchased via tablets has passed the ones purchased via traditional online channels for the first time since 2013 (Adyen, 2015).

What is clear now is that users are becoming dependent upon the Internet access anywhere (Pantano and Verteramo, 2015).

## WHAT IS NEEDED TO GO M-SHOPPING?

In the same context as accessing the Internet for the first time, a potential m-shopper requires certain platform elements. The principal platform elements of the m-shopping environment are a network and telecommunications hardware.

## Network

Suppose you were conducting a meeting in a restaurant and subsequently needed to book travel. The modern increasing network connectivity allows you to connect by mobile (smartphone) through an Internet mobile provider (i.e. 3, Vodafone, etc.) with an access speed varying according to the signal strength and type of connection (the speed of data connection does not affect the amount of data used and corresponds to ad hoc charges apart from the phone calls): GPRS, EDGE, 3G, HSPA+, and 4G. In particular, GPRS (marked on phone display by the letter "G"), the General Packet Radio Service, is the slowest data connection (114kbps) and it is only used if the phone cannot reach anything faster due to the interferences or location; EDGE (marked by the letter "E" and also known as eGPRS) has a theoretical speed of 400kbps; 3G correspondes to the third generation of the standard for top mobile data speed, with a speed up to 384kbps; HSPA+ (marked by the letter "H") stands for Evolved High-Speed Packet Access and can be 14.4 Mbps, 21 Mbps, or even 42 Mbps according to the network and device; 4G provides a speed up to 160 Mbps and, despite the higher cost if compared to the previous generation, their diffusion is increasing among users. Other alternatives are the wireless fidelity (Wi-Fi) networks, usually free of charge in many hotels, fast foods chains (i.e. McDonald's and Starbucks were the first ones offering this services to their clients), airport lounges and particular areas of cities (for instance, the city of Eindhoven in the Netherlands offers free Wi-Fi in all the squares).

---

**THINK POINT**

**How mobiles enter into our lives to add value for shopping**

Does all this seem familiar – low Internet access cost, many users and many places to use the service? Sounds as though this is becoming too diffused to be an integrative part of our lives.

In the past, there was a clear separation between the home life and the time for shopping, the task to buy a purchase was disjointed by the momento for collect information and purchase. The mobile devices enable a much richer experience that reduces or even eliminates the task for purchasing: through a mobile app, these devices assist you to complete your task (shopping), for instance you can research a certain product, scan the product code to get the best price, and then make the purchase immediately, thus you do not need to keep shuttling between the desktop computer, the electronics store, etc. (Nicol, 2013). You can buy anything, anywhere and anytime through mobile devices.

## FEATURES THAT DISTINGUISH M-COMMERCE FROM TRADITIONAL E-COMMERCE

Though a component of e-commerce, m-commerce has is own distinguishing elements which are listed below:

- **Mobile.** By its very nature, m-commerce is not restricted to a fixed telecommunications line (hard cable) that is linked to the Internet at a single location (desktop computer). M-Commerce users may carry their mobile communications device and use this device to make a purchase in any region that provides mobile/wireless communication coverage.
- **Ubiquity.** Mobile technology enables the user to access information wherever they are assuming the user is within the mobile communication broadcast region.
- **Personalisation.** Due to the limited memory capacity of the current mobile hardware, internal software enables a finer degree of information sorting and categorisation to meet the mobile user needs.
- **Flexibility and convenience.** The mobility of the mobile hardware delivers the early promise of e-commerce, that is "anywhere anytime" shopping. For example, mobile devices permit users to conduct transactions and/or receive information even when the user is engaged in another activity such as travelling or working.
- **Dissemination and localisation.** Retailers may deliver customized information to some or all m-shopping users that enter into a certain location through the automatic recognition of users' geographical position.

Using these features we can envisage that a local restaurant may broadcast their vegetarian menu (the personalisation) lunchtime specials within a few blocks of the restaurant (the dissemination) and this message would reach m-commerce–enabled users even if driving (the flexibility) in an unfamiliar geographic region (the ubiquity).

## CONTRIBUTORS TO THE GROWTH IN M-COMMERCE

The features of m-commerce are not themselves sufficient to expand its adoption. Other factors that are contributing to the growth of m-commerce include:

- Growth in smartphones usage.
  - Mobile communication devices are culturally entrenched. Smartphones have evolved from costly commercial sales tools to personal communication facilities with mobile apps able to support users in many tasks. To improve the adoption rates, many companies such as Samsung and Apple have developed a range of smartphones that are more fashion accessories that telecommunications hardware (i.e. iPhone).
- Declining costs of connectivity.
  - Competitive pressures between the communications providers and improving production systems have reduced costs of telecommunications hardware and transmissions.
- User incentives provided by telecommunications carriers.
  - Discounted hardware to encourage network usage.
  - Discounted airtime to increase network usage.
- User equity.
  - Potential m-shoppers that have a communication disability may use mobile devices to make a retail purchase using voice prompts; using a voice-navigated site.

## MOBILE PAYMENTS

Since mobile commerce includes the sale of goods, services and contents via mobile devices connected to the Internet without time or space boundaries (Kim et al., 2010), mobile payments service can be viewed as a new form of the electronic handling of the payments. It involves the transfer of monetary value for the purchase of a good by including the effective payment of products, services and bills authorized, initiated and/or realized through a mobile device (i.e. smartphone) (Schierz et al., 2010).

Depending upon the mobile device and available networks in the geographic region, a consumer has the option of making a mobile payment in one or all of these modes:

- **Short Message Service (SMS) charges.** The consumer keys in the SMS number that is assigned to the merchandise to be purchased and a charge appears on the billing consumer's bill account where SMS charges are normally listed. Coca-Cola have already stabling beverage vending machines that accept traditional coin payments and also display the SMS number for the particular machine. The beverage buyers call the SMS number from their own mobile device and once the vending machine receives the SMS signal, the

# M-SHOPPING

consumer may select the beverage to be dispensed. The charge for the beverage appears on the consumer's next SMS bill.

- **Direct charge to the billing to the account linked to the consumer's mobile device.** Mobile network devices today are fitted with facilities to transmit data to another computerised device in close proximity without making a telephone call. These data transmission facilities range from infrared (IR) beams, Bluetooth and Wi-Fi transmissions. The owner of the mobile device transacts the purchase sequence as they would do traditionally, that is, select the merchandise to be purchased and take it to the sales counter/checkout for payment. The only difference is that instead of payment by cash, EFTPOS (Electronic Funds Transfer Point of Sale) or credit card, the mobile device owner transmits the account details associated with the mobile device from that very device using one of the data transmission facilities noted above.

    Similar to the already described Coca-Cola SMS purchases, India's BPL mobile customer may send a message to 2233, which will be displayed on the LCD panel of the vending machine. The vending machine confirms the customer's mobile number then asks for the choice of chocolate and once selected, dispenses the chocolate and finally, the customer receives an SMS confirming the transaction. The vending transaction cost is debited from a pre-paid card, and added to the monthly bill of a post-paid customer (Hindu Business Line, 2003).

- **Using a clearing house service.** Intermediaries allow for payment authorities on behalf of the customer to pay for merchandise. One group, the Mobile Payment Services Association, is a coalition between Spain's Telefonica Moviles SA, Germany's T-Mobile AG and Britain's Orange SA and Vodafone Group PLC. The system of making payments through a mobile communications device is often referred to as a micropayment.

Benefits of micropayment to retailers:

- Billing the accounts linked to the mobile devices, e.g. cellular phone does not carry the charges associated with transfer of credit card funds.
- Reduced need to provide customers change for vending machines.
- Bill fraud is reduced. When a mobile device is stolen, the communications carrier usually disables network access for that device and so it cannot be used to make added micropayment.
- Extends the frequency of impulse purchases for items of small value.

Benefits for mobile consumer:

- Reduced dependence upon carrying cash and credit cards.
- Record or purchase appears on the account attached to the micropayment, e.g. cellular phone account.

## PROFILING THE M-SHOPPER

As indicated at the start of this chapter, the mobile shopping environment is still in its emergent stage of retailer development and shopper adoption. For retailers to tailor their market offering to the needs of the mobile shoppers, we should profile the current and intended adopters of m-shopping.

- **Buying behaviour.** Individuals enjoying mobile payments (Jayawardhena et al., 2009; Varnali and Toker, 2010; Gao et al., 2013; Gross, 2015)
  - Have a high desire for shopping convenience
  - Are innovative in shopping
  - Have a positive attitude towards non-store marketing
  - Have a positive attitude towards shopping through new technologies
  - Are price conscious
  - Are seekers of variety
- **Use of mobile communication technology.** This individual has a high level of ability to use the mobile devices, as it is demonstrated by their personal attachment towards the mobile, which they consider as an integrative part of their life.
- **Shopping and communication environment.** This shopper is confident in the parties that contribute to the shopping process and desires the convenience of m-shopping. In summary, this shopper:
  - Desires the convenience of mobile phone shopping
  - Enjoys mobile phone shopping
  - Has a low concern of financial risk from visited web retailer
  - Has a low concern of privacy risk from ISP
  - Is satisfied with mobile phone carrier
  - Searches for new hedonic shopping experiences

In addition, Dennis, Alamanos, Papagiannidis and Bourlakis (2015) found that m-shopping is particularly welcomed by shoppers with mobility disabilities, as an alternative to visiting physical stores. Mobile apps thus represent a useful channel for marketers to reach the growing, important (but otherwise difficult-to-reach) segment of disabled shoppers.

## CHAPTER SUMMARY AND CONCLUSIONS

It is often said that there is nothing new in selling, but that is not true for retailing. Retailing has evolved from face-to-face exchanges, to non-store hopping and now shopping on the go with mobile shopping (m-shopping). M-shopping requires the availability of a wireless network and a device that the shopper can employ to enter and use the wireless network to browse and shopping. The devices are not only used for placing orders for merchandise but may now be used to pay for goods and services that previously required cash or a credit card.

It is unlikely that m-shopping will displace the entrenched and growing cabled/desktop web shopping experience. But, the applications for m-shopping linked devices do present opportunities to provide existing and non-shoppers with facilities to access services that would have required the establishment of prohibitively expensive individual corporate networked systems to distribute the services and collect fees. For example, the large problem of shopping trolleys (carts) being removed and dumped after shopping could be reduced by linking the trolley to a mobile phone. The shopper keys in a code and the trolley is unlocked for use; if the trolley is not returned to a designated docking bay the same day, the cost of the trolley is passed on to the mobile phone account. It is just one application of the existing technology to adapt to the way people shop to save all parties from waste.

**Case study 11.1**
**IKEA "MAKE IT ALL COME ALIVE IN YOUR HOME" CATALOGUE APP**

The story of Ikea is a marketing success envied by many industries; it has even become a benchmark for growth, franchising and consumer sales. The story began in the early 1950s in Sweden with the idea of providing a selection of home furniture that was affordable for a wide segment of the population. The Ikea name combines the initials of its founder, Ingvar Kamprad (IK) with the first letters of the names of the farm and village where he grew up, Elmtaryad and Agunnaryd (EA), while the logo has been largely changed during the company history until 1967, which version remains the constant symbol of Ikea (they just changed the color in 1987 to introduce the Swedish color and promote worldwide the Swedish origin). The successful concept is to involve consumers for reducing costs: consumers assemble by themselves flat-pack products at home and provide the company with feedback on their experience. In the early 1980s it became a worldwide brand with stores in 20 countries and continued expanding, when the founder established the IKEA franchise.

As declared by Martin Enthed, IKEA Communications AB (Enthed, 2013): Where IKEA would like the industry to focus are among other things.

- A more generic definition of physically accurate material definition that could be portable/convertible between renderers.
- A more generic way of describing with physical accuracy how one 3D asset can connect to other 3D asset e.g. where a shelf can be placed in a cabinet. That then could be portable/convertible between interactive 3D tools.
- A way to easily and more accurately interact with soft 3D assets when building a set e.g. cushions, duvet, plaids and so on.
- Faster, Automated and more accurate ways of modeling/capturing a 3D assets and creating LOD levels
- ... and of course faster more interactive physically correct renderings. At IKEA we are continuously evolving and finding new use of the 3D assets to support the overall vision and business idea of IKEA.

One method being used to engage more consumers is the launch of a mobile interactive catalogue in 2011. This consisted of the annual catalogue accessible through the mobile app. Beginning with the information that 14% of clients have bought wrong-sized furniture and more than 70% were not aware of the real dimensions of their home, in late 2012 IKEA launched a new catalogue enriched with an augmented reality function that allowed consumers to scan the page to add contents like video, full-room views, decorating tips, etc. Finally, 1 year later, in 2013, they attend the 3D functions, under the challenge to find a good compromise between quality of realism (3D products reproduction) and speed. This app allows clients to (Figure 11.1):

- Place furniture in his/her own room
- Get inspired by IKEA proposal
- Collect updates on the new products
- Visualize 3D interactive products and environments

■ *Figure 11.1* IKEA mobile catalogue
Source: Ikea. http://www.ikea.com/ms/en_CA/catalogue-2015/index.html

As declared on the home page:

The IKEA catalogue app makes all the new inspiration and products move out of the catalogue and into your home, literally [...] fit in your everyday life. So, just download the app to your device, use it to scan the catalogue pages and let the home furnishing magic begin.

A recent investigation of consumers' response to these catalogues based on online reviews and university laboratory test (Rese et al., 2014) showed the extent to which consumers employing this new system appreciated its usefulness, but encountered some difficulties according to the unstable connection or amount of data to be processed/downloaded. Their results highlight the importance of this new typology of system supporting mobile shopping (including purchase decision) while still suffering technological limitations (performances of the adopted mobile device and speed of internet connection).The IKEA mobile catalogue is another way IKEA is trying to contribute to the changing lifestyles of its clients who are able to access more efficient and customized service.

## QUESTION

*Brief feedback to these questions is included at the back of the book.*

**Question 11.1** – It took half a decade to get a critical mass of users to adopt the Internet as a shopping environment. Which kinds of new mobile features will retailers need to provide to move consumers towards m-shopping?

## GLOSSARY

**4G**  Provides a speed up to 160 Mbps and, despite the higher cost if compared to the previous generation, its diffusion is increasing among users.

**EDGE**  (marked by the letter "E" and also known as eGPRS) Has a theoretical speed of 400kbps; 3G correspondes to the third generation of the standard for top mobile data speed, with a speed up to 384kbps.

**GPRS**  (marked on phone display by the letter "G") The General Packet Radio Service, is the slowest data connection (114kbps) and it is only used if the phone cannot reach anything faster due to the interferences or location.

**HSPA+**  (marked by the letter "H") Stands for Evolved High-Speed Packet Access and can be 14.4 Mbps, 21 Mbps, or even 42 Mbps according to the network and device.

**Hotspot**  A geographic area that receives a wireless network signal that may be accessed by hardware with the appropriate Wi-Fi transmission specification.

**Micropayment**  Micropayment is a methodology to generate revenue by offering pay-per-view webpages, web links, or web services for small amounts of money called "microcents."

**PDA**  First developed by Apple Computers as their Newton handheld device and later by the 3Com's as the Palm Pilot, the Personal Digital Assistant is a mobile computing device that incorporates diary facilities, word processing, e-mail and Internet access.

**Wi-Fi**  Short form of the term wireless fidelity (Wi-Fi) and is another name for IEEE 802.llb transmission specification. It refers to a non-wired connection between a wireless client and a base station or between two wireless clients. The term is most often linked to the Wireless Ethernet Compatibility Alliance (WECA). Wi-Fi is used in place of 802.11b just as we have come to know the term Ethernet in place of the IEEE 802.3 transmission specification.

## FURTHER READING

Pantano E and Priporas C V. (2016) 'Mobile retailing effect on consumption experiences: A dynamic perspective', *Computers in Human Behavior*, 61: 548–555.

## REFERENCES

Adyen. (2015) *Over 27% of Global Online Transactions Are Now on Mobile*. [Online] Available at: https://www.adyen.com/home/about-adyen/press-releases/mobile-payments-index-april-2015 [Accessed 20 June 2015].

Dennis C, Alamanos E, Papagiannidis S and Bourlakis M. (2015) 'Does social exclusion influence multiple channel use? The interconnections with community, happiness and wellbeing', *Journal of Business Research*, 69 (3): 1061–1070.

Enthed M. (2013) 'A retailers way into 3D: IKEA'. In *Proceedings of ACM SIGGRAPH Studio Task*, ACM, p. 1.

Gao T, Rohm A, Sultan F and Pagani M. (2013) 'Consumers un-tethered: A three-market empirical study of consumers' mobile marketing acceptance', *Journal of Business Research*, 66: 2536–2544.

Gross M. (2015) 'Mobile shopping: A classification framework and literature review', *International Journal of Retail and Distribution Management*, 43: 221–241.

Hindu Business Line. (2003) *Now You Can SMS for a Chocolate – Cadbury, BPL Mobile, E Cube Tie-up for Venture,* [Online]. Available at: allaboutvending.com [Accessed 20 November 2003].

Jayawardhena C, Kuckertz A, Karjaluoto H and Kautonen T. (2009) 'Antecedents to permission based mobile marketing: An initial examination', *European Journal of Marketing*, 43 (3/4): 473–499.

Kim C, Mirusmonov M and Lee I. (2010) 'An empirical examination of factors influencing the intention to use mobile payment', *Computers in Human Behavior*, 26 (3): 310–322.

Nicol D. (2013) *Mobile Strategy*, Upper Saddle River, NJ: IBM Press.

Pantano E. (2013) 'Ubiquitous retailing innovative scenario: From the fixed point of sale to the flexible ubiquitous store', *Journal of Technology Management and Innovation*, 8 (2): 84–92.

Pantano E and Verteramo S. (2015) 'Placeless store of Ubiquitous stores?', in *Proceedings of the 12th International Conference on e-Business*. Colmar: IEEE.

Rese A, Schreiber S and Baier D. (2014) 'Technology acceptance modeling of augmented reality at the point of sale: Can surveys be replaced by an analysis of online reviews?', *Journal of Retailing and Consumer Services*, 21 (5): 869–876.

Schierz P G, Schilke O and Wirtz B W. (2010) 'Understanding consumer acceptance of mobile payment services: An empirical analysis', *Electronic Commerce Research and Applications*, 9 (3): 209–216.

Varnali K and Toker A. (2010) 'Mobile marketing research: The-state-of-the-art', *International Journal of Information Management*, 30: 144–151.

WARC. (2015a) *Mobile Email Marketing Fails Potential*, [Online] Available at: http://www.warc.com/LatestNews/News/EmailNews.news?ID=34918&Origin=WARC

NewsEmail&CID=N34918&PUB=Warc_News&utm_source=WarcNews&utm_medium=email&utm_campaign=WarcNews20150615 [Accessed 15 June 2015].

WARC. (2015b) *Mobile Consumer Time Worth £7 a Minute*, [Online] Available at: http://www.warc.com/LatestNews/News/EmailNews.news?ID=34940&Origin=WARCNewsEmail&CID=N34940&PUB=Warc_News&utm_source=WarcNews&utm_medium=email&utm_campaign=WarcNews20150618 [Accessed 18 June 2015].

# Chapter 12

# U-shopping

### LINKS TO OTHER CHAPTERS

- Chapter 6 – E-store design: navigability, interactivity and web atmospherics
- Chapter 7 – E-service
- Chapter 11 – M-shopping

### KEY LEARNING POINTS

*After completing this chapter you will have an understanding of*

- Requirements for moving to u-shopping
- Consumer and retailer benefits for u-shopping
- Awareness of the developments in ubiquitous technologies and u-shopping

### ORDERED LIST OF SUBTOPICS

- Mobile retail evolution to ubiquitous retail
- How has u-shopping come about?
- What is needed to go u-shopping?
- Features that distinguish e-commerce, m-commerce and u-commerce
- Chapter summary and conclusions
- ❖ Case study
- ❖ Questions

- ❖ Glossary
- ❖ Further reading
- ❖ References

## MOBILE RETAIL EVOLUTION TO UBIQUITOUS RETAIL

As anticipated in the previous chapter, ubiquitous retailing emerges as an evolution of mobile stores based on the adoption of ubiquitous computing, by creating a new ubiquitous scenario for shopping from mobiles (Pantano, 2013): u-shopping, u-tail, u-retailing and u-commerce.

## HOW HAS U-SHOPPING COME ABOUT?

The continuous advances in computing capabilities and in mobile and wireless communication technologies, as well as the development of flexible software architectures and automatic identification systems provide new access to data that might be integrated in many application domains: the ubiquitous scenario (Kim et al., 2009; Pantano, 2012). In fact, the ubiquitous computing consists of the integration of computing in human activities as a pervasive penetration (Evans and Hu, 2006). As anticipated, it can be considered an extension of mobile computing based on the portable accessing technologies, such as the mobile camera, location-based service, ubiquitous sensor network, etc., which allows users to be always connected to a network while linked to web-based multimedia content repositories, which adapt the provided contents (and services accordingly). This is supported by the context-awareness characteristics which allow the system to adapt the response based on both the information on the users' state (i.e. geographical position, preferences, profile, etc.) and the surrounding environment on real time. This is in opposition to the traditional desktop computing, characterized by a system response based only on the environmental stimuli such as the users' requests (Kurkovski and Harihar, 2006; Kourouthanassis et al., 2007; Pantano, 2012). Hence, the main characteristics of ubiquitous computing can be summarized as (Lin et al., 2011; Kurkovski, 2005): (1) network accessibility (it is based on mobile devices constantly able to access the network); (2) device connectivity (it is based on the device possibility to be connected to the network through different systems such as wireless, etc.); (3) applications and input devices (it is based on mobile access to requested information through different input mobile such as mobile camera, GPS, etc., while the mobile application is based on a user-friendly interface providing several services and multimedia contents that can be easily shared and updated); and (4) context-awareness (it is based on the system ability to adopt its behaviour according to the people state, such as the recognition of the user actual location and the subsequent recommendation of places to see, etc.). As a consequence, consumers become ubiquitous consumers, always connected to a network for achieving/sharing contents, services, products (Pantano, 2012).

Another characteristic of the ubiquitous scenario is the low cost of the information in terms of access and sharing, thus it easily pushes towards an increased number of transactions, which can be based on customized services and complementary products, with benefits for the value creation (Kim et al., 2009). In fact, previous researches evaluated the acceptance of ubiquitous computing by focusing on the user intention to adopt these systems as largely influence by the emerging convenience (Pantano, 2012).

Due to the huge adaptability of these systems, ubiquitous computing has been successfully introduced in several different sectors, such as learning (especially for personalizing learning in higher education) (Lee et al., 2011), and cultural heritage and tourism (especially for destination promotion) (Wang et al., 2011). Similarly, in 2008 Wu and Hisa anticipated the adoption by retail industry, by predicting the u-shopping as a disruptive innovation able to make traditional e-shopping models obsolete, while forcing firms to reconsider internal resources and capabilities to fast reply to the changeable retail scenario.

## WHAT IS NEEDED TO GO U-SHOPPING?

Ubiquitous computing is introducing dramatic innovations in retail practices, by changing both the way users access and consume information, and the way firms reach clients, collect data on market trends and deliver the service product (Kim et al., 2009; Pantano and Viassone, 2015). In fact, the availability of these systems modifies the interface between clients and vendor, as well as the whole retail process, while providing new consumer-oriented services able to extend (removing) the boundaries of the physical space (Kourouthanassis et al., 2007; Pantano and Viassone, 2015).

This new kind of retail environment exploits the current advances on mobiles and wireless technologies, RFID (Radio Identification) systems, QR code (a sort of bidimensional barcode that memorizes information to be read by a mobile or smartphone), and on the new techniques for the fast moving of consumer goods (FMCG), for achieving the fast product recognition and delivery (Bennet and Savani, 2011). This technology is based on consumers' past knowledge of mobile applications that can be enriched with several functionalities. Hence, it is devoted to people who already have a smart mobile device (e.g. smartphone, tablet, etc.) and knowledge of the possible applications for these devices (both in terms of availability, installing modalities and main functionalities). In this way, the mobiles became a sort of interactive guide in the shopping environment anytime and anywhere. In fact, consumers use their own mobile for interacting with products, achieving more information, accessing personalized recommendations, etc., by focusing the camera on product's tag (or code) and exploiting the user-friendly interface of the ad hoc application.

From a managerial point of view, the ubiquitous computing provides a wide range of data on the single consumer, which can be exploited for the development of future (direct) marketing strategies. For instance, the user's geographical location system and QR code associated with each product are able to match his/her exact position with product preferences (i.e. purchased products, purchases frequency, total amount of purchases, etc.), personal profile (i.e. gender, education, personal address, monthly income, etc.), behaviour (i.e. place visited for how long, path to reach a destination, etc.), etc. (Bennet and Savani, 2011). Data on consumers can be easily collected in two situations: whenever a consumer purchases a certain good or visit a particular space embedded in the ubiquitous system and he/she focuses on a particular item (i.e. by focusing the mobile's camera on the item's tag). Furthermore, they solve consumers' dilemma concerning the comparison among different products, which is allowed in the online scenario, by extending this possibility also to the ubiquitous retail environment exploiting the network connectivity (Lee and Seo, 2006).

Since ubiquitous computing is based on mobile shopping, it overcomes the physical limitation of the user's own mobile by transferring the computing capacity on the ubiquitous system, thus it overcomes the limitations concerning m-commerce (mobile-commerce) related to the mobile technical characteristics such as memory size and computing capacity (Hejazinia and Razzazi, 2010; Yang and Kim, 2012). In fact, in this environment the technical capacities are not limited to the characteristics of the single device, but they are distributed for increasing the efficiency of the whole system, with benefits for the computing and memorization capacity of each mobile and for the quality of the final service for consumers. While in 2008 Wu and Hisa predicted the launch of ubiquitous scenarios for retailing, innovative platforms for u-tailing became available recently for testing their effectiveness with consumers. In fact, ubiquitous computing in retailing is a new concept; thus it needs to be further investigated for deeply understanding its impact on traditional offline shopping and on the emerging of new business models.

Preliminary prototypes of ubiquitous systems for retailing have been recently introduced in some zones with high pedestrian traffic such as

U-SHOPPING

metro and bus stops for preliminary tests with consumers, for example in Barcelona (Spain) (this case will be discussed later on throughout the chapter).

## FEATURES THAT DISTINGUISH TRADITIONAL E-COMMERCE, M-COMMERCE AND U-COMMERCE

In the past chapters we discussed e- and m-tailing, and thus it is possible to compare with the emerging concept of u-tailing concerning main features such as physical facilities, service, product displaying, and convenience. Concerning physical facilities, all three environments are flexible, customizable according to consumers' preferences (i.e. interface and product recommendation/visualization might be customized based on user past behaviour). Similarly, the three environments enhance the traditional service, by offering the possibility to access more information on the product on sale, compare online products and search for alternatives, etc.

Concerning product displaying, e-tailing supports the access through the desktop computer, while the m-store is accessed by a mobile device that usually has a small interface. The u-store provides a larger surface for visualizing the products, i.e. walls of metro stops, by offering a full-size virtual reconstruction of the products on sale. Finally, concerning the convenience, all the proposed retail environments require an Internet connection. While e-store is accessed through a desktop computer and m-store from mobile, u-store can be accessed only from the specific area where the new point of sale is located; it thus overcomes the boundaries related to the traditional stores opening hours, but not the physical boundaries.

### CHAPTER SUMMARY AND CONCLUSIONS

The present chapter reinforces the idea that retailing is evolving as prompted by the advancements in technologies. Retailing has evolved from face-to-face exchanges, to a non-store/distributed shopping environment largely based on new technologies (such as mobile and ubiquitous ones). U-shopping requires the availability of a wireless network, a device that the shopper can employ to enter and use the wireless network to browse and shop, and the consumer to be located in a certain area devoted to u-shopping. Similar to m-shopping, devices are used for placing orders for merchandise and to pay for goods and services that previously required cash or a credit card, and the product would be delivered directly to the home. Current progresses in 3D virtual reality will provide more realistic and efficient user-friendly interfaces, while the advancements in Fast Moving Consumer Goods will make the delivery process faster. Combining the advantages of e-shopping and m-shopping (i.e. a wider number of products, fast response to consumers' requests, open 24/7, possibility to quickly compare a huge number of items, etc.) and those of the physical store (i.e. the products are displayed on shelves with realistic dimension), offers an alternative to both shopping environments.

It is unlikely that u-shopping will displace the entrenched and growing m-shopping experience. But, the actual applications for u-shopping are quite limited around the world and mainly devoted to grocery.

### Case study 12.1
### SORLI VIRTUAL STORE AS THE FIRST EXAMPLE OF UBIQUITOUS STORE IN EUROPE

The Spanish Sorli Virtual is the first example of a ubiquitous store launched in Europe in July 2012 at the metro stop Sarrià in Barcelona (Spain) (Figure 12.1).

The functioning of this system is based on the QR code associated to each available product and on the consumer's mobile camera for scanning the code.

**Figure 12.1** Example of ubiquitous store in Barcelona, Spain

When the camera focuses on a certain code, the system transfers the information to the centre that calls consumers to proceed with the order and the payment. Afterwards, consumers will get the purchases directly at home.

The purchase process is based on the following steps: (1) each product is tagged with a code that memorizes the related information (i.e. price, quantity, etc.); (2) consumer focuses his/her mobile camera on the code to achieve information, the application interface guides the user into the process from the choice of quantity to the payment through credit card; (3) the system recognizes consumer's request and starts the payment procedure, by transferring the order to the distribution centre (that contains more products than a traditional physical store); (4) the centre confirms the availability of the chosen product and contacts the consumer for confirming the order, if the order is confirmed, the system completes payment and proceeds with the item delivery at home; and (5) the system updates consumer's information with the data related to the last purchased item(s) and consumer's behaviour (i.e. zone of access, visualized items before ordering, etc.).

The system is based on the item code, application interface and network connectivity through users' own mobile. For this reason, it can be easily adapted for a wide range of products, by modifying the code, improving the interface (and graphics) and updating the data repositories (by adding the information related to the new product).

## QUESTIONS

*Brief feedback to these questions is included at the back of the book.*

**Question 12.1** – Can ubiquitous retailing replace e-tailing?

**Question 12.2** – What are the main consequences of the u-shopping scenario for retailers?

## GLOSSARY

**Contactless technologies**  New technologies based on proximity sensor that allows payment without providing any pin or signature. For this reason, they are largely used for payment.

**iBeacon**  Small and low cost transmitting device, not requiring a minimum distance between the devices to set the transaction. This device might share data via Bluetooth connections, such as specific deals or product information, while tracking consumer location/route within the store (in-store location).

**Near Field Communication (NFC)**  Technology providing mobile devices with wireless two-way short-range connectivity up to a maximum of 10 cm.

**Quick Response codes (QR)** Bidimensional barcode able to augment the reality with contents and information by scanning it with a smartphone camera.

**Radio Frequency IDentification (RFID)** One of the first examples of contactless technology, consisting of a modern version of the barcode. It is based on a radio frequency transceiver (transmitter and receiver) attached to the item to be identified by a reader device (interrogator device) used to read the information stored on the tag.

**Ubiquitous computing** A sort of evolution of mobile computing based on the portable accessing technologies (i.e. cameras, Location Based Service, Ubiquitous Sensor Network, etc.), connected to a network anytime anywhere, and linked to web-based multimedia content repositories that adapt the provided contents according to users' characteristics such as location.

## FURTHER READING

Papagiannidis S, Pantano E, See-To E, Dennis C and Bourlakis M. (in press) 'To immerse or not? Experimenting with two virtual retail environments', *Information Technology and People*.

## REFERENCES

Bennet R and Savani S. (2011) 'Retailers preparedness for introduction of third wave (ubiquitous) computing applications: A survey of UK companies', *International Journal of Retail and Distribution Management*, 39 (5): 306–325.

Evans C and Hu B. (2006) 'E-commerce to U-business: A model for ubiquitous shopping mall', in *Proceedings of the First International Symposium on Pervasive Computing and Applications, IEEE*, pp. 427–432.

Hejazinia M and Razzazi M. (2010) Commercial activities through mobile phone distribution processing integrated with mobile agents. *Journal of Emerging Technologies in Web Intelligence*, 2 (3): 182–190.

Kim C, Oh E, Shin N and Chae M. (2009) 'An empirical investigation of factors affecting ubiquitous computing use and U-business value', *International Journal of Information and Management*, 29: 436–448.

Kourouthanassis P E, Giaglis G M and Vrechopoulos A P. (2007) 'Enhancing user experience through pervasive information systems: The case of pervasive retailing', *International Journal of Information Management*, 27: 319–335.

Kurkovski S. (2005) 'Using principles of pervasive computing to design m-commerce applications', in *Proceedings of the International Conference on Information Technologies: Coding and Computing*, IEEE, pp. 59–64.

Kurkovski S and Harihar K. (2006) 'Using ubiquitous computing in interactive mobile marketing', *Personalized Ubiquitous Computing*, 10: 227–240.

Lee H, Lee W B and Kweon S C. (2011) 'Examining consumer preferences for mobile devices to read digital content for the diffusion of ubiquitous learning in higher education', *Communications in Computer and Information Science*, 264: 324–331.

Lee K J and Seo Y H. (2006) 'A pervasive comparison shopping business model for integrating offline and online marketplace', in *Proceedings of the 8th International Conference on Electronic Commerce*, ACM, pp. 289–294.

Lin P-H, Huang K-S, Wu C-H and Hong Z-W. (2011) 'A resource management model for ubiquitous computing environments', in *Proceedings of the 15th International Symposium on Consumer Electronics*, IEEE, pp. 556–559.

Pantano E. (2013) 'Ubiquitous retailing innovative scenario: From the fixed point of sale to the flexible ubiquitous store', *Journal of Technology Management and Innovation*, 8 (2): 84–92.

Pantano E and Viassone M. (2015) Engaging consumers on new integrated multi-channel retail environments: Challenges for retailers. *Journal of Retailing and Consumer Services*, 25: 106–114.

Wang W-Y, Yang H-C, Chen W-W and Shih Y-L. (2011) 'Providing a ubi-Marketing platform using pervasive technologies to facilitate added-value services in lodging operations', in *Proceedings of the 15th North-East Asia Symposium on Nano, Information Technologies and Reliability*, IEEE, pp. 39–44.

Wu J-H and Hisa T-L. (2008) 'Developing e-business dynamic capabilities: An analysis of e-commerce innovation from i-, m-, to u-commerce', *Journal of Organizational Computing and Electronic Commerce*, 18 (2): 95–111.

Yang K and Kim H-Y. (2012) 'Mobile shopping motivation: An application of multiple discriminant analysis', *International Journal of Retail and Distribution Management*, 40: 778–789.

# Chapter 13

# Multi-channel success and the future of e-retailing

### LINKS TO OTHER CHAPTERS

- Chapter 4 – Understanding and communicating with the e-consumer
- Chapter 5 – Information search on the web
- Chapter 6 – E-store design: navigability, interactivity and web atmospherics
- Chapter 10 – E-retailing models
- Chapter 11 – M-shopping
- Chapter 12 – U-shopping

### KEY LEARNING POINTS

*After completing this chapter you will have an understanding of*

- How successful retailing principles are consistent across physical and virtual marketplaces
- How shoppers will develop their own service exchange situations with the aid of new technological developments coming in e-retailing and new multi-channel retail environments

**ORDERED LIST OF SUBTOPICS**

- Consumer buying decision process
- The hybrid retailer – the most likely winner in future retailing
- What can you expect to see and hear in e-retailing?
- Chapter summary and conclusions
- ❖ Case study
- ❖ Questions
- ❖ Glossary
- ❖ Further reading
- ❖ References

## INTRODUCTION

To the students at the University of Capetown South Africa, 6 June 1966, Senator Robert F. Kennedy said:

> There is a Chinese curse which says, 'May he live in interesting times'. Like it or not, we live in interesting times…
>
> (Kennedy, 1966)

Despite serious questions as to the origin of the phrase – that is, that the phrase is more likely to be of Western origin than Chinese (Editor, 2002), the sentiment *'living in interesting times'* holds true now and will continue to do so for e-retailing.

Changes in the retailing service exchange medium from bricks-and-mortar to an electronic medium have not endowed retailers with magical insights into the needs and buying processes of potential customers. This lack of consumer understanding was confirmed by the collapse of so many would be web e-retailers in the dot.com crash. What is needed is to consider the demands upon e-retailing from the point of view of the potential interaction between the website and shopping browser, without exploring the possibility for consumers to find and purchase products among different new channels (Pantano and Viassone, 2015).

### Consumer buying decision process

A potential e-consumer buying decision process will follow the established stages of need recognition, information search, information evaluation, purchase decision and post-purchase behaviour.

## Need recognition

An e-retail website is a combination of the traditional store display window, information desk, stocked display shelving, mood lighting/sound, promotional material that shouts out specials and the time-honoured barker/spruiker use to stimulate shopping interest. Such an e-retail site ought to elicit a need recognition response from any visitor to the site. A new or returning visitor should be treated to a combination of the four basic marketing elements – *price* (i.e. specials, discounts, interest free periods), *product* (i.e. new lines, clearance items, seasonal products, fashion and fad limited ranges), *promotion* (i.e. sales, seasonal specials, select shopper campaigns) and *distribution* (i.e. free delivery, lay-away, home installation) that accentuate the visitor's own need identification. Technology within the website, for example cookie files, capture data about the visitor's responses and what information was accessed. Such information then enables e-retailers to improve the rapport with the online customer by tailoring the site content to consumer demand. One positive application from such data collection is the inclusion of customer loyalty programs that encourage return visitation to the e-retailer site and increased purchases.

> **THINK POINT**
>
> Since we often choose to go to an e-retailing website rather than finding the site by accident or clicking through to the site, are we not already in a need recognition state at that point?

## Information search

Improved telecommunications technology and general population access to the Internet have transformed user availability to customisation of and digestion of large information volumes. Unlike the bricks-and-mortar retailer, an e-retail site has the facilities to make available such large volumes of information in a customised format to meet the immediate and potential queries of site visitors following the need recognition stage. Without personal embarrassment or the self-consciousness of asking a stranger (e.g. shopkeepers) for what may be an obvious or foolish product-related question, the e-retail site visitor can avail themselves of the online opportunity to obtain product brochures, price comparisons, frequently asked questions (FAQs), product applications, cleaning and repair information, an efficient search engine technology as well as specialised information via the e-retailer's e-mail system.

## Information evaluation

When seeking to evaluate the collected information on products and services, the potential shopper will often turn to the experiences and advice of family, friends and persons that have already experienced use of such merchandise. E-retailing gives the user added facilities to access evaluative experts and previous users of the merchandise in question to aid in the digestion and customisation of all this information. Many consumer groups act as such reference experts through the testing and personal evaluations of retailed products and then making these findings to others. Experienced e-retailers encourage interactions between previous, current and future shoppers by way of:

1. Online discussion groups.
2. Suggesting site visitors rate the available merchandise.
3. Suggesting site visitors express comments about this merchandise and the service exchange experiences.

Monitoring of the online discussions and visitor comments endows the retailer with invaluable knowledge regarding merchandise features and limitations that may be incorporated into promotional materials. To conclude, apart from all the benefits mentioned above, the e-retailer gains all this free information that would normally require expensive market research.

## Purchase decision

After a visitor to an e-retailer site has determined the merchandise to be appropriate for their needs, it is still not a certainty that this visitor will finalise a purchase. Commonly, an online customer nominates particular merchandise from an e-retail website and places those items in the online *shopping cart* (also known as a *shopping trolley*) for the checkout but later the customer discontinues the purchase process and leaves the e-retailer's site. This action of discontinuing an online purchase is termed *Abandoned Cart Syndrome* (Fenech, 2002; Belk et al., 2014; See-To et al., 2014). From his research into online cart abandonment, Fenech (2002) identified the principle contributors, as (in order of highest to lowest):

1. A lower level of education.
2. Higher frequency of web purchases.

3. Greater concern of online data risk and fraud.
4. Greater frequency of website service problems.
5. When shopping is used as a facility to see family and friends.
6. There are high levels of concern for online retailers tracking data.
7. Younger buying groups.
8. When shopping causes little arousal.
9. Higher frequency of browsing for a later purchase.
10. Higher fashion consciousness.
11. Higher frequency of web search for product information.

Although the e-retailer cannot yet duplicate the human interactions possible in a physical store setting, e-retailers may still empower customers in an attempt to reduce the incidence of online cart abandonment. One positive step to improve the e-retailer's customer interactions is streamlining the order process by

- Making improvements in the e-retailer's site navigation.
- Incorporating help links and interactive facilities to stimulate the shopper's arousal and fashion consciousness.
- Supplying the relevant merchandise information as needed.
- Greater use of online help facilities and screens prompts.
- Establishing chat rooms and customer discussion opportunities to share experience with family, friends and new acquaintances.
- Improved guarantees (including deliveries, data security, 30-day trials).
- Offline contact details (phone number, fax number, street address).

## Post-purchase behaviour

The key to a retailer's survival and success whether offline or online is to generate repeat purchase behaviour. For a customer to return to a retailer that customer needs to have confidence in the retailer. E-retailer confidence is often difficult to establish in light of online issues that have caused customers to make complaint and/or never return to the e-retailer. According to Cho et al. (2002), the online issues that often alienate customers and lead to complaints are the failure to meet customer *expectations* in relation to:

- Merchandise offerings.
- The e-retailer's storefront technology (this includes, but not limited to the website) that integrates:
  - Usability of the technology;
  - The technology failing to carry out a function.

- E-retailer information sources.
- Payment/settlement issues.
- Agreed conditions (including delivery timing).

To reduce the chance of customer expectations being unfulfilled, e-retailers will compensate for the lack of a face-to-face exchange by making available more information details than would otherwise be considered in a bricks-and-mortar environment. Dealing with each of the Cho et al. (2002) points, we suggest the following responses:

- **Merchandise offerings**
  - Define all dimensions of the size options, colour variations and accessories provided. One suggestion, to include the supply of actual colour swatches to reduce the colour errors often attributed to variations on computer colour monitors and be coherent with the last advances in graphics (including 3D graphics and augmented reality).

- **The e-retailer's storefront technology (this includes, but is not limited to the website)**
  - Providing sufficient technology to cope with peak buying periods such as Saint Valentine's Day and Mother's Day.
  - Redundant backup to take over when systems fail.
  - Facilities to store (file) partial orders for future use should the customer be interrupted and/or wishes to continue the shopping process in the near future.
  - Providing improved access facilities for the disabled/impaired computer user. Facilities may consist of:
    - Selectable larger display fonts;
    - Voice recognition commands;
    - Spoken responses imbedded in the webpages;
    - Written descriptions of displayed images (these can be read out to the non-sighted users even if they can't see the picture).
  - Alerts given by the e-retailer's site to advise users:
    - Pending specials;
    - Replenishment of merchandise that was out of stock;
    - Arrival of special orders.
  - Such alerts can reach the user through e-mail, phone short message service (SMS) or push notification, automated faxing, or other communications technologies.

- **E-retailer information sources** (the policies)
  - Information is to be detailed (even exhaustive), accurate and timely (not noticeably out of date).
  - Information is to be easy to find on the e-retailer site.
  - Include links to relevant or 'just interesting' sites shall establish the e-retail not only as an appropriate purchasing site but a point of reference or Web Portal for future enquiries in this area; thereby achieving a great milestone, being bookmarked as a favourite site in the user's web browsing software.
  - To contribute to a continued customer relationship after a purchase through:
    - Continued updates on the relevant and near relevant issues by e-mail or newsgroup. For example, the customer purchases an electric grill and then receives a monthly recipe; the e-retailer keeps the contact and the customer's satisfaction in the purchase is supported – space may also be sold to sponsors seeking to promote their ingredients.

- **Payment/settlement issues**
  - Not all customers want to reveal their personal details and movements to online parties. To aid these potential customers, e-retailers can now provide alternatives for the customer in the shopping cycle to minimise risk. For instance in many countries, such as Italy, Amazon started a collaboration with the national mail service which allows consumers to have their online purchase delivered to the preferred post office rather than to their home address. In this way the customer picks up the merchandise at a time that suits, conceals their personal address details while still gaining the advantages of shopping online.
  - Most courier organisations (i.e. DHL and FedEx) used by e-retailers have facilities for the purchaser to trace and track the merchandise while it is in transit. The e-retailer receives proof the item is 'on its way' and the client achieves the piece of mind of 'seeing' were the item is anytime they go online. Similarly, few e-retailers such as Amazon launched partnerships with the local post in order to set collection points within the local post offices, by giving clients the opportunity to choose the favourite one for purchases collection (within the standard office opening hours).

> **THINK POINT**
>
> For a retailer, traditional advertising communications devices cover such things as printed brochures, display signs and shelf display signs. New retailer advertising communication devices cover mobile app, presence on social media and the company website. If it takes effort by a retailer to update all these advertising communication devices, why do we consider that the web information is more up to date than the more traditional advertising devices?

## THE HYBRID RETAILER – THE MOST LIKELY WINNER IN FUTURE RETAILING

As discussed in Chapter 10, retailers today are not restricted to just *bricks-and-mortar*, *direct* and *virtual* categories of retailing but often opt for a hybrid business model. Hybrid retailers, sometimes referred to as **'multi-channel retailers'**, appear to be taking the greatest advantage of e-retailing opportunities.

In a study by Pauwels and Neslin (2015) online retailers introducing a bricks-and-mortar store were identified generated a higher frequency purchase, yielding the web gain in purchase revenue. Accordingly, Pauwels and Neslin (2015) estimated that 1.9% of consumers would have purchased through the online channel while the stores were closed, while this percentage decreased to 1.54 with the store openings.

When Kate Spade launched the partnership with eBay in the US, the store in New York gave clients the possibility to buy at any time products of the brand through the touch screen located within one of the four storefront windows enriched with the technology, and thus, customers were able to choose among the available products, while new products have been added each Saturday during the opening hours of the store (Pantano, 2016). Though the collaboration with a virtual retailer is emerging as something new, it is an early example of a continuing trend as offline retailers innovate for competing.

### Consumers' cross-channel free riding

Although previous studies provide evidence that in the emerging multi-channel scenario, consumers engage more purchases if compared to one-channel buyers (Dholakia et al., 2005 and Seck and Philippe, 2013), this context pushes consumers to adopt a new consumer behaviour that might be risky for retailers: consumer cross-channel free riding. This consists of the consumer tendency to use one channel for finding and comparing product information and a different one for purchasing, which can be managed by not linking each retailer (Verhoef et al., 2007; Hsieh et al., 2012; Pantano and Viassone, 2015).

## Retailer adaptation has always been a key to survival and growth

Long-standing bricks-and-mortar retailers are not only looking at a web presence as the means to become an e-retailer. To improve the relationship with their customers, retailers are adopting new electronic systems that complement their physical store presence. Nespresso in the Netherlands (http://www.nespresso.com) uses a system termed *'buy online, pick up at the store'* where the customer places and pays for an order with a credit card at the Nespresso website (or mobile app), but departing from other online procedures, the customer picks up the merchandise from the selected pick-up point (nearest Nespresso corner within the nearest department store or Nespresso boutique). E-mail is then used to advise the customer about stock availability at the time of the order and when the merchandise is ready for store collection.

Misunderstanding or ignoring a market position of strength is a failing that leads to the demise of some retailers. The availability of a new distribution channel is not an automatic indication of future success. Consider the US retailer Egghead (was http://www.egghead.com) that in the early 1990s had strong market presence with around 250 stores across the country. The retailer was well respected by its consumer market, had a solid brand image, and was profitable. Long before most other retailers, Egghead created an online presence for its technology minded customers in 1994. Effectively, this entry into a new distribution channel made Egghead one of the first multi-channel retailers. But as Lightfoot (2003) described, Egghead did not leverage its unique multi-channel position, rather it decided to abandon all of its offline stores in 1998 and exclusively sell online, evolving into a virtual retailer. Regrettably, a series of problems, i.e. much publicised hacking attacks on Egghead's website, technical failures in the e-commerce technology, failing customer loyalty and internal management problems, Egghead went the way of many dot. coms and exhausted its cash reserves and filed for bankruptcy in 2001 (Thornton and Marche, 2003). On the positive side for customers, the Egghead assets (including brand name and customer base) were sold to Amazon.com in 2001. To Amazon's credit, the new owner honoured the privacy policy of the previous Egghead clients as noted in the statement: *'Please note that if you are a returning Egghead.com customer, Egghead.com will not disclose any existing account information to Amazon.com, so you will need to re-enter all information necessary to complete a transaction. For information about how Amazon.com treats the information you give us, see Amazon.com's Privacy Notice'* (Amazon, 2003).

## WHAT CAN YOU EXPECT TO SEE AND HEAR IN E-RETAILING?

Improved customer education, availability of information, increasing usage of new technologies and increasing legislation have given rise to a new type of customer for this new millennium. Our new customers are more demanding, have higher expectations and are increasingly adversarial in their service exchanges with retailers. Part of the retailer response will be to empower the customer to tailor their own service exchange in the physical store and online.

### Greater individualisation

Just as web browsing technology learns and recalls a user's preferences for colour, fonts and items for inclusion, future stores will match their offering to learned customer experiences. Once the customer is identified to the store through a loyalty card or mobile app previously downloaded on his or her mobile phone, the technology will record the shopper's behaviour in terms of preferences for merchandise, delivery (i.e. home delivery, parcel pick up), time spent within the stores, products visualized, method of payment, etc. To save the customer time, the store system would forewarn the customer of difficulties (including stock outages) and then make suggestion for alternative merchandise that is either in stock or pending (e.g. new seasons stock).

### Greater reliability and convenience

New store technology will improve reliability for both customer and retailers. When a customer selects an item and adds this to the shopping trolley, the system (which can be based on a RFID reader, portable or fixed, or on the mobile phone camera) will read the merchandise's tag (RFID or QR code) and present the details to the shopper via visual display (integrated in the reader system or consisting on the mobile display running the ad hoc app). No longer will the customer be disadvantaged by the omission of shelf pricing or getting to the check-out only to be told that the product is *'not on the system'* and needs a delaying price check. Through the use of these technologies, the customer will be advised of these details at the point of merchandise access, the shelf, or bin stocking the merchandise.

Once the price information absence is detected, the retailer's system can search or calculate the price before the check-out is reached.

Aiding the retailer, this technology will indicate low or out of stock situations at the shelf as customers place the item into their trolley, long before the item is removed from the inventory system at the check-outs. Staff will have a perpetual inventory rather than depending upon physical stock updates.

Retailers use a *planogram* to determine what merchandise is displayed where and in what quantities throughout a store. Shoppers become familiar with their favourite stores but what do they do when a new merchandise line is added to the store and you are unsure where it is located? What is needed is a personal guide or in the future a mobile app to direct you through the store like a global positioning system (GPS) directs a car through traffic.

## Merchandise tracking

With delivery problems representing one of the main elements holding back the growth of e-shopping (see Chapter 7), merchandise tracking may be one of the essential development areas for the future. Early developments in bricks retailing followed research by Bernard Silver and Norman Woodland in the early 1950s. As a result, the barcode became a world standard for tracking and recording the movements of retail stock (Anonymous, 2003). A standard barcode is made up of dark (predominantly black) vertical bars broken up with light (predominantly white) spaces. To read the barcode a beam of light is passed over the code where the dark bars absorb the light and the spaces reflect it. The scanner (also known as a reader or detector) then turns the reflected light into electrical pulses that may be recorded on a data file.

While an excellent product identification system, barcodes have a significant and obvious limitation, that is, they need to be scanned to register stock movement. Stock may enter or be removed from the retailer's premises and if the barcode is not scanned with a reading laser, the stock is not identified and recorded so its movement is unknown. The solution is to have the stock *speak* up and identify *itself* to the retailer's electronic inventory management system. The stock speak, how? By adding to, or replacing the barcode with a miniature *Radio Frequency Identification* (RFID) tag or *QR Code*.

RFID (Radio Frequency IDentification) is one of the first examples of contactless technology, consisting of an enriched version of the barcode. It is the most common technology used to identify and localize objects from a distance. In particular, it consists of a radio frequency transceiver (transmitter and receiver) attached to the item to be identified by a reader device (interrogator device) used to read the information stored on the tag. RFID tags are also used to improve the in-store security, to enhance the rapid checkout of consumers, and to manage the shelf-life of products (i.e. by evaluating in real time the quantity of a certain product on the shelf).

QR Codes technology has become one of the most-used types of two-dimensional barcode. Developed in the automotive context, it is currently used in a broader context, including both tracking for logistics purposes and convenience-oriented applications aimed at enriching consumers' shopping experience through smartphones.

Bricks-and-mortar retailers have already piloted QR codes, such as Harrods (famous department store in London), which used QR codes as a tool for increasing its exposure in China, by being the first British retailer to lauch a WeChat social media account in 2013 devoted to interact with Chinese consumers accessible by scanning the QR code (Luxury Daily, 2013). Privacy becomes an issue when you consider that though the RFID and QR receivers were conceived to detect the movements of the tagged merchandise, they are in effect able to track the movements of the customer carrying the tagged merchandise within a shopping district that contains multiple RFID and QR scanners/receivers. Consider, if an organisation has more than one member store in the company's group (i.e. a supermarket, a bottle shop and a variety store all owned by one organisation) in the same shopping mall, radio triangulation by the RFID and QR receivers triggered by the merchandise's RFID and QR signal could detect the move of merchandise and therefore, the shopper, from one store to another and so on. The data from these movements could also interpret how long the shopper spent at various spots in the mall and all this data is collected *without* the shopper having given their permission. It is an *ethical* dilemma that will be debated for some time. Despite the debate, bricks retailers such as Tesco (www.tesco.com) are pushing ahead with RFID tags and QR codes for tracking supply chain movements and further trials in-store. As we argue below, the potential benefits are substantial, so we expect the development to diffuse into e-retail tracking as shoppers become more accustomed to it.

As applications of RFID tags and QR codes increase retailers may expect to fulfil management and marketing objectives including:

1 *Reduced retail fraud and theft*
   - Tracking products for clothing, grocery items, electrical merchandise and recorded music to reduce shrinkage.
2 *Asset supply chain control*
   - RFID tags and QR codes will track the movement of goods from one process centre to another, i.e. delivery dock and

warehouse storage. This is not limited to selling inventory but organisational assets that have in the past left the premises without authorisation or not entered in a log book, i.e. storage pallets and shopping trolleys.
3 *Inventory control*
   - RFID tags and QR codes will transmit inventory relevant information, i.e. batch number, unit code, number of items on the property and consumer-related merchandise information, i.e. product category, size and colour.
4 *Intelligent packaging*
   - RFID tags and QR codes can be linked to a sensor that recognises any tampering or deterioration of the merchandise while in transit and when that damage behaviour occurred. This damage may relate to a non-deliberate deterioration error, e.g. food storage temperature being outside of the recommended range. Equally, the sensor would detect malicious actions of third parties upon the merchandise, e.g. when a sealed lid on a container is removed and the subsequent replacement to disguise the tampering activity.

For *customers*, the expected benefits from a retailer using RFID tags and QR codes are

1 *Speedier checkout process* – in combination with intelligent shopping carts/trolleys, shoppers would have all their purchases totalled automatically as the individual product RFID tags and QR codes are read by the shopping cart and then provide the totals at the checkout point for payment.
2 *Security* – manufacturers will introduce RFID tags and QR codes into the components of final products so that if the components are removed they can be tracked. Consider the theft of car parts from a whole vehicle; in the past the panels would be almost impossible to detect and trace once removed from the original car.
3 *Tracking* – 'Where are the b----y car keys' – consumer RFID tag and QR code readers will become available to learn the tag codes of products that the consumer wishes to inventory. An immediate benefit is being able to locate the proximity of individual RFID and QR codes tagged items, such as the ever elusive car keys.
4 The RFID tags and QR codes provide the opportunity to include preparation and care information that will be understood by future appliances. Potential applications in this vain are:

- Allergens – Home health systems that are programmed for the individual's health requirements will 'listen' to the RFID tags and QR codes of grocery items. The tags may contain all the ingredients of the grocery items, even the complicated chemical codes, and notify the home health system of potential allergens that could be harmful to the customer/householder.
- For clothing – alerts the washing machine that the fabric is not machine washable or should be dry cleaned only.
- For frozen foods – RFID tags or QR codes alert the freezer display panel that the food is near or at its expiration date.
- For frozen foods – the RFID tag or QR codes pass cooking instructions to the microwave or convection oven to avoid over- and under-cooking.

### In-store interactive displays

Multi-channel e-retailers are not restricted to the sale of physical mechanise in bricks-and-mortar establishments but may also market digital products and services that were previously limited to virtual retailers. Through the use of interactive displays (or touch screen electronic kiosks), retailers will be able to offer such services as:

- Detailed product information
- Price checks
- Recipes and product application suggestions
- Dispensing ticket for events
- Reservations for events and activities
- Self-checkout to make purchases
- Personalised and targeted promotions
- Photo-finishing. This is a growing segment as customers bring in their digital camera cards and have the kiosks transfer the images to final photos
- Internet access
- Customer loyalty programs
- Banking and financial services
- Maps and direction services
- Human resource services, e.g. recruitment services.

Interactive displays generate extra revenue and because the customer is self-servicing, the variety of service exchanges are increased without added staff and subsequent drains on profits.

**Figure 13.1** Interactive touch screen displays come in a variety of styles
Source: Own source

## Greater use of contactless payments

Contactless technologies support the spreading of mobile payments, by offering the shift from the traditional magnetic stripe or "Chip and Pin" to contactless cards, where tag brought into close proximity substitutes the card sweeping or insertion into the reader (and the subsequent request of PIN or authorization for the payment), with benefits for the financial transactions in terms of time saving and ease of process, and the consequent reduction of the queues. For these reasons, contactless payment is particularly important to retail settings where speed and convenience of payment are the basic elements of the success, such as fast food and kiosks. For instance, in the US market, contactless payment is an established method especially in the fast food, leisure and sport industries (Olsen, 2008).

The implementation of these technologies creates benefits for both customers and retailers. Consequently, innovative ways for transactions at the point-of-sale are proliferating and mobile payments are one of the most investigated technologies in retail industry from both a scholar's and practitioner's perspective (Pantano and Viassone, 2015).

The continuous research in wireless technologies provides further systems such as NFC (Near Field Communication) and beacons, which are driving mobile phones to facilitate the access execution of several monetary transactions and are successfully employed for automatic mobile payments (Olsen, 2008). In particular, beacons consist of small and low cost transmitting devices, which do not require a limited distance between the devices to set the transaction.

These devices might share data via Bluetooth connections, such as specific deals or product information, while tracking their location/route within the store (in-store location). For instance, after downloading the mobile app, consumers may receive customized deals or special offers when they are within 50 meters of a specific shelf or mannequin. From a corporate perspective, retailers would obtain information about consumers behaviour such as time spent in a certain area of the stores, accessed information, consumers profile, etc..

**Mobiles as shopping assistant**

Communication technologies, and particularly mobile applications, can be considered as the fundamentals of the ubiquitous computing environment. From the systematic integration of the above-mentioned technologies, the features of this new scenario arise as follows: (1) embedding of computer hardware and software in other equipment and objects; (2) providing constant network accessibility and connectivity by user's mobile device (e.g. via wireless, Bluetooth, etc.); (3) supporting users through information services anytime and anywhere (accessing to the requested information via embedded input devices such as GPS or camera); (4) context awareness and adaptation of the system to current information requirements (i.e. the system replies according to consumers' location); (5) automatic recognizing and autonomous processing of repetitive tasks without user intervention (Kurkovski, 2005; Lin et al., 2011).

In fact, the increasing diffusion of mobile computing, based on the portable accessing technologies always connected to Internet for accessing to multimedia contents repositories (e.g. location-based services) (Lin et al., 2011), pushes retailers to provide mobile applications for consumers, with the aim to influence them to buy anytime and everywhere.

These apps show products through mobile interfaces supporting mobile purchase. In this way, the mobiles became a kind of interactive guide in the new retail settings. Therefore, mobile apps m-store offers a large convenience in terms of:

- Physical facilities, because app contents might be customized on users' requests and be constantly updated.
- Product presentation, because app offers a large variety of products and enhanced related information and the interaction with the available products (i.e. access to video, audio, 3D virtual manipulation, etc.). Resolution and interactivity are related to the mobile interface employed for the connection.

- Service, m-store offers mobile payment systems (for fast self-check out), access to personalized contents and recommendation systems, etc.
- Convenience, by offering a store accessible anytime and anywhere.
- Visual appearance, m-store provides 3D graphics, user-friendly interfaces, high interactive and realistic environments, which could be integrated within a real shopping environment as a supporting shopping guide (see the case of Ikea mobile catalogue in Chapter 11), etc.

*Figure 13.2* Regent Street app (Regent Street, London, UK)

### CHAPTER SUMMARY AND CONCLUSIONS

The dynamic nature of technology in the future will lead to costly investment decisions for retailers. To reduce the possibility of selecting inappropriate technology the e-retailer must keep in mind the buying decision process that follows the established stages of need recognition, information search, information evaluation, purchase decision and post-purchase behaviour. Not understanding the online customer's buying process has contributed to abandoned cart syndrome and e-retailer closures (for example in the dot.com crash). To overcome the lack of a physical store, e-retailers need to assist the online shopper's buying decision process through improved informational exchanges, i.e. newsgroups and FAQ webpages, Twitter and Facebook accounts. E-technology is not restricted to e-retailers but is being adopted by bricks-and-mortar retailers in the form of improved payment systems and merchandise identification through RFID tagging and QR codes. Bricks retailers are making great strides in modernisation. As a result, bricks-and-clicks retailers are increasingly making the running versus pure-play dot.coms.

In the introductory pages to this book, we quoted the (UK) *Sunday Times* journalist, Matthew Wall's personal experiences of life as an e-shopper. Matthew concluded that e-retailing is coming of age, but recognised his need to 'get out more'. Even the most committed e-shoppers still like bricks shopping and trust bricks brands and malls. Such shopper loyalty is likely to ensure that the high street will not be replaced by e-retail, but will more and more represent the physical presence of the successful multi-channel bricks-and-clicks retailers.

### Case study 13.1
### TESCO VIRTUAL STORE

*Sources: (Telegraph, 2011; Mobile Marketing 2014; The Creators Project, 2014; Tesco 2016)*

In 2011 in South Korea, Tesco (the British grocery chain) launched a new kind of store totally virtual within its South Korean chain Home Plus. Starting from the idea that South Koreans have little time for shopping, Tesco gave them the possibility to save time for shopping though plastering the glass walls of subway stations with pictures of their products, simulating everything they could expect in a traditional store. These "special shelves" featured QR codes which could be scanned by the consumers' mobiles, creating a shopping basket while waiting for the train and then purchasing. Moreover, deliveries were arranged to arrive in a few minutes or hours (rather than traditional "next day delivery" or "2–3 days" delivery) without the need for shoppers to wait in line to collect the purchases.

Following this successful trial, Tesco moved further with the adoption of advanced technologies for increasing the shopping experience, by launching a new project called "Tesco Pele" in collaboration with the Figure Digital company, which created a version of the Tesco store on the Oculus Rift headset. In particular, Oculus Rift is an innovative platform developed to enable people to build games and experiences with a high feeling of realism. Oculus Rift employs the most recent displays and optics designed specifically for VR. It allows developers to easily customize an optics system to provide a highly realistic visual presence in an immersive

# MULTI-CHANNEL SUCCESS

scenario. For the best usage, Oculus Rift must be associated with the following computer characteristics: Video Card NVIDIA GTX 970/AMD R9 290 equivalent or greater, CPU Intel i5–4590 equivalent or greater, Memory 8GB+ RAM, Video Output Compatible HDMI 1.3 video output, USB Ports 3x USB 3.0 ports plus 1x USB 2.0 port, OS Windows 7 SP1 64 bit or newer.

According to Tesco (Tesco, 2015), this project would synthetize the future of the supermarket, because

> Unlike the big plastic monstrosities you used to have to strap to your head for VR, the Oculus Rift is a far lighter, smaller and more comfortable headset. It works in conjunction with your computer and a pair of headphones to take you into virtual reality worlds – and with the improvements in computer graphics and screen tech over the last 20 years, those worlds can be startlingly realistic.

This project allows consumers to live a realistic experience in an empy supermarket, by exploring corners, visualizing shelves and products, etc. Tesco continues:

> Oculus Rift started as a Kickstarter project and surpassed its $250,000 target by some way – users pledged an astonishing $2.4 million. Then in March 2014, Facebook snapped it up for $2 billion. Clearly, they have big plans for virtual reality. "Let's say you have a friend getting married and you can't be there," Facebook's VP of engineering, Cory Ondrejka, told The Verge. "What if you could put a 360-degree video camera in the audience? Then, what you have is an ability to really feel like you're there and look around and see what's going on." It's early days, but we could be looking at a technology that has as much potential to change the world as the internet….

Accordingly, Figure Digital's managing director, Ben Paterson, declared: "We plan to create virtual experiences for brands that advertisers could only have dreamed about only a few years ago. We can now create 360-degree cinematic experiences and gamified interactive solutions that allow consumers to totally immerse themselves into a brand's message".

Therefore, Tesco is indicating how e-retailing will look in the near future and traditional retailers better take note.

## QUESTIONS

*Brief feedback to these questions is included at the back of the book.*

**Question 13.1** – Some workplaces are restricting Internet access due to high levels of online personal activities. How should e-retailers respond to this limited access threat?

**Question 13.2** – If a consumer can buy goods online to save money and then pick up from the retailer's bricks-and-mortar store (pick-up point) isn't this cannibalising the bricks-and-mortar store sales?

## GLOSSARY

**Abandoned Cart Syndrome**   This is an action of discontinuing an online purchase.

**Barcode**   This is a widely used graphic identification tag for merchandise using dark vertical bars for scanning and recording purposes.

**Cookie files**   Small computer files that record a website user's site visits to personalize information to improve online sales/services, enable subscribers to access a site without a password, record popular links, record demographics and track visitor search preferences.

**Contactless technologies**   New technologies based on proximity sensor that allows payment without providing any pin or signature.

**Cross-channel free riding**   Consumers' tendency of using one channel for finding and comparing product information and a different one for purchasing, which can be managed by not linking each retailer.

**Frequently Asked Questions (FAQ)**   A series of questions submitted by previous Internet users. The website owners then provide responses to these questions. The objective is to reduce the resources required to respond to the 20% of questions that are asked 80% of the time (the Pareto Principle 80/20 rule).

**Near Field Communication (NFC)**   Technology providing mobile devices with wireless two-way short-range connectivity up to a maximum of 10 cm.

**Oculus Rift**   An innovative platform developed to enable people to build games and experiences with high feeling of realism.

**Planogram**   Planogram refers to the placement of merchandise in a store in a specific arrangement to achieve a stated objective.

**Quick Response codes (QR)**   Bidimensional barcode able to augment the reality with contents and information by scanning it with a smartphone camera.

**Radio Frequency Identification (RFID)**   A miniature electronic device that can track the location of an item and perform many other tasks. The Association for the Automatic Identification and Data Capture (AIDC) gives a description of these electronic identification devices and their usage. www.aimglobal.org/technologies/rfid

**Shopping Cart (trolley)**   An electronic representation of the bricks-and-mortar shopping cart (a.k.a. shopping trolley) into which online shoppers place their prospective purchases before the sale is finalised.

## FURTHER READING

Friedewald M and Raabe O. (2011) 'Ubiquitous computing: An overview of technology impacts', *Telematics and Informatics,* 28 (2): 55–65.

Hopping D. (2000) 'Technology in retail', *Technology in Society,* 22: 63–74.

Huth C L. (2015) 'A privacy primer on beacon technology', *Journal of Internet Law*, 18 (8): 21–25.

Kang J-Y M, Mun J M and Johnson K K P. (2015) 'In-store mobile usage: Downloading and usage intention toward mobile location-based retail apps', *Computers in Human Behavior*, 46: 210–217.

Kaufman-Scarborough C and Lindquist J D. (2002) 'E-shopping in a multiple channel environment', *Journal of Consumer Marketing* 19 (4): 333–350.

Neslin S A and Shankar V. (2009) 'Key issues in multichannel customer management: Current knowledge and future directions', *Journal of Interactive Marketing*, 23: 70–81.

Sorescu A, Frambach R T, Singh J, Rangaswamy A and Bridges C. (2011) 'Innovations in retail business models', *Journal of Retailing*, 87 (S1): s3-s16.

# REFERENCES

Amazon. (2003) *Egghead Orders and Policy Info*, [Online] Available at Amazon.com: http://www.amazon.com/exec/obidos/tg/browse/-/776128/102-7635508-9796126 [Accessed 19 November 2003].

Belk M, Germanakos P, Asimakopoulos S, Andreou P, Mourlas C, Spanoudis G and Samaras G. (2014) 'An individual differences approach in adaptive waving of user checkout process in retail eCommerce', *Lecture Notes in Computer Science*, 8527: 451–460.

Cho Y, Im I, Hiltz R and Fjermestad J. (2002) 'An analysis of online customer complaints: Implications for Web complaint management', in *Proceedings of 35th Hawaii International Conference on System Sciences*. IEEE, pp. 1–10.

Dholakia R R, Zhao M and Dholakia N. (2005) 'Multichannel retailing: A case study of early experiences', *Journal of Interactive Marketing*, 19 (2): 63–74.

Editor. (2002) *The Quote 'May You Live in Interesting Times'*, 2003, [Online] Available at BBC: http://www.bbc.co.uk/dna/h2g2/alabaster/A807374 [Accessed 26 September 2003].

Fenech T. (2002) 'Antecedents to Web cart abandonment', in *Proceedings of Australian and New Zealand Marketing Academy Conference*, Melbourne.

Hsieh Y-C, Roan J, Pant A, Hsieh J-K, Chen W-Y, Lee M and Chiu H-C. (2012) 'All for one but does one strategy work for all? Building consumer loyalty in multi-channel distribution', *Managing Service Quality*, 22 (3): 310–335.

Kennedy R F. (1966) *May You Live in Interesting Times*. Cape Town, South Africa.

Kurkovski S. (2005) 'Using principles of pervasive computing to design m-commerce applications', in *Proceedings of the International Conference on Information Technology: Coding and Computing*, IEEE, pp. 59–64.

Lightfoot W. (2003) 'Multi-channel mistake: The demise of a successful retailer', *International Journal of Retail and Distribution Management* 34 (4): 220–229.

Lin P-H, Huang K-S, Wu C-H and Hong Z-W. (2011) 'A resource management model for ubiquitous computing environments', in *Proceedings of the 15th International Symposium on Consumer Electronics*, IEEE, pp. 556–559.

Luxury Daily. (2013) *Harrods Boosts Chinese Consumer Awareness via WeChat*, [Online] Available at Luxury Daily.com: http://www.luxurydaily.com/harrods-boosts-chinese-consumer-awareness-via-wechat/ [Accessed 14 January 2016].

Olsen C. (2008) 'Is contactless payment a reality for the retail industry?', *Card Technology Today*, 20 (11-12): 10–11.

Pantano E. (2016) 'Engaging consumer through storefront: Evidences from integrating interactive technologies', *Journal of Retailing and Consumer Services*, 28: 149–154.

Pantano E and Viassone M. (2015) 'Engaging consumers on new integrated multi-channel retail environments: Challenges for retailers', *Journal of Retailing and Consumer Services*, 25: 106–114.

Pauwels K and Neslin S A. (2015) 'Building with bricks and mortar: The revenue impact of openings physical stores in a multichannel environment', *Journal of Retailing*, 91 (2): 182–197.

Seck A M and Philippe J. (2013) 'Service encounter in multi-channel distribution context: Virtual and face-to-face interactions and consumer satisfaction', *Service Industries Journal*, 33 (6): 565–579.

See-To E W K, Papagiannidis S and Westland J C. (2014) 'The moderating role of income on consumers' preferences and usage for online and offline payment methods', *Electronic Commerce Research*, 14 (2): 189–213.

Tesco. (2016) *Tesco Tech Support*, [Online] Available at Tesco.com: https://m.tesco.com/mt/www.tescotechsupport.com/feature/oculus-rift-next-big-thing/ [Accessed 14 January 2016].

The Creators Project. (2014) *A Virtual Reality Tesco Is Opening Shop in Berlin*, [Online] Available at the Creators Project: http://thecreatorsproject.vice.com/blog/tescos-using-virtual-reality-goggles-to-possibly-allow-people-to-buy-groceries-from-bed [Accessed 14 January 2016].

The Mobile Marketing. (2014) *Tesco Goes Virtual with Oculus Rift*, [Online] Available at the Mobile Marketing Magazine: http://mobilemarketingmagazine.com/tesco-goes-virtual-with-oculus-rift/ [Accessed 14 January 2016].

The Telegraph. (2011) *Tesco Builds Virtual Shops for Korean Commuters*, [Online] Available at The Telegraph.co.uk: http://www.telegraph.co.uk/technology/mobile-phones/8601147/Tesco-builds-virtual-shops-for-Korean-commuters.html [14/01/2016].

Thornton J and Marche S. (2003) 'Sorting through the dot bomb rubble: How did the high-profile e-tailers fail?', *International Journal of Information Management* 23 (2): 121–138.

Verhoef P, Neslin S A and Vroomen B. (2007) 'Multichannel customer management: Understanding the research-shopper phenomenon', *International Journal of Research in Marketing*, 24: 129–148.

# Answers to chapter-end questions

Preliminary feedback is given to each question, but this should be seen merely as a guide. It is up to the reader to elaborate on the answer and in some cases maybe take quite a different tack to that provided by the authors. We do not imply that there is only one correct answer.

## CHAPTER 1: THE WORLD OF E-RETAILING

### Question 1.1
What do you think would be disadvantages of e-retailing for an independent baker like Botham's (www.botham.co.uk/)?
*Feedback* – May be put off by high set-up, investment and ongoing costs plus level of know-how and technology needed.

### Question 1.2
What do you consider are the main advantages of e-retailing for a small independent baker like Botham's?
*Feedback* – Location is unimportant; size does not matter; and reaches a larger audience.

### Question 1.3
Why do you think Screwfix is separately branded from B&Q even though both are under the same ownership, selling many of the same products?
*Feedback* – B&Q traditional store customers might consider they were being unfairly treated if e-customers of the organisation received a better deal.

### Question 1.4
Why do you think that the 7Cs of the e-retail mix represent a superior model to the traditional 4Ps and other versions of the retail mix?
*Feedback* – More customer-orientated than the 4Ps, emphasising **C1 Convenience for the customer** rather than a company's distribution network; **C2 Customer value and benefits** rather than a product a company sells;

317

# ANSWERS TO CHAPTER-END QUESTIONS

**C3 Cost to the customer** rather than the price set by the company; **C4 Communication and customer relationships** rather than promoting products with a hard sell. More specific to (e-) retail than the 4Ps, also including the essential elements of success and customer satisfaction: **C5 Computing and category management issues** needed to provide slick, reliable delivery without high stocks; **C6 Customer franchise**, i.e. the vital brand image and customer trust; and **C7 Customer care and service**, giving priority to looking after the customers' interests. Easier to remember than the traditional less-standardised versions of the retail mix.

## CHAPTER 2: THE BUSINESS OF E-RETAILING IN PRACTICE

### Question 2.1
Why are home electronics particularly suitable for online shopping?
*Feedback* – High on all three aspects of the de Kare-Silver ES test.
*Product characteristics:* low touch products, simple to deliver by post.
*Familiarity and confidence:* customers usually know exactly what they are ordering.
*Consumer attributes:* the typical buyers tend to be younger, better educated and in a higher socio-economic group than the general population.

### Question 2.2
Why is it surprising that groceries are among the biggest selling e-retail products in the UK?
*Feedback* – Low on all three aspects of the de Kare-Silver ES test.
*Product characteristics:* high sensory input in selection (visual, touch and smell), perishable, cannot be delivered by post.
*Familiarity and confidence:* Non-packaged products like fruit and vegetables can be variable in characteristics and quality.
*Consumer attributes:* On average, older and less educated than typical shoppers for products such as home electronics.

### Question 2.3
Why are groceries one of the main UK e-shopping categories?
*Feedback* – One of the first UK e-retail products, pursued by Tesco with single-minded determination to provide customer satisfaction, using an easy-entry, cost-effective e-retailing system.

### Question 2.4
How can online retailers reduce or avoid cart abandonment?
*Feedback* – State delivery charges and lead times up front; make the checkout process quick and simple, for example optionally available without registration; one-click ordering.

# ANSWERS TO CHAPTER-END QUESTIONS

## CHAPTER 3: INTEGRATION OF E-RETAILING INTO AN ORGANISATION

### Question 3.1
What do you consider to be the advantages and disadvantages that traditional retailers have in comparison with Internet pure-plays, in terms of online trading?
*Feedback* – This chapter outlines several advantages and disadvantages for traditional retailers integrating e-retail, that encompass for example, experience in the given product sector but often lack of experience in the e-commerce dimension. Further advantages and disadvantages are given in Chapter 1, Box 1.2.

### Question 3.2
Why do you think online customers may not be loyal to a particular company?
*Feedback* – Where online shopping is price driven, it is much easier to compare prices online and move from website to website, than it is to do the same with physical shops. Also, many aspects of the normal retail shopping experience, such as face-to-face interaction, are missing, which can increase the homogeneity among outlets of the online shopping experience.

### Question 3.3
What are the dangers of multi-channel operations from a company's perspective?
*Feedback* – A company must maintain a consistent brand, not just concerning for instance, standards for logos, colours and fonts, etc., but regarding values and message. Other factors include having consistent terms of business so that there is no conflict in pricing or returns policy for example.

## CHAPTER 4: UNDERSTANDING AND COMMUNICATING WITH THE E-CONSUMER

### Question 4.1
Why do people shop?
*Feedback* – To obtain useful benefits, but also for many other reasons. For example, to enjoy the process or to socialise with others.

### Question 4.2
Can e-shopping satisfy shoppers as much as bricks shopping does?
*Feedback* – E-shopping and bricks shopping are different and there is some evidence that e-shopping does not satisfy recreational motives as well as

# ANSWERS TO CHAPTER-END QUESTIONS

bricks shopping does. Even so, successful e-retailers can provide satisfaction for enjoyment and social motives.

### Question 4.3
How can the mechanistic process of e-shopping satisfy shoppers' social motives?
*Feedback* – For example, providing social experiences, communication with others having a similar interest, membership of virtual communities.

### Question 4.4
What can e-retailers do to provide enjoyment and social benefits for e-shoppers?
*Feedback* – For example, be present on social media (Facebook, Instagram, etc.) and engage with great content. Provide chat rooms and bulletin boards. Provide facilities for product reviews and suggestion boxes. Personalisation of offers.

## CHAPTER 5: INFORMATION SEARCH ON THE WEB

### Question 5.1
What is the *one* thing I can do to get my website noticed?
*Feedback* – Build a good Home Page, with a title, meta-information, no frames and with content pointing to what goods and services you are offering.

### Question 5.2
I've put up a good webpage some months ago, but nobody is accessing it much nowadays. What can I do?
*Feedback* – Change the content and keep them **updated**! People get bored by the same old thing. Put something relevant and timely for people to read. Moreover, share the contents through social media (i.e. Facebook), by sharing the link to specific content, etc.

## CHAPTER 6: E-STORE DESIGN: NAVIGABILITY, INTERACTIVITY AND WEB ATMOSPHERICS

### Question 6.1
Why do you think design issues are more important for e-retailers than offline (brick) retailers?
*Feedback* – Whereas design issues have some importance for offline retailers, they are just one of many components of the retail mix. In contrast, design issues affect just about everything in an e-retail context, including navigation, interactivity, relationships and atmospherics.

# ANSWERS TO CHAPTER-END QUESTIONS

**Question 6.2**
Two checklists have been presented in this chapter (a three-point list and a six-point list) to assist in the evaluation of the navigability of an e-retail site. How would you develop these two lists into a 'metric' that quantifies these points?
*Feedback* – A metric requires us to put numbers on the various aspects of navigability. So we have to develop numbers like a scale of 1 to 10 if you think the site performs well on that particular attribute. So a site might make it very clear where you are at the moment and you might give it 9 out of 10, but if it is very confusing about how to go forward to a particular location you might only give it 4 out of 10.

**Question 6.3**
How could an e-retailer use the metrics developed in question 6.2 to help improve its navigability performance?
*Feedback* – Providing you can work out a consistent way of measuring each aspect, then you can do this over time and get a good handle on which things are working and which things are not. The bad things identified by the metrics can be fixed through re-design of the website (for example, better directions on how to find a particular location, if it had only scored 4 out of 10). This should then lead to more satisfied customers.

**Question 6.4**
What is e-interactivity and how would you measure it?
*Feedback* – Interactivity refers to the interactivity between the user of an e-site and the site itself. The site is an ongoing entity, with a capacity to provide service, sell goods, transact money, be cheerful or grumpy, be there tomorrow for you, and so on. Chapter 6 includes a seven-item scale of interactivity, including for example, "site helps the viewer participate, learn and act" and "the site develops a close, personalized relationship with the viewer". Metrics can be applied to these items in the same way that you used metrics to measure navigability.

**Question 6.5**
How does interactivity help an e-retailer build a stronger relationship with its customers?
*Feedback*: Communication is seen as an important part of building any relationship. Given that e-interactivity is a communication-based interface, it seems likely that it could be important for developing e-relationships.

**Question 6.6**
Consider two different types of e-retailers. Name them. What sort of web atmospherics would be best for each of them, not necessarily what they are currently using?

# ANSWERS TO CHAPTER-END QUESTIONS

*Feedback* – The answer to this will depend on the examples chosen by the reader. No doubt some retail categories lend themselves more to the use of Web atmospherics. E-grocery shopping, for example, is primarily information driven, whereas online fashion buying has more need and potential for the use of atmospherics.

## CHAPTER 7: E-SERVICE

### Question 7.1
What is the difference between the macro and the micro view of e-services?
*Feedback* – Basically the macro view is a very broad view about what constitutes e-service and more or less equates e-service and e-commerce. The micro perspective sees it in terms of the provision of particular and varied detailed customer services within a site as part of the website-to-user interface.

### Question 7.2
Why do Moon and Frei (2000) prefer the co-production model (or co-creation) of e-service rather than the self-service model?
*Feedback* – Moon and Frei (2000) are concerned that self-service may be construed as a laissez-faire, free-for-all, in which the e-retailer takes a lazy approach and lets the user/consumer do all the work through self-service. This would prove frustrating for many (but not all) consumers, so instead they advocate a more cooperative or co-production type of approach to the provision of e-services.

### Question 7.3
Do you agree that the factors that contribute to *good* e-service are different from the factors that contribute to *bad* e-service? Why?
*Feedback* – The facts presented from the critical incident study in Chapter 7 are that they are quite different. Interactivity and information were seen as useful ways of developing higher levels of e-service, whereas the traps or negative service often come from things like poor delivery service or a poor returns service. One can see these in terms of "motivators" to get people to be positively motivated towards a site and hygiene factors for the negatives, things that may not get you really excited about a site but make you made if it does not work well.

### Question 7.4
Explain how e-service metrics can help an e-retailer better manage their business.
*Feedback* – Recall our answers to questions 6.2 and 6.3 because a similar approach is needed. There is no single best way of measuring these things. Numbers on a 1 to 10 scale could be used. Equally a critical incident is

ANSWERS TO CHAPTER-END QUESTIONS

either a yes or a no if that incident occurs (yes) or not (no). This is a simpler approach. Which one do you prefer? Two sections of Chapter 7 are devoted to e-service metrics as a performance tool.

## CHAPTER 8: BRANDING ON THE WEB

### Question 8.1
A common mistake to branding or the understanding of branding is to treat it very narrowly as a sign, symbol or slogan. What is wrong or limiting with this approach?

*Feedback* — First, lots of people make this mistake, so you should not feel too bad if you are one of them. Second, the use of a sign or slogan is a good start to branding, so it should be seen as part of a total branding approach. However it misses opportunities to use branding in a more powerful way. This will happen if we think of the brand in terms of its substance and essence and start to develop these ideas further.

### Question 8.2
Briefly summarise the three-stage approach for e-brand development outlined in Chapter 8.

*Feedback* — The three stages include brand concept (what is the basic idea of the brand?) as a start, followed by building the brand platform (including personality, purpose, point of difference and brand backup) and finally implementation through the brand elements (elements are all the points of contact between the e-retailer and their customers). More details are in Chapter 8.

### Question 8.3
The brand platform stage of e-brand development includes the need to develop the personality of the e-brand. Select a particular e-retailer and show how you would use web atmospherics to develop the brand of this particular e-retailer.

*Feedback* — Clearly the answer here depends on which e-retailer you have chosen. Chapter 6 gives you more ideas about the options for Web atmospherics. The key thing is to choose the right type of atmospherics to suit a specific brand. The matching process between the atmospherics and the brand is a critical branding principle, so be prepared to justify your choice of atmospherics.

### Question 8.4
Chapter 8 has really highlighted the importance of interactivity and trust as necessary for building strong e-brands. Why have these two aspects been highlighted in this role?

# ANSWERS TO CHAPTER-END QUESTIONS

*Feedback* – Chapter 8 gives more details, but a key answer is that e-retailers have *experiential* brands, thus interactivity is bound to be important. Trust is important for all brands, but is likely to be especially important because it takes a lot of faith that by clicking a mouse, money will be transmitted and goods will be delivered!

### Question 8.5
Why are Amazon.com and eBay regarded as such strong e-brands?
*Feedback* – Each of these e-retailers has had major financial (especially traffic and sales) success and stand above most of the remaining field. Several books and many papers have been written about them. They have played pioneering roles in their categories, though neither was the absolute (first) pioneer. They have each displayed leadership qualities in innovating and adopting progressive e-retailing practices. We will leave it to the reader to discover what they see as the best features of each of these two e-retail legends.

## CHAPTER 9: E-MALLS

### Question 9.1
What is important in managing conventional malls?
*Feedback* – It is important to mange the tenant relationship. It is important to manage the basics, like quality (though the tenant mix), service, atmosphere and infrastructure, as well as achieve the right overall image and position in the market. More details are given in the chapter.

### Question 9.2
How do you *translate* the principles in managing conventional malls to e-malls?
*Feedback* – The same principles apply, with just a slight change in the translation. The tenant mix remains critical, with a danger of having too many unknown pure (cyberspace) e-retailers. Big well-known click e-retailers are not a problem, but there are not too many of the trustworthy type.
A major finding of our original research in this chapter is that interactivity and trust, especially the latter, are extremely important for developing and building an e-mall.

### Question 9.3
Do you regard a shopping bot as an intelligent agent or a virtual mall? Why?
*Feedback* – The paper from Rowley (2000) and discussion in Chapter 9 indicate that you can interpret shopping bots either way. The chapter primarily views it from the perspective of a virtual mall because that chapter is mainly interested in e-malls but you may wish to reconsider it as an

# ANSWERS TO CHAPTER-END QUESTIONS

intelligent agent – that is like an intelligent shopping assistant. This alternative interpretation would require us to relocate the notion to Chapter 6, where we considered issues like navigation information search.

## Question 9.4
Why are e-malls less dominant in cyberspace than brick malls are in physical space?
*Feedback* – This is an important question and gets to the bottom of the entire rationale for e-retailing. A number of the authors' views are canvassed in the conclusion section of Chapter 9. Perhaps e-malls are a late starter at the beginning of its life cycle. This was also the case of conventional malls. There were very few conventional malls in the 1950s, with rapid growth since then. One view that we do favour is that most online shopping trips are focused on a particular category and therefore it would suffice to visit a particular e-retailer or a narrowly focused e-mall, whereas multi-purpose shopping trips are common and desirable offline and suit conventional malls. Of course, it could also be that each e-retailer often has their own website, which gives them more control, and thus the need to be part of an e-mall has diminished. However, this might change when virtual reality e-malls become more developed.

## CHAPTER 10: E-RETAILING MODELS

### Question 10.1
How would use of the retail participant groups in a retailer's environment help minimise channel disintermediation?
*Feedback* – By consulting with suppliers, partners and dealers the e-retailer will identify those distribution issues that may damage the relationship between the channel members before they occur.

### Question 10.2
If mobile apps are starting offering additional features to exploit the physical catalogues, why do many websites resist offering online catalogue?
*Feedback* – Part of the reason is habit and the confidence with mobile technologies, the online users are comfortable with what they have used for so long and see no great benefit from the mobile technology.

### Question 10.3.
Can a customer be in more than one of the A.C. Nielsen electronic shopper categories?
*Feedback* – As no person is ever a perfect fit for clothing, neither are they for categorisation, as helpful as the fit would be for the retailer. A person could be a Habit Die-Hard but because of their employment they can get

# ANSWERS TO CHAPTER-END QUESTIONS

to the mall for a special event present and so they have to consider the convenience of a non-store retailing channel, such as the Web.

## CHAPTER 11: M-SHOPPING

### Question 11.1
It took half a decade to get a critical mass of users to adopt the Internet as a shopping environment. Which kinds of new mobile features will retailers need to provide to move consumers towards m-shopping?
*Feedback* – Mobile communication technology is fustily improving with clearer display screens and polyphonic sound quality to emulate and almost duplicate the Web experience of using large computer displays. The integration with augmented reality feature would be able to provide a more realistic and enjoyable shopping experience. Fun and convenience (in terms of time and cost reduction) will catch consumers' attention.

## CHAPTER 12: U-SHOPPING

### Question 12.1
Can ubiquitous retailing replace e-tailing?
*Feedback* – Similar to the advent of e-retailing that did not replace the traditional (offline shopping), the complete replacement with u-shopping seems still unrealistic. Presumably, in a couple of years, the number of consumers using u-shopping will increase, without replacing the e-shopping or offline shopping.

### Question 12.2
What are the main consequences of the u-shopping scenario for retailers?
*Feedback* – Retailers have to be conscious of the new competitive environment, which includes the emerging channel base on ubiquitous computing. To this end, they could add this channel to their traditional offer, by handling more channels simultaneously.

## CHAPTER 13: MULTI-CHANNEL SUCCESS AND THE FUTURE OF E-RETAILING

### Question 13.1
Some workplaces are restricting Internet access due to high levels of on-line personal activities. How should e-retailers respond to this limited access threat?
*Feedback* – Work with the non-associated workplaces. This is not a new concept; social clubs at workplaces have often received preferred customer

treatment from retailer groups to encourage purchases at those associated retailers. E-retailers could offer employers and the employer's staff incentives (i.e. discounts or delivery specials) for using the e-retailer at specific times that limit interference with work operations.

**Question 13.2**

If a consumer can buy goods online to save money and then pick up from the retailer's bricks-and-mortar store (pick-up point) isn't this cannibalising the bricks-and-mortar store sales?

*Feedback* – Some cannibalisation is possible however, the service is intended and likely to generate sales that would not be made at the brick and mortar store, for example from busy people who do not get time to browse in a physical store and want to avoid crowds.

# Index

Aaker, D.: *Building Strong Brands* 216; *Managing Brand Equity* 216
Abandoned Cart Syndrome 298, 311
Abbey National: Cahoot 85
AbeBooks 39
Accenture: 'Beyond the blur' 217
AC/DC 44
adaptation 303–4
address, web *see* URL
Adidas 10
Adler, E.: '*Reverse Showrooming*' 20
Adobe Acrobat 260
adPointer 129
Advantage 94
advantages of e-retailing: for customers 7–8, 105–6, 109; for retailers 78–80
advertising 154, 253; banners 129; hype 213–14; interstitials 129; offline 125, 126; pay-per click 12; pop-ups 129
Advertising Standards Authority (ASA) 56
Aguiar, L.: *Digital Music Consumption on the Internet* 46
Alamanos, E.: 'Does social exclusion influence multiple channel use?' 279–80
Al-Hawari, M.: 'Measuring banks' automated service quality' 201
*All at Sea* 126
AltaVista 153
Amanda Wakeley 57
Amazon 11, 12, 16, 17, 22, 166, 171; app 64; Australia 225–6; Barnes & Noble and 38, 61, 219; Bookpages takeover 61; brand 219–20; category management 14; CDNOW and 41, 243; collection lockers 20, 65, 85; communication 65–6; computing 66–7; convenience for the customer 63–4; cookies 63; cost to the customer 65; customer care and relationships 36–7, 65–6, 67–8, 130; customer franchise 68; Dash 70; delivery service xxi, 14, 219, 301; 'department store' 234, 238; Echo 70; Egghead and 303–4; Elastic Computer Cloud "EC2" 67; 'e-mall' 230; FAQs 68; Fire TV 70; five-step approach 219, 240; founded 251; Fresh 49, 64, 70; growth 256; 'hedonic' 110, 113; Instant Video 45; as intermediary 150; Kindle 62, 69; Look Inside 69; market leader 37, 38, 60, 78, 145; market penetration 68–9; music downloads from 42; one click 219; Pantry 49; Pickup points 64; price cutting 40; Prime 6, 45, 65, 66, 70; Prime Air xxi, 109; retail mix 61–70; Same-Day-Delivery 6; secondhand market 39; Simple Storage Service "S3" 67; store-based retail outlet 252; Super Saver Delivery 6; Toys "R" Us and 14, 79, 85; Waterstones and 69; Web Services (AWS) 67; WHSmith and 14
Anderson, T.: *Brand Building on the Internet* 215, 216
Angus & Robertson 225–6
Ansoff matrix 68–70
AOL 186

# INDEX

API 97
Apple 22; integrated e-retailing 85; iPhone 277; iTunes 40, 42, 45, 171; Mac Forum 188; Music 40, 44; price cutting 40
Argos xxi, 20, 26, 36–7, 64, 67, 82, 93
Armani Exchange 55
ARPAnet *see* Internet
ASDA 48
*AskJeeves* 150
ASOS 10, 16, 26, 51, 53–5, 57, 236; Catwalk 54; Men 54; Outlet 54
atmospherics *see* web atmospherics
auctions: tips for 134; *see also* eBay
Auction Universe 220
Auctionweb 132
Audi 10, 17
augmented reality 168–70
Austin, Pat 133
autos, searches for 162
Avon 252
Ayden 274

Baidu 20
Bananalotto 129
BankNet 187
banners 129
Barcelona 290, 291
barcode 305
Barnes & Noble 38, 61, 219
Batiste 57
Bausch & Lomb 175, 176
BBC xxii, 115
beacons 309–10
Beatles, The 44
Become 235
Beighton, Nick 54
Belisario, Lester 175
Belleflamme, P.: *Digital Piracy* 46
Bell Legal Group 203
Benamati, J.: *E-Commerce Basics* 220
Benvengudo 155
Berkowitz, E.N.: 'In-home shoppers' 105
BestBookPrice 38
Best Buy 11
Bezos, Jeff 65, 70
Bienstock, C. C.: 'Measuring service quality in e-retailing' 200
Big W 212

Birch, D.: 'Entertainment-seeking shopping centre patrons' 232
Birmingham: Bullring 82
Bitcoin 187
BitTorrent 46
Black Friday 2015 66–7
Blackwells 84
bloggers 55–8, 128
Bluetooth 278, 310
Blu-Ray 44
Body Shop 57, 211, 212
Boohoo 55
Bookfinder4U 38
bookmarks 146
Book People, The 38
books 37–9, 48
Boolean search 149
Boots 67, 94–5, 145, 147
Borden, Neil 8
Botham's of Whitby 7
bots 235–6
Bourlakis, M.: 'Does social exclusion influence multiple channel use?' 279–80; 'To immerse or not?' 168
BPL 278
branding 211–26; approaches to 212–13; Australia 212, 225–6, 241–2; brand attitudes 241–2; brand concept 214–15; brand development 214–19; brand elements 216; brand identity 214; brand platform 215–16; interactivity 216–19, 224; optimal retail offer 222–3; overall retail offer 222; retail mix 220–1; social media 223; trust 216–19; UK 212; USA 212; web atmospherics 224
Braunstein, M.: *Deep Branding on the Internet* 217
brick-and-mortar retailer 8, 251, 255–61
bricks and clicks 14, 92, 143, 312
Bridson, K.: 'Online Retail Loyalty Strategies' 87, 88, 89
British Library 189
broadband *see* Internet
Brooks, P.: *Metrics for IT Service Management* 202
browsers 144, 146
Brynjolfsson, E.: 'Frictionless commerce?' 38, 65

**330**

# INDEX

B2B 2, 105
B2C 2, 78, 105
Buck, S.: 'From electronic money to electronic cash' 187
Burbank 35
Burberry 57
Burt, R.: *Capturing the Online Grocery Opportunity* 50
business models 248–69; assessment 254–61; categorizing 251; defined 248
buying decision process 296–302; information evaluation 298; information search 297–8; need recognition 297; post-purchase behaviour 299–301; purchase decision 298–9

Cahoot 85
call centres 201
Capetown, University of 296
Cap Gemini 106, 109
care of customer 16–17, 19–20, 25–6, 130; Amazon 36–7, 65–6, 67–8, 130; Compass24 125; Next 25; Texco 89, 130
Carpenter, P.: *E-Brands* 216
carrefour.fr 35
Carter, K.: 'Exploratory Assessment of Catalog Shopping Orientations' 105
catalogue retailing 252
Category Management (CM) 13–14, 19, 25; Amazon 14; Compass24 124; Next 25; Screwfix 16
catwalks 26, 54
CD 39, 41–2
CDNOW 41, 243
Céline 5
cellular phones *see* mobile phones
Centre for Retail Research 4
Chanel 5, 95
Charlton, G.: *Ecommerce Consumer Reviews* 101
Chicksand, L.: 'Overcoming the difficulties of selling "look and feel" goods online' 171–2; 'Selling "look and feel goods" online' 52
Childers, T.L.: 'Hedonic and utilitarian motivations' 110
Chip and Pin 309

Cho, Y.: 'An analysis of online customer complaints' 299–300
Choi, S.-Y.: *Economics of Electronic Commerce* 83
CKS Interactive 220
Clarisonic 57
click-and-collect 6, 82, 84–5, 95
click-and mortar retailer 252
clicks *see* bricks and clicks
click-through 253
Clinique 57, 95
clothing 50–3; ASOS 53–5; searches 161
cloud-computing 67
Coca-Cola 223, 277, 278
Cockett, W.: 'Measuring image' 232
co-creation 10
Cohen, A.: *Perfect Store, The* 220
Coles 166, 212
Collier, J. E.: 'Measuring service quality in e-retailing' 200
communication with customer 11–13, 15, 18–19, 25; Amazon 65–6; communications mix 122–31; Compass24 125; Next 25; Screwfix 15; on social media 25, 188
community 250; retailer's objectives for 259–61
Compass24 123–5
Compound Annual Growth Rate (CAGR) 2
computing 13–14, 19, 25, 67; Amazon 66–7; Compass24 124; Next 25; Screwfix 16
Connellan, T.: *e-Service* 202
Consumer Barometer 115, 116
consumers *see* customers
convenience for customer 9–10, 15, 18, 24; Amazon 63–4; Compass24 123; improved 304–5; Next 24; Screwfix 15
Converse 191
Conway, P.: 'Lasting Legacy' 92
cookies 13, 63, 65, 172
cost to customer 11, 15, 18, 25; Amazon 65; Compass24 124; Next 25; Screwfix. 15
Country Attire 6
craftinsure 126
Craigslist 239; 'e-mall' 230

**331**

# INDEX

Crank, A.: 'Virtual reality mall lets consumers shop alongside digital giraffes and zebras' 230
Cravens, D.: *Strategic Marketing Management* 184, 223
crawler 148, 149, 154
credit cards 22, 64, 103, 108, 119
Cristobal, E.: 'Perceived e-service quality (PeSQ)' 200
cross-channel free riding 302–3
Curulate 269
Cusack, M.: *Online Customer Care* 202
customer franchise 16, 19, 25; Amazon 68; Compass24 124–5; Next 25
Customer Relationship Management (CRM) 7, 12
customers: advantages of e-retailing for 24, 105–6, 109, 124; cross-channel free riding 302–3; customer franchise 16, 19, 25, 68, 124–5; customer relationships 11–13, 15, 25, 65–6, 125, 130; customer service 119, 120, 121–2; disadvantages of e-retailing for 106–9; expectations 299–301; gender of 113–15; individualisation for 304; loyalty 87–90; participant group 249; profile 103–5, 264–8; retailer's objectives for 254–6; value and benefits to customer 10, 16, 18, 24, 124; *see also* care of customer; convenience for customer
customization *see* personalization
Cuthbertson, R.: 'Online Retail Loyalty Strategies' 87, 88, 89

Dabholkar, P.: 'Measure of service quality' 199; 'Technology in service delivery' 191
David Jones 212
David Stead Orchids 153
Davis, L.: 'Atmospheric qualities of online retailing' 166
Davis, W.: *E-Commerce Basics* 220
dealers 250; retailer's objectives for 258–9
DealTime 88
debit cards 22
Deck, S.: 'Ease of navigation' 233
Deezer 40
de Kare-Silver, M.: *e-Shock* 37, 84; ES test 37, 41, 48, 83–4, 261–8

delivery: Amazon xxi, 6, 14, 219, 301; cost of 5–6; Next 24, 25; Nordstrom service 269; postpurchase issues 301; Screwfix 15; Tesco 96, 312
Dell Computer Corporation 14, 17, 22, 133, 191
Denbigh Farm Bed and Breakfast 167
Denison, T.: 'Men and women arguing' 115
Dennis, C.: 'Does social exclusion influence multiple channel use?' 279–80; '*E-business: Reality or Rhetoric*' 110, 145; 'Measuring image' 232; 'Piracy of the web' 46–7; 'To immerse or not?' 168
design, website 119, 120, 154, 160–79; described 160; importance 161; integrated approach 172–4; interactivity 163–5; navigability 162–3; objectives and strategy 174; purpose 160–1; scope 160–1
DHL 256, 301
Diesel 54
Digicash 187
DigiScent 172
Digital Economy Act 2010 (UK) 40
digital retailers 252
Dilmperi, A.: 'Piracy of the web' 46–7
Dior 5, 57
direct mail 126–7
directories 146, 147–8, 154
direct retailers 251–2, 255–61
disadvantages of e-retailing 5–7; for customer 106–9; for retailers 5–7
distribution channels 251–2
diversification 69–70
Dixons Carphone 36, 81, 133
DIY 14, 15
Dogpile 153
domain name 151
Domino's Pizza 81
Donthu, N.: 'Internet Shopper' 104
door-to-door selling 252
dot.com crash 79, 312
Dou, W.: 'Interactive functions' 188
Double Click 253
Douglas, A.: 'Advent of e-business concepts' 186
Dove 96

332

# INDEX

d-store 234
DVD 39, 44, 48
Dymocks 225–6

ease of use 194
Eastlick, M.A.: 'Influence of store attitudes' 105
Easy Exotics 153
EasyJet 113
eBay 20, 145, 150; brand 219–20; customer relationship 89; 'department store' 238; 'e-mall' 230; 'hedonic' 112, 113; how it works 133; market leader 78, 112; partnerships 302; profile 132–4; safeguards of 16; transaction fee 253
E-Color 172
eConsultancy 101
Eddie Bauer 26; Style Builder 172
EDGE 275
Edmunds 126
eDressit 53
Eduard, T.: 'Adding clicks to bricks' 248
Efficient Customer Response (ECR) 13
Egghead 303–4
Eindhoven 275
Electronic Data Interchange (EDI) 13, 66
Electronic Funds Transfer Point of Sale (EFTPoS) 278
Electronic Point-of-Sale (EPoS) 14
electronic shopping (ES) test 37, 41–2, 48, 83–4, 261–8
electronic signatures 186–7
electronic word-of-mouth 117–18
e-mail 148; marketing campaign 127, 274; spam 96, 127
e-malls 144, 230–45; Australia 234, 237, 240–3; conventional (brick) compared 231–2, 233–4; examples 237–8; interactivity 239, 240, 242, 243, 244; multiple category retailers 234; quasi 237; trust 239, 240, 241, 242, 243, 244
e-Marketer 150
English, Rosie 133, 134
enjoyment and e-shopping 105, 110, 112–13
Enthred, Martin 281
e-retail mix *see* retail mix
Eroglu, S.: 'Atmospheric qualities of online retailing' 166

e-service *see* services
Eshakti 53
eSkye 238
Esteé Lauder *95*
ES test *see* electronic shopping (ES) test
eToys 79
Etsy 5
Euromonitor 61, 67
European Court of Justice (ECJ) 38
European Union 40
Eurostats 8
experiential aspects of e-shopping 110–13
export 84
EZFace 172

Facebook 12, 57, 102, 145, 312; book tool 171; buy tool 150, 171; communication with customers on 25, 188; peer-to-peer communication on 117, 128, 188
Fanbuzz 172
Farfetch 51, 57
Fassnacht, M.: 'Quality of electronic services' 200–1
fast moving of consumer goods (FMCG) 288, 291
favorites 146
FedEx 256, 301
Fenech, T.: 'Antecedents to Web cart abandonment' 298–9
Figure Digital 312
file sharing 46
financial news 43
Fink, D.: 'Perceptions of website design characteristics' 144
Firetrap 54
Flight Centre 212
FMCG 288, 291
focus 146–7, 154
footwear 50–3
Force 4 123, 125
Ford 89
4G 81, 127, 275
frames 149
France 38
Francis, Aimee-Rose 55–6
Francis, J.: 'Exploratory and confirmatory factor analysis' 199; 'Model of quality determinants' 199

# INDEX

Frei, F.: 'Exploding the self-service myth' 189, 190, 191
Frequently Asked Questions (FAQs) 68, 87, 164, 194, 197, 297, 312
Fry, M.-L.: 'Corporate branding' 163, 217, 218
FTP servers 148
fulfilment 119

Galbraith, R.W.: 'Service-Marketing Perspective on E-Tailing' 165, 186
Gap 161, 212
Garcia, A.: 'Internet Shopper' 104
Gates, Bill 61
Gehrt, K.C.: 'Exploratory Assessment of Catalog Shopping Orientations' 105
gender and shopping 113–15
Germany 38, 44
Ghazili, E.: 'Constructing online switching barriers' 91
Ghose, S.: 'Interactive functions' 188
Gillett, P.L.: 'Profile of Urban In-Home Shoppers' 103–4
Gilly, M.: '.comQ' 199; 'eTailQ' 119, 200, 201
Giorgio Armani 57
Google 86, 123, 146, 150, 153, 186; analytics 253; Chrome 144; Express 49; market leader 148, 149; Play 42; + 128; Shopping 235
GPRS 275
Greenberg, E.: *Strategic Digital Marketing* 217
Griffiths, Quentin 54
groceries 35, 47–8; online 48–50; *see also* Tesco
Groupon xxii, 88
growth of e-retailing 2–5, 20–2
Guerlain 57
Gwinner, K.: 'Consumer perceptions' 199

Ha, H-Y: 'Factors influencing consumer perceptions of brand trust online' 217
Ha, L.: 'Interactivity reexamined' 188
Hahn, K.: 'Qualitative investigation' 187
Hall, E.: 'Viaweb store 4.0' 238
H & M 55
Harris, K.: 'Women on the Net II' 117

Harrods 306
'hedonic' e-retailers 110, 113
Herington, C.: 'E-retailing by banks' 201
Hermes 5
high street 5, 7
Hill, S.: 'To de-mall or e-mall?' 237
Hilton Nordics 152–3
Hisa, T-L: 'Developing e-business dynamic capabilities' 288, 289
hits 153–4
HMV 41
Ho, C. B.: 'Measuring the service quality of internet banking' 201
Hoffman, D. L.: 'Marketing in hypermedia computer-mediated environments' 188
Home Depot 212
home electronics 36
Home Page 146, 149
Homeplus 312
Homer, S.: *Consumer Behaviour in Tourism* 117
Homestead Electronics Ltd 86
hosts 5, 154
Hot Hot Hot 110
Howard, E.: 'Management of shopping centres' 232
HP 57
HSPA+ 275
Hulu 45
Hunter, R.: 'The role of atmospherics in influencing consumer behaviour in the online environment' 52
hybrid retailers 84–5, 252, 302–4
hype 213–14
hyperlink 260
HyperText Markup Language (HTML) 148

Ibuprofen 94
IKEA 191, 280–3; catalogue 281–2
Imation 172
indexing 152
Infonet 104
information 194; evaluation 298; search 297–8
information-only websites 84
infrared (IR) beams 278
Instacart 49

# INDEX

Instagram 12, 55, 56, 57, 67, 269; peer-to-peer communication on 117
instant messaging 148
integration of e-retailing 78–97; advantages 78–80; change management 91–3; resource implications 91–3; strategies 80–6, 87–90; switching barriers 90–1; switching costs 90–1
interactivity 160–79; electronic kiosks 308–9; e-malls 239, 240, 242, 243, 244; importance of 217; Nike 53
Internet: broadband 44, 81; hosts 5, 154; searching 143–56
Internet of Things (IoT) 82, 184
Internet World Stats 8
interstitials 129
Inthefrow 56–9
inventory 304–5
iPhone 277
Ireland 96
iSmell Personal Scent Synthesizer 172
iTunes 40, 42, 45, 171

James, E.: 'Interactivity reexamined' 188
Janda, S.: 'Consumer perceptions' 199
Jeffries 55
John Lewis 11, 36, 67, 85, 126
Joines, J.: 'Exploring motivations' 220
Jones, D. T.: 'Tesco.com: Delivering home shopping' 13
Jones, J.M.: 'Print and Internet catalog shopping' 103
Joseph, M.: 'Service quality in the banking sector' 201
Just Eat xxii
Just in Time (JIT) 13, 124

Kamprad, Ingvar 281
Kapferer, J.: *Strategic Brand Management* 216
Kates, A.: *Strategic Digital Marketing* 217
Kate Spade 302
Kearny, A. T.: 'E-business Performance' 13
Keller, K.: *Building, Measuring and Managing Brand Equity* 216
Kennedy, Robert F. 296
Kenzo 57
keywords 151–2

Kim, J. H.: 'Effects of web site atmospherics on consumer responses' 52
Kimber, C.: *Researching Online Buying's Offline Impact* 118
Kindle 62
King, T.: 'Piracy of the web' 46–7
Kingfisher 15
Knowles, R.: 'Overcoming the difficulties of selling "look and feel" goods online' 171–2; 'Selling "look and feel goods" online' 52
Knox-Johnston, Sir Robin 125
Koese, I.: 'Quality of electronic services' 200–1
Kolesar, M.B.: 'Service-Marketing Perspective on E-Tailing' 165, 186
Korea 96
KPE 129
Krasonikolakis, I.: 'Design visual examplars of 3D online store layouts types' 168

L.L. Bean 86, 109, 145, 155–6
Lands' End 6, 252, 256; My Virtual Model 172
laptops 81
Lastminute 85
Laupase, R.: 'Perceptions of website design characteristics' 144
Lauterborn, R.: 'New marketing litany' 9
Lego 231
Levine, E.: *Deep Branding on the Internet* 217
Ley Sinde (Spain) 40
Li, Y. N.: 'Factor analysis of service quality dimension shifts' 200
Libra 215
life cycles stages 116
Lightfoot 303
Like2Buy 269
Lin, W.: 'Measuring the service quality of internet banking' 201
Lindstrom, M.: *Brand Building on the Internet* 215, 216; *Clicks, Bricks & Brands* 217
LinkedIn 128
link popularity 130
Liu, M.: 'Influence of store attitudes' 105

log file 154
L'Oreal 57
LuisaViaRoma 57
Luxembourg 38
Luxottica Group 176
Luxury Daily 269

McCarthy, E. Jerome: '4Ps' 8–9
McDonald's 215, 237, 275
McGoldrick, P.: *Retail Marketing* 13, 16
Macleit, K.: 'Atmospheric qualities of online retailing' 166
Macromedia Flash 178
Mahoney, M.Y.: 'Electronic shoppers' 104
Malhotra, A.: 'Conceptual framework for understanding e-service quality' 199
Mall of America 231
Mall of the Emirates 231
malls: conventional 231–2, 233–4; *see also* e-malls
Manganari, E. E.: 'Store atmosphere in web retailing' 168
market development 69
marketing: e-mail 127, 274; permission 127; research 125–6; viral 128–9
Marketing Lion 152
Marketline: *Music and Video in Europe* 44
market penetration 68–9
Marks & Spencer 212
Marsland, D.: 'Measuring image' 232
Martens, B.: *Digital Music Consumption on the Internet* 46
Mathur, L.: 'Services advertising' 188
Maybelline 57
Megaupload 40
men and e-shopping 113–15
Mercedes Benz 130
merchandise, tracking 305–8
merchandise sales 253
Merrilees, B.: 'Corporate branding' 163, 217, 218; 'Do traditional/strategic concepts apply in the e-marketing context?' 225–6, 234; 'Entertainment-seeking shopping centre patrons' 232; 'Interactivity design' 165, 166, 188; 'Managing the mall relationship' 232; *Retailing Management* 191; *Strategic Marketing Management* 184, 223; 'Superstore interactivity' 191–2

metacrawler 150
meta-tags 152
Meteorological Office 124
micropayment 278–9
Microsoft: Internet Explorer 144
Miller, D.: *Retailing Management* 191; 'Superstore interactivity' 191–2
Millison, D.: *Firebrands* 216
Minitel 104
Mintel Reports: *Electrical Goods Retailing UK* 36; *Online Grocery Retailing UK* 36; *Try-Before-You-Buy* 37, 51; *Will Digital Video Streaming Wipe Out DVD and Blue-ray Discs?* 52
Mobile Index 274
Mobile Payment Services Association 278
mobile phones: 4G 81, 127, 275; MMS 127–8; m-shopping 273–83; prevalence of 21; as shopping assistant 310–11; SMS 127–8; 3G 275
models *see* business models
Mols, N.: 'Internet and services marketing' 188
Mondex 187
monitoring 153–4
Monnier Freres 57
Montemagno, Giulio 4
Moon, M.: *Firebrands* 216
Moon, Y.: 'Exploding the self-service myth' 189, 190, 191
Mota, Bethany 56
motives for e-shopping 110–13
Mozilla 144
m-shopping 21–2, 273–83; customer profile 105, 279–80; definition 273; development 274; e-shopping and 276; evolution 274–5; growth of 276–7; requirements 274–5; u-shopping compared 290
Muir, L.: 'Advent of e-business concepts' 186
Mukerji, B.: 'The role of atmospherics in influencing consumer behaviour in the online environment' 52
multi-channel retailing 20–1, 281, 302–3
multi-device shopping 82
multimedia message services (MMS) 127–8; *see also* mobile phones

336

multiple category retailers 234
Murphy, J.: 'Measuring image' 232
music 39–44; digital downloads 42; piracy 40, 46–7; streaming services 43–4
Mutum, D. S.: 'A review of customer relationship management' 184

Napster 46
National Westminster Bank 85
National Wine and Spirits, Inc. 237
natural language 150
navigation 160–79; aids 177–8; browsers 144; Ray-Ban 177–8; schemes 178
Near Field Communication (NFC) 273, 309
need recognition 297
Neslin, S. A.: 'Building with bricks and mortar' 302
Nespresso 177, 303
.Net 126
Net-a-Porter 16
Netflix 45, 67
Netscape 220
Netshop 86–7
networks, wireless 274–5
New Look 52
newsgroups 311
Next 6, 17, 22, 55; category management 25; communication 25; computing 25; convenience for customer 24; customer care 25; customer franchise 25; customer relationships 25; Directory 24; Directory Card 26; International Retail 24; Lipsy 24; market leader 85; Online Exclusives 24; profile 23–6; Retail 24; retail mix 24–6, 51; Sourcing 24
Nguyen, B.: 'A review of customer relationship management' 184
Nielsen, J.: *Web Usability* 147, 154
Nielson: *E-commerce* 21, 35; *The Future of Grocery* 47
Nike 191, 231; personalization 53
noise words 150
Nordstrom 17, 268–9; Haute-Look 269; Rack 269; Scan & Shop 269; TextStyle 269; Trunk Club 269
Notonthehighstreet.com 5

Novak, T. P.: 'Marketing in hypermedia computer-mediated environments' 188
Nurofen 94
nytimes 254

Ocado 48–50, 61
Oculus 230; Rift 236, 312–13
Ofcom 81–2
offers, targeted 96
Office for National Statistics (UK) 36–7
O'Hara, C.: 'Defense e-mall changes hands' 237
Omega 2
OneHydra 63
online paid content 43
Online Retail Relationship Matrix 87
online-to-offline (O2O) 20
Onsale Exchange 220
Opodo 113
Oracle 65, 66
Orange SA 278
Ordinary Least Squares (OLS) 196
Osoyou 102
ozeshopping 240–3, 244

paid content 43
Pantano, E.: 'To immerse or not?' 168
Pantone 172
Papagiannidis, S.: 'Does social exclusion influence multiple channel use?' 279–80; 'To immerse or not?' 168
Parasuraman, A.: 'Conceptual framework for understanding e-service quality' 199; 'E-S-Qual' 191, 199, 200; 'Technology Readiness Index (TRI)' 200
Parsons, A.G.: 'Non-functional motives' 102, 110
participant groups 249–51
partners 250; retailer's objectives for 258–9
Patel, T.: 'Measuring image' 232
Paterson, Ben 313
Pauwels, K.: 'Building with bricks and mortar' 302
Payflow Pro 187
payment: BankNet 187; Bitcoin 187; clearing house 278; contactless 309–10; credit cards 22, 64, 103, 108, 119; debit cards 22; Digicash 187; direct

# INDEX

charge billing 278; electronic 309–10; micropayments 278–9; Mondex 187; Next 26; Payflow Pro 187; postpurchase issues 301; SMS 277–8
PC World 67
peer-to-peer distribution 46
Peitz, M.: *Digital Piracy* 46
perceived risk of e-shopping 102–3
permission marketing 127
personalization 52–3, 172
Pinterest 25, 57, 128, 145
piracy, digital 40, 46–7
place 152
planogram 305
pop-ups 129
pornography 43
portals 148, 237
Porter, Michael 223
post-purchase behaviour 299–301
PriceGrapper 235
pricerunner 5
PricewaterhouseCooper 21
PrimeSense 52
privacy *see* security
Prodigy, The 42
products: categories 34–5; characteristics 261–2; customer confidence and familiarity 262–4; development 69; ES test 37, 41, 48, 83–4, 261–8; five senses and 263; suitability assessment 261–8
progress icons 177
promotion *see* communication with customer
publicity 126
public relations 126
purchase decision 298–9
Purchaser-Purveyor Loyalty Matrix 89–90
pureplay e-retailer 85, 251

QR *see* Quick Response codes (QR)
quality of service, e-retail 119–20
Quick Response codes (QR) 273, 288, 289, 291, 304, 305, 306–8, 312
Quill 14
QVC 252

RAC 204
radio frequency identification (RFID) 288, 304, 305–8, 312

Radiohead 42, 44
Ramazzotti, Eros 171
Ray-Ban 169, 175–9; e-store 176; images 178; navigation aids 177–8; navigation schemes 178; text 178; usability of website 177; virtual try-on 176; visual elements 178
Rdio 40, 44
RealMedia 129
Recording Industry Association of America 40
recreation, shopping as 104, 131
Reiss 55, 57
relationship with customer *see* communication with customer
reliability 119, 304–5
Rentz, J.: 'Measure of service quality' 199
RetailMeNot 4
retail mix 8–20; Amazon 61–70; care of and service to customer 16–17, 19–20, 25–6, 36–7, 65–6, 67–8, 89, 125, 130; category management issues 13–14, 16, 19, 25, 124; communication and relationship with customer 11–13, 15, 18–19, 25, 65–6, 125; computing issues 13–14, 16, 19, 25, 67–8, 124; convenience for customer 9–10, 15, 18, 24, 63–4, 123, 304–5; cost to customer 11, 15, 18, 25, 65, 124; customer franchise 16, 19, 25, 68, 124–5; Next 24–6, 51; value and benefits to customer 10, 16, 18, 24, 124
returns 194
revenue stream 251, 253–4
reverse showrooming 20
Revolve Clothing 57
Reynolds, F.D.: 'Analysis of catalog buying behavior' 105
Reynolds, J.: 'eCommerce: A critical review' xix
RFID *see* radio frequency identification (RFID)
Richardson, O.: *'E-business: Reality or Rhetoric'* 110, 145
risk: perceived 102–3; *see also* security
Roberts, J.: 'Managing the mall relationship' 232
Robertson, Nick 54

# INDEX

Rodgers, S.: 'Improved way to characterise Internet users' 144
Rohm, A.J.: 'Typology of online shoppers' 110
Rowles, D.: *Digital Branding* 217
Rowley, J.: 'Shopping bots' 235
Royal Yachting Association 124
Ryanair 113

Safari 144
safety *see* security
Sainsbury's 48, 85, 212
Samsung 57, 125, 277
Sanity 213, 214, 253
Scherer, C.: 'Exploring motivations' 220
Scheufele, D.: 'Exploring motivations' 220
Schloerb, D.: 'Quantitative measure of telepresence' 188
Schuh 6, 17
Screwfix 127; customer service 120–1; Express Shopping 15; retail mix 14–16
search engine marketing (SEM) 151–2
search engine optimization (SEO) 151–2
search engine results page (SERP) 151
searches: growth in 150–1; search engines 66, 146, 148–52; survey 144–5
Sears 133, 252
security 6, 22, 102–3, 119, 120, 194
See-To, E.: 'To immerse or not?' 168
Selfridges 52
self-service 189–92, 201
services 184–204; approaches to 185–9; critical incident approach to performance 192–7; metrics for 197–9; negative critical incidents 194–5; performance 192; positive critical incidents 193–4; quality 200
Shangri-la Hotel 171
shareholders 249; retailer's objectives for 257–8
Shehan, K.B.: 'Typology of Internet users' online sessions' 144
Sheldon, K.M.: 'Improved way to characterise Internet users' 144
Shih, C.: 'Conceptualizing consumer experiences' 188
Shim, S.: 'Electronic shoppers' 104
shipping *see* delivery

shopbots 235–6
shoppers *see* customers
shopping carts 298; trolley loss 298
Shopping.com 89
ShoppingMagic 96
shopping trolleys 298
Shopzilla 235
short message systems (SMS) 127–8, 277–8
showrooming 20, 51
Silver, Bernard 305
SimilarWeb 67
Siomkos, G. J.: 'Store atmosphere in web retailing' 168
Sit, J.: 'Entertainment-seeking shopping centre patrons' 232
Smith, M.: 'Frictionless commerce?' 38, 65
Smith, M. D.: *The Truth about Piracy* 47
Snapchat 57
Snapdeal 20
SneakerPlay 102
social aspects of e-shopping 110–13
social media 12, 17, 25, 102, 115; advertising on 128; branding on 223; communication with customers on 25, 188; consumers, engaging on 170–1; *see also* Facebook; Instagram; Twitter
sofcom 240–3, 244
Solo 108
Sorli Virtual 291–2
spam 96, 127
Spector, R.: *Amazon.com* 220
sponsorship 126
Spotify 40, 44, 46
staff 249; retailer's objectives for 256–7
Staples 69
Starbucks 275
Stephen H Smith Garden Centre 153
Sterne, J.: *Customer Service on the Internet* 202
Steuer, J.: 'Defining virtual reality' 188
sticky 177
Store locator 177
strategic options 82–6
streaming: music 43–4; video 45–6
Strom, D.: 'Building your online storefront' 238
Style Builder 26, 172

INDEX

subscriptions 253–4
Sugg, Zoe 56
*Sunday Times, The* 56; surveys xix–xx, 312
Superdrug 147
suppliers 250; retailer's objectives for 258–9
Svensson, G.: 'New aspects of research' 201
Swaminathan, V.: 'Typology of online shoppers' 110
Swarbrooke, J.: *Consumer Behaviour in Tourism* 117
Swift, Taylor 44
Swissmom 188

tablets 21, 81
Target 11
Tauber, E.M.: 'Why do people shop?' 105
T-commerce 81, 94
telecommunications: networks 274–5; see also mobile phones
Telefonica Moviles SA 278
telephone selling 252
television 252
Tesco 14, 17, 22, 67, 69; branding 212; Clubcard 12; customer care and relationships 89, 130; customer satisfaction 118–19; delivery service 96, 312; direct mail 126; Grocery App 96; market leader 48, 60, 85, 93; Pele 312; profile 95–7; QR 306; retail mix 35, 38; RFID 306; virtual store 312–13
Thomasville Furniture 172
Thorpe, D.: 'Measure of service quality' 199
3D body scans 52
3G 275
Ticketmaster 113
Tidal 44
*Times, The* xxii
T-Mobile 11
T-Mobile AG 278
Topshop 57
Toys "R" Us 14, 79, 85, 212
tracking merchandise 305–8
transaction fee 253

Travers, T.: 'Electronic trust services' 186–7
Trillenium 236
Trocchia, P.: 'Consumer perceptions' 199
trust, customer 240, 241, 242, 243; development of 239; importance of 217, 244
Turban, K.: 'Building your online storefront' 237
'turn the page' technology 189
24/7 236, 273
Twitter 12, 25, 56, 57, 128, 312

UK Customer Satisfaction Index (UKCSI) 67
UltraViolet (UV) 44
Unilever 96
Unipower 96
URL 146, 149, 153, 154, 224
u-shopping 287–92; characteristics of 287–8; m-commerce compared 290; traditional e-commerce compared 290
UX/UI (User experience/user interface) 10, 12

Value Added Tax 38
value and benefits to customer 10, 16, 18; Next 24; Screwfix 124
Van Riel, A. C. R.: 'Exploring consumer evaluations of e-services' 200
Varadarajan, R.: 'Interactivity in the electronic workplace' 217
Vargo, S. L.: 'On value and value co-creation' 191
Vauxhall 57
Verdana 178
Verdict 108, 109
Vestiaire 57
video 44–6; piracy 46–7
videotex 104
Vijayasarathy, L.R.: 'Print and Internet catalog shopping' 103
Viktor and Rolf 57
viral marketing 128–9
Virtual Reality (VR): grocery store 312–13; shopping centres 230, 236; try-on 168–70; see also e-malls
virtual retailer 251, 255–61

# INDEX

Visa 150
VisionDirect xxi
Vodafone Group PLC 275, 278
Vrechopoulos, A. 169; 'Design visual examplars of 3D online store layouts types' 168; 'Store atmosphere in web retailing' 168; 'Virtual store layout' 168; 'Who controls store atmosphere customization in electronic retailing?' 168

Waldfogel, J.: *Copyright Protection, Technological Change, and the Quality of New Products* 46
Walker, O.C.: 'In-home shoppers' 105
Walker, R.: *Strategic Marketing Management* 184, 223
Wall, Matthew xxi–xxii, 312
Wal-Mart 11, 191, 212
Walton, J.R.: 'In-home shoppers' 105
Waterstones 69
WayTech 172
Weaven, S.: 'E-retailing by banks' 201
web atmospherics 10, 12, 26, 130, 166–72; bells and whistles 167; branding 224
web-rooming 20
WeChat 306
Wedding Network, The 153
Wedgwood 231
Welch, R.: 'Effects of pictorial realism' 188
Westfield 230
WhatsApp xxii
White, L.: 'Exploratory and confirmatory factor analysis' 199; 'Model of quality determinants' 199
WHSmith 14, 81

Wi-Fi 81–2, 275, 278, 310
Wilde Rooms 51
Windham, L.: 'Overcome e-Business Barriers' 93
Wireless Application Protocol (WAP) *see* mobile phones
Wolfinbarger, M.: '.comQ' 199; 'eTailQ' 119, 200, 201
women and e-shopping 113–15
Woodland, Norman 305
Woolworths 212
Worldwide web *see* Internet
Wu, G.: 'Effects of perceived interactivity, perceived web assurance and disposition to trust on initial online trust' 217; 'Perceived interactivity' 188
Wu, J-H: 'Developing e-business dynamic capabilities' 288, 289

XML 66

Yachting and Boating World 124
Yadav, M. S.: 'Interactivity in the electronic workplace' 217
Yahoo! 146, 147, 148, 253
Yellow Pages 147
YouTube 55, 57, 128
Yudelson, J.: 'Adapting McCarthy's four P's for the twenty-first century' 11

Zalando 51
Zeithaml, V.: 'Conceptual framework for understanding e-service quality' 199
Zemke, R.: *e-Service* 202
Zoella 55
Zoom View 172
Zwillberg, Paul 129